Love, Sex, Death, and the Meaning of Life:
The Films of Woody Allen

Laurence Olivier On Screen

A Portrait of the Artist:
The Plays of Tennessee Williams

Joseph Losey

Who's Afraid of Edward Albee?

Elizabeth Taylor

The Hollywood Epic

Edward G. Robinson

George Kelly

The Dark Side of the Screen:
Film Noir

Harold Prince and the
American Musical Theatre

Acting Hollywood Style

The Boys from Syracuse:
The Shuberts' Theatrical Empire

Detours and Lost Highways:
A Map of Neo-Noir

Kurt Weill on Stage:
From Berlin to Broadway

A Method to Their Madness

A Method to Their Madness

FOSTER HIRSCH

THE HISTORY OF THE ACTORS STUDIO

DA CAPO PRESS

Cataloging-in-Publication data for this book is available from the Library of Congress.

Second Da Capo Press edition 2002
Reprinted by arrangement with W. W. Norton & Company, Inc.
ISBN 0–306–81102–2

Published by Da Capo Press
A Member of the Perseus Books Group
http://www.dacapopress.com

Da Capo Press books are available at special discounts for bulk purchases in the U.S. by corporations, institutions, and other organizations. For more information, please contact the Special Markets Department at the Perseus Books Group, 11 Cambridge Center, Cambridge, MA 02142, or call (800) 255-1514 or (617) 252-5298, or e-mail j.mccrary@perseusbooks.com.

1 2 3 4 5 6 7 8 9—06 05 04 03 02

CONTENTS

AUTHOR'S NOTE

"Hey, Stella!" a harsh, passionate voice cuts through the steamy Southern night.

"Hey, Stella!" hurled into the air, a primeval sound, like a wolf baying at the moon.

"Stella!" Arms outstretched pleadingly.

"You're tearing me apart!" the young man lashes out at his stunned parents, the frustrations of a lifetime engrained in the volcanic force of his attack. His eyes narrowed, his voice clenched in pain, his body contorted as his hands grasp the air, his handsome face scarred by the turbulence within, the man waits for an answer.

Marlon Brando, muscles rippling under a torn t-shirt, bellowing for the return of his wife in *A Streetcar Named Desire,* and James Dean, hunched over in adolescent agony in *Rebel without a Cause,* are two great moments in the history not only of American acting but also of American culture. With their quicksilver intensity and eroticism, Brando in *Streetcar* and Dean in *Rebel* seemed to herald a revolution in acting style as well as in sensibility. Raw, intuitive, and alive, they were like unstoppable forces of nature. They seemed more real, more private and neurotic than any actors had ever seemed before. Shredding accepted notions of actor's behavior, they caught us by surprise. Theirs was acting that had both unexpected size and immediacy, and the risks they took required us to take some risks of our own. To respond fully to the power they unleashed demanded that we give up some of our own safety: how was it possible to absorb these performances and not to peer, however fleetingly, into some of our own dark, unsuspected places? The vernacular American style with its jolting psychological revelations that Brando and Dean introduced has inspired several generations of actors.

On stage in 1947, Brando as Stanley Kowalski in *A Streetcar Named Desire*, mumbling and detonating, his back often turned audaciously to the audience, revolutionized American acting. And yet, like most revolutions, this one, too, had a lengthy pregnancy. Preceding Brando's explosion in *Streetcar* is an entire era in American theatre history—the story of the Group Theatre in the thirties—and preceding the Group is the history of the theatrical company that inspired it, the world's first theatre, the Moscow Art Theatre of Constantin Stanislavski. Brando's Kowalski, a landmark American performance in a landmark American play, had its true artistic origins halfway around the world in turn-of-the-century Russia; and the fresh, vital film acting of Brando and Dean in the early and mid-fifties represented in some ways a completion of an American theatrical experiment of the thirties and an ideal of truth in acting first codified by Stanislavski, the most searching, dedicated, and powerful teacher of acting in the history of the art.

A Streetcar Named Desire opened on Broadway on December 3, 1947. Two months earlier, in October, the play's director, Elia Kazan, had cofounded with Cheryl Crawford and Robert Lewis a workshop for actors called the Actors Studio. It was there, under Lee Strasberg's zealous thirty-year guidance, that the Method—the American adaptation of Stanislavski's original System that resulted in the intense, personal, realistic style exemplified by Brando and Dean—was defined, experimented with, and nurtured. Maintaining, like Stanislavski, an impassioned, lifelong interest in the nature of the actor and in the mysteries of the actor's creative process, Strasberg used the Actors Studio as the place where he held court on his favorite subject, what he called actors' problems. Strasberg was a great talker (his taciturnity in his private life was equally legendary) and what he had to say on what good acting is and how it is arrived at had reverberations far beyond the modest Studio theatre. Strasberg's Method became the most influential—and notorious—of all American acting styles, and, from the small room on West 44th Street in Manhattan where the Actors Studio is located, Strasberg's words reached out to and inspired actors all over the world. Of course, not everybody liked the man or his words (some ap-

The erotic intensity of Method acting: Marlon Brando, in *A Streetcar Named Desire*; James Dean, in *Rebel without a Cause*.

preciated the words, while resenting the man), but Strasberg's significance, and that of the actors' lab that he turned into the high temple of the Method, is undeniable.

Still thriving after the death, on February 17, 1982, of its artistic and spiritual leader, the Actors Studio is among the longest-lived, most important and controversial theatrical organizations in the history of American entertainment, and this book is an attempt to trace it origins, to define its artistic ideals, and to account for its impact—to evaluate its Method in theory and practice.

"Without the Group Theatre, there would have been no Actors Studio," says Cheryl Crawford. "And without the Theatre Guild," she adds, "there would have been no Group Theatre." She might also have said that without the Moscow Art Theatre there might not have been a Group Theatre. In Part One, I consider the historical and aesthetic links among the Moscow Art Theatre, co-founded in 1896 by Stanislavski and Nemiro- vich-Danchenko; the Group Theatre, co-founded in 1931 by Harold Clur- man, Lee Strasberg, and Cheryl Crawford; and the Actors Studio. All three organizations share an ideal of theatricalized realism, a presiding belief in acting as the artistic illumination of human behavior.

Part One concludes with the founding of the Actors Studio; in Part Two, I go behind the scenes on West 44th Street to report on how the Method is interpreted on home ground. In Part Three, I take a look at the results of Method training, as seen in the work of some of the most renowned of the Studio's members.

This book is a blend of theatre history, acting theory, and theatre and film criticism, spiced with personality profiles of a large and colorful cast from Stanislavski and Chekhov to Ellen Burstyn and Al Pacino (co-directors of the Actors Studio). Having outlined what I think I've done, let me quickly add what I haven't written: this is not, above all, a manual of the Method. I am not an actor, or a teacher of acting, and therefore I am not qualified to write a primer or a how-to-do-it book (even assuming this could be done). The would-be actor who consults these pages hoping to discover a detailed technical analysis of Stanislavski's System or Strasberg's secrets, or to find out how to get into the Studio, will be disappointed. After having attended sessions at the Studio and spoken to many Studio actors, I stand in awe of the actor's task, breathing the semblance of life into a writer's character. It is a responsibility that no one system or method can scientifically explain or precisely account for; certainly the art of acting cannot be summarized by a set of rules. The pursuit of good acting will always be treacherously elusive, arrived at through a magical combination of intuition and craft, and whatever assistance the body of knowledge called the Method can be to the actor is something only the individual actor himself can bear witness to.

I entered the Actors Studio as a watcher rather than a doer. Bringing with me the experience of twenty years of habitual theatregoing, I wrote down what I heard and saw, what I liked and didn't like, what I learned, and what I didn't. I'm an outsider, an observer, a "civilian" (which is the word Studio members use for someone like me). I write from the perspective of a member of the audience; as audience, I'm very good—I respond, I notice, I appreciate.

I make no pretense of writing technically about acting. Nor do I write objectively, as one who observes but has no opinions or preconceptions. I am in fact extremely opinionated, brandishing my biases wherever I can. Except for Neil Simon, Kabuki, and Brecht, I like almost any kind of theatre, but the kind I like best is the kind the Actors Studio trains its actors for: plays set in a real world, with characters who are complex, ambivalent, layered, recognizable, and every bit as neurotic as the people in the audience. Since its emphasis on psychological realism fulfills my own expectations of the type of material I most want to see, I approached the Studio as a friendly witness. I haven't, though, written a continuously smiling in-house account of Strasberg or of the Method, because I have a few genuine reservations about both. On the whole, however, I think the Actors Studio and the people who use it are quite special, and it is to consider and to celebrate that specialness that I have written this book.

A theatrical revolution: midway through Act I of *The Sea Gull* at the Moscow Art Theatre on December 17, 1898, Stanislavski's actors had their backs to the audience.

Part   1

BEFORE THE STUDIO

1

ACTING WITH BACKS
TO THE AUDIENCE

I t was a simple directorial touch, yet its implications were profound.

In the middle of the first act of *The Sea Gull* at the Moscow Art Theatre on December 17, 1898, a group of actors was seated on a long bench, placed at the front of the stage, with their backs turned to the audience. A gasp swept through the opening night crowd in audible response to this violation of theatrical rules. Actors turned away from the house, engaged in overlapping conversations – what could the director have been thinking of?

The director, Constantin Stanislavski, was thinking of nothing less than a theatrical revolution, a sweeping away of the conventions of nineteenth-century theatre. With so seemingly basic and trivial a gesture as seating his actors with their backs to the auditorium, as if the audience didn't exist, Stanislavski was declaring war on the kind of theatre in which star actors made sweeping entrances and exits, bowing to the cheers of their admirers as their fellow actors moved to the sides of the stage like the parting waters of the Red Sea to herald the arrival of majesty. In this kind of theatre not the play but the star was the thing; sets and costumes as well as scripts served merely as enticements for the glitter of star personalities. The shopworn farces, romances, and melodramas that were the staples of this star theatre were performed in a declamatory style—bombastic, artificial, and above all conventional.

"I'm not going to the theatre this winter. I'm sick of it," complains a character in Gorky's play *The Petty Bourgeois*, whose feelings echo Stanislavski's. "I can't stand those melodramas, with all their shooting and shouting and sobbing," she goes on. "It's all so false. Life twists people into

knots without any noise and shouting. Without any tears. Imperceptibly.
. . . It makes me sick to hear actors make love on the stage. It's never like
that in real life. Simply never!''

Trivial, riddled with convention, and disrespectful of both the rights
and talents of the actor, the ensemble, the director, the designer, and the
writer, the fraudulent glamour of this reigning style of nineteenth-century
Russian theatre had no roots in the Russian soil and temperament. Dependent on translations of fluffy French farces and stentorian melodramas, the
Russian theatre lacked Russian soul.

In the 1860s, in the work of Turgenev, Gogol, and Pushkin, Russian
literature found a powerful and distinctive national voice that was to reach
its fulfillment in the novels of Dostoevski and Tolstoy in the 1880s. But
Russian theatre—as theatre often does—lagged behind, with only an occasional national treasure such as Turgenev's *A Month in the Country*, Gogol's
Inspector General, and Griboyedov's *Wit from Woe* to interrupt the flow of
flaccid imports.

On that historic evening, then, when the curtain of the Moscow Art
Theatre rose on Act I of Chekhov's *Sea Gull*, Russian drama and Russian
theatrical production were in a shabby state. In the midst of so decadent
a theatre, Stanislavski's opening tableau was startling: Where was the star?
Where, for that matter, was the central focus of the scene? At what or at
whom was the audience supposed to look? Not only were the actors facing
the wrong way, they also seemed to be whispering their lines. Instead of
the booming tones audiences had come to expect, Stanislavski's actors
spoke intimately and conversationally, with a casualness that turned the
audience into eavesdroppers on Russian country life. A member of that first
audience later wrote, ''The spectator ceased to *watch* the performance, and
began to *live* with it.''

In place of the mimicry of the continental sophistication that Russian
audiences, feeling culturally and geographically isolated, looked up to,
there was the unmistakable accent and manner of the Russian gentry. And
replacing the anonymous, all-purpose sets, used as interchangeable back-
drops for imported farces and melodramas, was a realistically rendered
Russian scene.

Throughout Act I, Stanislavski's company was aware of a ghostly
silence in the house. They had been directed to focus their attention on
stage and as much as possible to forget about performing for an audience;

but it seemed, from the apparent lack of response, as if they were playing for themselves alone. When the curtain descended on Act I, Olga Knipper, the leading actress and soon to be Chekhov's wife, fainted, while all the other actors were convinced that their effort to modernize Russian acting style had met with failure. For a few awful moments, the audience remained silent, and then there was a roar. Quickly, the curtain was brought up as the distracted actors rallied to the thundering reception, managing to bow in near-unison as the curtain was raised and lowered, and then raised and lowered yet again, no fewer than seven times.

Ironically, at the time of this historic production, Stanislavski was only half-conscious of what he was doing. He did not fully understand Chekhov's play; and he had not even begun work on his System. In many ways, he was still an amateur. By his own admission, he was groping in the dark. He knew what kind of play and what kind of acting style he was opposed to, and he knew the kind of theatre he wanted to create. But he didn't know how to create it. Hating "the theatre in the theatre," he wanted "living, truthful, real life, not commonplace life, but artistic life" on the stage, as he later wrote in his autobiography *My Life in Art.* He envisioned an acting style that transmuted life into art, and he dedicated his life to finding out how emotional truth is captured within a theatrical framework. In 1898, he had no clear sense how this could be done.

He didn't know how to teach his actors how to act in the new style, and so he simply told them what to do. In frustration, he became a dictator, treating his actors like puppets as he placed them within a predetermined master plan. Unable to reach inside his actors or to create circumstances that might invite artistic inspiration, he worked in an entirely external way, beginning with costumes, makeup, accents, and movements that he hoped might lead to psychological insights. The way Stanislavski directed *The Sea Gull* violated practically every idea about acting that he was to discover at a later point in his long journey into the depths of the actor's art.

Faced with acting's great enigmas, Stanislavski adapted an autocratic style he was later to regret. He was also imperious toward Chekhov and his play. Chekhov insisted that he had written a comedy, and criticized Stanislavski's approach as too sentimental and too fussy: he was unhappy with the realistic sound effects and with the way the actors were so absorbed with objects, possessions, trinkets, things. Claiming that Chekhov didn't understand his own play, Stanislavski felt his direction made *The Sea Gull* stronger and more theatrical than it really was.

A director who misunderstood his playwright's intentions and who imposed his own lopsided interpretation onto a group of actors who had no definite technique and who resented his bullying manner—these hardly seem the ingredients for a theatrical revolution. And yet out of this mélange of bruised egos, accusations and resentments, and artistic and intellectual uncertainty emerged a historic evening, the beginning of a truly modern realistic performing style: the birth of the Method.

Constantin Stanislavski came from a prosperous mercantile family. Descended from peasants, his father owned a factory for making gold and silver thread; throughout the early part of his theatrical career, Stanislavski spent most of his days taking care of the family business. Remarkably tall, physically awkward, ill-spoken, Constantin Alexeyev (Stanislavski was a stage name) entered the theatre merely as an avocation, a retreat from his business responsibilities. By his own admission and that of eyewitnesses, he had no great natural gifts as an actor. But he did have a fierce will to improve and, even more important, he had an inventor's curiosity. He wanted to learn the secrets of great actors he had seen. How had Duse, Salvini, and Yermolova prepared for their greatness? What kind of training had they had? How much of their work was intuitive? How much was arrived at through conscious study? And how did they manage to hold on to their inspiration, performance after performance? The stagestruck young man who asked these questions, only to discover that acting was the only art form that had no codified system or guidelines to offer its practitioners, had no idea that finding the answers would take the rest of his life.

The well-to-do businessman fascinated by acting knew that some day he wanted to establish a theatre of his own, where a scrupulous realism in performance and production design would issue a challenge to the artificial conventions that were strangling Russian theatre. Stanislavski's love of realism was not, of course, something new in Russian culture. Pushkin, Russia's original literary hero and the father of the native realist tradition, wrote that the goal of the artist was to supply truthful feelings under given circumstances, which Stanislavski adopted as his lifelong artistic motto. And the Maly, the Small State Theatre, had a half-century tradition of realism by the time Stanislavski founded his first theatre. (The Maly was known as the House of Ostrovsky, as the Moscow Art Theatre later came to be known as the House of Chekhov. Unlike Chekhov, Ostrovsky does not translate well; the only play of his to become part of the world repertory is *The Storm*, a drama of annihilating passion. Most of his dozens of plays, local color studies of the middle class, are tame comedies of specifically Russian manners.) By the time Stanislavski had established his own Theatre, however, productions of Ostrovsky at the Maly had degenerated to a staid, official realism in need of drastic overhauling.

Although the Maly had become musty, having lost many of its original actors and having failed to develop a technique to assist the remaining ones to keep their work fresh, Stanislavski's first theatrical hero, the great comic Shchepkin, was an original Maly actor who, decades before Stanislavski began work on his System, had agitated for reform of traditional performing styles. "Seek your examples in life," Shchepkin admonished his fellow artists.

Aside from the isolated great actors he had seen and the diminished realism of Ostrovsky's plays at the Maly, it was a company of German players that gave Stanislavski a glimpse of the realist theatre he dreamed of. Under the iron-fisted direction of a man named Kronegk, the Duke of Saxe-Meiningen's company had been celebrated throughout Europe for the meticulous realism of its sets, the precision of its crowd scenes, and the ensemble work of its actors. Compared to contemporary Russian practice, the methods of the German troupe were indeed realist, though it didn't take long for the amateur Stanislavski to realize that the renowned foreigners were faking it. To camouflage the fact that their actors couldn't really act, Kronegk created spectacles. Sets, costumes, and mass movement, as in his famed production of *Julius Caesar*, disguised the impoverished acting and fooled most audiences into thinking of the Meiningen players as Europe's premier theatrical ensemble. The company's acclaimed "realism," then, was strictly external; the "truth" that it played was physical rather than emotional.

Aware of the director's tricks, Stanislavski nonetheless appreciated the company's surface realism, the careful period recreations, the skillful choreography of crowds—and these became the trademarks of his own early work in his first amateur Theatre as well as in the initial phase of the Moscow Art Theatre. The Meiningen productions were a director's show-case in which the actors were clearly at the service of the director's ingenu-ity; though he was to become the best friend actors have ever had, Stanislavski started out as something of a Russian Kronegk, hiding his actors' inadequacies beneath a finicky fidelity to scenic realism.

As a fledgling actor himself, Stanislavski was likewise addicted to externals. He was a compulsive imitator. Unable to generate inspiration from inner sources, he looked outward, at the great performances he had seen and remembered. And, without apparent shame—because he didn't know how else to get started—he tried to recreate the work of the actors he admired, slavishly copying the way they used their bodies, the way they threw their voices. He would practice for hours in front of a mirror, trying to see himself as an audience would see him. Like an athlete in training, he built up his voice and his body in an effort to turn both into supple instruments that he could "play" at will.

Attempting Othello early in his career, he worked from external models, patterning his interpretation on that of the great Salvini and going to Algeria to study the behavior of Arabs at first hand. He was a close student, of acting and of exotic locales; but the way he prepared the role resulted in a studied performance, a recreation of a vivid original. Something was missing in his method, he realized. "No one knows what will move his soul, and open the treasure house of his creative gifts," Stanislavski was to write in *My Life in Art*. "The creativeness of an actor must come from within." How to enter into and to stimulate that inner self became the theme of Stanislavski's epic quest. "Were there no technical means for a conscious entry into the paradise of art? . . . Where is one to seek those roads into the secret sources of inspiration? That is the question that must serve as the fundamental life problem of every true actor."

In 1877, Stanislavski organized his first amateur group, the Alexeyev Circle, producing a series of ephemeral farces, operettas, and melodramas until January 1888, when he founded a more ambitious company, the Society of Art and Literature. During the ten-year life of his second Theatre he put on plays by Tolstoy, Pushkin, Ostrovsky, Molière, and Goldoni, along with undemanding popular favorites. Stanislavski was still an amateur; yet his work was rich with enthusiasm and promise. And he began to develop a reputation that set his Theatre apart from the other circles of amateurs and dilettantes. As if in recognition of his achievements, on June 16, 1897, Stanislavski was summoned to a popular Moscow restaurant, the Slavic Bazaar, by V. Nemirovich-Danchenko, a leading professional man of

Stanislavski's *Othello* (1896): a realism of surfaces.

The co-founders of the Moscow
Art Theatre, Nemirovich-
Danchenko and Stanislavski, in
1923.

the theatre, playwright, critic, teacher, and administrator of the Philharmonic Institute. The historic meeting, which lasted from 10 A.M. until 3 A.M. the following morning, resulted in a proposal for a new Theatre, called (originally) the People's Moscow Art Theatre.

Nemirovich-Danchenko and Stanislavski had so much in common that they were both surprised they had not met before this. Both were idealists possessed of a religious conviction of the importance of the theatre. Both were visionaries who yet had the benefit of years of practical experience; they were men whose otherworldly tendencies were countered by shrewdness and plain good sense. Both had the leadership ability to translate ideals into realities. Neither was an intellectual, though Nemirovich-Danchenko mistakenly thought he was. Neither had a deep or secure understanding of plays as literature. Both were men of high temperament (as what true man of the theatre is not?)—proud, insistent, puritanical, and always quite prepared to stand on ceremony. Taskmasters and self-disciplinarians, they had powerful wills which sparked their many later conflicts and surely contributed to the fact that they never became close personal friends. In time, Stanislavski's fame far outshone that of his partner, yet Stanislavski had the grace both to feel guilty about that and to maintain throughout his career that there would never have been a Moscow Art Theatre without the vision, the persistence, and the administrative skill of Nemirovich-Danchenko.

At their first meeting, the two men divided up responsibilities: Nemirovich-Danchenko was to have final say in literary matters and was to attend to the daily running of the Theatre; Stanislavski was to have the last word in artistic and production concerns. It was a naive separation of powers, destined to provoke civil war. They agreed on basic principles, some of which have become theatrical legend: "There are no small parts, there are only small actors." "One must love art, and not one's self in art." "Today Hamlet, tomorrow a supernumerary, but even as a supernumerary you must become an artist." "All disobedience to the creative life of the theatre is a crime."

A period of sixteen months separates the first meeting of the co-directors from the opening night of their Moscow Art Theatre in September 1898. During this time, they assembled their company from the members of Stanislavski's amateur Theatre, from Nemirovich-Danchenko's students at the Philharmonic Institute, and from interviews with a wide range of professionals. How were actors selected for what was to become the world's finest acting company?

Stanislavski rejected a prominent actress of the time because "she does not love art, but herself in art." He wanted no egotists in his company. The new actor in the new theatrical world he was building would have to have goals higher than those of the old-fashioned star actors in love with themselves and fed by the adulation of audiences. The new actor would have to be able to feed himself. One actor interested Stanislavski because "he has ideals for which he is fighting. He is not at peace with present conditions. He is a man of his ideals." Another performer he rejected because, though talented, he had grown used to giving the public what it wanted. Commercial glossiness, theatrical fakery, narcissism—these qualities were to be outlawed in the new Theatre; Stanislavski and Nemirovich-Danchenko were more likely to admit less accomplished actors who were open to change. In assembling their original company, the two directors set themselves up as psychologists, evaluating the moral characters of prospective actors and making judgments about each actor's ability to adjust to a Theatre in which the group and the play counted more than the individual.

Since at this point Stanislavski had no System to rely on, he chose actors he thought he could mold; being asked to join the company was an invitation to become part of the world's first true theatre laboratory, whose goal was to discover creative laws for an art which, till then, had none.

The directors' choice as their Theatre's opening production, Count Alexey Tolstoy's historical drama *Tsar Fyodor*, reveals how far Stanislavski was from his ultimate destination. Serviceable—and superficial—the play dramatizes a war for control of medieval Russia. Tsar Fyodor, the saintly, unlikely son of Ivan the Terrible, is a feeble ruler whose government is fought over by two factions, one led by the Machiavellian Boris Godunov, the other by Prince Shouisky, an idealist who only reluctantly makes political compromises. Observed from the outside, as participants in a swiftly moving national pageant, the characters are vivid national types. In his seesawing emotions (siding now with Godunov, now with Shouisky), given to tantrums, wanting to escape and yet remembering from time to time who he is, impulsive, good-hearted, something finally of a holy simpleton, Fyodor is intensely Russian. In his contradictions and sudden reversals, he is the kind of psychologically complex character that led Stanislavski to the development of his inner technique. Boris and Shouisky are more thinly drawn, the craftiness of the former contrasted with the naiveté of the latter.

But it isn't the individual characters who are the focus of the play or of Stanislavski's production, but rather the pageant of Russian history in which the three principal figures assume their predestined roles. To bring the court of the ill-suited, sweet-natured monarch to theatrical life Stanislavski, his designers, and his actors became students of sixteenth-century Russia, combing libraries and museums and visiting provincial cities which contained relics from the period. They investigated Russian history the way they would later investigate characters; the result was a production that was a riot of colors, and of rich brocades, silks, and tapestries all certified for authenticity.

The company had rehearsed the play in Pushkino, a summer community where, away from the city and the regular pattern of their lives, they began to feel like a group united by common aims and values. The long rehearsal period that Stanislavski insisted on contributed to the emergence of a true collective spirit. Inevitably, though, despite the impeccable scholarship, despite the intense and protracted rehearsals, *Tsar Fyodor,* like the productions of the Meiningen players, was an example of external realism, a realism of manicured surfaces. Like Kronegk, Stanislavski camouflaged the rawness of his players beneath elaborate theatrical embroidery. By clever intent, the actors were upstaged by the sets and costumes, the historical and archaeological documentation. In *My Life in Art,* Stanislavski confesses that "we were forced for the time being to hide the defects and immaturity of our actors by the splendor of their costumes."

For all his genuine idealism, Stanislavski was also a sly fox who wanted to open his new Theatre with a good show, and in *Tsar Fyodor* he found a vehicle that remained his Theatre's spectacular signature production for the rest of his life.

To realize his goal of a deep, spiritualized realism, Stanislavski required a different kind of play. In Chekhov's *Sea Gull,* though he didn't know it at the time, he found exactly what he needed. Indeed, without Chekhov, Stanislavski might never have developed his System. Twenty-five years after he had directed *The Sea Gull,* Stanislavski was able to write that "Chekhov gave that inner truth to the art of the stage which served as the foundation for what was later called the Stanislavski System, which must be approached through Chekhov, or which serves as a bridge to the ap-

proach of Chekhov." In 1924, when he was writing *My Life in Art*, Stanislavski thus placed Chekhov and the System in symbiotic partnership, an
ironic conclusion in light of Stanislavski's first reaction to the plays and his
personal feelings about the man who wrote them.

The relationship between Chekhov, the greatest Russian playwright,
and Stanislavski, the greatest Russian director—a colossal mismatch that
resulted in wonderful theatre—has echoes of Chekhovian comedy. The two
men never felt comfortable with each other and, oddly enough, never quite
understood the other's art. When he first read *The Sea Gull*, Stanislavski
was puzzled and emotionally unaffected: he didn't know what to make of
it. Recalling his first impressions, he admitted later that it did not seem
"scenic," that it was "strange," "monotonous," and "boresome," adding
in an aside, "My literary ideals at that period were still dangerously primi-

A scene from *Tsar Fyodor,* the Moscow Art Theatre's opening production. "We
were forced to hide the defects of our actors by the splendor of their costumes,"
Stanislavski wrote in his autobiography.

tive." When Stanislavski reluctantly agreed to do the play, only because Nemirovich-Danchenko was so passionately committed to it, Chekhov was displeased with the results. Chekhov complained that Stanislavski never understood that his plays were comedies, and Stanislavski never understood what Chekhov meant by that.

"A man of letters must be as objective as a chemist," Chekhov wrote in 1887. "He must abandon worldly subjectivity and realize that dunghills play a very respectable role in a landscape, and that evil passions are as inherent in life as good ones." "In this world it is indispensable to remain indifferent," he wrote on another occasion. It is his indifference and objectivity that define Chekhov's comic point of view. Chekhov regards his characters' blighted idealism and failed romances, their lack of will, their unwarranted optimism about a future they will never see, their impulsiveness, their sentimentality, their unrealized dreams—in short, their struggling humanity—with a cool eye. He gently mocks their frailties and excesses and their assorted blindnesses—and his detachment is essentially an ironic posture. But (and it is an enormous "but") Chekhov's deep irony is mixed with compassion for all his characters, locked as they are in their private battles with their human condition. He laughs quietly at their shortcomings as he also loves them for the very weaknesses that make them human, and it is this delicate blend of ridicule and sympathy that is the backbone of his comedy. Chekhov's is the human comedy: comedy in its largest, most forgiving sense, and while Stanislavski could never bring himself to acknowledge Chekhov's plays as comedies, while he could never resist making the characters more overtly emotional and less foolish than Chekhov intended, he yet had an intuitive understanding of the unique Chekhov tone, call it whatever you will.

In a letter dated September 15, 1900, to Olga Knipper, as the Moscow Art Theatre was preparing *Three Sisters*, Chekhov wrote with evident concern: ". . . Four important female parts, four young women of the upper class; I cannot leave that to Stanislavski—with all due respect for his gifts and understanding. I must have at least a peep at the rehearsals." Chekhov distrusted Stanislavski's theatricality, his tendency to directorial overstatement, while Stanislavski could not adjust to Chekhov's untheatrical style, both personally and as a writer. They were a little in awe of each other. Stanislavski was always intimidated by major literary figures; he was tongue-tied in the presence of Tolstoy, for example, and while Chekhov was far less formidable, Stanislavski was nonetheless unnerved by his reputation. For his part, Chekhov looked upon theatre people as having a worldliness and glamour that he, a mere country doctor, felt entitled to admire only from afar.

After seeing a rehearsal or a performance, Chekhov would make cryptic comments to Stanislavski and other actors. All he told Stanislavski, after watching him as Trigorin in *The Sea Gull,* was that the character "wears striped trousers and boots out at heel, and smokes a cigar." Stanislavski was confused. Later, as he thought about the comment, he realized that it expressed Chekhov's disapproval of the way he had interpreted the character, a popular, womanizing author who observes people with detachment as possible material for his stories. Stanislavski had been playing Trigorin as a dandy, dressed nattily in a white summer suit, when what Chekhov had in mind was a man whose sloppy appearance revealed his tarnished soul.

After seeing Stanislavski play Astrov in a performance of *Uncle*

The final tableau from *Three Sisters* (1901) with, left to right, Knipper (Chekhov's wife) as Masha, Savitskaya as Olga, and Litovtseva as Irina.

Vanya, Chekhov had only this to say: "In the last act, Vanya sulks, but Astrov whistles." And to Leonidov, the actor who was playing Lopakhin in *The Cherry Orchard*, Chekhov said, tantalizingly, "Lopakhin does not shout. He wears brown boots. And he has a lot of money here [touching his breast pocket]."

In *My Life in Art*, Stanislavski presents Chekhov as a spouter of many such terse, enigmatic statements—a country bumpkin unable to explain what he has written. Yet we know more than Stanislavski; from Chekhov's letters to his editor and friend Suvorin, whom he considered his intellectual equal, we know that Chekhov could be shrewd and articulate about his work. Is it possible that he spoke to Stanislavski the way he did because that was his estimate of how much Stanislavski could absorb? Or, more likely, did Chekhov intend to stimulate the actor's imagination? In a sense, Chekhov was speaking to Stanislavski and his actors in their own language, giving them specific visual images that would help them get more deeply into their characters.

Stanislavski condescending to Chekhov as a writer who doesn't know what he has written; Chekhov complaining that Stanislavski had turned his dry-eyed characters into crybabies: this is the kind of ironic misalliance that might have leapt from the pages of a Chekhov story or play. Yet for all their literary and temperamental difference, the two men served each other splendidly and in time both came to realize it. Stanislavski could write as his final estimate of Chekhov that his work contains "the true aroma of Russian poetry." And Chekhov could say about Stanislavski (in a letter to Olga Knipper), "When he directs, he's an artist, but when he acts he's a rich young merchant who has taken it into his head to dabble a bit in art."

Finally, Chekhov and Stanislavski shared common goals and common enemies. Like Stanislavski, Chekhov was appalled by the theatrical conventions that dominated the Russian stage of the 1880s and 1890s. "Looking at Duse," he wrote to his sister in 1891, "I realize why the Russian theatre is such a bore." In a later letter, equally despairing, he wrote, "The drama must either degenerate completely, or assume a completely new form." It was with a vision of that "new form" that he began to write. After three apprentice full-length works (*Platonov*, 1881; *Ivanov*, 1887; *The Wood Demon*, 1889), he wrote four plays in his mature style that are among the greatest in the history of drama: *The Sea Gull* (1896), *Uncle Vanya* (1899, a reworking of *The Wood Demon*), *Three Sisters* (1901), and *The Cherry Orchard* (1904).

"One must write about simple things: how Peter Semionovich married Marie Ivanovna. That is all," Chekhov said. What was manifestly "new" about Chekhov's plays was the way his language, seemingly so threadbare, throbbed with a subtext, for while his characters seemed only to be talking of "simple things," their lives were often unraveling. "No one understood as clearly and as finely, as Chekhov, the tragedy of life's trivialities," Gorky wrote.

The enchantment of the unspoken permeates the plays, giving them their infinite subtlety. What his characters say often masks their true thoughts, and it was Chekhov's particular genius to suggest that beneath the surface of their words and actions his characters had rich inner lives they were afraid or unable to reveal directly. Dialogue rumbles with hints of turbulent inner monologues on the ache of romantic failures, the withering of ideals and dreams. In Chekhov's four masterworks, a vein of deeply private feelings flows continuously beneath words and actions.

It was precisely this subterranean level that Stanislavski had been trying to excavate in his search for truthful acting. Like Chekhov, he wanted to create characters with inner lives of the kind that people in real life have: characters, in short, who were more than the sum of their words. Throughout the crucial early period of the Moscow Art Theatre, as he was building a company of actors and selecting a repertory that would fulfill his ideal of theatricalized realism, Stanislavski embraced the "aroma" of Chekhovian poetry, and it was after he had lived with Chekhov's plays intensely and continuously from 1898 to 1904 that he began to construct his System. The subtlety and nuance of Chekhov's methods gradually filtered into his own —Chekhov's modern "inner" style became Stanislavski's inspiration and his goal.

Here are some examples of how Chekhov's method works. "A wife is a wife!" Andrei moans softly, at the end of Act III of *Three Sisters*. What a world of sorrow and disillusionment is mirrored in that bare declarative statement. Beneath the words is a glimpse of Andrei's recognition that he is married to a woman not of his class who has systematically and ruthlessly displaced him and his sisters from their own home and who is cheating on him with the head of the school board. Up to this moment in the play, Andrei has seemed the dull member of the family, sightless in the face of his wife's niggardly, conniving actions. Yet this one sentence, spoken as if to himself, reveals with a lightning flash a true measure of his self-awareness.

When he first wrote this scene, Chekhov provided Andrei with a litany of complaints. In rehearsal, Chekhov ordered Stanislavski to cut the entire speech and to replace it with that plain and hopeless "a wife is a wife." It was therefore left to the actor, submerging himself in the character, to invest those few stark words with all the feelings that had been written into the original aria-like outpouring.

In the last act of *Three Sisters,* clandestine lovers Masha and Vershinin have one final moment together before he must depart with his regiment. "Goodbye," he says, extending his hand in a furtive gesture. "Goodbye," Masha whispers. With characteristic strictness and reserve, Chekhov allows the lovers no more than this flat exchange. No poetry and no melodramatic embellishments, yet beneath the two words, in what is left unsaid, there is a rush of passion.

"Goodbye"–"Goodbye." No more than this and yet, in the theatre, played by performers who understand Stanislavski's System (and who thereby understand Chekhov's), the moment can be devastating. Actors who know how to use the inner technique can suggest in these two words a sense of their characters' fleeting rapture and the grim future that awaits them. Vershinin, saddled with a hysterical wife and four daughters, has wrested some rare happy moments in his short affair with Masha; now, with the departure of his regiment, he faces a life of possibly terminal bleakness. Masha, trapped in a loveless marriage to the boring village schoolteacher, has seized a glimpse of a larger, finer life. The leavetaking of her handsome soldier means a return to the pettiness of a provincial life. In saying goodbye to Vershinin, she feels she is saying goodbye, possibly forever, to her own higher self. One simple word, stated and answered, and two souls are revealed.

In the last act of *The Cherry Orchard,* in a brief scene that seems squeezed into the major action of the family's departure from their ancestral estate, Lopakhin and Varya have a hurried interview. She enters in a burst of energy, chattering about having lost something in her luggage. "I packed it myself and don't remember where." A pause. Lopakhin asks her where she will go; she answers briskly that she has been engaged—"as a sort of housekeeper." Lopakhin mentions, with apparent nonchalance, that her

new place of employment "is nigh on to seventy miles." Another pause.
"And here ends life in this house," escapes from him, almost as an afterthought to the factual statement about geographical distance. Still preoccupied with the luggage, Varya exclaims, "But where is it? Either I put it
in the trunk, perhaps" and then, in the same breath, as if it is part of the
same concern, "Yes, life in this house is ended—it won't be any more—."
After Lopakhin says where he will be going, he talks about the weather.
"Last year at this time it had already been snowing, if you remember, and
now it's quiet, it's sunny. It's only that it's cold, about three degrees of
frost." "I haven't noticed," Varya answers tersely. Another pause. "And
besides our thermometer is broken." As if in rescue, a voice from the yard
calls out to Lopakhin. "This minute," he says, in evident relief. Sitting on
the floor and laying her head on a bundle of clothes, Varya cries quietly.
Her mother, Madame Ranevsky, enters. Varya, already recovered, speaks
in her usual clipped style. "Yes, it's time, Mama. I can get to Regulin's
today, if we are just not too late for the train." Through the door, she calls
out to her sister, "Put your things on!"

Urged by Madame Ranevsky, Lopakhin had come to ask Varya to
marry him. Yet, as we've just seen, he makes no mention of marriage—
indeed, in either the words or the actions of both characters, there is no
suggestion of romantic feeling. On the surface, two people who are clearly
awkward in each other's presence talk nervously, with false animation and
tremulous pauses as the Ranevsky household is dismantled around them.
"Our thermometer is broken," Varya says, when it's really her broken heart
she is talking about. Luggage, distances, weather—this seemingly bland
exchange has momentous consequences for both characters. For Varya, not
being proposed to is a sign that she will likely remain a lifelong spinster;
to Lopakhin, not asking Varya to marry him is further evidence of his
inferior social status, his separateness from the aristocratic family whose
estate he has bought and whose beloved cherry orchard he is razing in order
to build rental property. Beneath her bustling efficiency—she runs the
house with a will of iron—Varya is deeply insecure about her womanliness,
and so she presents herself to Lopakhin as a kind of sexless wonder, a
household nun. For her, more than for Lopakhin, who sees that he doesn't
love her, that in fact she won't allow anyone to love her, this is a tragic
moment in which her darkest fears about her unlovableness are confirmed.
And yet the end of a part of her life—will Varya ever again get this close

to a proposal of marriage?—is presented almost as a comic footnote to the play's central action. Broken thermometers, and broken hearts: Chekhov's subtle comedy is touched with tragedy.

"To act Chekhov's plays on the stage, there must not be people only —glasses, chairs, crickets, military uniforms and wedding rings must also act," wrote the playwright Leonid Andreyev in a cunning assessment of Chekhov's art. "All the theatres, in which only human beings act, and objects do not," he continued, "cannot act Chekhov's plays. Where there are no wonderful pauses, where time has not learned to act, there is no Chekhov. . . . The dialogue is transferred from human beings to objects, from objects back to human beings and from human beings to time, to stillness or noise. Everything is alive, has a soul and a voice. Oh! how far removed his theatre was from the intolerable naturalism which had been grafted on the stage, and which knows *objects* only."[1] Andreyev's is the best description I know of Chekhov's spiritualized realism in which everything on stage from the simplest objects and sounds to the most seemingly casual conversations is wonderfully, magnetically alive and charged with unexpected significance.

Chekhov's method, then—the writing between the lines, as it were, where the true drama is being enacted; the filled silences; the interactions among a closely knit group of characters; the special charged reality of words, actions, objects, sounds, and place—demands an echoing method from actors. To bring to life characters who have a life beneath their words, in magnetized subterranean vaults, actors have to look beneath their own surfaces. To release their full flavor, Chekhov's plays require actors who share a past and know how to work from within. When he directed the four great plays, Stanislavski had an instinctive sense of how to translate their poetic realism into theatrical images, but he had no systematic means of training his actors. When inspiration struck, as, given the nature of his extraordinary, hand-picked actors, it often did, it was accidental, without true technical foundation.

It wasn't until 1906, several years after he had directed *The Cherry Orchard*, that Stanislavski had a System sufficiently thought through to be usable in production. Turgenev's *A Month in the Country* was the first play on which Stanislavski applied his theories in a conscious way. Written in 1850, Turgenev's play is an ideal Method text, the kind of comedy-drama of muted passions that anticipates Chekhov and that, especially considering when it was written, is astonishingly modern. Still, it's curious that Stanislavski chose *A Month in the Country* rather than a play by Chekhov as the first formal demonstration of his System. Was he still downplaying his attachment to Chekhov? Was he still underrating Chekhov's impact on the development of his own ideas about acting?

In *A Month in the Country* (subtitled *Scenes from Country Life*) feelings are expressed as obliquely as in Chekhov. Natalya, a country woman bored with her husband and suffering from some indefinite malaise, falls in love with her stepdaughter's tutor. Because this love crosses boundaries of age, class, and marital status, it dare not speak its name, although Natalya, being willful and devious, manipulates all the other characters in a doomed effort to claim it for herself. Her sudden tantrums, her abrupt shifts from exuberance to depression, are but the surface eruptions of a tumultuous inner life. Alternately charming and peevish, mercurial, and destructive, Natalya is a full-blooded Russian: emotions rush through her like wind through the trees.

Stanislavski instructed his actors to remain absolutely still as they spoke, in order to focus their concentration (as well as that of the audience) on what was happening inside their characters. "Let the actors sit without moving . . . let there be only a bench . . . and let all the persons in the play sit on it so as to display the inner essence and the word picture of the spiritual lacework of Turgenev": these were Stanislavski's monastic directions. He hoped that stasis would transmit a sense of the characters' private thoughts. Watching that first self-conscious demonstration of the System must have been like attending a wake.

Once he felt secure enough in his System to be able to use it as a rehearsal technique, he met with powerful resistance. In the absence of any rules or guidelines, his actors, like all actors before them, had devised their own individual systems, whether they could consciously articulate them or not; they regarded Stanislavski's new enthusiasm as one more interference from their despotic director. Stanislavski was not to be talked out of his new ideas, however much protest he encountered; he was so certain that he was on to something important that he established a studio in order to train actors in the fundamentals of the System.

2

BUILDING THE SYSTEM

How does the actor act? In simplest terms, that was the question that haunted Stanislavski. Actors before Stanislavski had of course thought about how they work but it was the rare actor, then as now, who could be articulate about it: the actor's art, after all, is in speaking other people's words.

Admiring the work of the great actors he had seen and eager to learn their secrets, the young Stanislavski discovered that for the most part the great actors carried their secrets to their graves. There were fragments here and there, but even these concerned ends more than means, intentions over technique. The great actors worked intuitively and were therefore above rules. Where did that leave actors of genuine talent who were less than geniuses and who therefore needed to supplement their natural instincts with a consciously worked-on technique? To his amazement, Stanislavski realized that he was in love with an art that had no laws and few written traditions, an art that seemed dangerously to depend on accident and chance.

"If the ability to receive the creative mood in its full measure is given to the genius by nature," Stanislavski wondered, "then perhaps ordinary people may reach a like state after a great deal of hard work with themselves —not in its full measure, but at least in part." How can the actor learn to inspire himself? What can he do to impel himself toward that necessary yet maddeningly elusive creative mood? These were the simple, awesome riddles Stanislavski dedicated his life to exploring. Where and how to "seek those roads into the secret sources of inspiration must serve as the fundamental life problem of every true actor."

Stanislavski thus set out to find some ground rules for an art that seemed to have stubbornly resisted them. Aware that a process as mysterious and individual as what an actor does to merge his being into the playwright's character can never be reduced to a single formula ("Is it necessary to say there can be no system for the creation of inspiration or system for creation itself?"), he yet wanted to define ideas about creative method that might be useful to all actors. "In the realm of psychic life there is a great deal that is necessary for all men, and the approach to which is the same for all men," Stanislavski was able to write in 1924 after almost thirty years of investigation. "These organic laws of creation, common to all mankind, and perceptible to our consciousness, are not many in number."

In identifying these "organic laws," Stanislavski was simply codifying what actors before him had thought but had never analyzed as thoroughly as he was prepared to. Rather than inventing or discovering, Stanislavski summarized a vast unwritten body of knowledge, recording procedures good actors had always instinctively followed, in a form that has continued to be useful and provocative. His work assures actors that their elusive art has a craft basis, that technique to some extent can control accident and the randomness of inspiration. As a reference and a guide rather than as a set of rules, Stanislavski's System legitimized the art of acting by providing it with a written tradition.

"True talent is deeply hidden in the soul," Stanislavski wrote. How to discover a conscious means for releasing the treasures we all have buried in our subconscious was the heroic quest that he embarked on. "THE SUPERCONSCIOUS THROUGH THE CONSCIOUS!" That was Stanislavski's creed, "the meaning of the thing to which I have devoted my life since the year 1906, to which I devote my life at present, and to which I will devote my life while there is life in me," he wrote in 1924.

The high task he set himself—how can the actor enter "the paradise of art?"—was one he knew he could never complete, and unlike some of his zealous disciples he never thought of his System as finished. It was, rather, a beginning, a whole series of beginnings, as can be seen by the number of times Stanislavski changed the emphasis and direction of his work. Always willing to consider new means of releasing the actor's expressiveness, as he moved from external to internal enticements, Stanislavski was continually evolving.

He hoped that the results of his lifetime of exploration in the vast subcontinent of creative nature would assist the actor in moments of difficulty, would offer guidance and support, clues and hints; but he never felt that the System was or could become a code of laws to be observed with orthodox piety, and he certainly never felt that mastery of it would create talent in the untalented or unleash inspiration in the uninspired. Rather, following some of the procedures he outlined, the innately gifted actor, faced with difficulties in bringing the author's character to life, might be able to edge himself into a creative mood.

The desired creative state that Stanislavski writes about so insistently is in a way trancelike. To arrive at it, the actor has to be relaxed and concentrated—he has to be calm, clear, and open. Stanislavski noticed that all the great actors he had seen shared a quality of "physical freedom. . . . Their bodies were at the call and beck of the inner demands of their wills." Over the years Stanislavski devised exercises to help the actor rid himself of muscular tensions and thereby open himself to the possibility of entering the "paradise of art." Once he is physically relaxed, and therefore more able to respond to feelings and impressions, the actor must direct his attention to an object, to a sensory or emotional memory, to his partner, or to a part of the stage—in short, to whatever he needs to focus on in order to arouse his own belief in the circumstances of the play and diminish his awareness of the audience.

Properly relaxed and concentrated, the actor has a chance of slipping into a creative state, where he can begin to reach the usually obscured depths of his subconscious, there to discover a stream of pure, flowing, usable emotions, memories, and images. At ease, focused, and ready to work creatively, the actor must now find some way of making himself believe in the reality of his character and of the action of the play. ("Scenic truth is not like truth in life, it is peculiar to itself," Stanislavski wrote.) How the actor is to stimulate his commitment to the playwright's fiction has been a hotly debated issue. Stanislavski himself changed his ideas about it, at one point emphasizing an external approach, at another an internal one.

For Stanislavski, the problem if not the solution was simple: to convince himself of the reality of the author's made-up world, and thereby to act truthfully the actor must learn to develop his imagination. The actor must ask himself: *What if* the situation in the play were really happening

—how would I react? Should I think of parallel examples from my own life? Should I find all the ways in which I am similar to the imaginary person created by the playwright? Would knowing how my character moves, what he wears, what he had for breakfast, who his parents were, help bring me closer to him? "Everything must be real in the imaginary life of the actor," Stanislavski noted. "From the moment of the appearance of *if*, the actor passes from the plane of the actual reality into the plane of another life, created and imagined by himself. Believing in this life, the actor can begin to create."

As he continued to experiment, Stanislavski modified his ideas about how actors could strengthen identification with their characters. His first, controversial approach was through affective memory,[2] in which the actor would recreate a vivid experience from his own life that might help to arouse emotions he needed for a scene. If the memory were sufficiently strong, Stanislavski found it could be used indefinitely, each time stirring the actor in the same way. In time, Stanislavski moved away from the intense focus on the actor's own life that was required for the affective memory exercise toward a concentration on the behavior and actions of the character. This later phase resulted in what is called the method of physical actions. Although they seem opposite, the affective memory technique and the method of physical actions have the same goal, to coax the actor toward the innermost source of his creativity. Whether the preparation starts with inner work—the actor combing his past in the search for emotional stimuli —or with physical actions, its aim is to lead the actor to an artistic recreation of "the life of the human spirit"—to acting that is immediate, fresh, alive, natural, organic, and truthful.

How to heighten and rearrange life-truths into theatrical ones and, once a semblance of the actual has been caught on the stage, how to make it seem as if what is happening is for the first time were the entwined goals of Stanislavski's quest as he shifted his course from affective memory to the method of physical actions. At the same time he changed his focus from the actor's inner work to the actor's work on the given circumstances provided by the playwright. Although the methods shifted, the end— capturing "the life of a human spirit" during the two hours' traffic of the stage—remained the same. Eager disciples, less catholic and more doctrinaire than the Master, have taken up firm battle positions, insisting that one or another of Stanislavski's approaches—the affective memory, the magic *if*, or the method of physical actions—is the only route to tapping the actor's creative roots. It is a battle that scarred the Group Theatre and, a half century later, continues to rage, with believers in the Actors Studio's use of affective memory lined up on one side, as detractors join ranks with an answering militancy on the other.

Stanislavski called all of his methods examples of psychophysical technique: all of Stanislavski's investigations of how actors create can in fact be seen as a continuing dialogue between body and spirit. In approaching a play, Stanislavski looked for the subtext pulsing beneath the text; so in his work on his System he always linked the actor's physical presence —the way he looks and sounds and moves—to something beyond it, his higher spiritual self.

Like Freud, who was conducting his own experiments at about the same time and whose ideas matured just as Stanislavski began to codify his System, the Russian director's concern was in reaching the subconscious. Like Freud, Stanislavski asked: What truths lie beneath our conscious minds? How do gestures express feelings? What meanings are buried in words a character speaks? Stanislavski's aim, left uncompleted at his death, was to construct a System for the actor which would forge links between text and subtext, reason and emotion, body and soul, life and art. He was after nothing less than a grand synthesis between the worlds of the flesh and the spirit.

Although Stanislavski's studies were concerned with the creative problems of the actor, his comments have a universal reference. Any artist, regardless of medium, indeed anyone who lives (or wants to live) expressively, can recognize and profit from the truths Stanislavski uncovered. His real subject was the enigma of man's creative nature, and to begin to fathom this he became, in various measures, psychologist, laboratory scientist, teacher, and writer.[3] Stanislavski's goal was to enliven the actor's "instrument," and his suggestions about ways to sharpen sensory responsiveness, memory, and self-awareness, and about how to gain greater control over physical and emotional reactions, can be instructive to us civilians as well; they can, in fact, be seen as comprising a guide to living more creatively. From the pages of Stanislavski's many books springs a bracing sense of well-being. Having mastered his System—its lessons had become second nature to him, both offstage and on—Stanislavski exuded sensitivity and control. Stella Adler, who studied with him for six weeks in Paris in 1934, remembers him as a man of "enormous size, a giant spiritually as well as physically." In photographs, invariably, he is a towering presence, his radiant face bathed in the light of a special vision. He looks indeed like one who sees: a Russian mystic tied to the earth by a core of terrific common sense. An extraordinary patience and kindliness emanate from him, and a deep wisdom. Here is a man who knows, the photographs tell us, confirming the impression created by his books; here is a true leader and guide.

He wouldn't have defined it exactly this way, but Stanislavski was a missionary, a bringer of light. I am myself a rationalist and something of a skeptic, yet I can feel Stanislavski's spiritual force; it's there in the writing, and in the testimony of his colleagues and disciples, and its intensity reaches out to me, a non-actor and an American, across the decades and over the boundaries of national sensibility. Stanislavski bequeathed more than a craft legacy to actors, he gave them a sense of the dignity and the responsibility of their profession. He told them, both in his work and in the way he lived his life, that ultimately truthful acting can flow only from truthful living; that to be able to act realistically, honestly, freshly, and intuitively is to be able to live those qualities too, at a deep instinctual level, beyond the need for practice or for rules. The highest acting comes from the highest living: this simple connection emanates from every page of Stanislavski's written legacy. A student of human behavior, the Stanislavski actor must cultivate keenness about himself and others as a way of life, and must be able to translate his life-observations into theatrical truth. "Let the artist live," Stanislavski's voice rings out, "but let him at the same time learn to recreate his life and his emotions into art." It's no wonder that Stanislavski warned his actors that mastery of his System was the work of a lifetime.

In 1896, when Stanislavski and Nemirovich-Danchenko drew up their agenda for their Theatre, they were theatrical rebels, brandishing psychological realism as their battle cry. In less than a decade, and certainly by the time of the Bolshevik Revolution in 1917, they had evolved into theatrical elder statesmen temporarily overshadowed by upstarts who denounced them as dry-as-dust conservatives. The militant new theatrical leaders, several of whom had emerged from the ranks of the Moscow Art Theatre itself, dismissed Stanislavski's continuing interest in realism as sterile and confining.

Given the Russian love of dialectic, Stanislavski's fervent dedication to realism inevitably provoked a counterreaction. Theatre companies were organized expressly to oppose the art-reflects-life theme that dominated the Moscow Art, and during an extraordinary Golden Age of Russian theatre that lasted for approximately twenty years, from 1905 to 1925, a number of radical companies were formed, each with its own strident agenda, each passionately convinced that its own particular "-ism" was the "correct" one.

Shrewd theatre man that he was, Stanislavski realized that any style, and especially realism, which is the largest, most difficult style of all, required frequent refueling. He recognized that to keep the house style fresh and to prevent its degeneration into the kinds of clichés that he had from the beginning opposed, his Theatre needed to be open to experiment.

"Those who think that we sought for naturalism on the stage are mistaken," Stanislavski answered his critics. He denied, and rightly so, that the Moscow Art Theatre was a "realistic theatre only, that we were interested only in local color, and that all that was abstract and unreal was uninteresting to us. And yet who had been the first to produce plays of the latter character in Russia? Who was it who was really interested in the quest and creation of the abstract? But once an idea gets into the mind of the public, it is hard to dislodge it," he wrote, irritated at being typecast.

Although Stanislavski's deepest interest and his highest achievement were firmly rooted in the work of the Russian realists, from the start of his career he had been charmed by other possibilities. Acting and production design may be "realistic, conventionalized, modernistic, naturalistic, impressionistic, futuristic," he wrote. "It is all the same so long as they are convincing, that is, truthful or truthlike; beautiful, that is, artistic; uplifted, and creating the true life of the human spirit without which there can be no art." In his youth, he had studied to be an opera singer, and he maintained a lifelong devotion to this most exaggerated of performance styles. (In 1918, he founded his own Opera Studio.) From his amateur days, he retained a passing taste for melodrama, throwing himself into the direction of *The Two Orphans,* for instance, a potboiler about the French Revolution, with greater enthusiasm than he had orignally had for Chekhov. "I like to create deviltry in the theatre," he said with pride. "In the realm of the fantastic, the stage can still do a great deal." Symbolism, allegory, constructivism, futurism, fantasy, abstraction, poetry—modern Russian and foreign "-isms" of varying stripes were all welcomed at the Moscow Art Theatre.

Stanislavski's spectacular 1903 production of Maeterlinck's fantasy *The Blue Bird* was among the most successful and long-lived in his Theatre's repertory. The Moscow Art housed overblown allegories like Andreyev's *Anathema* and *The Life of Man;* classic Russian satires like *The Government Inspector* and *Wit Works Woe;* stylized foreign plays by Goldoni, Molière, Hamsun, Hauptmann, Ibsen, and (never successfully) Shakespeare.[4] In a gesture that decades of theatre historians have read as a token of his open-mindedness, Stanislavski invited the visionary anti-naturalist Gordon Craig to direct *Hamlet.* Spouting his heretical notion that actors should be replaced by marionettes, Craig barged his way into the Theatre that Stanislavski had erected in honor of the art of the actor. The production that emerged from the inevitable clash between the two strong-willed directors pleased neither, but was remarkable for having been undertaken in the first place.

Realizing the need for a workshop where modernist styles that had invaded Russian poetry, painting, and music could be tried out for their theatrical fit, Stanislavski founded a Studio in 1905. "The principle of the new Studio . . . was that realism and local color had lived their life and no longer interested the public." When he established the Studio, he was willing to acknowledge that "the time for the unreal on stage had arrived."

To direct this experimental outpost, Stanislavski selected an actor from the Moscow Art company who had been the original Treplev in *The Sea Gull* and the original Tusenbach in *Three Sisters,* a man whose name would in time become as legendary as that of the Master himself: Vsevolod Meyerhold. "Meyerhold and I sought for one and the same thing . . . that impressionism which had already been established in the other arts, but had not yet been applied in ours," Stanislavski wrote.

Two plays were rehearsed, but neither was ever publicly performed because Stanislavski was not pleased with the work. Although he disbanded the Studio, this first failure led the way to the formation of a series of Studios where, under the shadow of the Moscow Art Theatre, avant-garde, anti-realist ideas could be fought over, tried out, discarded, or absorbed into the life blood of the parent company. These Studios became, in effect, labs where young actors could be trained in the System, and where fledgling directors like Meyerhold could gain the experience they needed in order to challenge and sometimes to break away from their patrons.

Meyerhold's career indicates how the Studios helped to change the character of Russian theatre. A skilled realist actor, Meyerhold quickly grew disenchanted with the Moscow Art style and soon after Stanislavski closed the Studio he embarked on a peripatetic, far-reaching career that was to end in 1939 with his execution in one of Stalin's concentration camps. Like all Russian leaders, Meyerhold was a fiery polemicist who thrived on debate, hammering out his theatrical beliefs in defiance of the realism he had been trained in at the Moscow Art. A born theorist, Meyerhold seemed to receive a lifetime's injection of energy from his heated denouncements of Stanislavski's aesthetic; rebelling against his first director gave his own work a sharp focus.[5]

If the goals of Stanislavski's theatre can be seen (in *The Sea Gull*) in a group of actors with their backs to the audience, Meyerhold's aims are revealed (in a production of *Wit Works Woe*) in an equally powerful counterimage. Here a stageful of actors are seated behind a banquet table that extends the entire width of the proscenium. Far from turning their backs, Meyerhold's actors stare insolently at the audience. Theatre is not life, they seem to be saying; it is a spectacle. An entire stageful of actors placed behind an outsized table: Here is the audacious signature of a director in active competition with the playwright, a director determined to proclaim his ingenuity. What bravado is announced in that tableau, and what a luxurious sense of theatre!

Though Stanislavski indeed explored other styles, he always returned to his beloved realism, whereas Meyerhold remained a theatrical knight errant jousting at windmills. Fueled by his contempt for Moscow Art austerity—its plain auditorium; its refusal at one point in its history to allow applause or curtain calls; the pious atmosphere that Stanislavski cultivated, as if going to the theatre were like going to church—Meyerhold wanted to return theatre to its Dionysian roots. To put theatre back into the theatre, to recharge it with an air of carnival and bacchanal, to scrub away the propriety that Stanislavski overlaid on all his productions, Meyerhold experimented widely and freely with a variety of avant-garde notions, approaching each with an almost childlike wonder, and never settling for long in any one style. He had a go at cubism, impressionism, and expressionism. He used ideas from the commedia dell'arte and the Japanese Noh theatre. Sometimes he put his actors in masks and had them move in ceremonial

A scene from Maeterlinck's fantasy *The Blue Bird* (1903), Stanislavski's most successful departure from realism.

processions. Anticipating some of the methods of Brecht's alienation technique, he broke up texts into a series of episodes announced by placards,
kept the lights on during performances, and had the curtain removed so
audiences entering the theatre immediately saw the playing area. To bring
the play closer to the audience, he would send actors scurrying up and down
the aisles.

His methods changed, but he always held on to his belief that realism
(he called it naturalism) was dangerously wrong-headed. He declared war
on Stanislavski's dramas of language and psychology, insisting that the
essence of theatre was movement and that the actor's art lay in the precise
and knowledgeable use of his body. To serve that idea, he developed his
own counter-System, called biomechanics, in which his actors worked on
their bodies in the same rigorous way that the Stanislavski actor examined
his soul. Biomechanics became the basis for a drama of ritualized movement, of gesture and mime, to oppose Stanislavski's lifelike picture-frame
stage: a body theatre to challenge a theatre of words and faces.

While Stanislavski remained aloof from politics—for him, plays served art rather than the state—Meyerhold moved in and out of politics like a jack-in-the-box. Originally as uncommitted as his mentor, Meyerhold joined the Bolsheviks after 1917, rejecting the pictorial pomp and lushness of his pre-Revolutionary work for a stark, abstract, constructivist style. With its asymmetrical arrangement of bare platforms, the new look of Meyerhold's work seemed to herald a brave new world of sleek industrial efficiency and proletarian briskness. In time, once Stalin began to subvert the Bolshevik ideal, constructivism, along with a host of other radical styles that had flourished in agitated response to "bourgeois realism," was branded formalist and decadent.

Passionate embrace of one "-ism," or system of belief, followed by decisive turnabout was a common pattern in Russian arts, reflecting a deep need for clash and counterpoint, of which Meyerhold, unlike the imperial Stanislavski, was a victim. Once socialist realism was declared the official style—the only style acceptable to the state and, in a sense, no style at

Meyerhold, the most daring of Stanislavski's challengers.

all—Meyerhold was a goner. He made weak statements of adherence to the new cultural orthodoxy, but at a directors' conference in 1939 he spoke in a way that showed his true and only identity, as a theatrical firebrand and maverick, an artist rather than a Party member. Within a month, he died in one of Stalin's camps, and his wife was found murdered in their apartment; "the victim of a burglary," read the official report.

In the years leading up to and following the Revolution, Russian theatre, then, was as polarized as Russian politics: the forces of the old and the forces of the new faced each other behind a volley of theory and pronouncement. Out of this melee of raised voices one person would emerge to reconcile the extremes of Stanislavski realism on the one hand and Meyerhold theatricality on the other. Although this mediator, Eugene Vakhtangov, doesn't carry the fame of his two predecessors, he is still regarded reverently in theatre circles. Like Meyerhold—like everyone who attained theatrical stature in the Russian theatre's Golden Age, for that matter—Vakhtangov received his training at the Moscow Art, at its Third Studio (now known as the Vakhtangov Theatre). Like Meyerhold, Vakhtangov never spoke in a negative way about Stanislavski, who remained his benefactor even as Vakhtangov began to modify the Master's precepts in the few productions he directed before his early death in 1922. Vakhtangov based his work on a foundation of Stanislavski realism, adding elements to it rather than, like Meyerhold, erecting a performance style over the ashes of its destruction. Stanislavski approved: "Vakhtangov understands my ideas at a deeper level than anyone else," he said.

At the height of his powers in the years immediately following the Revolution, Vakhtangov felt an obligation to connect theatre with politics; since no worthy Bolshevik plays had yet been written, he returned to established material with a fresh eye. One of his most celebrated productions was a radical reinterpretation of Chekhov's long one-act comedy, *A Wedding*. In 1921, in the aftermath of political upheaval, Vakhtangov could not react to Chekhov's bourgeois intelligentsia with the poised acceptance that Stanislavski had shown two decades earlier. Because Chekhov's wedding celebrants seemed to him to inhabit a different world, he turned them into figures of Hogarthian caricature, grotesque embodiments of pre-Bolshevik bourgeois decadence.

Constructivist setting and stylized movement in Meyerhold's 1922 production of
Tarelkin's Death.

Vakhtangov's colors were more primary than Stanislavski's, his "realism" expressed in a broader, more extroverted style. There were vaudevillian touches in his work and political lampoon, all with the Master's blessings.

In November 1917, a few weeks after the October Revolution, an American theatrical press agent sat huddled against the Russian cold in a corner of a Moscow train station while "out on the street in front of the station the rattle of small arms rose and fell with all the realism of a well-staged Western melodrama." Oliver Sayler had traveled halfway around the world to sample at first hand the treasures of the Russian theatrical renaissance. Although theatres were closed when he arrived, in less than a week they had resumed their normal schedules. With the contours of the new society only dimly perceivable beyond the rumble of gunfire, Russians continued to go to the theatre as if theatregoing were an immutable natural right. As Sayler admiringly noted in *The Russian Theatre*, the inspiring book that recounts his journey, Russian audiences looked to the theatre for something other than entertainment or temporary relief, wanting instead to confront, through the mirror of dramatic art, their own deepest impulses. "The Russian theatre has persisted through the days of anxiety and the Terror," Sayler wrote. "Out of their sorrows the Russians have [built] all their art. And in the days of their profoundest gloom, they return to it for the consolation which nothing else affords. The Russian theatre has persisted, therefore, not because it is a relief from life, an underground retreat where one could escape the agonies and the duties and the burdens of life. To the Russian, the theatre is rather a microcosmos, a concentration and an explanation of life."

The theatre activity that bedazzled Sayler throughout the tense winter of 1917 was surely the equal of the theatres of ancient Athens, Renaissance Italy, Shakespeare's England, and Molière's France, where the art of the drama occupied a place of central importance in the life of the community. The Moscow Art Theatre and its various Studios were first on Sayler's list, but he was also impressed by productions at the Maly, the guardian of Russian classicism, and at the many thriving alternate theatres—the anti-Stanislavski companies like the experimental Kamerny, under the direction of Alexander Tairoff and Alice Koonen (a refugee from the Moscow Art), whose cubist production of *Salome* was a great hit; Balieff's *Chauve-Souris*

(The Bat), Moscow's equivalent of American vaudeville and cabaret (Balieff, Russia's premier clown, had also trained at the Moscow Art); and the adventurous Kommisarzhevskaya Memorial Theatre. In Petersburg, he saw Evreinoff's radical monodrama and Meyerhold's productions of *Don Juan* and *Masquerade.* Positioning itself somewhere along the Stanislavski-Meyerhold axis, each theatre was wedded to its own proudly announced agenda, armed with its own visionary aims. Each theatre not only trained its actors but also imbued them with its philosophy. With their clear-cut sense of mission, their players unified in training and beliefs, and their almost daily changes of program, the Moscow theatres were pure examples of what Oliver Sayler had never been able to see on native grounds: full-fledged repertory companies.

Joyfully, Sayler returned to New York to write up his impressions (the first edition of *The Russian Theatre* was published in 1920) and, along with the Russian-born theatrical impresario Morris Gest, he began to beat the drum to bring the first theatre of the world to America. On January 21, 1923, amidst delirious anticipation, the Moscow Art Theatre opened at Jolson's 59th Street Theatre, and American acting has never been the same.

3

STANISLAVSKI
IN AMERICA

Tall and princely, looking like a visiting dignitary, Stanislavski was jolted by his American reception. On their arrival, he and his company were given a brassy welcome and then hurled into a vortex of publicity. Lionized, fêted, interviewed, photographed, and wined and dined, the Russian artists were inundated by American know-how and fanfare: the circus might have come to town. "I like New York and its inhabitants," Stanislavski said. "The city is rather tawdry—but comfortable."

Beneath the hoopla Stanislavski could see that there was a genuine respect for his work. "Some of the famous actors and actresses seize my hand and kiss it as though in a state of ecstasy," he said. "We have never had such a success in Moscow or anywhere else. No one here seems to have had any idea what our Theatre and our actors were capable of."

"What an embryonic stage art is in here and how eagerly they snatch up everything good that is brought to America," Stanislavski noted with more condescension than truth, for in New York in the early twenties, a time of unparalleled prosperity and expansiveness, American arts were beginning to flourish. Americans still felt culturally inferior to Europeans (as Russians had in the nineteenth century), but writers, composers, and painters were also discovering distinctive American styles and subjects. When the Russians came to town in January 1923, the American theatre was already launched on what was to be the most glittering decade in its history. The theatrical twenties set records in sheer quantity that will never be broken, and the quality was often pretty good too, certainly better than it had ever been before. Frequently gaudy, almost always energetic, American theatre in the twenties reflected American pace and verve. Until 1920,

51

theatre in America had been as backward and tradition-bound as the nine-teenth-century Russian theatre that had disgusted Stanislavski and Chek-hov; then, as if by historical design, in February 1920 a good play by a new American playwright —Eugene O'Neill's *Beyond the Horizon*— was produced on Broadway, a significant first step in the creation of a serious native dramatic literature. At last America had a playwright to boast about, and as if inspired by O'Neill's example, other writers throughout the decade mingled their voices in a hardy theatrical chorus. Before 1920, the best the American theatre had produced was Clyde Fitch, craftsmanlike but inescapably provincial, the playwright as carpenter, and David Belasco, whose idea of realism was to reproduce a section of a Child's Restaurant. But in the twenties a group of writers, among them George Kelly, Philip Barry, George Kaufman, Sidney Howard, Elmer Rice, Ben Hecht, and Maxwell Anderson, began to write about the American scene in a tangy, homegrown style. Whenever they had wanted to get serious, American producers before 1920 had had to rely on imports and revivals of classics. Now, on the other side of *Beyond the Horizon*, they began to have a fund of authentic American originals to choose from.

In the twenties, the American theatre had money and technical know-how so that it could afford sets and costumes and lighting that the visiting Russians couldn't hope to match. It had directors like Jed Harris and George Abbott and George Kaufman who knew how to keep a show moving at a trim, neat clip. It had high-minded impresarios like Morris Gest (who sponsored the Moscow Art Theatre), producers of taste like Arthur Hopkins (who presented important foreign plays), and barracudas and flesh mer-chants like Al Woods, who made fortunes peddling trash. It even began to develop critics like George Jean Nathan, Alexander Woollcott, and Stark Young, who were personalities in their own right. And, as only in America, it had a wealth of popular music—in the sumptuous, girl-glorifying Ziegfeld Follies, in George White's Scandals, in the Passing Shows, in Irving Ber-lin's Music Box Revues, in shows like *The Blackbirds* that brought the rhythms of Harlem to midtown, and in musical theatre that told stories like *No, No, Nanette* and *Showboat*, to take a low and a high example of this uniquely American genre.

And, perhaps above all, the American theatrical twenties had stars ("The whole theatrical business in America is based on the personality of the actor," Stanislavski noticed): Katharine Cornell, the Barrymores, Marilyn Miller, Jane Cowl, Laurette Taylor, Pauline Lord, Helen Hayes, the Lunts, Paul Robeson, Ina Claire, Jeanne Eagels. There were stars with glamor and style, with sex appeal and ready-made personalities, whose names alone were enough to sell tickets, and there were stars, like the Lunts and John Barrymore (occasionally), who could even act.

But what the American theatre didn't have, and could barely even envision, was a true repertory company, a band of players who had the benefits of similar training, years of practical experience in working together, a body of distinguished plays to draw from, and agreed-upon aims and ideals. Only in the Provincetown Players and the Theatre Guild had the American theatre produced something similar to the Moscow Art; but in 1923 the Provincetown, which had fostered the early work of O'Neill, was on the point of disbanding and the Theatre Guild, though embarked on what was to be a long and distinguished history, was not really a company at all, and certainly not in the Russian sense. It did not present its plays in alternating repertory, but in open-ended runs, according to what the market could bear. Although it had actors under contract, it kept losing them to Hollywood, or to the more lucrative offers of other producers. Too, the Guild built its prestige on foreign plays—Shaw was the favorite house dramatist—and did virtually nothing to encourage American writers. But most significantly, the Guild had no fundamental, sustaining ideas about theatre, and unlike Stanislavski's company, no system of training to weld its performers into a genuine ensemble. To be sure, it had some first-rate actors who, very much in the American grain, proved to be dedicated more to their own advancement than the Guild's. This was a company of would-be stars, for the most part, rather than a disciplined ensemble devoted above all to their theatre and their art.

In the twenties as now, an American actor in love with acting and indifferent to the big break might not long survive in the cutthroat New York theatre. The kind of economy on which Broadway always has and always will be run has produced some wonderful theatre, but because it is unlikely ever to produce an American equivalent of the Moscow Art, the Russian company was a revelation.

The visitors opened with their signature production of *Tsar Fyodor*, followed by *The Cherry Orchard* and *Three Sisters*, *The Lower Depths*, and three scenes from *The Brothers Karamazov* together with Turgenev's one-act comedy, *The Lady from the Provinces*. By this time in the company's history,

Stanislavski had been instructing his actors in his System for over fifteen years and so the performances Americans saw had an even greater stylistic consistency and a deeper and more secure inner life than the premiere performances of these plays had had. Americans were witness to the culmination of a quarter-century of Stanislavski's experiments in truthful acting and, stimulated by the adulation that swept over them, it may be that in New York in 1923 the Moscow Art players were at their inspired best.

"The emotions of the audience rose to match the emotions on the stage. At the close there were such cheers and shouts as New York had never heard—even the chilliest of Anglo-Saxons were swept up in it," reported the *New York American,* in a breathless account of opening night, January 9, 1923. "The Moscow Art Theatre proved for perhaps the first time in America that culture can sometimes be as exciting as a football game." What was it that American audiences so appreciated? What did they see in the Russian actors that they could not find in American ones? What struck them as so new and important?

First, I think, it was the strong sense of a group of actors sharing the stage that American theatregoers noticed. The measure of how much an impact the ensemble playing had can be seen in the grumbling reaction of an American xenophobe, a dim reviewer named John Golden. "The ensemble work is an accident of the Russian character," he snorted. "The Russian is accustomed to an atmosphere where complete and indeed servile obedience is required from one class to another. He is willing to yield himself utterly to the director's orders. The American actor has too much independence, too high a degree of individuality, to make this possible." Even to a bigot, then, the company's group unity was palpably evident. It was the sense of give-and-take among the actors, the charged interplay, the unified performing style, that audiences commented on. In ensemble theatre, every role, including extras in group scenes, is filled with vivid, life-giving details; indeed, the company's group scenes—the gypsy tavern revelry in *The Brothers Karamazov,* the court pageanty in *Tsar Fyodor,* the stageful of loungers and talkers in Chekhov—were applauded for their vitality and spontaneity. In ensemble theatre, actors who listen are as crucial in sustaining the lifelike illusion as actors who have the lines. One critic commented on how intently Olga Knipper paid attention throughout her scenes in *Tsar Fyodor,* as if she hadn't been hearing exactly the same dialogue for the past quarter of a century.

Surely it is no accident that *Three Sisters, The Cherry Orchard, The*

Part of the ensemble in *The Lower Depths*. Stanislavski is at center, leaning against the table. "The ensemble work is an accident of the Russian character," an American critic grumbled.

Lower Depths, and *Tsar Fyodor*—the jewels in the Moscow Art's crown—are about groups of characters: extended families, as in Chekhov; political units, as in *Fyodor*; socioeconomic units, as in Gorky. What any individual character does affects the group, while the group supplies the arena against which each individual action resounds. There are no heroes in the American sense, no one character who either has primary claim on the attention of the audience or rises up from the crowd to triumph over circumstances. In these Russian plays, the characters go down for the count—together.

The ensemble was extraordinary, but the company's actors also had true star calibre. To the Russians, a repertory theatre meant not what it often has in America, a company of commonplace actors who couldn't make it on their own, but as Stella Adler says, a company where every actor "played like a big star. That's what ensemble is—a *group* of stars like the Moscow Art Theatre had. You'd go to see every one of their actors; every single actor in the company had the ability to be a star." The names of some of the original Moscow Art players—Moskvin, Katchaloff, Leonidov, Knipper-Chekhova, Stanislavski—have become like talismans to actors who care about good acting. Although they never violated the unity Stanislavski insisted on, and never used acting as self-advertisement, they performed with authority.

In the 1923 season, there were two scenes (in *The Brothers Karamazov*) of virtuoso acting that became the talk of the theatrical community: Katchaloff as Ivan, in an extended monologue in which the two parts of the character's typically divided Russian soul engage in tortured debate; and Moskvin as Smerdyakof, who, in refusing money from Ivan in recompense for the brutish way Dmitri has treated him, became the image of a lost soul retaining one last, tragic claim to honor. These scenes stood out from the ensemble in a blaze of actorly incandescence.

"Our actors smirk and ogle and are quite at home with the gathering before them," wrote Alan Dale in the *New York Journal.* But "these Russian actors evinced complete oblivion to an audience. . . . Here were people concentrated upon their work. . . . taught to sink their personalities." Dale was struck by "the utter self-forgetfulness of the actors." American audiences, used to seeing stars transporting a prefabricated personality from role to role, were delighted at being unable to recognize the Russian actors in different parts. Playing (metaphorically more often than literally) with their backs to the audience, the actors submerged themselves in their parts, hiding out beneath costumes and makeup. In *Tsar Fyodor,* Moskvin had a regal bearing; in *The Lower Depths,* as Luka, unrecognizable behind a tangled beard and flowing cap, he seemed to have shrunk; in *The Brothers Karamazov,* he assumed yet another face, that of a defeated, humiliated old servant. As the cynical Satin in *The Lower Depths,* the absentminded, avuncular Gaev in *The Cherry Orchard,* and the handsome, lovesick soldier Vershinin in *Three Sisters,* Stanislavski seemed to inhabit three separate bodies. Like Moskvin, he transformed himself physically, vocally, and spiritually for each of his roles, growing shorter, taller, stouter, handsomer, or sillier as the parts demanded. Neither actor carried an identifiable persona from one character to the next: they seemed to remake themselves for each play.

"Most Americans lead a decent, clean, and happy life": our friend John Golden again, speaking up for the American way, and again, his obtuse vehemence is a gauge of how sharp an impact the Russians had. "Most Americans do not have any contact with the degraded individuals, morbid, neurotic, and vicious, seen in so many Russian dramas." If we can't accept Golden's "morbid" and "vicious," we would have no question about the "neurotic" element. Indeed, the Russian repertory was awash with characters wracked by neuroses—characters with inner lives far richer and

Stanislavski as Satin in *The Lower Depths,* and as Gaev in *The Cherry Orchard.* With each role, Stanislavski seemed to assume a different physical and spiritual presence.

more troubled than any that had yet appeared on the American stage. (It wouldn't be until the early plays of Tennessee Williams in the forties that American characters as layered and gnarled as those of Chekhov would appear, and it's not by chance that Williams's work would be interpreted most persuasively by Actors Studio actors, trained in the American version of the Stanislavski System.)

Golden might dismiss the Russian characters as sick and unwholesome, but a more enlightened American viewer, John Corbin, writing in the *New York Times,* identified the charged atmosphere as "realism of the spirit," "intensity of soul revelation , . . . a characteristically Russian quality manifest in every page of Tolstoy and Dostoevski." "Every actor is aglow and vibrant with it. . . . We have not the Slavic gift of the persistently incandescent soul, of the persistently illumined countenance." "Spirit," "soul," "revelation," "incandescence," "illumination"—these words are written with awe, as if the critic is in the presence of something beyond the American grasp. Reviewers as well as audiences didn't have ready words for what they saw, though they knew they weren't merely seeing a transcript of life; the Russian actor behaved in a surpassingly natural way (one writer said that you felt like joining in during a card game in *Ivanov*), but audiences felt that something beyond photographic realism coated the performances. Many American critics could find no better way of expressing the luminous acting and so openly borrowed Stanislavski's own phrase to describe what they had seen: "the revelation of the life of the human spirit."

New Yorkers would not let the Russians go and so by popular demand (which for once was not a mere public relations phrase) the company returned for a second season in the fall of 1923 after having toured. This time, their repertory was not exclusively Russian, and it included three comedies to show what they could do in an uncharacteristic light vein: there was one Chekhov, the early *Ivanov*; two Russian comedies of manners, both in the satiric spirit of Gogol, *The Death of Pazukin* and *Enough Stupidity in Every Wise Man*; a full-length version of *The Brothers Karamazov*; and three foreign plays—Ibsen's *Enemy of the People*, in which Stanislavski played Stockmann, a part for which he said he didn't have to use the System because it came to him intuitively, Goldoni's high-spirited *The Mistress of the Inn*, and *In the Claws of Life*, Knut Hamsun's romantic melodrama which absolutely nobody liked ("it is no more Russian than you are," Alexander Woollcott sniffed).

"In two seasons, Stanislavski's players have said farewell as often as Bernhardt did in a decade," reported the *New York Times*. But finally, on May 12, 1924, after two engagements in New York and a tour of principal cities, mostly in the East, the company did offer a farewell gala. Stanislavski as Brutus and Katchaloff as Marc Antony delivered the funeral orations from *Julius Caesar*, Madame Knipper-Chekhova read Chekhov's *The Student* followed by *The Marriage Proposal*, Katchaloff performed a scene from *The Death of Ivan the Terrible*, Moskvin and Valdimir Gribunin acted in a short farce, *Surgery or the Village Dentist*, and the company performed several scenes from *The Brothers Karamazov*.

Having been on special leave from the Russian government, the actors departed—except for two, who remained behind in response to impassioned requests from the American theatre community to bring the gospel according to Stanislavski to the New World.

"At Richard Boleslavski's American Lab Theatre, you were flooded with clarity and health and values," Stella Adler recalls. "Boleslavski was a brilliant speaker who carried on the tradition of Stanislavski and Chaliapin. They were all giants on the stage, powerful forces in the theatre. Like Russian music, they were strong and big—you got this Moussorgsky quality from the men—it wasn't an English quality, I can tell you that!"

Stella Adler remembers going to the new American Laboratory Theatre to see Boleslavski's production of a play called *The Sea Woman's Cloak.* "It was important, I knew that at once. It had size and background. It was in a tradition. It represented the kind of acting that hadn't been seen in America before." Already a working actress, Stella Adler nonetheless enrolled in the school that was attached to the theatre because she wanted to absorb "the spiritual aura that all the Russians have." Her father, the great Yiddish actor Jacob Adler, was a Russian Jew, so some of the Russian "size and spirit" she admired was already flowing in her veins. "People who loved the theatre knew that theatre in Russia was great," Adler says. "We all went to the Lab hoping some of that greatness would spill onto us. The Russians are deeper than we are, and an artist in Russia was of the highest degree. We didn't have that tradition here."

The Lab, originally called the Theatre Arts Institute, was founded in 1923 as a school for young American actors like Stella Adler who wanted something "bigger" than what the commercial American theatre offered. Providing a full three-year program to specially selected students, the Lab promised more than technical instruction; it aimed to be a theatrical holy ground, a place where the spirit dwells and is given flight. As such, it was a significant first step in translating Stanislavski's ideas into an American idiom.

Impressed by the Moscow Art performances, a group of wealthy American patrons led by Miriam Stockton approached Boleslavski to become the director of a school for "the encouragement and development of native talent and genius in the theatre arts." Boleslavski agreed, provided that the organizers understood that it would be impossible to "impose any foreign ideal upon American soil"; he cautioned them that American actors could not become like the Russians they had admired merely by studying Stanislavski's System. Working together with Boleslavski, the founders of the Theatre Arts Institute adopted a platform:

1. This theatre must grow here by itself and must get its roots into American soil.

2. It must begin slowly, training young Americans for the stage in all its departments.

3. It must be recognized and organized as a living social force, recreating itself each generation from the thoughts and material of its own times.

The sponsors called their school "an unpretentious effort to implant a new cultural force in America."

Since Boleslavski wanted to impress his eager American students with the fact that the glistening acting they had seen in the work of the Moscow Art Theatre was the result of years of dedicated practice and that intuition no matter how ennobled it might be had to be harnessed to a conscious technique, students began their studies at the beginning, with classes in diction, voice production, and body rhythm. Only after a year of classroom exercises and practical study did the school evolve into a workshop of scenes and play production.

The American Laboratory Theatre bulletin for 1924–25 boasted that in its first season it had created among its twenty American students "an organic group, similar to the Guild of medieval times, which, in the collective practice of its craft, has become a living theatre—that is to say, a theatre in which each actor strives to act his part, however humble, as if it were a major part in the play but harmonized toward a perfect ensemble." With a fervor that must surely have struck some of his American students with its distinctly un-American sentiment, Boleslavski idealized the benefits of group training. Here he is, sounding alarmingly militaristic: "It is not generally understood how important it is artistically to train a group of actors by the collective method. The weak and inefficient will not survive the test of collective work, leaving the field to those who have genuine talent. Only through the inspiration of a keen collective effort based on what I like to call 'noble competition,' is the soul of the actor disciplined by his art, the soul which is the source of all art."

The first result of this "collective method" was *The Sea Woman's Cloak*. Working with his students on it for ten months, first in classroom exercises, then in a workshop lab, and finally in full production before paying audiences, Boleslavski came up with a winner. It was a performance that Lee Strasberg would often refer to with deep respect in sessions at the Actors Studio, a performance that inspired Stella Adler to enroll in the

Lab's school, and one that prompted the dramatist Rachel Crothers to write this ecstatic letter to the *New York Times* (May 3, 1925): *"The Sea Woman's Cloak* is an awakening to the depth and breadth and boundless possibilities of the art of acting . . . young people playing old women and men without makeup, and looking old because they have become old through absolute understanding and feeling and the quickening of dramatic imagination to such a flame that they are transported into the little seacoast village of Ireland—actually living the lives of these in the play—people as remote from these young Americans as anything can be." Crothers found the acting "so much greater and more sincere than one usually finds in the professional theatre that it is amazing and unbelievable."

The production was terrific advertising for the Lab's school: "Is this what happens when young actors are trained in the Russian manner?" admiring audiences asked. Apart from Boleslavski's rhetoric about "the group" and "the soul," and the pervasive references to Stanislavski, I don't

Richard Boleslavski, who introduced Stanislavski's System to American actors.

know that the training was specifically Russian, but it was comprehensive, and as such an oasis in the history of the teaching of acting in America. "It was marvelous training," Stella Adler says with a warmth that leaps across the intervening decades. "It was thorough and complete, well-rounded and systematic, at an unmatchable level. And remember, we all had the recent model of the Moscow Art Theatre players to goad us, and to inspire us."

Far from being a lab in which the actor examined his feelings, the school compelled the actor to work on his voice, his body, and his intellect, too, in the belief that the actor must know how to speak, to move, and to think, in addition to being able to transmit emotions. Of the many extraordinary teachers at the school, Stella Adler remembers with special fondness Mordkin, a star of the Russian ballet, who adapted ballet lessons to the needs of actors in a course called Plastique and Mimeodrama; Margareta Dessoff, "a marvelous teacher of voice production"; and, above all, Maria Ouspenskaya, who along with Boleslavski had chosen to remain in America after the Moscow Art's departure—her course, the Technique of Acting, was the school's most famous. "Her English was limited, so she couldn't help you there," Stella Adler recalls. "When I was playing Ophelia I went to her house and acted for her for hours. I knew if I did it for her I couldn't go off track. I watched her eyes. She knew the truth—from a Russian sense, not an American sense." She was a superb teacher, Adler suggests, because she didn't "bring in any self or personality. She had relinquished all that at the Moscow Art Theatre."

(Despite her high reputation, I have my doubts about Ouspenskaya. "She was not a very good teacher," says Beatrice Straight, "though she was a wonderful character. Another Moscow Art émigré, Tamara Dayakhanova, with whom I also studied, was a wonderful teacher. It was she who really understood the System." Unlike Boleslavski, who radiated personal warmth, Madame Ouspenskaya was austere and remote, and so fiercely critical that some students felt crippled by her. She also drank, from a cup she tried to disguise in a paper bag. Some days she was incoherent not because her English was inadequate, which it plainly was, but because she was inebriated. Although there is no connection between being a good teacher of acting and being a good actor, Madame was an uneven actress, as can be seen in the bits and pieces she performed in Hollywood films of the thirties and forties; far from embodying Stanislavski's ideals, she is archly theatrical, "Russian" in a sentimental, what-the-market-wants manner.)

Madame Elizaveta Anderson-Ivantzoff taught ballet; Oscar Berner, the principles of makeup for the stage; John Mason Brown, the development of the drama; La Sylphe, ballet and corrective gymnastics; James Murray, fencing; Margaret Prendergast McLean, the science of phonetics; Elizabeth W. Perkins, observation through drawing; Professor William Tilly, problems of stage speech; Professor Douglas Moore, appreciation of music; and, "through the courtesy of Henry W. Kent and Huger Elliott of the Metropolitan Museum of Art," the school offered a special course in surveying the great artistic movements. With art, music, speech, phonetics, ballet, and the history of the theatre, the curriculum has a wonderfully old-fashioned flavor, and the Waspy, finishing-school patina is emphasized by the very proper-sounding Anglo-Saxon names of some of the faculty. But overseeing the entire course of study were the defiantly Russian Boleslavski and Ouspenskaya.

"Boleslavski didn't do much classroom teaching," Stella Adler says. "He lectured—passionately and eloquently—to large audiences" of anyone interested in the Art of the Theatre (which was the name of his course). It was in these lectures that Boleslavski transmitted the Stanislavski legacy to America. In 1933, after the Lab had disbanded, and he had moved on to directing films in Hollywood, where his Russian spirit was entirely submerged, Boleslavski published a distillation of his famous lectures which he called *Acting: The First Six Lessons.* Aside from Stanislavski's references to his work embedded in *My Life in Art,* Boleslavski's book was the first appearance in English of aspects of the System. (Stanislavski's *An Actor Prepares* wasn't published until 1936.)

Concentration, memory of emotion, dramatic action, characterization, observation, and rhythm are the subjects of the six lessons, couched in the form of a series of encounters spread over a number of years between an "I" and an eager, initially naive aspiring actress, a disarming young woman called (in those pre-feminist days) the Creature. Threaded through the lessons is Boleslavski's reiterated catechism that acting is a high and exacting art that demands control of the body, the will, the intellect, the emotions, and, crucially, the soul. (If "soul" sounds too formidable, Boleslavski suggests substituting imagination.) Boleslavski stressed the actor's spiritual training as the most important part of the work, and he developed a series of what he called "soul exercises" in relaxation, concentration, and training the affective memory, which, stripped of the spiritual overlay, were to supply the foundation for Lee Strasberg's work at the Actors Studio.

Throughout his lessons, Boleslavski alerts the actor to his inner riches, the "golden box" of observations, impressions, and sensory and emotional memories, both conscious and unconscious, which the actor must learn how to use in affective memory exercises for assistance in building a character. "Boleslavski called affective memory memory of emotion," Stella Adler says. "He told us how Stanislavski had changed his emphasis, and that it no longer held the central place in his theories that it once had. Following Stanislavski, Boleslavski asked actors to focus more on the given circumstances of the play rather than on their own circumstances."

As Stanislavski's emissary to America, Boleslavski took care to stress the deep links between the actor's internal and external tools, the almost spiritual correspondences between the resources of his mind and body. He warned that the actor's inner work was only a means of preparation, not an end in itself, and that the actor's awareness of self was useless without being translated into expressive dramatic action.[6]

Maria Ouspenskaya, a legendary and controversial teacher.

"Many of the outstanding productions of the last five years have come from foreign sources, the Moscow Art Theatre, the Reinhardt productions, the Irish Players," announced the first bulletin of the American Laboratory Theatre. "America has not [yet] supported an art theatre of its own. Failures to establish an art theatre have been many but they fail to prove America will not accept and support a creative theatre of its own. On the contrary, the very failures have been responsible for a new era of the theatre in America." Organized to fill in the gap, to become America's first "native, creative theatre," the American Lab must be accounted yet another failure in America's attempts to keep pace with the best of European theatre. Although it produced challenging new plays and classics not likely to be presented by commercial managements, none of its later work achieved the same imaginative reach of *The Sea Woman's Cloak*. Following this initial success, the Lab presented (for its 1925–26 season) *Twelfth Night* and a dramatization of *The Scarlet Letter*. For 1926–27, it selected *The Straw Hat* by Labiche; *The Trumpet Shall Sound* by Thornton Wilder; *Granite* by Clemence Dane; and *Big Lake* by Lynn Riggs. For 1927–28, the repertory was *At the Gate of the Kingdom* by Knut Hamsun; *Much Ado About Nothing;* a pantomime by Arthur Schnitzler called *The Bridal Veil; Dr. Knock* by Jules Romains; and *Martine* by Jean Jacques Bernard. For its last season, 1929–30, its first Russian drama, *Three Sisters; Where It Is Thin, There It Breaks* by Turgenev; and, in commedia dell'arte style, two seventeenth-century vaudeville farces by Cervantes, *The Pretended Basque* and *The Jealous Old Man*. This was an ambitious and noble dossier, which nonetheless failed to honor one of the terms of its original agenda, the establishment of a *native* art theatre. Creative the Lab certainly was, offering a repertory which stretched the actors who had been trained in its school; but where was the American drama it had intended to foster? A mediocre adaptation of a classic American novel *(The Scarlet Letter)* and two immature plays by new American writers (Wilder's *The Trumpet Shall Sound* and Lynn Riggs's *Big Lake*) were not a promising beginning.

Despite Boleslavski's insistence that the Lab had to be a theatre built on native grounds, it never stopped looking like an import, as it presented plays by foreign playwrights acted by students trained primarily by Russians. His theatre failed, but Boleslavski is nonetheless a crucial figure in the story of Stanislavski in America. He planted seeds that the American founders of the Group Theatre caused to grow. He was a stirring speaker

—indeed, people who heard him lecture nearly sixty years ago light up in remembrance of his fiery style. He helped American theatre people to think of their work in idealistic terms, to regard themselves as artists with special sensitivities that they needed to learn to respect and cultivate. As Stanislavski's American ambassador, an embodiment of the Russian theatrical spirit, he is to be honored. But as a teacher and director, his record, frankly, is cloudy.

Miriam Stockton was often unhappy with him, claiming that he did not comply with either the spirit or the letter of his contract. After the first few years, he was absent for long periods of time; he did very little classroom teaching and by and large delegated to others the job of running the theatre. When the theatre folded, Boleslavski in a fit of ill-temper blamed "America," announcing that art was possible only in Russia. He decried Broadway's rampant money-mindedness, yet to supplement his income he did not hesitate to direct shows on Broadway, popular pieces like *The Vagabond King* and ephemera that didn't even have merit as popular entertainment. Stockton complained about his frequent "defections" to the world of commerce, as he defended himself in terms of survival and practicality. There were then distinct limits to Boleslavski's idealism. Far from being only a high-minded theatrical visionary, he was also a practical man who could, and quite readily did, compromise.

Boleslavski left the Lab for Hollywood to direct a series of mostly mediocre movies which (including *Rasputin and the Empress* starring all three Barrymores as a trio of unlikely Russians) could well have been the work of a conventional American craftsman. As a director, in both commercial and experimental projects, he was noted more for his crowd scenes than for his handling of intimate passages. Ironically, it was the external touches of his work that received most attention.

For all his human and artistic shortcomings, there is no question that once he stepped onto the lecture platform Boleslavski radiated enthusiasm, idealism, and farsightedness. Two young men, fired by his talks, began to think about founding the kind of theatre that the American Lab was supposed to become but never did, a theatre devoted to the production of new, socially significant American plays of literary merit performed by a company of actors trained in an American adaptation of Stanislavski's System.

4

ON NATIVE GROUNDS:
TRIUMPH

I n the beginning was the word, or rather many words, almost all of them Harold Clurman's. One of the great experiments in American theatre history began with Clurman talking at a series of Friday night lectures open to anyone who cared to listen. "Those Fridays were exciting," says Group member Margaret Barker. "We knew we were in on something terribly important." Held first at Clurman's room in a West Side hotel, the talks were moved to Cheryl Crawford's larger apartment in response to the increasing size of the audience, and finally to the Steinway Hall at Fridays at 11:30, after everyone's show had let out.

What drew young actors and theatre people to these gatherings was the contagion of Harold Clurman talking about his favorite subject, the theatre. With a passion that invaded his listeners, Clurman announced his idea for a theatre that would present good new American plays that reflected the temper of the American moment and that would be performed by a handpicked company of actors united by training and values.

"We were like animals in a jungle coming to a watering place," Morris Carnovsky says. "We felt the need for something which we did not in the beginning recognize as the Group Theatre. We wanted a common basis in an understanding of the rules of acting. We wanted to talk the same language."

Stella Adler says charmingly that Harold Clurman can't be compared to Stanislavski or Boleslavski or indeed to any other theatre man because "he floated down from on high with a dream of founding a truly American theatre. He was a miracle. He fell down from a bright star into a theatre that couldn't distinguish itself as theatre." Nonetheless, Clurman's ideas for a possible theatre had been influenced by the Russian example, for like every theatre lover in New York he too had seen the Moscow Art's ensemble work and its repertory of great national dramas and he too went to the American Laboratory Theatre to listen to Boleslavski in order to learn more about the Russian System.

When Clurman first began to talk, in 1928, he was working as a script-reader for the Theatre Guild, the American theatre's closest approximation of the Moscow Art. It was, indeed, the distance between the two organizations that encouraged Clurman to want to set up his own company. The Guild represented Broadway at its best, and while it was a worthy outfit, producing a series of mostly intelligent, mostly foreign plays, it was not the kind of theatre Clurman thought Americans were entitled to. The Guild didn't have the vision or the theoretical fervor of the Russian groups; its management lacked the conviction of a Stanislavski or a Meyerhold that theatre could enlarge and perhaps even alter the quality of life. "The Guild just wanted to do good plays," says Morris Carnovsky, who acted in some of them. "They were not organic with the society we lived in. They had an extraordinary number of good actors, but like acting in general in the twenties, it was hit or miss. It was instinctive and imposed by commercial necessity."

For all its polish and taste—perhaps indeed because of them—the Theatre Guild wasn't an essential part of the life force of New York; the links between actor and play and between play and audience weren't deep. The Guild put on plays by leading European writers like Shaw, Pirandello, and Coward. Later in the twenties, it produced O'Neill but only after O'Neill had been nurtured by the Provincetown Players. The Guild's most famous actors were the Lunts, the exemplars of a glamorous star theatre. "Lunt told me once, 'Lynn and I have our own group,'" recalls Morris Carnovsky. "They were in a starry firmament all by themselves: Castor and Pollux. It worked well for them." But the Lunts skillfully trading quips in a Coward drawing-room comedy was not Clurman's idea of theatre at its highest level.

The Guild was fine after its fashion, Clurman conceded; but he didn't much care for the fashion. It was too external, too airy; it had too high a tolerance for continental froth.

Yet the Guild's management, Theresa Helburn and Lawrence Langner, encouraged dissident youngsters like Clurman, and even set up a theatre for them called (with echoes of the Moscow Art) the Theatre Guild

Lee Strasberg, Harold Clurman, and Cheryl Crawford, the founders of the Group Theatre, at Brookfield Center, 1931. Clurman is clearly the guiding spirit.

Studio. Their first and only production, presented in December 1929 at the Martin Beck Theatre, was a play about life in contemporary Russia called *Red Rust.* "It's pretty bad, isn't it?" Cheryl Crawford said, when I told her I had located a copy of this long-forgotten curiosity. "I guess you could put it down as an example of our youthful folly." Certainly this immature piece —"a ten-twent-thirt melodrama," said the *Herald Tribune;* "as artless and crude a sample of playmaking as one could ask for," said John Mason Brown—could not inspire confidence in the literary judgment of the people who were to organize the Group Theatre.

Because, then, of what the Moscow Art Theatre was and the Theatre Guild wasn't, Harold Clurman started talking. And like-minded people, dissatisfied with the present state of the American theatre, started listening.

If you've ever had the pleasure of hearing Harold Clurman talk, you'll know the kind of excitement his Friday evening sessions generated. His arms flailing in continual animated motion, his voice rising to ungentlemanly volume, and with occasional leaps in place for emphasis, Harold Clurman loved making a public spectacle of himself. He had the gift of gab, to be sure, but he had a lot more, the gift of sharing his power so that after listening to him you felt a surge of energy. When he spoke, with no regard for moderation or for his own dignity, Clurman had the ability to alter lives.

Clurman's delivery, deeply fused with his messianic theme—his dream of founding a socially aware American art theatre—had the force of manifest destiny. Each week, he delivered a jolt. "He wrecked all my idols," recalls Margaret Barker, who was appearing at the time on Broadway with Katharine Cornell in *The Barretts of Wimpole Street.* "I had always wanted to be a star on Broadway, like Kit Cornell. But when I started listening to Harold, my outlook on theatre changed. I went to those early meetings with questions. I felt I was fighting for Cornell."

The man who talked the Group Theatre into being was an extraordinary mixture of characteristics: an intellectual with drive and showmanship, an idealist with a clear sense of economic and political realities, an uplifting speaker who was also a doer, with the common sense to translate high-flown theory into practice, a man of destiny who was witty, homely, accessible, earthy, warm, not excessively neurotic, and a shrewd and for the most part kindly judge of character.

This practical-minded idealist was a native New Yorker who came from a prosperous upper-middle-class Jewish family where moral values and intellectual accomplishment were deeply respected. From the age of six, when his physician father had taken him to see Jacob Adler perform in *Uriel Acosta* in Yiddish at the Grand Street Theatre, Clurman had been in love with theatre. Although his propriety-conscious family had some reservations about Harold's flamboyant style, they encouraged him, giving him a fine education and the opportunity to travel; as a student, he inhaled the culture of both Paris and New York in the twenties. Behind Clurman's flair for selling ideas, then, holding it up and keeping it honest, was a solid intellectual foundation.

Clurman had the drive to create a theatre in his own image, but as the very name of his Theatre suggests, he didn't do it alone. When it was incorporated in 1931, the Group Theatre had three directors. In addition to Clurman, there were two friends he had met in the Theatre Guild: a grave, quiet young woman from Akron, Ohio, Cheryl Crawford, and an equally grave young man with a wide forehead, a studious, masklike face, and a harsh voice that carried a trace of a foreign accent, the great hero-villain of our story, Lee Strasberg. "Harold needed someone like me, someone who could remain calm," says Cheryl Crawford. "Harold and Lee both got along much better with me than they did with each other." Although they shared ideals, the three Group directors had quite dissimilar personal styles. "Oh my yes, we were very different," Cheryl Crawford admits, with a rueful smile. "There we were, two Old Testament prophets and a Wasp shiksa. They had seduced me into the idea of their theatre, metaphorically speaking. At the time, Lee was an enigma to me. He hardly spoke, and so I couldn't believe it when Harold told me, in 1927, that Lee knew more about acting than anyone else in the world. He seemed to be carrying some ulcerating pain, which he never talked about. He never cried out."

At first, the directors' personal qualities seemed complementary, Clurman's brashness balanced by Strasberg's and Crawford's soberness, his public personality in startling contrast to the privacy of theirs. Strasberg and Crawford appeared severe, emotionally pinched and stingy, whereas Clurman seemed to be embracing the world. Offstage, however, Clurman was as deeply private as his colleagues. "He was a public man, he had no talent as a private man; the marital state was not for him," says Stella Adler, who made the mistake of marrying him. For all his quietude, Strasberg had titanic explosions, and Crawford, for all her seeming lack of ego, was hurt by her failures as a director. All three were jealous of their power, and eager for recognition. Their partnership foundered finally in 1937, when Strasberg and Crawford resigned, leaving Clurman in sole charge of the Group; in truth, the directors had never been entirely easy with each other.

And yet it was through the clash and interplay of these three high-powered theatrical missionaries that the Group Theatre was forged. Like Stanislavski and Nemirovich-Danchenko at the Moscow Art, the Group directors claimed areas they would specialize in. Clurman, naturally, became the Theatre's spokesman, its chief public relations officer; given his academic background, he was its literary adviser, too, casting the deciding vote in the selection of plays. Strasberg, intensely interested in acting problems and in interpreting Stanislavski's System, was placed in charge of actor training and directing. To Cheryl Crawford fell most of the dirty work, the day-to-day administration, raising money, negotiating for theatres, and running interference between her two colleagues.

On the subject of theatre in general, and the Group Theatre in particular, all three were possessed of the kind of concentrated idealism that had been responsible for the creation of the Moscow Art Theatre some three decades earlier. Whether you preferred Harold to Lee or Cheryl to either was finally less important than the fact of their moral and artistic passion. For all their personal shortcomings, the three directors were people of vision sustained by their belief that in the midst of a commerce-ridden theatre a vital American ensemble could be erected, a "native, creative" repertory theatre of the kind that had been promised in the original charter of the American Lab.

As observers of their careers, we may wish that they had been a little different at times, had made different artistic and literary choices at times, had been less temperamental or personally difficult. They made mistakes; they hurt others and were wounded in return. But they built the first and so far the *only* true American theatre company, a company of American size and American passions that, against all the odds, in the face of a national depression, an often hostile and ignorant press, financial and artistic defeats, and many personal feuds and jealousies within the ranks, produced, in a new acting style, twenty-one plays that spoke to and about the American scene. "I can't believe we did it," Group member Ruth Nelson says, fifty years later. "And we were on Broadway too!"

There were no auditions to become a member of the Group. Instead, actors were interviewed by the three directors, who based their decisions on an intuitive sense of who would and who would not fit into the kind of theatre they envisioned. "They judged actors as people," Group member Phoebe Brand says. "They judged us in interviews, not auditions, and made their choices with that peculiar producer's instinct they all had. Their final choice was one of intuition." Like the founders of the Moscow Art Theatre, they turned first to people they already knew—young actors from the Theatre Guild like Morris Carnovsky, Phoebe Brand, Sanford Meisner, Franchot Tone, and John Garfield, who had been attending Clurman's Friday nights; Stella Adler, Ruth Nelson, and Eunice Stoddard, from the American Laboratory Theatre; and Margaret Barker, from Broadway. "I remember the day I heard I had been chosen," recalls Phoebe Brand. "It was one of the great moments of my life. I knew we were all in on something very important."

Joining up with the Group meant making economic sacrifices. It meant being willing to enter a theatrical experiment whose rules had not yet been clearly defined. It meant, perhaps most difficult of all for these young actors, giving up ideas of becoming stars. "When they asked me to join, I went to talk to Kit Cornell," Margaret Barker remembers. "We spoke all night. I told her I wanted theatre rather than stardom, and plays that spoke to our time. A lot of the old guard had hackles up about the upstart youngsters, but Kit said to go ahead. She said if she had been ten years younger that's what she would do too. Franchot Tone told me, 'If you want to be a star, don't come; if you want to be a good actress, come.' Cheryl told me, 'If you want to be cast always as a hysterical ingenue, don't come.' " To Stella Adler, who already had vast experience performing with her father's company and starring on Broadway, the Group's non-star policy was particularly painful, and she never did adjust to it. "The Group wrecked some people's lives," Ruth Nelson says. "We didn't join to serve ourselves; we served the playwright; we served the theatre."

Because they had no models, the Group fought about how to run a theatrical collective. As engrained American individualism confronted the idea of ensemble theatre, there were continuous eruptions. Far from feeling like participants in a true democracy, some of the actors were later to accuse the directors of being arbitrary and dictatorial. During their summers in the country early in their history, and the time when some Group members lived communally in an apartment in town which they called Groupstroy, the Theatre had a real cohesiveness. For the most part, however, the Group's team spirit was regularly eroded.

But in 1931 the young theatre people (whose average age was twenty-seven) chosen to participate in Clurman's experiment were proud and eager, and more united than they were ever to be again. As self-styled reformers, they were determined to startle the American commercial theatre. Almost as soon as they became the Group they left town for the summer, as if to announce their distance from the theatrical mainstream. By car and train, they departed for Brookfield Center, Connecticut, where for ten weeks they established a commune, getting to know each other, developing a common technique through Strasberg's instruction in Stanislavski's System, and rehearsing what was to be their opening production to be presented in September at the Martin Beck Theatre, Paul Green's *The House of Connelly*.

Instead of rehearsing a play in the usual rushed Broadway manner, the Group was taking the luxury of working on it for an entire summer. Instead of a pickup cast, creating their roles without the benefit of a unified method (or in most cases of any method at all), here was a carefully chosen company trying out a new System, and if that meant discarding everything they knew, overturning the bad habits, the shortcuts, and the tricks of the trade they had acquired as an almost inevitable result of working according to the American "system," they were willing to do that—to start from scratch, if need be.

"That first summer, we were like a family," Morris Carnovsky remembers. "We loved each other, for the most part. And, at first, we believed the Method could change our lives." "That summer was so exciting," says Margaret Barker. "We'd all do it again. I remember the first night, when we got together, there was to be no smoking. We were so pure and idealistic, when we started."

To me, the image of the Group that first summer in Brookfield Center studying, living together, earning their keep by performing skits for guests at the summer resort, and training for their Broadway debut is the most inspiring in the history of American theatre. Gazing into that long-ago summer, I am moved by the idealism and ardor, the discipline, the wonderful, saving joy and innocence. (Why hasn't anyone ever written a novel or made a movie of it, that first historic summer when, with terrific will and focus and ebullience, a group of young actors and directors transformed themselves into the legendary Group Theatre?)

Clurman told the Group that the drama of American life in the throes of the Depression demanded a theatre of courage and commitment. His call for relevance had special relevance at the time: the Group and the society it came from were well-matched. Clurman's messianism, his all-things-are-possible stance, attained particular urgency in the face of the potential collapse of American society. One wonders, did the Group need a national catastrophe like the Depression in order to come together as it did?

Contrary to popular assumptions, Clurman's listeners in Brookfield Center were a disparate group: they weren't all poor, they weren't all from the Lower East Side, they weren't all Communists, and they weren't all Jewish. Except for Friendly Ford, who had been selected for his natural-ness, but who couldn't act (after a season, he returned to his native Texas to sell cars), they *were* all talented, however, and they all believed in what Clurman and (in the beginning) Strasberg told them. In one of the historic photographs from that summer, Harold Clurman sits on a lawn, a pointer in his hand, holding forth as the company, grouped around him in a loose semicircle, listens intently. On a porch, seated off to the side, holding her head in a reflective pose, sits Stella Adler, not quite one with the others. She wasn't the only "outsider." Margaret Barker had the "disadvantage of wealth" (as Mordecai Gorelik says, a half-century later); so did Dorothy Patten and Franchot Tone. Ruth Nelson had a strict convent upbringing. Art Smith and Cheryl Crawford were from the American heartland, Midw-esterners through and through. Far from being a group of New York Jews, as they were sometimes described, the company represented a cross section of America.

From the beginning, Strasberg stressed improvisation and work in affective memory, which were new techniques to everyone except the actors who had been at Boleslavski's Lab. In 1931, five years before the American publication of *An Actor Prepares*, Strasberg had to depend for information about the System on what he had absorbed from Boleslavski's lectures, on untranslated articles from Russia, and on Stanislavski's comments on his technique in *My Life in Art*. Strasberg's attendance at the Lab had been irregular and confined for the most part to 1923 and 1924, when Boleslav-ski's emphasis on affective memory was more pronounced than it was to be at any later period. Along with Boleslavski, most of his listeners at the Lab grew disenchanted with the technique—but not Strasberg, who was drawn to it because it confirmed his readings in Freud and because he felt it led to the kind of truthful acting style he was interested in. Although he always referred to Boleslavski as "my teacher," Strasberg took from him what he wanted to, hearing what he wanted to hear. His interpretation of Stanislavski, as filtered through his partial understanding of Boleslavski's talks, comprised a minority of one; and in the face of often belligerent opposition, Strasberg continued to use affective memory as a cornerstone of his method.

Strasberg relied on the techniques of affective memory and improvisation as ways to liberate the actors from the text, to stimulate their imaginations, and to coerce them into examining their own feelings. With *The House of Connelly* in the distance, Strasberg had his actors invent their own scenes, write their own dialogue, and investigate their own lives for emotional equivalents and substitutes. "I allowed myself to experiment with the affective memory," Morris Carnovsky recalls. "I discovered some things of value in it. But as a rehearsal method, or as a technique useful in performance, I soon found it had no value. And could be harmful."

Photographer Ralph Steiner instructed members of the Group to pose as "The Thinker." (Clurman and Strasberg at upper right.)

"I got to the point where I couldn't stomach the affective memory," says Phoebe Brand. "I lent myself to it for a while—it is valuable for a young actor to go through it, but it is too subjective. It makes for a moody, personal, self-indulgent acting style. It assumes an actor is an emotional mechanism that can just be turned on. Emotion can't be worked for in that way—it is rather a result of truthful action in given circumstances. Lee insisted on working each little moment of affective memory; we were always going backwards into our lives. It was painful to dig back. When we worked on actions, it was all right. The technique of summoning and wooing emotions from your own insides doesn't make as much sense to me as getting emotion through objects. Lee crippled a lot of people," she adds. "Acting should be joyous, it should be pleasurable and easy if you do it right; but it wasn't with Strasberg. A good teacher doesn't cripple."

"I remember that Lee asked me, the first time I met him, whether I had a strong emotional memory," Margaret Barker says. "He had me do an enormous amount of emotional memory work on my role in *Connelly*. He had me going over and over a painful experience—my roommate had been killed the year before—until I thought I was going to crack. He did an enormous amount of improvisations. There were one-word exercises where we had to create an object. And we did a lot of work on animals—I remember watching white rats. This way of going about acting was new to me. On Broadway I had never questioned why I was being asked to do something. To ask was to be thought arty-warty. On one of the last rehearsals, I flung my purse in Strasberg's face. He had me doing an emotional memory, and I felt I wasn't playing the play."

Strasberg's work in 1931 had emphasized preparation: how the actor uses his past to place himself in the right mood for his role; in 1932, he paid more attention to the play's circumstances rather than the actor's. "That second summer we had speech and body classes," says Phoebe Brand, "and Lee worked with us on actions and objectives. What did the emotional memories we had been working on have to do with action? It was complicated. Here was emotion and sense memory, there was action: 'I'll never be able to join them,' I thought." In 1932, at Dover Furnace, gesture, mime, and the use of the voice and body were taught by experts brought in to supplement Strasberg's work. Clearly a split was developing between those who believed in the value of the inner work that was Strasberg's specialty, and those primarily interested in training their voices and bodies to project their roles. Borrowing from Stanislavski the concept of the actor as his own instrument, the Group began to be divided about how that instrument could best be tuned.

Because the Russian theatre was their inspiration, members of the Group visited their artistic homeland whenever they had the money or time. In 1934, Clurman and Adler, then married, went on one of these pilgrimages, and, as Oliver Sayler had been in 1917, they were amazed by the variety and virtuosity, the energy, commitment, and rich aura of tradition of the Russian stage. For one Group Theatre, the Russians had a dozen companies, all with their own philosophy of theatre and their own conservatories. On their way back to New York, the Clurmans stopped in Paris, where they met Stanislavski. "Meeting him was simply an accident of life," Adler says now. "He knew about the Group, and he knew about me because of my family. He admired my father's work and had asked to meet him, when he had been in New York in 1923." She and Clurman talked with Stanislavski a few times; although he had been ill, and was recovering from an operation, they found him gracious and attentive, a true gentleman. Clurman had to return to New York on Group business, but Stella stayed on and, in the chance of a lifetime, studied with Stanislavski daily for a period of five weeks.

"I was always a scholar," she says, "and I brought along someone who could take shorthand." Stanislavski asked her about the part she had just played (Gwen Ballantine, a woman of wealth who falls in love with a bohemian in John Howard Lawson's *Gentlewoman*). "He started to work with me on it, on some problems I had with it.

"I told him that in using the Method I had stopped enjoying acting, and he said, 'If my System doesn't help you, don't use it . . . but perhaps you're not using it correctly.' He told me about how he acted Stockmann in *Enemy of the People*, which he felt was his most successful performance, and then he worked with me on my role in *Gentlewoman*. At this point in his work he no longer emphasized affective memory. Instead, he concentrated on the given circumstances supplied by the playwright. He wanted to take the actor deeper into the play rather than into himself. And he stressed what was called the method of physical actions: how starting from the outside, from creating the outer line of a role, planning it in terms of a series of actions, would take you inside a character's mind. He led me to use the physical stage, the physical circumstances. We did exercises to make it clear—to help me *use* the circumstances of the play."

Like an apostle to the Gentiles, Stella Adler returned to the Group to share what she had learned. "Stanislavski said we're doing it wrong," she announced, in what was to prove a historic confrontation.

"Stanislavski doesn't know," Strasberg bellowed. *"I* know!"

At that moment, Strasberg alienated some of the actors permanently. "Such arrogance," Morris Carnovsky bristles, half a century later. "I had no further use for him after that." "Oh, the battles we had the summer Stella came back from Russia," recalls Margaret Barker, sighing. "They were hair-splitting. I remember we argued about 'can I really feel a fly crawl up my face?' "

Affective memory or no affective memory, to the members of the Group this was a life-and-death matter, the occasion of a bitter civil war that continues to the present. Stubborn, high-strung, querulous, deeply committed to their art, Group actors were people for whom a craft issue became a battle cry; being on opposite sides of the affective memory standoff was enough to sustain a lifetime of animosity.

"Affective memory induces hysteria," Stella Adler, its most vocal opponent, insists. "It's polluted water, and yet Americans, typically, continue to drink it. Stanislavski himself went beyond it. He was like a scientist conducting experiments in a lab; and his new research superseded his earlier ideas: the affective memory belonged to the older, worn-out ideas. But Lee always thought it was the cornerstone of the Method, and in this way he became a laughingstock."

The continuing debates over acting method, with Strasberg and Adler forming their own coalitions, were backstage news. The Group, after all, was a theatre not a conservatory and from the beginning it was judged on results. How effective was its method on stage? To what extent were Group actors successful apostles of a new realism?

A cold January night in 1935 at a Sunday benefit performance at the old Civic Theatre on 14th Street supplies an answer. The play: *Waiting for Lefty,* by a member of the Group named Clifford Odets. A one-act play about a taxi strike, it was presented at the end of an evening of political sketches and cabaret on the stage of the Theatre Union, the foremost radical theatre of the thirties. As the play began, a jolt cut through the audience. On a bare stage, six or seven taxi drivers sat in a semicircle as a fat man,

"The birth cry of the thirties," *Waiting for Lefty* (1935), with Elia Kazan leading the cast and audience in the call for a strike.

their union leader, shouted: "You're so wrong I ain't laughing. Any guys with eyes to read knows it. Look at the textile strike—out like lions and in like lambs. Take the San Francisco tie-up—starvation and broken heads. The steel boys wanted to walk out too, but they changed their minds. It's the trend of the times, that's what it is." The language was jabbing, staccato, vigorous; the characters on stage looked and sounded like most of the people in the audience. When a character named Joe stepped out into the spotlight, he seemed to be speaking directly to the working-class listeners. "You boys know me. I ain't a red boy one bit! Here I'm carryin' a shrapnel that big I picked up in the war. And maybe I don't know it when it rains! Don't tell me red! You know what we are? The black and blue boys! We been kicked around so long we're black and blue from head to toes. . . . What's this crap about goin' home to hot suppers? I'm asking to your faces how many's got hot suppers to go home to?"

Five separate flashbacks dramatize incidents from the lives of taxi drivers who've come to the meeting to wait for Lefty, the chairman of their workers' committee. Showing how workers are victimized by bosses, the five episodes pile indignation on defeat, hammering at the audience like successive punches. When the action returns to the present, and the workers learn that Lefty isn't going to arrive because he was just found with a bullet in his head, an enraged cabbie steps to the podium to deliver a thundering NO! to the way things are. "Hear it, boys, hear it? Hell, listen to me! Coast to coast! HELLO AMERICA! HELLO. WE'RE STORMBIRDS OF THE WORKING CLASS. WORKERS OF THE WORLD . . . OUR BONES AND BLOOD! And when we die they'll know what we did to make a new world! Christ, cut us up to little pieces. We'll die for what is right! Put fruit trees where our ashes are! (To audience): Well, what's the answer?

ALL: STRIKE!
Agate: Louder!
ALL: STRIKE!
Agate and others on stage: AGAIN!
ALL: STRIKE, STRIKE, STRIKE!

Starting at high voltage, the performance built to this seismic climax with actors moving to the front of the stage, their arms uplifted, as the audience rose to its feet to answer with tumultuous cries of its own. More than a theatrical event, this was "the birth cry of the thirties," as Harold Clurman wrote in *The Fervent Years.*

"I've never seen anything like it," says Sylvia Regan, who was in charge of audience development for the Theatre Union. "I don't think anyone had expected anything like this. It was only part of a series of Sunday evening benefits, when our theatre would give its stage to other companies, mostly workers' theatres. As soon as the play began, you felt something special was happening. And when it was over, the audience was on its feet cheering and yelling. They wouldn't let the actors go. It was incredible. Unforgettable!"

"The audience felt reborn," says Morris Carnovsky, who acted in the play that evening. "They had been seized in a way they never had been before. They were too excited to go home to sleep, and stood outside the theatre, in the cold, talking excitedly. Odets had written the play in two or three weeks, as a piece of propaganda for the taxi strike, but his writing had such passion and force—there was a submerged poetry in it—that it transcended politics."

It was with a vision of this kind of play, and this kind of performance, that Harold Clurman had begun his talks in the late twenties; this performance of *Waiting for Lefty* on January 5, 1935, signaled the true birth of his Group Theatre. Whatever his theatre had done before and whatever it was to do in the remaining six years of its life was overshadowed by the night at the Theatre Union when his dream of a relevant American theatre was triumphantly fulfilled.

It had taken the Group almost five years—nearly half its life—to find its full voice. When Clurman organized his Theatre, he had, with characteristic impulsiveness, placed the cart before the horse. He had said that he was forming a theatre to present important American plays, but when the Group was founded it had only one play in the till (a present from the Theatre Guild), its opening production, Paul Green's *House of Connelly.* The struggle to find worthy plays was continuous, and until the emergence of Odets in 1935 the Group's literary record was uneven.

"It's a lovely play, I don't know why no one has revived it," Cheryl Crawford says about *The House of Connelly.* Set in the South in the late nineteenth century, the play enacts a Chekhovian struggle between a fading aristocratic way of life and an emerging new class. The Connellys are a family of misfits saved from ruin by the energetic daughter of their tenant farmer. When this new woman, bristling with modern ideas, marries the Connelly heir, she represents a new middle class come to revive a wasted privileged one; in the mingling of these traditionally antagonistic groups a renewal of the American South is prefigured. Originally, Green ended his play with the death of the new woman; but at Clurman's insistence, a conclusion of social promise replaced the earlier defeat.

The play has a worthy theme and some chiseled dialogue, but finally it seemed more like the kind of play that would be produced by the stuffy Theatre Guild than by a company of young upstarts. In performance, it had an attenuated effect perhaps because the material was outside the personal experience of the cast. *The House of Connelly* didn't come from their marrow

The Group Theatre's first production, *The House of Connelly* by Paul Green (1931). Clockwise from left, Eunice Stoddard, Stella Adler, Morris Carnovsky, Mary Morris, and Franchot Tone.

the way *Waiting for Lefty* would four years later. Paul Green's well-made play wasn't the organic expression of their heart's desire, as Odets's work would prove to be.

Nonetheless, *The House of Connelly* received better reviews than almost any of the Group's twenty later productions. "We had twenty-two curtain calls opening night," Cheryl Crawford remembers with pride. "At the sixteenth call, the audience started yelling for the author. I was sitting with Paul Green in the upstairs lounge at the Martin Beck—we were both too nervous to sit through the play—and I urged him to go down to the stage. When the reviews came out the critics seemed to sense we were trying to do something different."[7] In the *New York Times* (October 4, 1931), Brooks Atkinson wrote that "this new band of actors, who give themselves the dull name of the Group Theatre, have done an extraordinary thing. They have been arrogant enough to regard acting as an art. . . . Like the Moscow Art Theatre, whose memory they hold in humble and hopeful reverence, they play in the light of a common inspiration. Nothing so luminous, so clearly imagined, so immediately responsive as their current performance has been seen on the New York stage in recent memory. . . . They are self-conscious at present. They play at a tempo that is almost dull, and in order to keep their performance honestly subdued they are frequently hard to hear in a large auditorium. . . . Directly the curtain goes up you feel enkindled. . . . Excess of spirit may paralyze them. They may force the soul too much. And it will take years to achieve a standard of mood and diction. But nothing since the founding of the present Theatre Guild thirteen years ago has held out so much promise of revitalizing our stage."

John Mason Brown, in the *New York Evening Post* (September 29, 1931), wrote that "they received the kind of rafter-rocking cheers which are all but unknown at first nights nowadays. . . . In the Group Theatre jaded Broadway seems finally to have found the young blood and new ideas for which many of us have been praying."

1931, the Group's second production, was blatantly relevant. A kind of Depression vaudeville, it presented a series of skits about unemployment, and as such was a precursor to the Federal Theatre's Living Newspapers and to the agitprop theatre that was to be the staple of the decade's numerous left-wing companies. Though most critics disdained it,[8] the play had an audience—in the balcony, where people who couldn't afford seats downstairs recognized the play's situations as reflections of their own. In concept, *1931* was the kind of pertinent theatre Clurman had been talking about, but it needed a real writer—it needed Odets—to give its litany of complaints life on the stage.

All the Group needed was a first-rate play set in contemporary America to show off its Method, but from 1932 until *Waiting for Lefty* it never really found one. The Group kept choosing plays about larger-than-life anti-heroes who gain the world only to misplace their souls—dramas like Maxwell Anderson's *Night over Taos,* a stillborn historical piece in blank verse about a Mexican dictator who loses his kingdom, and Melvyn Levy's *Gold Eagle Guy,* about a self-made American millionaire in boom-town San Francisco. These inflated period plays might have provided bromides for thirties audiences, assuring them that the quest for money and power comes to no good in the end, but they were not challengingly linked, in language or spirit, to the training Strasberg had been providing. These were not promising Method texts; these were not the kind of play with which to build an American national theatre.

Men in White, produced in 1933, wasn't that kind of play either, but it was something the Group badly needed for the morale of its actors and producers: it was a hit. It was the play that kept the Group alive. "It wasn't a very good play, I think we all realized that at the time," says Margaret Barker, who had the starring role, that of a young woman of social position who interferes with her fiancé's career as a doctor. "But it *was* beautifully done." Sidney Kingsley's drama, about a brilliant young surgeon who, tempted by Mammon, ultimately chooses service to humanity over self-advancement is a fake, a manufactured, old-fashioned melodrama.

It was meticulously and lovingly directed and acted, however, with an earnest realism that had the force of something new. *Men in White* was Strasberg's best work for the Group. "It was the play that established him as a director," Cheryl Crawford says. In later years, both Strasberg and Kingsley, who became lifelong friends, would often refer to *Men in White* as one of the milestones in the American theatre. Kingsley recalls that when he got off the bus at Green Mansions, the Group's home base for the summer of 1933, to deliver the script of his play to this band of "wild, woolly, incongruous nuts that I wanted to become a part of," he little suspected that he was "to meet my destiny."

Throughout the summer of 1933, Strasberg drilled his actors like a sergeant, taking them through exercises and improvisations on hospital

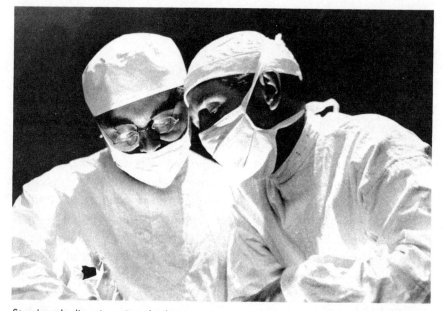

Strasberg's directing triumph: the operating room scene from *Men in White* (1933).

routine. It was a historic case of directorial overkill, but it paid off: the production gleamed with ensemble give-and-take, creating the illusion of a miniature world, a bustling microcosm. The comings and goings of patients and staff were rendered with exacting detail and with incidental natural sounds, background chatter, bells, sirens, doctors being paged. Strasberg composed many of the scenes in deep focus, with action upstage to provide a counterpoint to the foreground drama and to suggest that the scene was only a fragment of an ongoing reality, the daily life of a metropolitan hospital. The big set piece was a wordless operation that was a symphony of calibrated movement. "The operation scene was like a ballet," Margaret Barker says. "Strasberg really choreographed it. My brother, who was a doctor, came to rehearsals to make sure the actors were doing it right."

In writing and performance, *Men in White* was literal photographic realism. Despite its movie sale,[9] its good notices, the Pulitzer Prize that it won, the busy box office, and the aura of greatness that has clung to it over the years, *Men in White* was not what Clurman had had in mind. For all its good intentions and its final uplift—its hero facing a brave new world

—putting on a play like this hospital melodrama was not why the Group Theatre had been established.

There were, however, two pre-Odets plays—*Success Story* in 1932 and *Gentlewoman* in 1934, both by John Howard Lawson—that came closer to fulfilling Clurman's aims. "Lawson was a man, and he wrote like a man," Morris Carnovsky says. "When he refused to cooperate with the Congressional committee that was hunting Communists, he went to jail for his manhood. [Lawson was one of the Hollywood Ten.] He represented a social and emotional life that was very attractive." Unlike most of the early Group choices, the two Lawson plays are contemporary; authentic period icons, filled with local color and lifted by a charged vernacular poetry, they are about what money does to people who have it and what it does to people who don't. Lawson was an imperfect craftsman, but at his best he writes with the urgency of a disaffected radical.

He never wrote the great political play that his interests seemed to promise, but in *Success Story* and *Gentlewoman* he created characters of genuine moment. As Clurman notes in *The Fervent Years*, Lawson had a direct influence on Odets. Much of the Jewish flavor of Odets's work, the New York intensity of his characters, can be traced to the two plays of Lawson's that the Group produced while Odets was working through successive drafts of *Awake and Sing!* In a voice of protest and challenge (we're in a terrible fix, his plays cry out, and what are we going to do about it?), he was the first Group writer who really answered Clurman's call for socially alert plays of literary value.

In *Success Story*, Lawson created a scrappy American anti-hero who ought to be much better known than he is. Sol Ginsberg is a proletarian rebel in whom the heartbeat of a generation can be felt. Poor Jewish boy and sometime radical, smarter and tougher than his Gentile boss, Sol thrusts his way to the top of American big business in an orgy of buying and selling, wheeling and dealing. For good measure, he even wins the boss's shiksa girl friend. But a secretary, the young woman who's been with him since the old days when they attended radical meetings together, tries to keep him honest by reminding him how he has betrayed his youthful idealism. When she finally realizes that Sol will soil her too, the way he does everyone else, she shoots him, in an out-of-control finale that prevents the play from being first-rate.

Sol is like one of those gangsters in thirties movies who invert the

American dream, grabbing for all the good stuff—money and sex and power
—for all the wrong reasons, and with a ruthlessness that poisons the soul.
Here he is, confronting the former boss he has ruined:

> Sure, personally I'm crazy—even should I lie down on a piece of toast and
> tell you I'm a poached egg, my money mind keeps right on working—when
> I get violent put me in a straitjacket, but I'll still be able to guess the market!
> . . . I'm being fair, Raymond, but I want my own way and I'm going to have
> it. . . . Sure it's rotten, don't I know it? If a man's in business, he's got to
> use the methods that fit: I got no choice, business is rotten from the ground
> up! . . . I was a radical once, a boy . . . a fool of a boy—I murdered him,
> and he's waiting round every corner to murder me now—

And here he is, brashly facing his death:

> My God! This business of dying is the bunk like everything else. . . . Let me
> look at you, Aggie . . . you'll be a snappy widow and rich too . . . change your
> name from Ginsberg to Grinnel, like we talked about, and don't . . . don't
> spend money too fast. . . . One time there was a Jew named Christ dressed
> up in a rainbow, he told the world plenty, maybe there'll be some more like
> him. . . . Me, I don't care! I'm only thinking of myself. Put me in a solid silver
> coffin with gold cupids—don't matter what it costs . . .

As Sol, Luther Adler (Stella's brother) was like a caged tiger, frantic
to the point of delirium, and as Sarah, the woman who loves him and kills
him, Stella Adler was equally electric. Here at last were characters Strasberg and his actors could relate to: here were the Adlers, smart, hot-blooded
Jews tied to each other by strong family bonds, playing volatile Jewish
characters bound together by a lifetime of powerful feelings. In *Success
Story,* the Group actors didn't have to contend with high-falutin' Maxwell
Anderson rhetoric, as in *Night over Taos,* or to struggle with Southern
accents, as in *The House of Connelly,* but were free to speak in the voice
they knew best, that of impassioned, complaining New Yorkers, a voice shot
through with irony and self-pity and a woolly romanticism.

In *Gentlewoman*—the Group wisely going to bat with Lawson for a
second time—the bohemian anti-hero Rudy Flannigan doesn't speak with
the same staccato snap as Sol. He doesn't have Sol's rough-and-ready idiom,
or his scalpel-like wit, or his turbulent Jewishness. But he is a considerable

character nonetheless, a potent thirties prole, a man of the people with ruddy charm and a way with words. The play is something of a Depression-era *Candida* as it traces the misalliance between a woman of wealth (who loses it at the end of Act I) and a big city hobo. After a shaky marriage during which he tries to become middle class, Rudy realizes that, like Shaw's Marchbanks, he must rise above entangling domestic arrangements. To serve his class, the working class, he must return to it, alone, rather than dally in the haunts of the respectable. Leaving his aristocratic wife with their child (an ideal child of the remade future who will carry in his genes his mother's breeding mixed with his father's revolutionary idealism), Rudy goes off, the rugged democrat, untamed and untamable, to speak, to organize, to change the world.

In *Success Story* and *Gentlewoman,* the actors found the kind of play that suited their hyper-realistic style. But the fire didn't roar because Lawson's work just missed the sustained intensity that would show off their method at full tilt. In Odets, they found their man, and no mistake about it. Odets was part of the family, a member of the tribe. In his writing, if you listen, and if you know, you can hear the rhythm and swing, the fast, nimble wit, of Odets's best friend, Harold Clurman. Odets's plays were writing themselves, gathering form and focus, in the depths of his sub-conscious as he listened to Clurman's messianic talks and as he delved into his own emotional memories at Strasberg's insistent requests. And over it all he was washed by the heightened real-life drama of the period in which he struggled to artistic maturity, the era in response to which the Group had been formed. The thirties—the America of bread lines and soup kitch-ens, of strikes and unemployment, of union meetings and Communist cells —quickened Odets's artistic imagination the way the twenties—the decade of parties and good times—had aroused Fitzgerald's.

When after several false starts Odets presented finished plays to the Group, they were the expression of the Group's own passion, a distillation of Harold's harangues and Lee's method and of the earthy, idealistic tem-peraments of Odets's fellow actors. As a part of the Group, Odets found his voice, and in return he gave the Group its artistic identity. In one extraordi-nary year, 1935, the Theatre presented four Odets plays that unleashed four years' worth of the Group's psychic and artistic energy. *Waiting for Lefty, Till the Day I Die, Awake and Sing!,* and *Paradise Lost* were dramas made to order for a company of players. In the vast panorama of the

American theatre, Odets is the only truly company playwright, a writer with a theatre of his own. Odets evolved his style within the Group, living at Groupstroy, going away with the company for summers in the country, and inhaling the Group's conflicts and attachments, its language and its spirit. After such an apprenticeship, it follows that he produced a play like *Awake and Sing!*, an intense claustrophobic drama of Jewish family life.

Odets writes in a tone of Jewish irony mixed with Jewish exaltation. His characters, deeply scarred by the times, victims of an American system gone haywire, have, like Harold Clurman, a way with words: they're sustained by their ability both to talk and to feel and by their remembrance of a better past, their projection of a better future. In the midst of woe, as their lives are falling apart, they are yet capable of envisioning utopia. They are ecstatic sufferers, wedded to bitterness. Bad luck, despair, betrayal, and ostracism have been their fate, and from the debris they have learned to patch together a life.

Awake and Sing! and *Paradise Lost,* the two essential Odets plays, are about roomfuls of Jewish strugglers huddling in kitchens or cramped living rooms who meet each day with a growl and a wisecrack and who feed on the expectation that if things are bad now they will only be worse tomorrow, though in the end, somehow, everyone will survive. The families in these two high Odets dramas, the Bergers in *Awake and Sing!* and the Gordons in *Paradise Lost,* are equal parts victims and yea-sayers. Myron Berger and Leo Gordon are the sweet-natured husbands and fathers who leave to their wives, Bessie and Clara, all the messy business of tending their families. Ruling the roost, doing battle with enemies, protecting their own, the women are tougher and more realistic than their husbands. Life has hardened them, made them sharp and wary, prepared them to expect the worst, but in their hearts they still have dreams. Disappointed in their husbands, who grow daily more remote and private, fearful of what's to become of their children, the women have constructed their homes as fortresses against the haphazardness of the outside world. Myron can't earn a decent living; Leo is swindled blind by his partner of many years, Sam Katz. And as if that isn't bad enough, the fates of their children offer further proof of the world's rottenness. Bessie's Hennie gets pregnant by a guy who disappears. Bessie's Ralph is choking at his mundane factory job, and his girl is leaving him because they don't have enough money to make a life together.

Clara Gordon's kids are buried even deeper in the rubble of shattered hopes. Ben is a former Olympic champion with a bum heart who marries a tramp, drifts into a life of petty crime, and gets killed in a shootout with cops. Julie, with visions of Wall Street investments dancing in his head, is slowly wasting away from a fatal disease; Clara sees in his gradual deterioration a constant reminder of her cursed fate. Paula is a wonderful musician who must surrender her piano when the family, wiped out, piles its belongings in the street.

The Bergers and the Gordons wear their suffering with honor. It is their shame, yet it is also their identity. Through the financial and emotional setbacks, the blasted romances, the stalled careers, and the accumulated woes of what it means to be poor and Jewish and dispossessed in urban America in the 1930s comes at last deliverance. Their lot is one of Biblical calamity—the misfortunes visited upon Odets's families would indeed try the patience of Job—and like the Old Testament sufferers they are transformed, purified, in the very process of their travail. At the end, there is, for the survivors, renewal. Hennie runs away from her unloved husband and child to be with Moe Axelrod, Bessie's star boarder, a veteran who lost a leg in defense of his country, a wastrel and a rake, but a real man for all that, a guy who sees life hard and straight and whose sexual energy will lift Hennie out of the muck of a loveless marriage. Ralph's fate is less decisive but more exalted. He will remain at home but he will awake and sing, building himself into the apostle of a future utopia, the new society envisioned by Jacob, his politically radical grandfather.

With two of their children dead, their business destroyed, evicted from their home, the Gordons are also possessed of a vision of a new life. Heavy as it is, their grief has not bent their spirit. They've been tested and tried beyond reasonable bounds and they have endured, their honor intact, their optimism miraculously reborn.

"It seemed to me, sitting high up in the second balcony of the Belasco Theatre, watching Julie Garfield, J. Edward Bromberg, Stella and Luther Adler, and Morris Carnovsky in Odets's *Awake and Sing!*, that it would at last be possible for me to write about the life I had always known," Alfred Kazin recalls, in his impassioned memoir *Starting Out in the Thirties*. "In Odets's play," he continues,

> there was a lyric uplifting of blunt Jewish speech, boiling over and explosive.
> . . . Everybody on that stage was furious, kicking, alive—the words, always
> real but never flat, brilliantly authentic like no other theatre speech on

Clifford Odets as Dr. Benjamin in *Waiting for Lefty* (1935).

A group scene from *Awake and Sing!* (1935), Odets's high-strung play of Jewish family life. Left to right: Roman Bohnen, Morris Carnovsky, Stella Adler, Art Smith, J. Edward Bromberg, Alfred Ryder, Sanford Meisner, and Phoebe Brand.

Broadway, aroused the audience to such delight that one could feel it bounding back and uniting itself with the mind of the writer. . . . Odets pulled us out of self-pity. Everything so long choked up in twenty thousand damp hallways and on all those rumpled summer sheets, everything still smelling of the cold shadowed sand littered with banana peels under the boardwalk at Coney Island, everything that went back to the graveled roofs over the tenements, the fire escapes in the torrid nights, the food, the food, the pickle stands in the shadow of the subway and the screams of protest—"I never in my life even had a brithday party. Every time I went and cried in the toilet when my birthday came"—was now out in the open, at last, and we laughed. . . .

Sitting in the Belasco, watching my mother and father and uncles and aunts occupying the stage in *Awake and Sing!* by as much right as if they were Hamlet and Lear, I understood at last. It was all one, as I had always known. Art and truth and hope could yet come together—if a real writer was their meeting place. Odets convinced me . . . the actors of the Group Theatre had all the passion. I had never seen actors on the stage and an audience in the theatre come together with such a happy shock.

Giving American Jewish audiences a truer image of themselves than they had ever had before, Odets's plays had a quick, fresh quality. Through the power of their language and the solidity of the Group actors, American lives were raised up to art, where bitterness, loss, and sorrow are annealed and soothed and even at times made triumphantly comic.

Realist? No, Odets was not that. He was too high-strung for that. He elevated homely details and accuracy of observation into a realism sprinkled with the poetry of Jewish inflection and Jewish emotionalism. Odets's characters like Chekhov's are representative of a particular social class and of a particular era; but unlike Chekhov's, they are not at the end of a line, the last remnants of a privileged order, but rather are harbingers of an energetic American future. As in Chekhov, Odets's confined settings have reference to a larger reality; the ravages of Depression America seep in through every crack in the walls, coating the rooms and their inhabitants. Like their true mentor, Harold Clurman, the plays are bigger than life, fiercely sentimental, buoyed by their coiled, feverish, overemphatic language.

Beginning with the echo of realistic speech, Odets stitches a quilt of folk poetry and streetcorner philosophy; big city argot mixes with Yiddish intonations as words and phrases are repeated like leitmotivs in a symphony. For all its seeming verisimilitude, the language is dense, thickly textured, and shrewdly theatrical. Odets's characters speak in a lingo of their own, a compound of metaphor and inversion, as short jabbing sentences, alive with colloquialisms, alternate with longer speeches of operatic intensity. Here is an Odets sampler:

Where's advancement down the place? Work like crazy! Think they see it? You'd drop dead first.

The country's all right. A duck quacks in every pot!

Christ, you could a had a guy with some guts instead of a cluck stands around boilin' baby nipples. . . . That's the stuff you coulda had. Put up at ritzy hotels, frenchie soap, champagne. Now you're tied down to "Snake-Eye" here. What for? What's it get you? . . . A 2 × 4 flat on 108th Street . . . a pain in the bustle it gets you.

There is more to life than this! Everything he said is true, but there is more. That was the past, but there is a future. Now we know. We dare to understand. Truly, truly, the past was a dream. But this is real! To know from this that something must be done. That is real. We searched; we were confused! But we searched, and now the search is ended. For the truth has found us. For the first time in our lives—for the first time our house has a real foundation. Clara, those outside are afraid. . . . Let them look in our house. We're not ashamed. Let them look in. Clara, my darling, *listen to me.* Everywhere now men are rising from their sleep. Men, men are understanding the bitter black total of their lives. Their whispers are growing to shouts! They become an ocean of understanding! *No man fights alone.* Oh, if you could only see with me the greatness of men. I tremble like a bride to see the time when they'll use it. My darling, we must have only one regret—that life is so short! That we must die so soon. Yes, I want to see that new world. I want to kiss all those future men and women. What is this talk of bankrupts, failures, hatred . . . they won't know what that means. Oh, yes, I tell you the whole world is for men to possess. Heartbreak and terror are not the heritage of mankind! The world is beautiful. No fruit tree wears a lock and key. Men will sing at their work, men will love. Ohhh, darling, the world is in its morning . . . and *no man fights alone!*[10]

   "No one else but us knows what is in those plays," say Morris Carnovsky and Phoebe Brand, speaking for the Group actors who appeared in

Awake and Sing! and *Paradise Lost.* "They don't know their tremendous inner life, their poetic values. Other people don't see the underside of Odets. The plays are so intertwined and so rich. So much is happening between the lines. We talked about inner meaning. No one can play them the way we did. No one. We knew the playwright; Harold knew the playwright better than the playwright knew himself. He helped Odets shape the plays."

Odets's young spirit—he was only thirty in 1935—tapped the Group's young energy, releasing the style of overheated realism they had been exploring. The exercises in improvisation and sense memory, and in finding experiences in their own lives that corresponded to those of their characters —everything, in short, that Strasberg had been teaching them—pointed toward the kind of acting Odets's plays demanded, acting in which psychological realism is pushed to the heights of a lyric intensity.

5

ON NATIVE GROUNDS:
DEFEAT

1935 was the year of Odets. Photographed, interviewed, written about as the wunderkind of the American theatre, he was sought after by society matrons and Hollywood moguls. Sadly, for him and his theatre, nothing he wrote after that banner year was ever to be as good. After 1935, Odets contributed three additional plays to the Group roster: *Golden Boy* in 1937, *Rocket to the Moon* in 1938, and *Night Music* in 1940.

A good show, in a way that earlier Odets plays hadn't been, *Golden Boy* was the greatest commercial success in the Group's history. Though it was acted with the magnetic realism that was now the Group's hallmark, the play is a setup job, manufactured and self-conscious. Should Joe Bonaparte be a prizefighter or a violinist? Is he to live by the fist or the fiddle? This is the play's central question, its nagging spurious premise. Joe's moral crisis, as he struggles with a choice between a life dedicated to great music or to brute strength, has always seemed ludicrous to me. He's clearly a special case, a man too talented and too lucky to be believable, and I don't see how his story has any of the social significance that Odets seems to think it does. Who in the Depression, or at any other time, had such luscious options as between a stellar career on the concert stage or heroism in the boxing arena?

Odets's Jewish moaners have a wider reference than this Italian winner who blows it; the articulate, disaffected, undefeated characters in *Awake and Sing!*, *Waiting for Lefty*, and *Paradise Lost* are the impassioned conscience of a generation, brought to a sizzling theatrical boil, whereas Joe Bonaparte reveals more about Odets's strictly personal conflicts between art and money, between holding on and selling out.

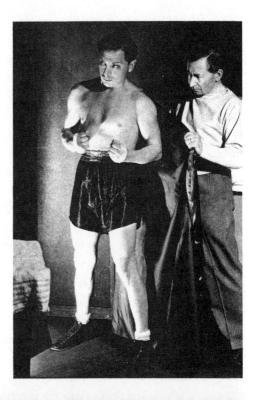

Luther Adler as *Golden Boy* (1937), with Art Smith, in the Group's most commercially successful play.

Scenic realism, with real fruit or the table, in *Golden Boy*. Phoebe Brand, Morris Carnovsky, and Frances Farmer.

In *Golden Boy*, Odets is working on a smaller canvas. Although the play contains an echo of the verbal thunder of 1935 (and certainly Odets rewarded Group actors with colorful roles), *Golden Boy* shows Odets beginning to leave the tattered, spacious world of Depression America that he seemed to require as a creative impetus. For all its showmanship, the play anticipates the narrowed focus and diminished power of the work to follow.

The dentist's office where *Rocket to the Moon* takes place seems especially claustrophobic and out of touch with any outside world. Caught in a loveless marriage with a cold woman, a dentist is rejuvenated through his affair with his assistant, Cleo Singer. His worldly father-in-law, trying to prolong his vigor, is also infatuated with Cleo, while Cleo herself, an Odetsian optimist, ultimately rejects both men to go off on her own. Sealed off in a world of private feelings, crying out to love and be loved, the characters don't have the moral earnestness or the emotional size of the taxi drivers, the Bergers, and the Gordons. Odets tries to lift this meager romantic drama to the level of social allegory, but the play's action and its small trapped characters can't support the inflated title. The contemporary America that he wants his characters to represent isn't a tangible part of the play's fabric; it doesn't stain the furniture the way it does in *Awake and Sing!*

Night Music even more than *Rocket to the Moon* seems like a play without a country. A drama of rootless characters, wanderers in an amorphous nighttime city, *Night Music* itself has no home base. In this episodic Saroyanesque fable, Odets's young walkabouts are sustained by their love and their idealism as they confront a hard-bitten world. The oratorical flashes—swelling, passionate outbursts, fervid pronouncements of a utopian future—that are periodically sprayed over the flimsy action seem like mere stylistic exercises, form without substance, both echo and parody of the high-flying Odets of only a few years earlier.

After the Group dissolved in 1941, Odets wrote only four other plays: *Clash by Night* (1941), a domestic melodrama; *The Big Knife* (1949), about the corruption of a Hollywood star; *The Country Girl* (1951), about the comeback of an alcoholic actor; and *The Flowering Peach* (1954), in which the Biblical Noah and his wrangling family talk pure Odets. Like *Rocket to the Moon* and *Night Music,* these are plays without a theme or a context large enough to warrant the hyped-up quality of Odets's writing. The two actors in *The Big Knife* and *The Country Girl* are too parochial to uphold the battles of conscience that Odets has thrust upon them. In these plays about theatre people, Odets's own disappointment, his lingering sense of having been corrupted by American commerce, his sorrow at his inability to continue the power and the purity of the work of 1935 can be read.

Odets's earliest family plays opened onto a clanging American panorama; his later family plays retreated to more autobiographical concerns. Although he could always create conflicts on stage—his husbands and wives conduct ongoing pitched battles as they grapple with betrayal, compromise, and disillusionment—he never again found a subject and a period that inspired him as much as being poor in America in the early thirties did. When, after 1935, the country's and his own fortunes improved, something crucial went out of his writing; the vernacular poetry that ennobled his three strongest plays faded, never to be fully revived.

To a remarkable degree, Odets's success and decline paralleled the Group's. His glory was their glory; his failure was their failure. When they charged into *Waiting for Lefty*, *Awake and Sing!*, and *Paradise Lost*, the Group set a performing standard against which excellence in the American theatre continues to be measured. After Odets left the Group for Hollywood, the original Group began to dissolve, and in 1937, in anger and frustration, Cheryl Crawford and Lee Strasberg resigned. The Group became what some claimed it had been all along, Harold Clurman's personal theatre. After Clurman took over as sole director, the Theatre had its greatest box-office success and a series of disappointments until, early in 1941, it quietly passed away, after presenting the prophetically titled *Retreat to Pleasure*, which featured in its cast only two original Group members.

1935 had been the Group's year, as it was Odets's. After that, though it did some good work, the Group was never quite the same. 1936 was a disaster: two stylized plays for which the actors' training had not adequately prepared them. The first was *The Case of Clyde Griffiths*, Erwin Piscator's adaptation of *An American Tragedy*, a crudely didactic rendering of Dreiser's novel as a condemnation of American capitalism. *Johnny Johnson*, a collaboration between Kurt Weill and Paul Green, was an anti-war musical fable about a holy innocent who holds onto his sweet naiveté as he's bombarded with evidence of man's folly and cruelty.

Requiring a presentational acting style, ironic and objective, these two neo-Brechtian pieces had a drastically simplified approach to character.

With *Johnny Johnson* (1937) by Kurt Weill and Paul Green, the Group tried a Brechtian-style musical, and failed.

What mattered was what the plays said, while characters were merely pawns in the service of the plays' raw ruling ideas: capitalism corrupts; war is insanity.

"Lee liked *The Case of Clyde Griffiths* for the chance it offered to do something spectacular with it in production, but it was a poor play," Morris Carnovsky says. "It was the first stylized play we did," Margaret Barker recalls. "The improvisations we worked on for it were exciting. Helen Tamiris was our dance instructor. She was a very strong director; she beat a drum and you were to do some fabulous leap. We had period costumes and were to walk in rhythm to music. I walked like my arms were in slings. Lee's direction was patterned after Meyerhold productions that he had recently seen. But I remember that in a half hour working with Stella Adler on that play I knew more about it than from all the rehearsals."

Johnny Johnson was so poorly planned—rushed through rehearsal, it was booked into much too large a theatre—that it helped precipitate the schism of 1937. "I developed the play along with Kurt Weill and Paul Green," says Cheryl Crawford. "It was the only musical the Group ever did —wisely, I think, because none of the actors were really singers." "On

Johnny Johnson, our designer Donald Oenslager was given to grand designs," recalls Morris Carnovsky. "He was going for the smallness of human life against a background of war, which went against what we were working for in our performances. But when we argued, Lee silenced us with, 'Donald knows!' "

In 1939, the Group experimented more successfully with another stylized play, Saroyan's *My Heart's in the Highlands.* Whimsical, in a way uniquely Saroyan's, a fable about a dreamy little boy, his impoverished poet-father, and a bugle-playing refugee from a local asylum, a former Shakespearean actor gifted with special insight, the piece has art theatre "masterwork" written all over it. It's an impossible play, cloying, sentimental, fruity. To direct this new kind of material, Clurman chose Robert Lewis, one of the company actors, who had trained with Eva Le Gallienne at the Civic Repertory Theatre, and who, more than anyone else on the Group team, had a fondness for fantasy. Directing a company of newcomers— there were no Group regulars in the cast—Lewis worked for quite different values than Strasberg had. Whatever the script's literary atrocities, the performance had a lighter touch, a more fanciful quality, than any earlier Group effort. It felt like an authentic departure from the usual Group colors.

After Odets left for Hollywood in 1936, the two writers Clurman was most loyal to, writers clearly in the Lawson-Odets camp, never got the hang of the medium. Irwin Shaw and Robert Ardrey went on to be successful in other areas—Shaw became a popular novelist; Ardrey wrote screenplays. The four plays they contributed to the Group—*Thunder Rock* and *Casey Jones* by Ardrey, Shaw's *Gentle People* and *Retreat to Pleasure*—are a sorry lot. Ardrey's *Thunder Rock,* a fable (yet another!) about American isolationism on the eve of World War II, was certainly the most boring script in the Group's history. Set in a remote lighthouse, it concerns the retreat from the world of a man of affairs. During his sojourn, he meets the ghosts of pioneers from an earlier age, who while fleeing from religious persecution had smashed into the lighthouse. From their example, the lessons of the past, the hero resolves that he must rejoin his country as it prepares for war. As a paradigm of American uncertainty on the brink of entering the World War, the play has some historical interest, but flat dialogue defeats its symbolic intentions.

In Shaw's *Gentle People* as well, the language and the characters aren't grand enough to sustain an allegorical framework. In the action of two old fishermen who rise up to slay a crime boss who has humiliated them, we are meant to see the heroic revolt of the common man against fascist terrorism.

"What did he think the Group's audience was? I asked Lee Strasberg at one meeting," Mordecai Gorelik, one of the Theatre's principal set designers, recalls. "He said, 'The American people.' I said I thought that was too grand, and too general, that the audience was the professional middle class. 'Oh, call me anything,' he snapped. 'Call me knockwurst.' Well," Gorelik concludes, "I think that was a problem, the Group not defining its relationship to a specific audience. They weren't political enough. Some of the members, notably Morris Carnovsky and Elia Kazan and Robert Lewis, were more radical than the directors wanted to be. I too wanted the directors to try more daring things politically, but they didn't. And so I joined with a group that was more truly political, the Theatre Collective."

In the thirties, plays—like everything else—were scrutinized, then applauded or denounced, on the basis of their politics. What a writer had to say about what was wrong with America and how to fix it was often more to the point than how he said it. At left-wing theatres, plays were put on because they had a politically acceptable approach to issues of the moment. In agitprop dramas like *Stevedore, The Sailors of Catarro,* and Brecht's *Mother,* produced at the Theatre Union, political revelation was more important than literary finesse.

When *Waiting for Lefty* exploded on stage at the Theatre Union, it looked as if the Group had joined the Marxist brigade. In *The New Masses,* orthodox radical Mike Gold saluted Odets, a gesture he was soon to withdraw after seeing *Awake and Sing!* and *Paradise Lost* and realizing that Odets wasn't really political. Like most hardcore leftists, Gold dismissed Odets and the Group as bourgeois at heart, more interested in emotion than politics, more dedicated to revealing character than to promoting Marxism.

If the Group was too far to the right to please the disenchanted, it was too liberal, too consistently critical of American pieties to satisfy most of the Broadway reviewers. In the popular mind, Group actors were Marxist revolutionaries who mounted plays that attacked the American way.

Individually, some Group members were deeply leftist. "I later learned that thirteen members of the Group were Communist," says Mordecai Gorelik. "Communism drew various types, from Morris Carnovsky, one of the finest people you'll ever meet, to Kazan, always quick on the trigger to know what to belong to when." After he left the Group, John Howard Lawson became a leading Communist spokesman in Hollywood. Odets belonged to the Party from 1934 to 1936. Gorelik claims that the Group's lawyer, Andrew Overgard, was a Communist.

"Once the Communist thing took hold, strong class distinctions emerged," recalls Margaret Barker. "I went to cell meetings, but I was never in the Party. I was considered bourgeois because my father was a doctor. Like most people in the Group, I too thought the Russian experiment would be the answer to everything, but I think that the Group became too involved in politics that were strangling them all."

Individual Group members may have been intensely political, but the Group Theatre never descended to propaganda; its plays never offered specific solutions to specific problems. (As an example of what he considered the Group's political aloofness, Mordecai Gorelik cites a conversation between Sidney Howard and Harold Clurman at Dover Furnace in the summer of 1932: "Howard asked, 'Is your theatre going to be a Marxist theatre?' Harold said, 'We're not going to be limited by that,' to which Howard responded, 'Marxism is a very roomy philosophy, Harold.' ")

The Group was run by people who thought good acting and writing were more important than political causes. "The theatre had no political policy," says Morris Carnovsky. "Lee talked a lot of politics, but he steered clear. Once he asked his brother to come and give us some lessons in Marxism. A lot of us had leftist feelings—you couldn't help it in those days —but the Group never made any public statement."

The last-minute optimism in *Awake and Sing!* and *Paradise Lost,* where Odets's unnerved heroes pledge themselves to building a better America, is typical of the level of the Group's political thinking. Odets's final uplifts are purely rhetorical, making up in theatrical bravura for what they lack in ideology.

If it was not political in any narrow or militant sense, still the Group was no art-for-art's-sake ivory tower organization either. In the broadest— and I think the best—sense, the Group was a social theatre, producing plays that illuminated the turmoil of the American thirties. "We were very aware of our social responsibilities," says Margaret Barker. "What can we say to the world through this play?—was a through-line for each play we did. The image of people standing in bread lines had an enormous impact on us. We felt we had something to set the world on fire. Harold always had held out to us the inspiring idea of contributing your creativity to better the world."

"All of our plays were an acknowledgment of the difficulty of living in our time," says Morris Carnovsky.

Money figured importantly in all of the major Group Theatre productions. Whether the characters had it or didn't have it, money remained a fixed central part of the American experience that the plays chronicled. Money was temptation, corruption, dream, and necessity. Without it, you couldn't survive; with too much of it, you were driven crazy. The Group's most vocal in-house critic, Mordecai Gorelik, says that a recurrent theme in Group plays—What does it profit a man to gain the whole world if he loses his soul?—was beside the point for the Group's audience, most of whom had trouble enough earning a meager living. "Gaining the world was fantasy, and I thought the Group should find a new metaphor. But they never did."

The Group took sides, as over and over again its plays supported the common man against the capitalist machine. Repeatedly bamboozled and confounded by the system, the average man, the lone individual, whose soul the Group pledged itself to reveal, rises up to challenge the way things are by his strength of character, his will, his integrity, his ability to conceive of a fairer system, and his capacity to have dreams. The power to turn dream to reality was Harold Clurman's personal legacy, imprinted on most of the plays presented by his theatre.

Not only was the Group a theatre that reflected the times, it positively required the times to do its best work. Coming to life during the unprecedented suffering of the early thirties, it was distinctly a Depression-era outfit, one that depended on the struggles created by the Depression to sustain its own artistic momentum; in the late thirties, as the economy began to revive and the country prepared for fighting fascism, the Group splintered, losing its artistic focus and impact. "My image of the end was when I saw Harold alone in a field, wringing his hands," says Morris Carnovsky. "His face was haggard. He was alone, and agonized. I knew then the Group was finished."

As a group experiment, the Group never really worked. Heated battles over politics, money, the Method, sex, class distinctions, power, and success caused ill feelings which fester in Group members to this day.

The directors wanted to run the ship with minimum interference from the actors. "We were a thorn in their side, but we had opinions about everything," Morris Carnovsky recalls. In 1937, a group of angry actors served each director with a white paper. "There were a lot of things the actors needed to fight for," says Margaret Barker, "but I thought the papers, which criticized each of the directors individually and personally, and which caused Lee and Cheryl to resign, were grossly unfair. Both Cheryl and Lee had been terribly burdened by responsibilities, while Harold had been terribly involved emotionally with Stella. It was all too much for Lee; he was in bed for weeks after a production. The militant actors put the finger on the three people who had carried us for seven years."

"The actors wanted too much control. That's no way to run a theatre," Cheryl Crawford says.

"Early on the actors had a voice, but as time went on they had nothing to say, and financially everything was in the hands of the directors," says Mordecai Gorelik. "It was a tough job for the directors to keep the Group alive, and they did it at the expense of the actors. I always liked working with the Group creatively—but when it came to money, that was another matter. The actors got the lousiest salaries of anyone on Broadway. I was told by Cheryl that since this was a group endeavor, and everyone was making sacrifices, there was no reason why she had to pay me regular union rates. I told her I wasn't charging more than the lowest union rate. I finally told her I could not design for her under union rates, I would be thrown out, but that after getting my salary I would invest it in the Group."

Gorelik also had acrimonious relations with the Group directors over whether or not he was a Group member. "When I asked them if I was in or not, they called a meeting. They didn't want me, because if I was a member there were things I could do. Harold and Lee told me that to be a member you had to have the Group spirit. At the meeting (in 1934) Odets took the chair. Art Smith stood up and said, 'Of course you're a member.' Next day, I walked into the office and said I want to see the books. Harold said, 'You'll see them over my dead body.' Lee said, 'The group members are those who have faith in the directors.' They were having such a tough time holding it together, and they felt I was in the way. That summer I received a letter, signed by the three directors, telling me I was no longer a member of the Group. Once I was no longer a member, they asked me to design their next show. So we got on fine again, though I still had a few sore spots."

Margaret Barker says she will never forget how she learned she was no longer a part of the Group. "In 1937, there was a sign on the door: 'Nobody is in the Group Theatre except the cast of *Golden Boy.*' Since I wasn't in the play, that meant I was out of the Group. It was terribly cruel, in a death-striking way."

"For me the Group was a miserable experience," Stella Adler says. "I wasn't a part of it, ideologically or any other way. I am not a group member: I only joined because I believed in Harold."

"Strasberg always thought I was an ingrate for turning against him," Morris Carnovsky says. "He felt he taught me everything I know."

"They thought men would change the world; women were slighted in the Group, to be kept in their place," Margaret Barker says.

Aside from Odets, and to a lesser extent Lawson, the Group produced no major new voices in American drama. But Stella Adler, bristling, says that "any four-year-old would understand that a theatre doesn't survive by masterpieces. It's a mistake constantly to look for great literature: a theatre cannot survive only on great plays. Stanislavski directed *The Two Orphans*, a melodrama, for God's sake. And my father played in commercial junk along with Shakespeare, Gorky, and Tolstoy. All the plays put on by the Group had merit—they had a right to be seen, they were wonderfully staged; I felt it was amateurish to make literary judgments. Theatre is not always to be judged as literature."

But when the good new plays the Group was looking for didn't materialize, ought they to have applied their Method to revivals? In 1940, a production of *Three Sisters* was cast and put into rehearsal. Clurman was going through a personally difficult period, however, and feeling listless; and a production that could have been a turning point for the theatre was abandoned. "We just didn't have the money to continue," says Phoebe Brand. "Or a director. And there was so much inner dissension. It just fell apart, which is a shame, because it would have been a lovely production. We were doing Clifford's version. Frances Farmer played Olga. She was a lovely person, and she adored the Group, but there was something driving her. Stella played Masha, I played Irina. Lee Cobb and Sandy Meisner were also in it. It's a pity it didn't get on."[11]

By and large, the Group Theatre was not a great critical success. Press reaction to what the Group was trying to do and to what it represented in the history of the American theatre was not enlightened. Occasional flashes of outright hostility toward the Group are startling to read, a reminder that its fortunes were often decided by writers whose ignorance matched their arrogance. Ironically, the Group's strongest acclaim was in London in 1938, when it performed *Golden Boy* and was accorded the kind of adulation the Moscow Art Theatre had received in New York in 1923.

"We revamped English acting," says Stella Adler.

"We were an absolute sensation," Morris Carnovsky says. "They stood up and cheered. They really tore the place down. We could have stayed there indefinitely. They referred to us as 'those darling Americans,' and told us they understood every word we said."

Like most Americans, the Group respected success, even if sometimes they said they didn't. In *The Fervent Years*, Clurman writes proudly of the theatre's two moneymakers, *Men in White* and *Golden Boy*. But Group members also knew that success, like money, could contaminate, making you forget why you joined the Group.

Odets's bouts with financial and artistic recognition were indicative of the Group's paradoxical relationship to making it. Odets wanted the kind of acclaim that O'Neill had received in the twenties, but he also craved popular acceptance. He wanted to please both *The New Masses* and the Broadway crowd, and more often than not wound up finding favor with neither. When he became the thirties' answer to O'Neill, Hollywood tempted him with offers of huge amounts of money. Odets capitulated, thinking all the while that he was betraying his theatre colleagues. "In the beginning Cliff was beautiful and passionate, but when he went to Hollywood, he ate himself up from within," says Morris Carnovsky. "He became disillusioned, and corrupt. He protested, 'I'm not falling for that Hollywood crap, I know what's happening, they're making too much over me.' But he fell for it. He maintained a shrine within himself for members of the Group. He would give us things—records, paintings. He loved us all. But he never got over the feeling that he had sold himself to the highest bidder, which was the movies."

Relations between Hollywood and the Group were never easy. Once they arrived in California (and almost every Group member went out there at least once some time during the thirties), they found the studios had nothing for them to do. They were given vague titles, and then sat around, observing. Even Stella Adler went West, changing her name to Ardler, and appeared in a few Paramount B pictures; her most famous role is that of a millionaire's mistress in *Love on Toast.*

Only two Group actors, John Garfield and Franchot Tone, had regular movie work, and both were made to feel guilty for having deserted the Group. "When he was a youngster in the Group, Julie was pure in heart," Morris Carnovsky remembers. "But then when he went out there, money happened, and lots of women, and he became a mess. He didn't grow after he left the Group." Margaret Barker told me that Franchot Tone was the best actor in the Group, but there's no evidence of that in his movie work. Once in Hollywood, Tone too went the way of all flesh, becoming increasingly alcoholic and having the misfortune to marry Joan Crawford.[12]

Their opposition to movies united the Group as no other issue ever managed to. Later, Strasberg and Kazan would relax their antagonism to movies, but most of the Group members held to their original view of them as anti-art. When performers like Sylvia Sidney and Jane Wyatt who had made careers in films were imported for a single Group production, Group members were resentful. Among the refugees from Hollywood only Frances Farmer escaped censure because of her own scorn for movies and her commitment to the Group's ideals.

Financial defeat; an erratic literary record; no big stars except for John Garfield; bitter internecine warfare about acting and politics; failure to establish a repertory structure, or a true theatre collective: as Cheryl Crawford says, the Group bit the dust on many counts. But the Group, the bravest and single most significant experiment in the history of American theatre, lives on, a vital part of the theatrical community. For, in addition to the example it set, what the Group produced above all was a corps of actors who were such perfectionists that many of them retreated from acting, as if in awe of the demands of their profession, in order to become master teachers. Generation after generation, Lee Strasberg, Stella Adler, Sanford Meisner, Robert Lewis, Elia Kazan, and Morris Carnovsky have passed on to their students a deep regard for the actor's art that they themselves acquired as part of their experience as Group members. Variously interpreted, the spirit of the Group continues, in the classes of Stella

Adler at her Conservatory, at the Neighborhood Playhouse which Sanford Meisner has directed for nearly fifty years, in the Strasberg Institutes in New York and Los Angeles, and in that most famous of all American acting places—where both the ideals of the Group and the lessons of Stanislavski are intently, passionately honored—the Actors Studio.

KEN WEINBERG

Part 2

BEHIND CLOSED DOORS:
INSIDE THE ACTORS STUDIO

6

A PHILANTHROPIC GESTURE

"House is open!"

It is 10:50 on a Tuesday morning at the Actors Studio. People are filling in downstairs, into the front office and reception area, greeting each other and talking shop. The atmosphere is friendly and casual, but anticipatory. Conversations continue as the members go upstairs to the Lee Strasberg Theatre, where the sessions are held.

On stage, twining a ball of rope, an actor is already in place. He is seated at a cluttered desk surrounded by objects—a ladder, a toaster, crutches, a wheelchair—which seem to invade the stage. The actor himself looks like a prop among a warehouse of props. As Studio members enter the theatre, they glance distractedly at their colleague on stage, taking his presence for granted. The actor in place takes no notice of his gathering audience. As he concentrates on twining rope with undivided attention, you get the impression that for him there is no one else in the room, there is no reality other than the one he has created for himself out of the clutter on the stage. He is alone up there, lost in his private thoughts.

There are only seven rows of seats in this theatre, and they are quickly filling up. At 10:59, the moderator enters, walks to a seat in the middle of the front row, picks up a card lying on a small table, and announces that this will be a scene from *American Buffalo.* At 11:00 precisely, the house lights are lowered and the scene begins.

Which means that the actor simply continues to do what he has been doing for the last ten minutes, working that rope as he's deep in thought. A bedraggled young man enters, shuffles some cards, fiddles with papers on the desk, seems about to speak, retreats into silence, begins cracking and eating nuts. Then, finally, a voice, low and growly, emerges from the debris. "So?" the man at the desk says, continuing his wrapping.

The actors speak quietly and slowly, with long pauses in and between speeches. As they talk, they go on with their own separate and private activities, the young man cracking and eating, the man at the desk wrapping and twining.

The set is dark, the voices are often a blur, as if the actors are plunged in intricate inner monologues. They are obviously not playing to the audience, but instead are conducting their own personal investigation of the material.

After about ten minutes of this faltering, hesitant exchange, the actor at the desk calls "Scene!" He then turns to the audience, acknowledging the presence of others for the first time. House lights go up. The audience, having been as intent as the actor with his twine, now move in their seats, cough, relax; the hushed atmosphere that has prevailed throughout the scene lifts. The actor at the desk looks at the moderator in the front row and begins to speak, louder and more fluent than he had been when in character. "We did it two months ago for Lee Grant, and she said to allow the paternal instinct to come in this time. The energy was less this time, maybe because of that; it wasn't as angry as it had been before. I made a prior life for the character."

"My character is an ex-junkie," the younger actor says, "so physical things happen to him."

"How does the scene relate to your own work?" the moderator interrupts.

"What I need to do is be more specific with choices I make. I made the choice to give the character an itch, and I got his speech pattern through one adjustment, rubbing my tongue. My prior life was a little weak, though; last time I had a through-line."

"Did your choices take over for you?" the moderator asks. "Did they feed you? Maybe you didn't give yourself sufficiently personal answers. . . . OK, let's have some comments."

"You didn't seem to think so much about the actor working this time," a member says to the young actor. "You seemed more open to just letting things happen, rather than worrying about fulfilling the tasks you set for yourself."

"To wrap twine and to eat peanuts violates the given circumstances," another observer says. "I saw marvelous atmosphere, some of the behavior was nice, but I didn't see any situation. I saw card playing but for no reason. The prior circumstances weren't attended to. What's the scene about?"

"I liked it better the last time," the older actor says. "I went more with my own reactions then. The parental choice dampened it; the colors of desperateness were very much down this time."

"Other comments?" the moderator asks, before launching into his summary.

"The behavior was general, a little conventional," he begins. "I didn't feel that the inner life you worked out really took over. The actor has to have his imagination impelled, but the tasks you set didn't really seize your imagination. What does the card game do for you in remembering? Where does it help you to be emotionally? I didn't understand the long pantomime that preceded the first word: why did you need to speak then, at that moment? For both of you, the behavior was too withdrawn, there wasn't enough of yourself there."

The moderator calls a five-minute break before the next scene. As some members go downstairs, for coffee or to use the rest rooms, while others stay in place lighting cigarettes and talking, assistants clear the stage as the actor for the second scene sets up. Unlike the actors in the first scene, who have the advantage of preparing before the house is open, he has to relax and to get concentrated during the break, as the audience unwinds. He stands at a podium, his only prop, taking glasses on and off, fidgeting with a sheaf of papers, and visibly screening out everything but his own thoughts. He claims the space immediately around the podium for himself, creating a small invisible circle behind which he retreats into his character.

After the audience has settled down, the moderator announces that the next scene will be Chekhov's monologue, *On the Harmfulness of Tobacco.*

The actor clears his throat, removes his glasses, glances furtively off to the side. Slowly, in a hushed tone, as if his voice is rising to the surface from a vast cavern, he begins to speak. "I feel like screaming," he says, in a barely audible whisper. Is this the actor, sharing with us his own frustrations, or is he delivering the playwright's dialogue? For a moment, he seems about to stop the scene. But no, it turns out, he's just being natural. He's doing the piece, but in a way that makes it seem as if he's just talking to us as himself in his own words rather than saying words that have been written down in a finished form by someone else. He scratches his ear. Then his chest. Again, he looks nervously to the side. The actor's offhandedness begins to acquire a subtext, as his voice grows more distinct. But his approach remains primarily internal, as he protects his casualness, which is clearly the most important element of his work.

At the end, he sits down on stage, sighs, and laughingly says, "After a scene is over, we're all better and more relaxed, more believable."

"I didn't want you to see the work," he says. "I didn't want you to catch me acting, I wanted you to catch me at a lecture hall. I wanted to give myself permission to take my time, to think about what I was going to say. I've got to make this guy me, yet I've never experienced what the character, this hen-pecked husband and failure, experiences."

"You confront failure daily, don't you?" someone from the audience suggests. The actor, startled at first, agrees. "So you know the character very well!"

"Comments?" the moderator asks.

"It's casual, it's relaxed, it's nice," someone volunteers, "but I don't care. It lacks immediacy. Chekhov mounted it in an immediate situation, and you don't explore this."

"You have a wonderful wry sense of humor, and I wish you'd give yourself permission to use it."

"You always sell yourself short. I don't know why you don't fly to the moon."

"Why the hell did *you* want to do this piece?" the moderator calls out. "You have to be alive to something you want to do. You have to *start* with what excites you about the material. Allow yourself to dive in where you dive deepest; you are trying to keep lids on a lot of things, so you can be easy and relaxed, but to do what? You suspect that if you really let go, you'd get the wrong reaction.

"The value of work is that it should open response in you, it should arouse you to a place where you need to be, to be alive and open. Go to where your instinct indicates, and don't worry too much about 'working' correctly, which will stop you cold. Be as bold as you can be. It's still a kind of performance here, you know: the mystique of leaving that element out is a mistake. When this method was put together at the Moscow Art Theatre, problems were worked on during the day and performed at night. It wasn't done in abstraction, as it often is here. For us, the work has become something of a monster, divorced from performance and production.

"C. S. decided to write a book about the problems and make some money."

"Who?"

"Constantin Stanislavski. He started all this. Ok, it's one o'clock, time's up. That's it for today."

The audience applauds the moderator (who today was Frank Corsaro) as they continue conversations started two hours ago.

In language, atmosphere, and general procedure, what I have just described is a typical, closed-door session at the Actors Studio: two scenes, followed by the actors' statements about what they wanted to work on, and then comments from the observers.

The Actors Studio was founded by three Group Theatre alumni as a workshop for professional actors. Quite unlike the Group, which came into being with a great flourish and a battery of burning manifestos, the Actors Studio had a modest start.

"Gadge [Elia] Kazan and I were at a coffee shop in the theatre district," recalls Cheryl Crawford, "and we remarked that there was no place in New York where a working or professional actor could go to work on his craft. We regretted that actors had no opportunity to develop their skills, and so, on the spot, really, we decided to organize such a place. It was as simple as that."

Kazan and Crawford, who had remained good friends since the Group Theatre days and who met for just such lunches as this from time to time, were both in a particularly generous mood in the autumn of 1947. Crawford had just produced *Brigadoon*, the biggest commercial hit of her career, and Kazan was the most exciting young director in town, with stunning reviews for his direction of Arthur Miller's *All My Sons* and with a new play he had directed, *A Streetcar Named Desire*, already the talk of the new season on the basis of its sensational out-of-town notices. Kazan and Crawford had always been concerned about the welfare of actors, and here, riding high in their own careers, they had the chance to do something about it. "The Actors Studio was begun as a philanthropic gesture," Cheryl Crawford claims.

The founding of the Actors Studio seems almost accidental, improvisatory. And yet the seeds for such an enterprise had been planted in the Group Theatre. When the Group faded away, the impulse it had fostered did not fade with it. Some Group members wanted to start another theatre while many of the alumni wanted a place where they could continue to explore acting problems and teach others what they had learned during their unique experience in Clurman's company.

In 1940 as the Group was winding down, Elia Kazan, Bobby Lewis, and Sylvia Regan from the Theatre Union tried to start a Dollar Top Theatre that, in spirit, was an attempt to go on with the work of the Group. "The concept was that if you got a big enough house, with every seat a dollar, you could attract enough of an audience to make a profit," says Sylvia Regan. "We wanted the kind of people who had come to the Theatre Union, where tickets were cheap (the top of the balcony was thirty cents) and where we made the effort to create good theatre for people who had never been to the theatre. At the Dollar Top, we wanted people to come in off the street, as they had at the Theatre Union. We wanted to do good new plays that would have appeal to a mass audience—a people's theatre—as well as revivals. Theatre business was not good at the time, and Gadge and Bobby Lewis, who were both darling guys, thought of the Dollar Top as a way to stimulate theatre business, as well to keep the spirit of the Group alive. But unfortunately, we never got beyond the planning stage."

The motive that the Group had stimulated—to have a gathering place for theatre people serious about the theatre—was fulfilled during the forties in Erwin Piscator's Dramatic Workshop at the New School. "There wouldn't have been an Actors Studio without Piscator's Workshop," says Jack Garfein who, at seventeen, was its youngest student. Although it never got beyond an amateur status, the Workshop was a theatrical nucleus of course work and productions that perpetuated the Group's idealism. To teach at the Workshop, Piscator, a German émigré who had worked with Brecht, invited "people who had something to offer, whether or not he agreed with them," says Maria Piscator, his widow. Because "Piscator liked debate, and thought of school as a confrontation," he invited Strasberg, Sanford Meisner, and Stella Adler to teach for him, even though he had basic disagreements with their ideas.

While the Group alumni taught their individual versions of the Method, which Piscator thought was "sugared realism, not real realism," "the branch of the tree and not the tree itself," he instructed the school's young actors (among them Rod Steiger, Maureen Stapleton, Marlon Brando, Montgomery Clift, and several others later to join the Actors Studio) in his own theory of objective acting. "The idea of this," Madame

Piscator says, "is to learn to see the world not through the senses only, as in Stanislavski, but to move away from the individual, as in Brecht. In objective acting, we do not judge. And we put more of an emphasis on the power of the gesture than in the Method. We're interested in conveying ideas more than emotions.

"Piscator respected the theatre of Chekhov and Stanislavski, but he felt that the times—his times—demanded something more, and something other. After World War I, he had been surrounded by death, he had seen hunger in Russia and Germany, which conditioned his thinking about the theatre. He fought against the sentimentality and the bourgeois mentality of the romantic and the realist theatres."

Piscator and Strasberg had many battles about the Method, objective acting, and Brecht (whose work at that time Strasberg felt was falsely theatrical and lacking in human dimension). The Workshop was the place where debate was not only encouraged but was necessary for maintaining alertness. "Piscator took the best from each style, to create the Wall Street of acting," Madame Piscator says proudly. "He thought an actor should be able to do anything, to play any style, to be a dancer, a choreographer, a scholar."

"Piscator's hero was Meyerhold, and he expected an actor to be an athlete as well as to be in touch with his inner being," Jack Garfein recalls. "Piscator wanted the actor to be an *über*-artist, and to be able to go from Chekhov to gymnastics. He was not against realism: he was against *only* realism: he was against limitation. He felt there was so much in the human instrument that actors who limited themselves to realism were closing off. He believed that actors should have a psychological approach for things that needed it, but that they should also be able to jump rope when needed, and not ask questions about motivation."

In the Group, actors had been trained to work on their inner lives in order to animate their characters, and thereby to fulfill the playwright's intentions. Piscator, however, believed above all in a *director*'s theatre; he thought of himself as a master conductor, and he wanted an orchestra of perfectly trained musicians who could play anything he asked them to. "He was an ultimate conducting artist," says Jack Garfein, "and all of us who grew up with him learned that theatre is not a democracy. Piscator thought the director was the spokesman for the playwright, and that it was the actor's job to carry out the form and vision of the director. He didn't have the actors to carry out his vision because the psyche of American actors won't permit them to give themselves up so totally to the ideas of a director."

It was inevitable that Piscator's director's theatre and the theatre of highly sensitized actors which was the Group's legacy would clash: Brecht's alienation technique and Stanislavski's System could not cohabit peacefully under the same roof for any extended time, and in the late forties Strasberg and Adler left the Dramatic Workshop to begin teaching on their own. Strasberg taught a class in directing at the American Theatre Wing, where he didn't have to contend with any rival ideologues, and Adler founded her own Conservatory. It's important to record that when Group people didn't have a home base once their Theatre dissolved, Piscator had welcomed them to his Workshop. "There would have been no Actors Studio without the Group Theatre," Cheryl Crawford says emphatically, but between 1941 and 1947 Piscator's Workshop, an often overlooked link between the Group and the Studio, helped to perpetuate the Group's spirit.

Although it shared the Group's allegiance to Stanislavski, in at least two ways the Actors Studio was quite unlike the parent organization. The Group produced plays, whereas the Actors Studio was intended as a workshop only, a place for actors to practice their craft apart from production concerns. "We were opposed to production," Cheryl Crawford says (though others claim the Studio did have its sights set on becoming a producer). "We never thought of the Actors Studio as putting on plays, and for that reason we didn't need much money." While the Group became the focus of the professional and personal lives of its members, the Studio was to be a place where actors could come and go as they pleased, as they pursued independent careers.

One Group member berated me for suggesting a continuity between the Group and the Studio, arguing that apart from their shared interest in Stanislavski and some of the same personnel, the two organizations were quite distinct. In fiery tones, my informant said that the Studio was preoccupied with the smallness of self while the Group, infused by Clurman, had been formed to serve an idea, a high, selfless vision of theatre. "The Studio is a commercial enterprise, dedicated above all to creating stars," I was told. The Group's focus was the play and the ensemble, whereas the Studio was set up to assist the individual actor. As such, the Studio had a more realistic agenda than the Group, one that faced the facts of the American entertainment marketplace where actors are not hired en bloc but for their individual worth. But I don't see that this emphasis on the individual makes the Studio venal, even in comparison to the Group; the way the Studio serves actors' needs seems to me as idealistic and as far removed from commercial taint as the way the Group worked toward its ensemble selflessness.

Many Group members, in fact, out of aversion either to Kazan or Strasberg, or both, have never set foot inside the Studio while others have had only sporadic or peripheral involvement. The Studio became yet another rock to split on for the querulous Group. Those who had broken with Strasberg in the thirties regarded the Studio as the place where he continued to preach his lopsided version of the System, and in more than one interview with Group members, I sensed a resentment of the Studio as courting fame for itself while pretending to shun it, and both creating and welcoming stars while nominally serving the technical needs of talented actors whether known or not.

As I see it, what mainly separates the Studio from the Group is the fact that it is a lab rather than a theatre, a workshop where actors can tinker with their instruments apart from the pressures of professional production. As a result of that, the atmosphere at the Studio is far more theoretical and abstract than that at the Group, where the primary concern was putting on plays. Built and sustained by people passionate about good acting, good writing, and good theatre, the two enterprises for all the differences between them do represent a genuine continuity: both share a commitment to artistic excellence that transcends narrow commercial concerns and that's based on the necessity of continual self-renewal.

As a "workshop for professional actors," the Studio's agenda was certainly more modest than the Group's. It was the very simplicity of its aims that made it unique. "The Studio was, and is, *sui generis,*" Elia Kazan says proudly. Beginning in a small, private way, with a strictly off-limits-to-outsiders policy, the Studio quickly earned a high reputation in theatre circles. It became the place to be, the forum where all the most promising and unconventional young actors were being cultivated by sharp young directors from the Group Theatre.

When it first opened in September 1947 in an old Union Methodist Church on West 48th Street (the Studio didn't settle into its permanent home until 1955, but moved about among a series of makeshift locations), it offered two classes, an advanced class conducted by Robert Lewis that met for two hours on Monday, Wednesday, and Friday, and a class led by Kazan for younger, less experienced actors that met on Tuesday and Friday from 11 A.M. to 1 P.M. (As she had for the Group, Cheryl Crawford scouted for rehearsal space and for money.)

In that first year, the Studio was unlike what it was ever to be again. First, as Kazan and Lewis introduced the actors to the Group's interpretation of Stanislavski, the emphasis was on exercises rather than, as in later years, work on scenes. Too, rather than audition, actors were asked to join because one of the founders was familiar with their work; and any actor could be asked to leave if he or she wasn't measuring up. (After the first year, actors have had to audition, and once they are admitted, it's for life.) At the end of the year, when Lewis left because he wanted the Studio to become a producer, the class system, dividing actors into groups according to experience, was dropped.

The first year, as the young actors were feeling their way in what was to them a new acting method, the Studio was Kazan's property. It belonged to him, it was his place the way the Group Theatre had been Clurman's. It was his growing reputation as a brilliant actor's director that lured actors, and it was his version of the Group's method that they received.

"Gadge drew me to the Studio," recalls June Havoc. "I'd worked with him twice. We'd done a Sam Behrman play for the Theatre Guild, and then a film, *Gentleman's Agreement,* and I wanted more of what he had to offer. He warned me that it would be dirty, sweaty work at the Studio. It was, and it was wonderful. Kazan was a symbol to me of the daring, exciting part of the theatre; if you weren't ready to be daring, forget about working with him at the Studio. The years with Gadge were so formative for me. He was there for us as creative artists. He had the answers. He knew how to look at us, to make us come alive. Gadge *was* the Studio to me; it was never the same for me after he left."

Kim Hunter remembers that when she was on the road with *A Streetcar Named Desire* Kazan told her, "Get yourself to the Studio. He'd already sent Brando and Karl Malden [also in the play] there. His say-so was enough to get me in. We had used some of the Method on *Streetcar;* we had done many improvisations, so the work at the Studio wasn't that surprising to me, though a lot of the vocabulary was new to me. We did a lot of sense memory exercises that first year. And improvisations. And work on animals. It was Kazan's vocabulary: I remember he stressed action, always asking us, 'What is your action? What is your action? What are you trying to accomplish in the scene?' That whole first year he was orienting us to the Group Theatre's point of view about acting.

"Everybody was shy about getting up, but Kazan wouldn't wait for volunteers. 'Get up, do it!' he'd say. It was like being thrust into a lake. He pushed people as far as they could go, and oh he was marvelously exciting. All year, he kept everyone excited about the work. Kazan said the doors at the Studio should be open at both ends, and maybe some of us should leave. He then went off to make a film, and when he came back, he found us all in a state; we'd all taken what he said personally, and had begun to compete for our place in the Studio. Kazan said we couldn't compete with each other. 'You're here because you're glorious individualists,' he told us. 'No one else can be Marlon Brando—you'll only be second-rate Marlon Brandos.' Now of course there's no longer that kind of concern among the actors for keeping their place, because once a member, always a member."

"Kazan mentioned the Group more often than he talked about Stanislavski," Joan Copeland, a member of Kazan's first-year class, recalls. "He presented the Group to us as the spiritual parent of the Actors Studio. Marty Ritt was Kazan's assistant, and he had also been part of the Group, toward the end. The first time we met, nobody really knew anyone else. We were all sitting at children's desks—I guess the room was used for a Sunday school class—and Kazan asked people what animal another person reminded you of. I looked at Nehemiah Persoff, and said baboon; then he had to do an improvisation as that animal. Nehemiah said I reminded him of a cat. That was the way we were introduced to each other. It was all very split second, and Kazan kept it moving. He wouldn't let anyone hold back. Teaching us what he had learned at the Group, he forced us to work at digging into ourselves. It was often painful. There was nothing casual about Kazan's method—it could be joyful, but it wasn't fun.

"Bobby Lewis's class had more fun. Bobby has an off-center panache and brings a lot of color to his work. He's interested in heightened, stylized plays, just as he is himself beyond realism. He's like a caricature, bigger and broader than life. He's sweet and kind and dear and patient—with him, acting is fun: not with Kazan."

All year, Kazan had been looking for a play that his students could act in together. When he found a provocative psychological study about army wives called *Sundown Beach*, he cast it and began rehearsal. When it was presented, first in the summer of 1948 at the Westport Country Playhouse and then in New York in the fall, it was like a graduation exercise for his first-year class.

As a working director—as, in fact, the busiest, most sought-after director in New York and Hollywood—Kazan couldn't keep up with the demands of teaching on a full-time basis. After the first year, with Lewis gone and his outside commitments swelling, Kazan brought in other directors, like Daniel Mann and Martin Ritt, to help with classes. It was soon apparent that the Studio needed a full-time person, someone interested more in teaching than in pursuing his own career "on the outside." In 1949, in a historic move that saved the Studio, Kazan invited Lee Strasberg, his Group Theatre mentor, to join his fledgling workshop.

Once Strasberg took over, the heart of the Studio became—as it has remained ever since—the Tuesday and Friday morning meetings where, from eleven to one, Strasberg would talk about acting. These were not classes but sessions, and the actors who performed scenes for Strasberg were not students but professionals. Strasberg said he was not a teacher but a moderator working along with Studio members in a close study of actors' problems. Strasberg made it clear that the Studio was not a school but a lab for actors who have already had voice and body training and who were now ready to do inner work on themselves to see what was getting in the way of a fluent expressiveness.

Over the years, the Studio became Strasberg's personal domain, his citadel and his temple. In his nearly thirty-five years of working with Studio actors, he talked himself into a role for which he was superbly cast: high priest of the Method. Strasberg's twice-weekly scrutiny of actors' problems has had a resounding impact on American acting, in films and television as well as theatre. Under Strasberg's artistic leadership, the Studio popularized the revolution in American acting that had begun in the Group and established a style that has come to be identified as quintessentially and uniquely American.

7

STRASBERG'S METHODS

N ow, in a montage of twenty-three scenes—fragments culled from twenty-five years of Acting Unit sessions—let's look at Strasberg and his actors at work. Here are some things to notice: language—the Studio has its own, distinctive code words and phrases that are repeated over and over, with incantatory insistence; the way Strasberg takes charge, orchestrating each encounter with a spray of polemic, invective, wit, therapy, and philosophy; the way Strasberg's mind works—the play of allusion, the movement from specific example to abstract theory, from local to universal reference; the combativeness, the love of a good fight, the rough-and-ready frankness, the enduring concern for the idea of good acting and for the actors who are trying to attain it; the hushed, tense, intoxicating atmosphere of inquiry and experiment that permeates each thrust and parry between Strasberg and his eager, sometimes feisty, sometimes overwrought acolytes, the actors who year after year entrusted him with the care and feeding of their talent.

I have adapted these snapshots from the Actors Studio tape collection on deposit at the Wisconsin Center for Theatre Research in Madison. Although I have snipped, condensed, and rearranged the comments for continuity and (I admit) dramatic value, I have not changed or added any words: the good dialogue is all transcribed from life. Under my editorial guidance, the Strasberg who emerges from the following fragments is terse, pithy, and epigrammatic, qualities Strasberg certainly possessed, along with his fabled prolixity. *That* Strasberg, wandering off onto tangents, sliding into digressions within digressions, negotiating a route back to his original point through a tangle of repetition and circumlocution, is barely glimpsed here. My aim is not to provide a documentary thoroughness but rather an impression, necessarily fragmentary, that is nonetheless true to the spirit and that captures the vinegar and the tang of the father of the Method as he operated on home ground.

1. Shelley Winters, work on *Sweet Bird of Youth*

"I don't know how to act this character," Shelley Winters wails after playing Alexandra in a scene from Tennessee Williams's hothouse drama. "She's not like me at all. She's a movie star, and I'm a movie star, but we're so different. I'm basing my idea of the role on a movie star like Joan Crawford, who can chew up two directors and three producers for breakfast."

"With very little left over for lunch," Strasberg adds, not missing a beat.

"To help me get into the part, I'm wearing a dress of Marilyn Monroe's, and I'm relating to Marilyn being thirty-six and her fears of getting old, just like my character has her own fight with age: she's a star whose stardom depends on the appearance of youth."

"Look, darling, you always make things hard for yourself," Strasberg offers. "You've got more of the character inside you than you think."

"My psychiatrist says I am not the character."

"Your psychiatrist doesn't know as much as I do."

"My image of myself is a weak lady, not a gorgon, a dragon lady like Tennessee's character. I'm more comfortable playing victims. I feel ashamed to reveal nasty aspects of myself—I was afraid to play an unsympathetic character in *A Patch of Blue;* I thought I was lousy, and I won the Oscar."

"You tell yourself in advance you can't do it, and that's why you can't. Look, darling, you can play this bitch very easily."

2. Shirley Knight and Keir Dullea, work on *Private Ear*

"I got a ticket this morning on the way to the Studio," Keir says, following the scene. "And I used my feelings about that in the scene. It was right for the character."

"Yes," Strasberg agrees. "Often what is aroused in the actor is right for the scene. If you're nervous or angry about something in real life, don't cut off those impulses, but bring them right on the stage with you. Actors are first of all human beings, and actors are usually the first ones to forget that. Bring your human, real life feelings onto the stage."

"I was in a terrible state this morning," Shirley says. "I shied away from work in private areas. I am very lost in my work in general. When I think I'm overdoing it, you say that I'm doing it right; when I think I'm being natural, you tell me I'm overdoing it."

"That's a basic problem for the actor: to find at what moment his awareness of what is taking place coincides with what *is* taking place."

"I'm just terribly nervous whenever I work here, Lee. I'm more nervous doing a scene at the Studio than I am in front of a camera or when I audition or even opening night on Broadway."

"Then why the hell do you come here?"

Inside the Actors Studio, with Lee Strasberg and a session of the Acting Unit.

© SYEUS MOTTEL

3. STRASBERG DISCUSSES CHRISTOPHER JONES'S INTENTIONS IN A SCENE FROM *NATURAL AFFECTION*

"I haven't seen your work before," Strasberg says. "Where do you come from?"

"The South."

"Where have you studied?"

"Uh—well, not much, you know."

Christopher Jones (who was to marry Strasberg's daughter Susan) sits on the stage in a cocoon of moodiness and sultriness. There seems little separation between him and the dumb, sexy, inarticulate character he has just played. He is deeply uncommunicative, yet Strasberg is strangely drawn to him.

"Your work seems interesting enough so that I want to find out about you, about where you come from."

"Yeah."

Shelley Winters listens intently to Strasberg after she has completed a monologue.

"You are very easy and natural on stage, but remember that ease and naturalness are *for* something; they are to serve the play."

"Uh-huh."

"You are very much to be encouraged. Don't let anything we said here throw you."

4. Estelle Parsons, work on *Hamlet*

Flushed from her brash attempt to perform one of Hamlet's soliloquies, Estelle Parsons explains how she tried to work her way into the difficult material. "I thought I'd do a private moment and let the words come out of that. Then I thought I'd do sensory things and let work come out of that. Then I got to the words through physical relaxation, relating to my surroundings moment to moment and coordinating verbal expression with my feelings. I was concerned with inner expression." A sigh, a gathering of breath. "I haven't got to the point of creating Hamlet."

"We shouldn't encourage you to play Hamlet," Strasberg says, poker-faced as always. "Problems can be faced more legitimately in other parts. Your procedure is not right. You got away from a verbal pattern, but when emotion struck, I didn't understand what you said.

"If you want to see what you can do with words, pick something totally unrelated to the scene, and see how the words come out from whatever it is you're doing. In the early days of the Group, we'd find different situations with the same words. In one improvisation, Robert Lewis said the words to *I Sing the Body Electric* without worrying about what meaning the lines would take on. He played a little clerk taking a cold shower: the purpose was to show that the event gives meaning to the words. The emotional experience can wash the words.

"It took you a half-hour to say the first word (I'm exaggerating, darling): the sound was beautiful, a good tone, but each phrase was separated. Sing it, to get away from words at a simple logical level. You seemed deliberately to be interfering with yourself, I didn't know why. As if you were doing something with yourself in between the phrases."

(When I mentioned to Estelle Parsons that I had listened to her Hamlet tape, she laughed good-naturedly. "I did it right after my father died; at the time I felt very close to Hamlet's 'to be or not to be' soliloquy. My work was coming out of my grief, which is *not* the way to work.

Strasberg felt that using a recent emotional experience turns the work into a kind of therapy. Your emotions have to be controllable. You can't deal with emotions that are fresh. Lee told us to use memories from at least seven years ago. He said I shouldn't have done Hamlet at the time I did it, for the reasons I did it, and he was right.")

5. Steve McQueen mumbling his way through a scene from a play called And All That Jazz

He stops and starts, and speaks so quietly that he can't be heard clearly in the front row. In May 1956, McQueen is at the raw beginning of his career, and yet it's possible to detect talent, an interesting and unconventional presence, even through the blurred voice, the poor speech. Strasberg asks him where he studied.

"At the Neighborhood Playhouse. For three years."

In a rare moment, Strasberg is caught off guard. "They didn't work on your speech?" he asks, not attempting to disguise his incredulity. "I'll give you some exercises."

Strasberg launches on one of his least favorite subjects. "When the actor is acting properly, there is no problem with projection. Vocal energy for the actor is different. Actor's energy is more than the human being has to begin with; it is more than it would be in life.

"It is a separate thing to work on. It won't take away from your concentration. And by the way, the idea that the actor has to work so concentratedly that he doesn't know what's happening is crazy—that's hysteria and possession. Volume is something that has to be worked on. We give it its due, contrary to popular belief. It's a simple mechanical thing.

"From the audience point of view, Steve, a great deal of what you do would be lost. But the actual work is coming well—the handling of the girl was very sound; it had a natural, believable quality, it was never forced. There was definite progress in relation to what we've seen before."

6. Sensory work, in a scene from Three-Day Blow

"You left out something simple," Strasberg tells one of the actors who has just completed a scene. "It's raining out; when the character comes in, he's wet. You didn't completely take in the reality of the three-day blow. Along the same lines you didn't concentrate on handling the glass—a simple act which requires terrific concentration and will. You want to act, that's your temperament, but now it is a vague desire: I want to act, I WANT TO SING. But it is too general, to act you have to first know to create for yourself the reality of the glass and of the rain outside.

"You look puzzled," he says to the actor, who seems to have caved in. "I'm not here to stop people from acting. I want to commit suicide when I hear this. I am here rather to lead you to believable and true and exciting and dramatic acting: I don't want less acting, I want *better* acting.

"Which is why it's important to work on sensory reality, on relating to objects. Then other senses begin to function, you are at ease, the actor is the character, he is creating something.

"Let me tell you about the Peking Opera as an example of what I mean. They have a high degree of craft and technique in dealing with inanimate objects. They are accomplished on a flabbergasting level. I saw an actor make the movement of being in a rocking boat. In the end, I rocked along with her. I wouldn't rock with a *real* boat on the stage: the created reality was greater, more real to me, than the tangible reality.

"It's that kind of concentration and conviction, that degree of physical reality, that you need in your acting. Emphasis on physical tasks leads to relaxation, the actor is concentrated, and then things—the emotional reality—happen by themselves. Work on the objects leads to internal reality."

Recalling the work of the Peking Opera puts Strasberg in a ruminating mood. "Acting is the most human of the arts," he says, as if he's beginning a soliloquy. "It's also the strangest, the weirdest. Human beings are affected unconsciously by a variety of impulses going on inside them: to express one of them can lead to a moment of reality on the stage. How ticklish, sensitive, wonderful our impulses are: how can we make the bird do what we want? That's our aim here. We cage it, lock it up, train it."

7. STRASBERG TALKS TO ANNA MIZRAHI (WHO WAS TO BECOME THE THIRD MRS. STRASBERG) AFTER HER FIRST PERFORMANCE IN A SCENE AT THE ACTORS STUDIO

"You are subject, like so many actors, to panic reaction, which sets up an emotional state which interferes with the functioning of the will and energy.

You have to get over your fear. Your instrument is ready, but your will is now too weak.

"You're lazy. You haven't activated yourself, in life and on the stage. You always give way to your sense of doubt.

"You don't want to take my forty years' experience as guaranteed; I put a kosher label on it. Look, darling, if we trust our technique, it rewards us."

8. Keir Dullea, working against type, as a prizefighter in a scene from *Return to Kansas City*

"I worked for what fighting this man meant to me and personalizing my partner. We did a lot of improvisations. I felt today like I wasn't acting."

"I didn't personalize," his partner Maya says. "I just tried to work with Keir, to respond to what he was doing moment by moment. I didn't do enough work on the room."

"OK, what would you say?" Strasberg asks, in a bored, uninviting voice, his usual way of soliciting comments from the house.

"Keir's relaxation was wonderful," someone volunteers eagerly.

"Maya works too much for results," another voice says, "and I didn't know where she came from."

"You made a big breakthrough today, both of you," Shelley Winters says. "You were better than you were in *David and Lisa*, Keir. You have a tendency to intellectualize, and to pull everything in. But not today. The emotion was right. You did all the right things in terms of preparation."

"I must caution you that there is a danger here of watching scenes as scenes," Strasberg intervenes. "We are not an audience, but fellow craftsmen. The reason we ask people to explain what they are doing is to confine our comments.

"I was interested in seeing you do this kind of scene," Strasberg turns his attention directly to Keir and the work just seen. "We want you to stop being concerned with creating sensitivity. Many of your emotional colors are tense and confined, and the scene offers you a chance to live a life of pure physical response. But I didn't see any prizefighter in what you did. A whole physical life of the character is needed, something that goes beyond the simple demands of the scene. The scene was concerned only with the scene. You need to learn to live on the stage simply and believably, within the logic of the character: you need to provide a basis for yourself, of how *you* would be inside that character."

9. PAUL NEWMAN, WORK ON *THE TAMING OF THE SHREW*

"This is worse than any opening I've been through," Paul Newman says.

"Yes," Strasberg readily agrees, "because here you have a different type and kind of observation. Here, the actor has a different sense of himself —he must be very precise, in terms of his own intentions. There is nothing to be achieved here. We are concerned about ourselves: what did you intend to do?—not whether or not we like you. It's a healthy kind of nervousness.

"It stems from a fear of ourselves. This self-feeling of the actor is very important; it's the only thing the actor has in his work, how he felt in relation to carrying out what he wanted. What we're trying to develop here is that the actor becomes the critic of his own sense of truth.

"You began to create a whole situation, but you rushed to the words. And once you use only the lines, you're stuck to the lines. You permit yourself to be led by the word, so your imagination is tied before it comes alive. You found events to stimulate the imagination; it's the event, the situation, that has to be brought alive: the actor then is embarked on the use of himself.

"Words are not easily part of our background. But that can be overcome, by the actor's sense of being a character in an event on a stage. You began to use physical logic, which is good, because how much can you do in the words after a while?"

10. DEFINING INTENTIONS

Many of the actors have trouble saying exactly what they were working for in a scene. Today, however, the actress who has just completed work on *Exit the King* is as good a talker as Strasberg, and her crisp, rapid statement of what she wanted to achieve and what she thought she did achieve is a refreshing departure from the usual hesitations and self-effacements. Perhaps her statement is a little quick, though, a little too glib. . . .

"This is the first time Andreas and I worked together . . . I see everything in life from my point of view; the straightness with which I see things makes me go toward the words. I see everything too personally; Andreas sees it too overall. We were in conflict, but it makes a good team."

Strasberg guffaws. "Your evaluation of your own work is completely cockeyed. This shows how you sensitive people are so concerned with your insides that you don't know what's coming across. You don't work personally, and he doesn't work generally. It's the other way around."

11. AL PACINO, AS HICKEY AND HAMLET

For his first scene at the Studio (January 17, 1967), Al Pacino performed a terrific stunt, moving from a monologue in *Iceman Cometh* to a soliloquy in *Hamlet*. After, the audience broke a long-standing tradition at the Studio by applauding. They were clearly impressed, and a little aghast, at the audacity of the experiment. Himself fired by the actor's courage, Strasberg asks Pacino to switch characters, to play Hickey as Hamlet and Hamlet as Hickey.

"We don't say much on the first occasion," Strasberg says, his voice, uncharacteristically, revealing pleasure at the work he's just seen. "We all understand the tension. You chose a tough problem, an unusual confrontation, and you had a real acting courage here. I know nothing about you, where you come from. The actors' applause for you corroborates the judgment of the directors, who are happy to see our choice is verified. The kind of talent you showed today is the kind we admire and like to help. I would almost prefer not to comment at this time, but . . ."

The house laughs, knowing that a Strasberg discourse is about to be launched. "When you did Hamlet, there were many casual, unnecessary movements—yours, not the character's. Naturalness pours out of you without regard for its significance. What seems lacking is a sense of a situation. You're aware of an audience, of people around you.

"Your body has an experience beyond your mind. You trust your body. But when I asked you to do it in a chair, it was to show you that you didn't need so much movement, and to focus your concentration.

"Your behavior was too general. You need to work on behavior within situations. There is a freshness and spontaneity in you, but now they need to serve a greater aliveness, the playwright's situation.

"I assume you knew it was a dangerous confrontation. Your choice implies a willingness to use yourself. The courage you have shown today is rarer than talent: that kind of courage tends to die subject to the pressures of career.

"So good luck to you. And we hope to see your work soon again."

12. UNUSUAL CASTING

Today, intense silence washes over the house as, believe it or not, Shelley Winters is playing Juliet. The scene over, Strasberg is quick to express his pleasure, not so much for how successfully Shelley embodied Juliet, but for her technical development, which she can apply to work on any role, in any medium.

"There was much less fussing around than usual for you; you often do too much, and it is difficult for you to repeat, because you work through emotional understanding. When it doesn't hit you emotionally, you don't know what to do. You've used the emotion to mask the weaknesses you've felt: you've placed too much on the emotion rather than the simple doing.

"We didn't get the logic of the events here, only the logic of the sequence of the words. There was no behavior of the character leading to the things you express. You need more logical behavior on the stage.

"Next time, speak as little as possible. It should take thirty-five minutes, not fifteen. You'll be getting undressed, and as you try to live within the image of Juliet, sing. Later we can trim it down to actual performance time."

"But . . . ," Shelley starts to protest, but today Strasberg doesn't give her a chance. "You argue with such haste and violence, that no one ever agrees with you. No director can ever stop to listen to you. You argue very well, but people are in a dither when you argue."

13. PRIVATE MOMENTS

On stage, with head bowed and legs planted apart, a seated Anne Bancroft is steeped in silence. Seemingly unaware that there is anybody else in the room, she slowly rises from the chair and . . . begins to mime taking a shower.

The young Al Pacino, working with Allen Goorwitz (Garfield) and Sally Alex during an Acting Unit session.

Covered with stillness, a statuesque Dennis Tate lifts his head, as if in response to some imaginary sound, and sniffs the air, inhaling an aroma that seems to stir memory and thought. You can see the imprint of an inner monologue in the subtle shift of expression that passes over his face, and in his flickering eyes.

Jittery, responding to noises both inside and outside her room, Shelley Winters is recreating being alone and frightened in her apartment. Her agitation rises until she is on the verge of hysteria.

These actors, at three separate sessions, are working on private moments, an exercise Strasberg developed from a suggestion of Stanislavski's that the actor must learn to be private in public. Because it is an exercise rather than a scene, the private moment releases the actor from any obligation to a text or for that matter to an audience. Working from material called up from his own experience, the actor needn't do anything dramatically effective; he needn't in fact do anything at all that is perceivable to an observer. The private moment exercise is one of the foundations of Strasberg's inner technique.

"Often the private moment is of use to the person doing it, not to the observer," Strasberg explains. "The moment—the action—is connected in the actor with privacy and difficulty. But the private moment is not intended to deal with something so private we shouldn't see it, with something that gives us a sense we shouldn't be watching."

To Dennis Tate, Strasberg says, "It was good for you to sit before us, to smell an aroma, and not to do anything physical, but to focus only on what you're doing with your concentration. Just to sit there listening to something, and to absolve yourself of the need to do things for us is good for you because usually in life and on the stage you are so anxious to make your point."

As Anne Bancroft begins to explain her private moment, "I remembered a dream . . . ," Strasberg quickly interrupts. "Don't tell me too much

Madeleine Thornton-Sherwood
working on a private moment.

in public, darling. Some things I permit only for myself. The observer cannot know what the private moment is.

"The private moment was good for you, Annie. You're always active, but it isn't you. It's God's business, and even God doesn't know unless he has Freud at his side. You always seem to be more vivid than necessary. I begin to think, something's not kosher, what is she hiding beneath the need to fight for expression. You have an acting problem that relates to a personal thing; you can't sit at ease on the stage as you did here in the exercise, because you have the actor's basic sense that he can't himself amount to anything. You think that when you don't do anything you are nothing. You have a problem with tension, which is relieved by trying to get to a sense of yourself."

"Now don't give me psychoanalysis," Strasberg chides Shelley Winters, as she tries to explain how she recreated a condition of fright. "The private moment exercise has for you a peculiar terror. The fact that you are here is a great achievement. Even when I saw you come in here, you weren't sure. These exercises do involve revelation, which has a scary quality for the actor. Here, there is no acting. There is only work for yourself. The actor is not brought here to deliver in the private moment exercise: if it doesn't work, it doesn't work. The human being performing it is most able to judge himself if it is working; it establishes the actor's best sense of truth: is he doing what he wants to do well enough?

Because the actor can't know in advance how it will turn out, what he might learn about himself during it, or what images or feelings it might arouse, the private moment exercise is a kind of therapy. It can rip through the actor's defenses, release tensions that have built up over years, and help to free the actor physically and vocally.

"I remember a young actress who had trouble expressing what she felt," Strasberg reminisces. "She brought in a private moment where she was lying in bed listening to Turkish music. She started to dance. Hot dancing! In a way that was startling. From that point on, her voice on the stage started to change, she had more vocal colors, and we began to get a fullness of response.

"The private moment shouldn't be done before other exercises in concentration," Strasberg cautions. "It should be done in a sequence. It can be powerful. The person can relive a moment and not be able to stop it. In my entire experience of over forty years, however, only once was there a dangerous effect. The actor didn't seem like a person who had *any* private moment, his work was so overt and technical. He relived a thrilling human moment, and then he couldn't stop. He had to go to the doctor. I didn't know the person had psychologic difficulty.

"I have kept away from doing private moments with persons with mental problems, until recently. When you know the people, it may not be dangerous, especially when done in the sequence of the work.

"Washing, taking a shower, listening to music, anything you do daily is food for the private moment. *You, you, you!*—not a fictitious character. Bring things from your environment. See if you can be impelled by memory and how simple tasks gain luster thereby."

Giving luster to simple tasks is one way of describing Strasberg's entire Method.

14. AFFECTIVE MEMORY

"What is an affective memory, and how does it work?" is a question Strasberg was often asked by members of the Studio as well as by outsiders. Today, Strasberg is going to step out of his customary role as moderator in order to guide an actor, Pete Masterson, through the step-by-step procedure of building an exercise in affective memory.

The silence in the room is thick, almost eerie. Observers know that what is about to happen, a reawakening of an experience that has been stored in the actor's unconscious, will feel like a seance.

The actor is in place, seated on the stage in a trancelike posture, his arms dangling at his sides. You can feel Strasberg's excitement and anticipation: he's a doctor demonstrating a new theory to a select group of interns. He has his jacket off, his sleeves rolled up; he's in the lab, eager to get to work.

"You have picked an experience that you would like to remember. Keep in mind that emotion cannot be directly stimulated; you can't say, I WANT TO LOVE. In working an affective memory, if you anticipate the result, you choke the emotion. The actor should be relaxed, and ready to go with what is happening.

"First, relax. Professional relaxation, with no tensions anywhere in body and mind. Relax your chin, Pete." Here, Strasberg gets up from his chair and goes over to check the actor's face and body for points of possible

Strasberg leading a session in warm-up exercises prior to work on affective memory.

© SYEUS MOTTEL

tension. He touches him with the ease of an experienced doctor on the lookout for malfunction.

"When you're ready, tell me where you are, what you see and touch. Tell me only the sensory realities of which the event is compounded. OK, where are you?"

A long pause. The actor is beginning to breathe heavily. When he speaks, it's as if he's emerging from sleep. "I'm in a house." ("Notice the wonderful resonance of voice induced by relaxation," Strasberg crows like a proud parent.) "I'm in a room."

("I don't know what a room in a house is . . . I don't want the words.")

"It's dark—brown—there's a lamp by the couch. Brass. A plant in it. I see light green, light yellow. I'm wearing rough cotton. I feel hot. Sticky heat. Throat dry. Pants holding heat in. A cold wind on my hot face from the air conditioner. My legs feel heavy. There's a musty odor."

("I don't know what musty means. I have to look it up in the dictionary.")

"I see a person, heavy in hips and chest. I hear a voice."

The actor pauses. "Keep going. Go ahead," Strasberg urges. "Don't worry about emotional things."

"I'm touching the dog."

("Relax the mouth. Take it easy. Don't tell me in words what you see. Keep that to yourself.")

The actor moves on his chair as a low growl forms in his throat.

"Do you want to make a sound? Go ahead, relax the face and eyes."

Somewhere from deep inside, the actor emits a low, sustained groan, a mixture of anguish and release that seems to express both the climax and the expulsion of the memory.

"OK, Pete, good boy. Open your eyes. Now sit up. In my classes, I know the strengths and weaknesses of the actors. How far they can control themselves. I didn't know this about you.

"Recalling these experiences, which we push away, and which condition our emotional behavior, is good for human beings, not just for actors. It opens response. The key is in the concentration on the object. For all of us. Usually we don't think of the detail, yet that is the key to the reliving. The memory does not fade, take my word for it. I don't know why. Our experiences are literally engraved in the nervous system. They are woven into the fabric of our existence, and can be relived, though we usually don't like these things awakened. We deal with the subconscious and unconscious and memory: contrary to popular belief, our work is really Pavlovian, the conditioned reflex theory, rather than Freudian.

"About half a dozen things serve for all kinds of emotional experience. You use six, eight, ten things until they become second nature, like a conditioning factor—you respond to a certain stimulus without volition.

"An actor who masters the technique of using the affective memory begins to be more alive in the present. I use this technique in production as well as in training. Without this in production, purposes of the training are not utilized. Of course, the way we do it here is not the way we do it in a play. Here we talk about it; in a play, to reexperience the event shouldn't take more than a minute or two. One of the catch phrases in the Group Theatre was take a minute.

"With affective memory work, you choose an experience of your own that is parallel to a particular moment in a scene. You have to practice it, or else worry about it will create tension. The exercise doesn't help you in a scene unless you practice it at home, in the shower, at the same time other things are being done.

"Using the affective memory, which the great actors used unconsciously, makes it possible for us to join in the great tradition of acting. When Kean in *Hamlet* picked up the skull of Yorick, he cried, because he said he always thought of his uncle. The ancient Greek actor Polis brought on the ashes of his own recently deceased son when he delivered Electra's funeral oration."

Strasberg concludes by contrasting two basic types of actor: the actor of experience, trained in the inner technique derived from the work of Stanislavski, and the actor of skill, proficient in externals. "This knowledge of inner technique and craft formulated by Stanislavski solves the problem of acting. External technique, which I do not emphasize, does not solve an acting problem, it helps the instrument. Of course, nobody denies the importance of external technique."

If Strasberg's defense of affective memory has an edge of urgency, it's because he alone among the Group Theatre's scholars of acting continued to believe in its usefulness. Perhaps in citing its virtues, he relived an affective memory of his own, one of the Group's bitter clashes over this most controversial aspect of Stanislavski's System.

15. Singing the Words

Like the private moment, the song exercise is Strasberg's own invention, an outgrowth of his work in developing techniques of relaxation and concentration. In it, the actor stands absolutely still, looks directly at the audience, and sings. As Strasberg acknowledges, it's a tough exercise that exposes the actor's uncertainties about himself. Today, the performer in the hot seat is that volatile good sport, Shelley Winters. Strasberg is guiding her through the exercise, so that the session becomes a demonstration.

"OK darling, you're standing self-consciously. Try to relax. You are real and we are real, you're doing an exercise, not an acting thing. You can't hide behind a character, because the song exercise confronts the actor and the audience in a direct way."

"I'm scared, Lee. I'm not a singer."

"That's why this is good for you. Relax, now. Stand still. Look at the people, really see them. The audience really sees us and we are really aware of the audience, no matter what goes on.

"OK. Ready? Don't move, darling; all the impulses go out the back when you move. Now, when you make a sound, it must be full. Commit to a full sound."

She starts to sing, with unsteady pitch and a wavering volume.

"You're pulling in, a sign of retreat," he calls out to her. "Be aware of the tension: the relaxation takes place with the mind, without moving."

She continues to sing, gaining in volume. Then she falters.

"Keep going, come on," Strasberg coaches from the sidelines.

Shelley renews her energy, but the words are muffled. "I can't follow the song." She sings louder, her voice becoming fuller as she gains confidence.

"You're trying to sing too much," Strasberg interjects after she tries a vocal flourish.

"You see it's not that difficult," Strasberg assures her when she has finished. "You're still alive."

"I could feel the tension in my eyes. I was worried that the melody would go out of my voice, which is what happened when I auditioned for a musical."

"This exercise was not intended for a musical audition. This is a basic exercise in control of energy. It starts as a trap: no involuntary impulse can come out. If we stand still and vibrate the voice, things build up inside, you get frustrated, then thought allows impulse to express itself. So this is a good exercise for people who have difficulty between impulse and expression: it traps all the hidden impulses, brings impulses closer to awareness. Impulses will always find their expression, like water finds its own level."

"I don't understand how it works."

"Darling, nothing here can be understood. You have to do it."

16. STRASBERG DIRECTS

In his role as moderator, Strasberg seldom performs the functions of a director. Commenting on the work only after the actors have finished, he does not focus on interpretation or characterization (director's concerns) but on the actor's work on himself. Occasionally, however, he will direct a scene, assisting actors to make choices and to sharpen motivation.

Today, he is directing Viveca Lindfors and Anne Bancroft in *The Stronger*, a tour de force by Strindberg in which Anne's character remains silent as Viveca's unleashes a boiling stream of words. Interrupting the scene, going onstage to demonstrate gesture and behavior, and even giving line readings, Strasberg is in constant motion.

"Whatever you do at the beginning should not give away the end. Do you see what I mean, Annie?"

"No," she says dryly, with a mischievous glint in her eye. There is general laughter that (for a moment) dispels the tension in the room.

"Don't give it away too soon. There should not be unconscious anticipation, which depletes the work. Viveca, you're anticipating the whole scene. If you come in and look at her that way, that's the play. You're too anxious to make it happen.

"Look, darling. You played the first part on the basis of the cold. You came in for hot chocolate, remember, now you don't pay attention to it, which shows you are more interested in acting.

"Put in your own words, if you want to, or stop talking.

"Annie, you're responding too vulnerably. Make a sound if you want to speak: the not-speaking should arise from the character, not seem like a trick of the author.

"Enjoy the hot chocolate, darling."

Moving back and forth between the two actresses, Strasberg cajoles, reminds, fine-tunes, soothes, hones, ignites (drives crazy).

"Don't give it away, Annie."

"You mean I should sit here and take that from her?"

"Behave in the continuity of the character. The character is not you or me.

"Take your time, Viveca. Don't rush with the words. Inside, go on with your own sequence of thought before you come to the next words. Each thing is an hour.

"Hot chocolate, darling, hot chocolate. Don't just stay with the emotions."

Anne, pinned to silence by Strasberg, visibly chafes under the restriction. As Viveca's character continues to goad and challenge her, she emits a series of grunts and growls, of low moans and wheezes, which have an unexpected eruption: she strikes Viveca, who, stunned, and to protect herself, strikes back. They struggle. The audience gasps. Strasberg is delighted.

By the end of the session, Viveca is black and blue.

17. Improvisation

Al Pacino has just improvised a scene from *The Hairy Ape*, finding his own words and actions as substitutes for those supplied by O'Neill.

"The value of improvisation is to see how much the actor knows about the character and about the character's past," Strasberg begins, a note of disapproval entering his voice. "I couldn't tell from the improvisation about the character's past, about what impelled him into the scene. The character comes onstage from a set of circumstances. I didn't see them."

Taking off from Pacino's failed improvisation, Strasberg lectures on the value of spontaneity in acting. "Human beings improvise all the time. Improvisation may uncover things which the author may only suggest. Don't only follow out what the author tells you to do. There's more power in you that comes out in what *you* do. Do whatever you feel like doing.

"Stanislavski said that little by little, through repetition, a production will become progressively dead: 'I will show you how to keep youth in the play,' he told his actors. And he had them improvise, to keep freshness of reaction. During a run, actors have to retain the sense of improvisation, in order to come onstage with what an American actor named William Gillette called 'the illusion of the first time.'

"Anticipation is one of the great occupational hazards. In Group Theatre rehearsals, we worked out small adjustments which would be changeable in each performance, and that made all the difference. In the work of the great Russian actors and Duse, each performance was slightly different in result, though the essential values, intentions, shape, and outline remained the same, like a human being. The nature of art is not spontaneity; art is composed. But to make art alive, there is the need for spontaneity."

18. As if

"I used the 'as if' on unsexing Lady Macbeth," the actress says, explaining her approach to a scene. "I personalized that my goal was 'to get' Macbeth . . ."

"You misunderstand the 'as if,' " Strasberg interrupts. A reprimand is on the way.

"The attendance is so in and out here that people go away with the weirdest ideas of what we are or are not concerned with. It's incomprehensible how you misunderstood the 'as if.' The verbiage we use gives us a sense of security, yet people often use the wrong words.

"Look, darling, 'as if' doesn't paraphrase the words. It is to arouse your conviction to a greater extent than the imaginary thing in the play. If it is not personal or concrete, it is of no value. Make yourself a given circumstance, that's an 'as if.' All these things—affective memory, 'as if' —are personal, they're a way of recreating personal experience, so you will always get results, though they may be the wrong ones."

19. Duse

Frequently during the course of his comments, in an attempt to link the Studio's work to acting traditions, Strasberg would refer to great actors of the past. The one performer he consistently held up as a model of greatness, as in fact the patron saint of the Method, was Duse, an artist who made instinctive use of the inner technique that Stanislavski codified.

Today, at the opening session of the 1959 season, Strasberg's remarks about Duse are especially heightened.

"Duse on stage was terrifying. There was a sense of revealing the innermost parts of herself. The essential thing the actor reveals at the moment the audience is seeing is his own emotion. Through her suffering, Duse's performances summarized the search for inner and outer truth. She did more than bring on reality and conviction in behavior and inner experience. Each moment was a design in terms of the reality of the human being.

"She arrived at a fusion of the inner and external that we haven't achieved. Here, we do the inner but we don't pay enough attention to the external. She summarized unconscious and subconscious processes of creation, and she added a classical quality.

"Her inner technique was intense, her outer expressiveness was beautiful beyond description, but it was never beauty on its own. She used her hands to evoke the flickering realities of the human being. Her hands were like the flight of birds. Her work had meaning and reality and conviction greater than any in the entire history of the theatre. It will take

The young Eleanora Duse. "It will take the next one hundred years of the theatre to deal with her accomplishment," Strasberg told Studio members.

the next one hundred years of the theatre to deal with her accomplishment."

20. Welcome to New Members

For a few moments today, Strasberg becomes a genial host as he makes his annual welcome to new Studio members. Each year he says much the same thing, adding minor variations to lend a spontaneous touch to what had become a Studio ritual. After calling out the names of the inductees, Bruce Dern, Avra Petrides, and Inga Swenson, he welcomes them and cautions them.

"We applaud you, and want you to know that whatever we say from here on is meant kindly. The final thing we judge by here is talent, but it takes more than talent to wish to audition, it takes courage. In our world, we have plenty of talent, but there isn't as much courage to use the talent continuously and consistently. When talent is recognized, it usually dies, to settle for imitation and repetition rather than creative progress.

"So welcome, and remember, from here on in, there is no more applause, only brickbats."

21. A EULOGY FOR JAMES DEAN

"I saw *Giant* the other night, and when I got into the cab, I cried," Strasberg says, and as he speaks tears well up in his eyes, and he stops. Shocked by Dean's sudden death, Strasberg holds up the actor as a symbol of the many young, talented, self-destructive people who come to him for help in developing their craft.

"I cried for pleasure and enjoyment in seeing Jimmy on the screen. I didn't cry when Jack [Garfein] called to tell me Jimmy was dead. But I cried when I saw him on the screen. I cried at the waste, the waste in the theatre, the senseless waste of the talent. The strange kind of behavior that not just Jimmy had, but a lot here had: the drunkenness now that you really made it. It's terrifying. Laziness I can forgive, but this thing. What to do. Once we get to the point where the talent is usable, then comes the self-destruction. I knew it about Jimmy—there was something destructive in him. I went through it with Franchot Tone in the Group. We let him go. The utter waste of Jimmy. And what could I do? I feel helpless. We can feed the talent, can combine it with other talents, have a place for it, but what we haven't been able to do . . . the personal self-destructiveness. I see personal problems, but I feel it would be an intrusion to call someone in. Oh, the stories I read in the paper. What does this have to do with the talent? Where does the talent go?

"People at the top start to go; the most talented are the most vulnerable. When you become successful, at that moment, it dries up, deserts, becomes arid. It becomes Marlon Brando and big business, and you can't get anyone on the phone.

"What are you working for?

"Talent has to be maintained with personal progress and combined with a contribution to the theatre."

22. A COMMENT FROM A FAMOUS OBSERVER

Wrapped in mink and wearing no makeup, Marilyn Monroe sits timidly in the back row, having arrived a half-hour late for the session. She sits, as always, in a silence that is profound and reverent, attending to Strasberg's every word. Today, for the first time, after a scene has been completed and Strasberg invites comments from the audience, she raises her hand to speak. Strasberg turns, ashen, afraid she might say something that would embarrass him, and calls on her.

"I just wanted to say," she murmurs, in her breathy, fearful voice, "that it was . . . just like life."

23. THE ACTORS STUDIO IN THE WORLD

An inveterate theatregoer, Strasberg always took pleasure in sharing his worldwide theatre experiences, comparing the work at the Studio with a variety of international theatre styles. ("I know as much about the theatre as anyone in the world," he says. "I've read so much, spent so much money I didn't have.") It is fall, 1956, and he has just returned from seeing productions in Germany, France, Italy, and England. Delighted and amazed, he reports the enormous curiosity about the Studio in London theatre circles.

"It's as if the Actors Studio was a magic kind of thing. It takes weird propaganda to achieve that. This is the only time in the history of the theatre that an organization not involved in production has achieved that kind of reputation. There is a feeling, a sense of excitement, about the Studio. That things are happening here, that we have a contemporary kind of theatre, a contemporary kind of acting. I found myself denying that the Studio was magical, that it was just a lot of hard work. I tried to combat a sense they have there that the Actors Studio has some kind of secret retained in its recesses and that people receive the rays of the magic stone as they pass by.

"It was a rather flabbergasting experience to realize how much the eyes of the world are focused on this little place here."

8

A PORTRAIT OF
THE MASTER TEACHER

When, in January 1982, one month before his death, I asked the Studio secretary what would happen when Strasberg was no longer around, she simply looked at me in open-mouthed amazement, as if such a situation were inconceivable, as if Strasberg were both immortal and irreplaceable. Strasberg in fact trained no successor, and the "official" position of both Strasberg and the Studio Board was the mystical one that in the course of time someone would inevitably come forth who would assume the responsibilities of artistic director. New member Gayle Greene told me, "Lee always said that this is an autocracy and that someone will arise organically: 'You can't plan it. Art doesn't work that way.' "

To grasp the significance of the Actors Studio, we first have to decipher the character of the man who spent his life probing actors while defending himself against similar invasions. Who was Lee Strasberg, and what was he really like? In a single afternoon, I was given the following clues. "He was like Jesus," a Studio member told me in June 1982, five months after Strasberg's death, tears welling in her eyes. An hour later, I was offered a different opinion. "Strasberg always thinks . . . well, he doesn't think at all anymore, thank God! He was a vicious man. Vicious!"

Here are some further opinions. "He was a gigantic genius, a consummate master teacher, but a flawed man," says Madeleine Thornton-Sherwood. "Why couldn't he be different?" asks Lois Smith. "But he wasn't, and that's the way it was." "Along with Stanislavski and Brecht, he was one of the major names in twentieth-century theatre," says Viveca Lindfors. "Olivier is great, but he hasn't made an original contribution the way Strasberg has." "His artistic contributions were extraordinary," said Carl

Schaeffer, the Studio's treasurer until his death in the fall of 1982, "as far as his personal qualities, that's another matter." "He has been a rock to my life," Shelley Winters cried as she delivered a eulogy at Strasberg's funeral. "I've absolutely been shaped by Lee," says Estelle Parsons. "He changed the direction of my life," Ellen Burstyn says.

Over and over, I heard these provocative comments about Strasberg: resounding praise for his work as a teacher, often followed by grave judgments about his personality, dark hints or outright condemnations that made him begin to seem positively Mephistophelian. To some loyalists, he was clearly the best of men; to some defectors, the worst; and to many who knew him, he was a bewildering combination of good and evil, of lofty idealism and base ambition. I didn't talk to anyone whose reaction to Strasberg was neutral: he had the uncanny ability to arouse strong responses in everyone.

In the course of many interviews, with members of the Group Theatre as well as of the Studio, I was told that Lee Strasberg, in addition to being "like Jesus," was Buddha, Moses, Oedipus, Rasputin, God, the Pope, Pontius Pilate, Hitler, Jim Jones, a sectarian, a cult leader, a doctor, a lawyer, a scientist, a guru, a Zen master, Job, a rabbi, a high priest, a saint, a fakir, a badger, a Jewish papa, the Great Sphinx, a talmudic scholar, a Hassidic scholar, and a human being.

For over twenty-five years, often twice weekly, in good weather and bad, Strasberg went to the Studio on Tuesday and Friday mornings at eleven to comment on the work of actors. (In the early 1970s, after he had established the Lee Strasberg Theatre Institute, and become something of a movie star, he confined his work at the Studio to the Friday session; from 1975, he divided his time between New York and Los Angeles, spending fall and winter in the East, spring and summer "on the Coast," where he acted in movies, conducted master classes at the Strasberg Institute in Los Angeles, and moderated sessions at Actors Studio West). Although he gave less time to the Studio as his own fame as both teacher and actor grew, his enthusiasm never wilted. He loved talking about acting; it was a subject that stirred him every time he sat in his front row director's chair and began to share his observations on the work he had just seen. From that chair, he encouraged, harangued, coddled, yelled at, soothed, and inspired several generations of the most talented actors in the history of American theatre.

Like Clurman, Strasberg thought of himself as a voice in the wilder-

ness, a theatrical seer speaking a gospel that had the power not only to stimulate art but also to save souls. Like Clurman, he clearly loved to hear himself talk and often said too much. Neither man felt he had to measure his words. "Lee certainly talked a lot," an actress who left the Studio told me, with a sigh. "But someplace in this long talk something would mean something to you: there'd be a gem for that hour."

Out of the ocean of words with which Strasberg sprayed each session, there would always be brilliant illuminated passages. If he had a tendency, forever indulged, to go on and on, he also had a gift for the pithy phrase and the *mot juste* that would highlight the core of an acting problem, and that would be precisely the thing the actor needed to hear.

It was a long-standing, though seldom-acknowledged fact of life at the Studio that many actors (especially newer members who hadn't yet decoded the passwords) had trouble understanding Strasberg. "When I got in, I soon realized that I didn't know what he was talking about," says Madeleine Thornton-Sherwood. "When someone has the magical, insightful, informed ability Strasberg has as a teacher, it's upsetting that sometimes he wasn't clear," Lois Smith says. "He's dangerous to many actors because he was hard to interpret," June Havoc says. "He was often inexact and self-repetitive, and matters which are clear became obfuscated by his explanation," Arthur Penn says, adding that "nonetheless there was a first-class mind operating."

It was one of the great ironies of Strasberg's career that this powerful teacher for whom words were the currency of his gift to actors had trouble with verbal clarity and precision. "He felt that no one understood his work fully, and that no one was a true product of the work, that he hadn't fully explained his work to anyone," says David Garfield, a longtime Studio member (and the author of a fine book on the Studio).

Listeners ready to hang on every word the man says (even if they don't understand his every word); a speaker flailing to communicate his ideas to people who aren't receiving them the way he wants them to: the situation is fraught with mordant comedy, as the guru and his disciples are separated by a verbal standoff. But for all his obscurities, his dependence on code words, his faulty grammar, his repetitions, his serpentine wanderings, Strasberg had a genuine feeling for the inflections of spoken English. For all his verbal foibles, he was (like all demagogues) a powerful wielder of words, employing them with often remarkable skill to wound and to cure, to strike and to soften, to goad, galvanize, berate, to arouse and to silence. He presided over a world-renowned theatre workshop for nearly thirty-five years precisely by his power to speak and to communicate.

Yes, he was a terrible speaker; and a great one.

Strasberg's words often seemed at odds with his looks. His words were intense, alight with artistic fervor and the joy of experiment, but his face was defiantly inexpressive, a mask that instilled terror in generations of brilliant American actors. Solemn and inscrutable, Strasberg appeared locked in thought. His face issued the challenge to keep away. Yet for all its ostensible blankness, Strasberg's poker face suggested a busy inner life.

"You could never tell what his reaction was," says longtime Studio observer Syeus Mottel. "Yet people would look to see what Lee was thinking of the work. People wanted to penetrate his mask—it was a perennial challenge."

Strasberg as master conductor, with actors Maya Kennan and John Ryan.

© SYEUS MOTTEL

Strasberg seemed markedly different in and out of session. During session, he was extraordinarily generous, voluble, sharing; when session ended at one o'clock, he seemed to retreat at once into a private world. Encased in silence, his immobile features became truly intimidating, and to actors whose work he had just scrutinized with enormous concern, he had not a word to say.

"When you worked for Lee, there was nothing else in the world; no one else existed except you and your problems," Gayle Greene says. But when the work was finished, the bond snapped, and the teacher would rarely even greet his student. "It became a gamble when you said hello to Lee if you'd get a hello back," Marcia Haufrecht says. "But I would gladly sacrifice getting a hello for his deeper caring about me. Lee didn't believe in passing the time. He didn't have time for social amenities. He said, 'What is there to say hello about?' "

New Studio member Katherine Cortez sees his social remoteness as a way of "being able to deal with our emotions in session, without adding an extra charge." Martha Coignay, the Studio's secretary from 1956 to 1959, who got Strasberg "to say 'good morning' after six months on the job," and who had phone conversations with him where "there could be ten minutes of silence," feels he was "totally concentrated, not rude or shy."

Although Strasberg's not saying hello might have been a deliberate strategy for protecting the work, or might have indicated extreme shyness, social insecurity, or preoccupation, still it was a disconcerting eccentricity which some people couldn't accept. Alice Hermes, who taught a speech class at the Studio in the fifties, recalls that she would regularly pass Strasberg on the stairs. "For four years I would say, 'Good morning, Mr. Strasberg,' and not once did I ever get a response. He knew perfectly well who I was. He knew I hadn't come to sweep the floor, though even if I had, I'd have expected an answer."

I wonder if Strasberg's remarkable unfriendliness, like his face from which normal human reactions seemed to be erased or withheld, was a way of controlling people. The silence and the numb face seemed to provoke others into wanting a response from him.

Off the job, then, Strasberg was a profoundly private man. Social ease, affability, glad-handing—these were qualities he didn't have, and was not interested in cultivating. He had the good sense to marry women who did his socializing for him. The first Mrs. Strasberg, an actress named Nora Krecaun, died in 1936; the second Mrs. Strasberg, Paula Miller, a minor actress in the Group Theatre, and the third, Anna Mizrahi, an actress Strasberg met when she joined the Actors Studio in the mid-sixties, became celebrities in their own right. Both women proved to be wonderfully complementary to the withdrawn sage they had married: they were outgoing, aggressive, adept meeters and greeters; skillful hostesses who, like their husband, sparked powerful and wildly contradictory reactions.

"Paula was the great interceder, and would supply the dialogue for Lee to the world for three months at a time," Martha Coignay recalls. "She had a great deal of warmth." "Paula always offered you a bowl of chicken soup," Gordon Rogoff, the Studio's chief administrative officer in the late fifties, says. "She was an imposing woman, and when it came to guarding the zoo, she was a great lioness." (At this writing Anna Strasberg is engaged in a bitter court battle with the Studio. She claims that the tapes of Strasberg moderating are the property of the Strasberg estate. The Studio maintains that the tapes belong to the Studio, an educational tool for its members.)

If Strasberg allowed his strong wives to gain control of his personal life—to dictate his relations with his children, and with the outside world—he alone ruled the Studio. "Lee was a damn near despotic and frightening figure," says Arthur Penn. "There was a gory ten years where Lee ruled with a capricious iron fist." "A terrific sense of terrorization and intimidation came from him," says Gordon Rogoff. "There was a double tyranny we suffered from: the tyranny of the reputation and the tyranny of the real man. He attracted actors who seemed to require cold-blooded tyranny, terrorism rather than freedom."

"I like to argue," Strasberg frequently claimed, and indeed he cultivated an image as a Jewish haggler, someone who relishes the clash of opinion. He was a Talmudic *gribbler*, quibbling over nuance and inflection, but it was often with himself that he argued as he staged mock combats, stating on his own an argument's thesis and antithesis, its point and counterpoint. In theory, he was certainly the kind of fellow who liked good rows, but in practice most of the time he was too authoritarian, or too insecure, to entertain them.

Until the middle seventies, he would regularly ask for comments ("OK, what would you say?") in a bored tone of voice, and would then rarely address himself to what was said unless he violently disagreed;

rather, he seemed to use the time when others spoke to gather his own thoughts. In his last seven or eight years, he dispensed altogether with soliciting comments from observers, as if he sensed that time was running out and that, considering his vast experience, only his remarks mattered anyway. He knew, and everybody else knew, that those sessions belonged to him, and in his final years he seized the time, with increasing possessiveness, to say what he had to say.

"I don't believe theatre is a place for democracy," says Joanne Linville, a sometime moderator who approved of Strasberg being the sole respondent to the work. "I don't know about that sitting and talking from lots of people; I want to be told by one person who knows. Three-fourths of the comments are meaningless and destructive. Lee would shut people up who didn't know what they were saying."

From time to time, he would pay lip service to the idea that in a Studio, as contrasted to a production, there ought to be disagreement and debate. In a production, he said, there is only one director, and his voice must be the decisive one, while in a studio there is room for several voices. But in fact Strasberg needed to be in sole control, and he sought weaker people to agree with him and bolster him. Unwilling to collaborate, to delegate responsibility, or to tolerate serious differences of opinion, Strasberg was the boss. The Studio was his domain, his fief, his spoils—the place where he held court; and it may be that he maintained so tight a grip over it because it hadn't been his in the beginning.

"I founded the Studio, along with Cheryl Crawford and Robert Lewis," Elia Kazan told me, as if to remind me. It was Kazan who, in 1949, invited Lee Strasberg to join the Studio, two years after it was founded, when he realized that the Studio needed a full-time teacher. Kazan knew he needed someone who was not working actively in theatre or films, and he turned to Strasberg.

The question remains, why wasn't Strasberg part of the original team? One reason is clear. Even though Strasberg resigned from the Group in 1937, the wounds hadn't healed a decade later; Strasberg had earned a reputation as a poor risk in a group effort since he was hot-tempered and authoritarian. "In 1947, when the Studio was being put together, Kazan had said, 'Lee Strasberg must be kept away!' " Gordon Rogoff reports. But whatever personal doubts Kazan continued to have about him, he also knew that Strasberg was a gifted teacher, and that his particular skill—close examination of scene work—was exactly what the Studio setup required.

Strasberg entered the Studio at the invitation of the younger man, his protégé in fact, who had begun to direct Group productions after his own departure. To accept the job was in a sense humbling, though the Studio represented a resting place after years of wandering on the margins of the theatre. After he resigned from the Group, Strasberg was a peripatetic and far from successful director, a man without an artistic home. He had taught directing at Piscator's Dramatic Workshop and at the American Theatre Wing and had worked occasionally on Broadway, most notably as director of two Odets plays, *Clash by Night* and *The Big Knife.* Between his sporadic Broadway assignments, he went to Hollywood, where he directed screen tests. Now, in 1949, at a low point in his career, Strasberg was brought in to save the Studio, and what had originally been Kazan's Studio soon became Strasberg's. In 1952, he was named Artistic Director, and for the next thirty years, his attachment to the place was unbreakable. He thought of the Studio as compensation for what the Group had done to him, and

Strasberg with Anna Mizrahi Strasberg, his third wife.

© SYEUS MOTTEL

for all those years of obscurity and of feeling like an outsider in the business about which his knowledge was encyclopedic and his ideals empyreal.

"Everyone talked about Strasberg's emotional needs and problems with respect to the Studio," Gordon Rogoff recalls. "There was a faction at the Studio that looked at Lee Strasberg as having been victimized by the Group Theatre, and that felt Kazan was getting recognition as a director that Lee had been denied," Jack Garfein says. "Everything seemed channeled toward the fact that Lee Strasberg had been victimized, and that we at the Studio were to make it up to him. We championed him with a zeal you find only in religion. Kazan felt we were making Lee a heroic figure, that we weren't seeing other sides, that the man was not faultless. Kazan felt this veneration would boomerang—a warning that was prophetic."

Born in Austro-Hungary, and emigrating with his family to the Lower East Side when he was three, Strasberg spoke in a voice that retained the hint of a foreign accent. It was neither a pleasant nor a trained voice, it was simply his voice, the one he had been born with: the voice of his people, untutored, monotonous in pitch and inflection, rough-edged, plebeian. Strasberg decidedly did not sound like an actor; is there perhaps a link between his unpolished speech and the notorious mumble that has always been part of the popular image of the Studio he controlled? He was often accused of underselling the importance of speaking well, but, as Michael Wager says, "How would Lee have known what good diction was? It would have sounded false and untrue to him."

Listening to him, you can't help but notice striking contrasts between his harsh, ethnic, working-class voice and the theoretical abstractions that often issued from his lips. He sounded like a Damon Runyon character, tough and slangy, or a folk prophet, a streetwise man of humble origins; but what he said was often tinged with a loftiness derived from Stanislavski. Strasberg's idiom was a disarming blend: part intellectual theory, part knowing practice; part Stanislavski idealism, part smart-talking Broadway vernacular; part mysticism, part shrewd common sense.

Strasberg's verbal schizophrenia reflected a genuine split in his personality. On the one hand, he was a true scholar of the theatre; on the other, he was pure American show business. A man with little formal education who loved to read, he amassed one of the world's great collections of theatre books. Books on any kind of theatre from any period and any place in the world fascinated him. His apartment was overrun with books: books tumbled from the walls and swelled in intimidating piles up from the floor. Visitors often joked that because of all the books a walk from the foyer to the living room could be treacherous.

Strasberg's bookishness, his true and continuing love of learning, which he so generously shared with his actors, was mixed with his love of show business. "He grew up in this country, and despite all his idealism, he wanted money and success too," says Jack Garfein. "Like everyone else, he was seduceable. When the opportunity came to be popular, he took it, which is what he counseled us against."

It was Strasberg's shifting, ambivalent, compromised attitudes toward popular success, and his increasingly apparent worship of those who had attained that success, that caused more ill feelings among his students than any other facet of his personality. As on virtually no other issue, Strasberg students and associates are united in this disappointment about his stargazing. "Whenever a star called, Lee went running," Carl Schaeffer told me. "Lee was in love with stars," says Estelle Parsons. "Lee knew his reputation was based on movie actors he produced," says Madeleine Thornton-Sherwood.

In the early years, Strasberg consistently warned his actors about the dangers of going out to Hollywood and becoming movie stars. "Lee and Paula talked some of the actors out of accepting plum movie roles," Jack Garfein remembers. "They talked Albert Salmi out of the lead role in the movie version of *Bus Stop,* and they wouldn't let Nancy Berg play the role in *Around the World in Eighty Days* that went to Shirley MacLaine. These were parts that could have changed their careers; instead, Lee persuaded them that they owed it to their artistic development to stay in New York and study, rather than go off to make movies. But we began to realize, in the mid-fifties, that the ones who made the sacrifices for art were not the Rabbi's favorite; those who *made* it were the Rabbi's favorite."

Strasberg's fatal attraction to the limelight first began to be noticeable in 1955, with "the shock wave" of Marilyn Monroe descending on the Studio. "Though she had certainly sold out early in her career, Marilyn was innocent, she was not to be criticized, but for us she became a sign of Lee's lust for success," says Jack Garfein.

To Studio regulars, Strasberg seemed caught in a trap: he had been cautioning them against going to Hollywood, yet here he was treating a movie star, probably the most famous movie star in the world, like visiting royalty. For Monroe, all the Studio rules were suspended. Though technically she was never a member, Strasberg had told her she didn't have to audition and that she could become a member any time she wanted to.

The relationship between the movie star and the acting coach was fascinating, positively mythic. (Norman Mailer was so intrigued that he wrote two books in which the Monroe-Strasberg connection is central.) Clearly, the two saw each other in powerfully symbolic ways: Strasberg was the father that Norma Jean Baker had never had, and Monroe was Strasberg's passport to the national fame that he secretly coveted. She wanted to be taken seriously as an actress, and how better to assert her seriousness than to absorb what Strasberg had to say in the shelter of the Actors Studio on West 44th Street, at the other end of the country from Twentieth Century-Fox, another kind of studio altogether that wanted to imprison her in the sexy image she reviled.

People at the Studio liked Marilyn, who was as shy and insecure as she was reported to have been. Arriving late, she was usually dressed in a large coat and wore dark glasses, and she sat modestly in the back like a country cousin. She performed only one scene, the opening from *Anna Christie*, with Maureen Stapleton as her partner, which has passed into legend in the Studio's history; the consensus was that her work was sensitive, hushed, tremulous. What created discomfort in the Studio was not Monroe herself, but the kind of publicity that she automatically attracted. Suddenly the Studio was invaded by journalists—the actor's sanctuary became a matter of public curiosity, a news item, a subject for gossip columns. Whether Monroe deserved to be there, whether she could act or not, was beside the point: she represented a world to which all of the Studio's ideals were opposed. The Studio was New York, serious acting, the theatre, artistic individuality, heavy realistic drama; Monroe was Hollywood pastry, a glamorous confection who transported a winning personality from one prefabricated role to another. And here was their mentor telling them she had the makings of a great actress, that she could play Grushenka in *The Brothers Karamazov*, or that she would be a splendid Cordelia in *King Lear*. ("I can't consider that woman was an artist," Estelle Parsons says. "Strasberg convinced himself that she was, but he sometimes confused a disturbance with a gift.")

Talent as opposed to fame was all anyone ever needed to get into the

Studio, but dating from the Monroe era the famous began to receive special treatment. "Strasberg did not treat Anne Bancroft the same way he treated an unknown actor," Michael Wager recalls. "When a star was working, Lee was terrible," says Mathew Anden. "It created a lot of bitterness over the years. On the coast, at Actors Studio West, I remember when Barbra Streisand did a scene from *Romeo and Juliet.* Her diction got in the way, of course, but Lee told her she was wonderful."

In the late fifties, Strasberg gave an interview in Los Angeles in which he said movie stars like Gary Cooper who always behaved naturally and who seemed to be drawing on their true personalities were unconsciously using the Method. Many Studio actors felt betrayed: isn't Cooper simply playing himself, they asked? Isn't he merely behaving, instead of acting? Isn't he just cashing in on his ability to be natural in front of a camera? The more or less official position at the Studio in the fifties was that while it was certainly all right to act in Kazan movies (which were cast mostly with Studio actors), movie acting in general was not good for you. Yet here was their artistic leader publicly praising movie stars, and upholding their ease and naturalness as the fulfillment of Method training. Strasberg answered objections with his usual strategy, claiming he had been misunderstood. The Method was useful to film acting, he said, but acting in films should not be seen as its goal or as the highest embodiment of its lessons.

Strasberg's star-gazing caused major upsets at the Studio on three further occasions: in the sixties, during the time the Studio ventured into production; in the seventies, when Strasberg himself became a movie star; and in the eighties, when he allowed Cindy Adams to write a celebrity biography about him.

When he assumed the direction of the Actors Studio Theatre, Strasberg made it clear that he wanted to cast the plays with the biggest names he could get—an intransigent position that angered many Studio members who felt that in going after stars Strasberg was undermining the ensemble ideal that he had always spoken about as the foundation of a true repertory company. In 1975, Al Pacino asked him to appear in *The Godfather Part Two;* Strasberg accepted, and gave a startlingly good performance that led to a series of movie roles. Because it necessarily limited the time he could devote to the Studio as well as to his private classes, Strasberg's new career caused considerable resentment.

But by far the most disturbing of his celebrity exploits was his pro-

Frank Corsaro, Michael Gazzo, Marilyn Monroe, and Lee Strasberg in a Broadway diner in 1955, shortly after the opening of *A Hatful of Rain*.

longed association with Cindy Adams, a New York gossip columnist who
courted him with a proposal to write his biography. Prodded by his wife
Anna, Strasberg, who had never been liberal in granting interviews, and
who was withal an intensely private man, mysteriously and uncharacteristically granted full access to Adams for an astounding two-year period,
permitting her to attend sessions at the Studio, to accompany him and his
wife to parties and openings, and to listen to his thoughts about acting, the
American theatre, and his personal life. Adams, whose chief claim to
literary distinction was as co-author of a book about Jolie Gabor, and her
husband, a saloon-circuit comic, Joey Adams, played up to Strasberg, giving
him star treatment. After a lifetime of being behind the scenes and after
decades of helping to develop stars, Strasberg evidently enjoyed being
treated like a star himself.

Lee Strasberg: The Imperfect Genius of the Actors Studio, the book that
emerged from his prolonged personal contact with Adams, was exactly what
anyone could have predicted, a potpourri of gossip and anecdotes that
repaid Strasberg's generosity with irrelevant and often queasy glimpses into
his private life. The book sent waves of shock and revulsion through the
Studio and offended anyone who valued Strasberg's work regardless of what
they may have thought of him personally. "It's a filthy book," one Studio
member told me in angry recollection. "It's a ridiculous book, full of
made-up conversations and preposterous imaginings." "That Strasberg let
that woman into his house was the shabbiest thing he ever did." "He was
an old man, who cares about what his sex life was like?" "How could she
have interested a major publisher with her drivel?"

In February 1982, three days before he died, Lee Strasberg appeared
on the stage of the Radio City Music Hall in a benefit performance for the
Actors Fund of America called The Night of 100 Stars. Strasberg came on
near the end of a very long evening—in a chorus line, kicking his legs in
a lineup of million-dollar talent, some of them, like Al Pacino and Robert
De Niro, Studio members he had deeply influenced. (Imagine Stanislavski
in such a setting!)

Strasberg managed to preserve his dignity. When he was introduced
in the star chorus, he made not a single concession; while every one else
managed a professional smile, Strasberg was unyielding, his face frozen.
Refusing to act like a celebrity, he looked like a Talmudic scholar about
to discourse on chapter and verse. But still, there he was, participating in

a garish show business pageant. "It was like the end of *Don Giovanni*," Michael Wager says. "He died dancing with celebrities. How ironic, and how appropriate, in a ghastly sort of way. The punishment fit the crime."

In a way, Strasberg was the victim of his own idealism. He had spoken for so long and with such conviction about standards, craft, respecting talent, about acting as a high demanding art, that his own excursions into the real world beyond the shelter of the Studio seemed like violations. Having cast himself in the role of theatrical law-giver and visionary, he came to be imprisoned by it: the actors that he shared his insights with didn't want him to be like everyone else, desirous of fame and money, and most of them were shocked whenever he actually descended from theory and analysis in order to direct a play, act in a movie, or head a theatre company. For his sake, as well as their own, they wanted him to remain above the smell of the crowd. As his own personal ambitions emerged, as it became obvious that he was impressed by fame (even though he held on to a steadying skepticism about fame's great risks and pitfalls, its power to corrupt talent), Studio members who thought of themselves as his disciples were seriously disillusioned, and scandalized by the Messiah's worldliness.

"He became a celebrity of the kind you wouldn't associate with the Group Theatre or the Actors Studio," says Jack Garfein. "At his Institute they offer classes in commercials; and at an Actors Studio benefit in 1981, he talked of the Studio's contribution to the industry: imagine, Lee Strasberg talking about the industry. I cringed." (Garfein, who is artistic director of the Harold Clurman Theatre, adds that Clurman was the one Group leader who never compromised. "He was the one who held on to his original purity and integrity—he was the one who managed to combine the practical and the idealistic. Lee Strasberg took the easy way." John Strasberg, Lee's son, told me he was sorry Clurman wasn't alive so I could talk to him, because Clurman really loved the theatre in a pure way, whereas he felt that his father had made compromises.)

Speaking at Strasberg's star-studded funeral, Al Pacino said, haltingly and intriguingly: "Lee . . . was what he was. We will miss him."

What was he, finally, this man who was so beloved and so hated? To many Studio regulars, Strasberg was more than a teacher, he was also a shaman, a man of special insight, a spiritual guide, a genius who spoke scripture. To an outsider like me, the adulation he evoked in people of accomplishment and absolute integrity is daunting and a little frightening. The pseudo-religious and cultist overtones that for many years had been apparent at Studio sessions surfaced dramatically in the months after Strasberg's sudden (and despite his age) quite unexpected fatal heart attack when several actresses claimed to have had visitations from him, in which he shared with them the secret of the Method, and when many who had held him in awe felt genuinely bereft by his absence.

Why did Strasberg's words mean so much to so many intelligent and talented actors? A negative word from Strasberg could seriously undermine an actor's confidence, make him consider changing careers; Strasberg's praise or encouragement could sustain an actor for years, perhaps even for a lifetime in the theatre. How did one man gain so much influence over the creative spirit of generations of actors, and why did so many yield so much of their own power to him?

First, I think, it was so simple and intangible a matter as the way he presented himself. "When he walked into the room, everyone stood aside," says Mathew Anden. "He had an aura you respected." Even in Group Theatre days, Strasberg had an elderly appearance; he looked like a wizened scholar, soberly engaged in the pursuit of ideas, and with age this schoolmasterly quality ripened.

"He cultivated a patriarchal, European attitude," says Sabra Jones. "We were Strasberg's children," Michael Wager says, "and being at the Studio was like participating in a terrible Jewish family romance, with all the goy actors wondering what was going on. Such intensity I've never seen. Strasberg was a substitute parent who validated your existence, as a human being and as an artist: what more powerful thing is there? Many of us had a father-son, love-hate relationship with him. I loved Lee, and I despised him," Wager says, his voice trembling with feeling.

As a demanding, wrathful, Jewish paterfamilias, Strasberg was indeed brilliantly cast. Hiding behind his masklike face, he was a father who rarely smiled or responded in any overt way to the behavior of his children, but who sat observing them with intense concentration. Imagine the thrill of eliciting a smile, a nod or word of approval, anything at all, from so ungiving a parent. Surely Strasberg's stillness lent him his knowing aura; coming from the mysterious recesses of that great stone face, words acquired a special significance.

His stern manner made many actors want to do their best to please him. "When you worked at the Studio for Lee you set extremely distant limits for yourself, and you tried to reach those limits, testing yourself against yourself," Joan Copeland says. "It was because of Lee, what he projected. When other people took over, there wasn't the same sense of expectancy." "His gift was to inspire people to function at their highest level," Estelle Parsons says. "He created an artistic climate in which I felt free to work. He was able to create some feeling in the room so your instrument could go."

Strasberg's ability to engender loyalty was of course based on more than his remote, patriarchal image, intimidating (and, to many, inspiring) as it was. It was based, too, on his intense belief that, as Michael Wager says, "acting is an art that means something. He had a capacity to instill respect for art and craft. That was a powerful magnet in a theatre that paid no attention to art. It's what kept me there for ten years. The dignity and self-respect he gave the actor was more important than anything he taught." "He treated every actor as an artist," says Estelle Parsons. Speaking at Strasberg's funeral, a grieving Shelley Winters said, "Through Oscars and lousy pictures, I always knew there was a place where I could go and be well: listening to Lee Strasberg at the Actors Studio made me aware of the honor of being an actor."

Part of Strasberg's appeal to the artist lurking within every actor was his emphasis, as Jack Garfein says, on "great inner treasures. He made us all feel that we were special beings, and it was a major part of the work to make us become aware of—to know how to tap—those inner riches. A bad or dangerous result was the 'inner circle' psychology that this could lead to: the defensiveness, the sense that we were all initiates in a private club."

"Lee loved talent, he truly worshipped it, perhaps because he felt he didn't have it," says Sabra Jones. Indeed, respect for talent permeates the air at the Studio: you can feel it as an almost palpable element. And to actors adrift in a hazardous profession, Strasberg's votive offerings to the idea of talent and to its development were heady and intoxicating, a purifying alternative to the hard practicalities of the Broadway show shops.

In an industry where the law of the jungle prevails, where contracts, money, and deals are the daily currency, Strasberg talked about art and ideas and made his actors aware of a great tradition which they formed a part of. "In being close to him, we felt close to all the greatness of the theatrical past," says Jack Garfein. "His power lay in the mysticism of the past. He was bringing us close to Edmund Kean, Garrick, Duse, Stanislavski. That was the magnet that drew us, that sense of being part of a great historical process."

Although there were gaps in Strasberg's knowledge ("he hid behind the intellect he created to make up for feeling like an inadequate immigrant who hadn't finished school," Sabra Jones says), a good part of Strasberg's power derived from his presentation of himself as an intellect. "It was an extraordinary experience to meet someone with such a rich mind," says Mary Mercier, who runs Actors Studio West. "I was overwhelmed. He's a lesson to all people to remain intellectually alert."

Yet, perhaps more than anything, it was Strasberg's great skill in sizing up the actors who worked for him that created such strong filial attachments. He was remarkably intuitive about actors as people; he could read beneath their facades, unearthing their strengths and insecurities. He was an incisive lay therapist, shrewd in not giving the individual actor more than he could take—contrary to popular impression, he never seriously trespassed into private areas. As Madeleine Thornton-Sherwood says, "Lee always told us there are other places you can go to have your problems attended to."

Strasberg knew what the individual actor needed to do to unlock his creativity. "He believed everyone could be expressive, and in fact he could extract expressivity from a stone," says Michael Wager. "The trap was that he set himself up as having papal infallibility, that he and he alone had the power to unleash your expressivity and turn it into art. Some actors began to feel they needed him to reach their expressiveness."

"Lee knew what *you* needed to do to open up your instrument," says Eva Marie Saint. "I had a Quaker father, and we didn't show too much emotion at home. Lee sensed this about me the first time he saw me work, and he gave me emotional, angry scenes to do. He opened floodgates for me in a kind, constructive way." Geraldine Page says Strasberg "forcibly deprived me of what made me comfortable in my acting. He worked hard with me—relentlessly—to break me out of my mannerisms, out of the fluttery spinster thing I kept doing in the fifties and this helped me to get the part of Alexandra del Lago in *Sweet Bird of Youth*, which changed my career. He knew what I needed to *undo* to move ahead. He did me worlds of good, but it was like having to face an acid bath. He could be cruel; he was like a Zen master."

"Actors thought he was a god because he could mobilize emotions through the sense memory exercises he had worked out so methodically," says Sabra Jones. " 'Do this, and feel something,' he said. And that was very powerful, especially for those who were not in touch with how they felt. Because of this, they made transferences to him the way they did to a therapist. I know this is the real reason for his great success as a teacher."

Sensory work and the inner nature of the Method compelled a close relationship between Strasberg and his actors: it was as if, in working on themselves, discarding their emotional and physical blocks, they weren't so much preparing a performance for Strasberg as revealing their souls. And in that charged context, Strasberg became father confessor, surrogate therapist, and soothsayer. Many actors I talked to expressed a gratitude to Strasberg that went beyond matters of craft. Strasberg, they said, had helped them to life-changing self-discoveries. Although I couldn't help wondering if some of the disciples hadn't mistaken Strasberg's acute psychological insights for generosity of spirit and his dedication to laboratory experiment for compassion, I had no question at all about the fact that he had assisted many talented people to unchain their talent, and that he had provided an atmosphere in which to confront both self and craft.

Good acting is important in the world, and great acting is exalting to performer and audience: this was the subtext of everything Strasberg said and did, and this conviction, lit with promise and the joy of discovery and creativity, shone through the flaws in his personality. It was his sustaining, life-affirming gift to those who came to listen to him, and, realizing this, you arrive at an understanding of why so seemingly cold and formidable a man was so truly beloved as a teacher.

9

THE BEST AND THE BRIGHTEST:
STRASBERG'S MODERATORS

"In a way, Lee's death is a freeing thing: the children have to grow," Marcia Haufrecht told me, sensibly enough. "In the last years, he became more and more restrictive." But it was clear from the sessions I observed in the spring of 1982 that the work of the Studio would continue as a monument to its master teacher and that in a quite forcible way both the letter and the spirit of Strasberg's many words on acting would be carried on by moderators like Ellen Burstyn, Estelle Parsons, and Arthur Penn he had himself chosen.

Gordon Rogoff recalls the first time Strasberg was replaced by another moderator. It was a bitterly cold January morning, and the unthinkable happened: Strasberg, who never missed a session, was too ill to come in. Rather than simply cancel, Rogoff, as the Studio's second in command, took it upon himself to try to find a substitute, and he began making calls to people he felt would be qualified to sit in for Strasberg on this one occasion. Arthur Penn, a long time member of the Studio with a deep understanding of the work, took the session.

"Strasberg was incensed," Rogoff remembers. "You would have thought I had committed a murder. Lee was never the same to me after that. The freeze began. It took a year to get rid of me. After I left the Studio in 1960, I never talked to him again."

In the seventies, as his own acting career caught fire, and as he began to divide his time between Los Angeles and New York, Strasberg could no longer moderate two sessions a week. He agreed to take Fridays, leaving Tuesdays to a rotating panel of "guest" moderators. Far from feeling threatened by other moderators, Strasberg in this later period welcomed them as an absolute necessity. Without them, the traditional twice-weekly meetings would have had to be curtailed; and the season would have had to be shortened as well, to allow him the six months a year that he wanted in Los Angeles. After having been at every session for the better part of a quarter of a century, Strasberg became something like a visiting celebrity, fitting the Studio into a busy schedule.

At the time of his death, there were fifteen people Strasberg had approved as moderators, among them Shelley Winters, Frank Corsaro, Arthur Penn, Estelle Parsons, Ellen Burstyn, Eli Wallach, Lee Grant, Vivian Nathan, and Elia Kazan. In Los Angeles, at Actors Studio West, there was another list, including Martin Ritt, Sydney Pollack, Martin Landau, Bruce Dern, Joanne Linville, and anyone from the New York list. These were the best and the brightest, the people who talked Lee's language, speaking the words he wanted spoken. Faces and personalities changed from session to session, underscoring what many members had always felt about the Studio's dangerous absence of structure and continuity, but Strasberg's Method prevailed.

When Strasberg moderated, any Studio member no matter how famous might be likely to work for him. When other moderators took over, no matter how successful they might be in the outside world, they were in a sense sitting in for Lee, saying what he might say, using the vocabulary that they had absorbed over the years from listening to him; and most of the famous Studio actors didn't, or wouldn't, work for these moderators, as to do so seemed to violate unspoken Studio protocol. As the Oscar winners and the celebrated moved up to moderator rank, working if at all only for Lee, a tendency that had been developing since Strasberg's own movie stardom seemed to harden: the Studio was no longer quite the workshop it had been since 1949, when everyone, star and novice alike, brought in work for Lee, but a place where those who had made it "on the outside" commented on the work of those who hadn't. This power shift doesn't diminish the value of what the Studio offers its members, but it does call into question its own designation as a place where talent alone counts. No, at the Studio (though here it is often more subtle and perhaps for that reason also more insidious), as in the hustling show business world that it sets itself apart from, the star system is in full swing.

The moderators I saw most frequently—Ellen Burstyn, Arthur Penn, Estelle Parsons, and Eli Wallach—had quite different personal styles, and the atmosphere in the Lee Strasberg Theatre would shift noticeably according to which of them was taking the session that day. Individual variations aside, it was clear that they shared certain general assumptions about what good acting is and about how the actor can work toward achieving it, and both in what they had to say about the work of the actors and in the language in which they said it they were manifestly Strasberg's disciples, speaking party doctrine.

In the following pages I would like to share my impressions of each of the four moderators and then look closely at some further scene work, gathering evidence for my conclusions about how the Method works and what its aims are.

Ellen Burstyn always walked into the room with a proprietary air. Pleasant and accessible offstage, once she entered the Studio's inner sanctum she became almost transcendently grave. To the working actors, she offered absolute concentration and respect, like Strasberg radiating a belief in the *moral* value of the search for good acting. Closer to Strasberg at the time of his death than anyone else, Burstyn has become the principal keeper of the flame. "I want to be careful what I say because I'm not speaking only for myself now, but also for the Studio," she told me.

"Lee insisted I learn to teach," Burstyn says. "Lee was the extension of Stanislavski, and he taught me to continue that line of teaching and thinking about acting. Moderating is so outer-directed, while acting is so inner-directed that I'm not sure how I'll be affected as an actor. I feel that I have the ability to help actors—at least I hope so." When I asked her why she thought she was effective, she said: "I understand the process. I studied with Lee till the day he died; I never stopped working for him. I was scheduled to work for him the week he died. I have a lot of respect for the actors. I know how hard it is to do, how difficult the task is, and I have compassion."

This certainly tallies with what I observed about her, but I think her impact, her real power and brilliance as a moderator come from her sense of the work as a sort of spiritual pilgrimage. "You work on your being here; if you want to change your acting, you have to change your being. The root of religion is to reunite with yourself, which is what we do here. The word 'religion' comes from a root word that means to 'bind back,' which involves, as our work does, a *remembering* of yourself. We're working on ourselves here, cutting through all the conditioning. There is a spiritual component

In *Resurrection* (1980), Ellen Burstyn heals a crippled woman played by Studio member Madeleine Thornton-Sherwood.

to the work, but Lee would never allow spiritual language to be used so I try not to."

In session, Burstyn has much the same kind of illuminated quality she had in *Resurrection*, where she played—unforgettably—a woman with supernatural healing powers. As in the film, she is wonderfully calm. When she speaks to the actors in a clear, quiet voice, it's like the laying on of hands. She is extremely sharp about people ("the good actor learns the motivating forces of human behavior," she says). More than with anyone else I talked to, I could sense Burstyn making intuitive judgments about me, gauging how far she could trust me.

She has the born teacher's gift of summary and synthesis, and she can light on just the word that will lead the actor to an insight about himself and his work. Demanding that actors be precise in stating their intentions, quizzing them intently to hone down exactly what tasks they have set, Burstyn conducts sessions as an intense colloquy between her and the working actors, with little space left for observations from others. Protective of the actors who've just worked, she can be short with the house. "May I make a comment?" a non-member asked. "No, you may not," she answered, as a gasp escaped from the audience. On another occasion, a member tried to comment on an actor's interpretation of a role, but Burstyn quickly cut him off. "They're not doing the scene at that level, and so we don't need to address their work in that way." She treats the working actors as though they are a sacred trust—she's remarkably caring.

At one session, I was impressed by her responsiveness to an actor who was blocked both in his scene and in his ability to make statements about it. Moved nearly to tears by his problem, Burstyn said, "You have been stamped by Lee Strasberg as a talented actor. No one will ever again receive that seal of approval. Honor Lee's faith in you! I want what you have to offer, I want to see the faith Lee had in you borne out." The actor agreed to do the scene again, to see if he could break through his resistance. This time, with Burstyn's encouragement ringing in his ears, he came almost magically alive; where he had been physically inert the first time, he was now free in using his body. As he began to improvise, forcing his partner to make spontaneous adjustments, the scene gathered energy and dramatic conflict. "Fed" by Burstyn, the actor had opened up, discovering unexpected humor and power in himself.

Where Burstyn comes in trailing an air of solemnity, Estelle Parsons enters with a crisp matter-of-factness. "I don't like to moderate, I like to act," she told me. "When I moderate, I'm always aware that nobody should tell an artist what to do. I try to be open to what the actor is trying to do, not to press on the actor what I think he should be doing. One must be gentle, encouraging, help the actor to gain courage, to find his way. The materials we deal with resemble what a psychiatrist may deal with, but the person you're talking to is an acting instrument, and that's different from the person himself." Perhaps to underline her statement that she doesn't know any more than any other member, Parsons doesn't remain seated during her comments, but works the room, moving from one side to the other, speaking out from odd corners and tangents.

She eagerly solicits comments from the audience, even from the non-member observers, who are traditionally not permitted to contribute. "I'd like to know what some of you in the back have to say; after all, somebody let you in here!" Where Burstyn's moderating is steady and balanced, Parsons's is delightfully quirky. And where Burstyn talks in a low, soothing voice, Parsons alternates between whispers and roars. Sometimes, her voice goes dead and she becomes practically inaudible. "We can't hear you, Estelle," someone called out, at a moment when she had noticeably faded. Parsons's next sentence came out with a blast that you could hear on 44th Street.

Though clearly she doesn't want power the way Burstyn does, though what she says doesn't have the firm outline or the rhetorical finish of many of Burstyn's comments, Parsons is in fact a first-rate moderator in her own way. She's more relaxed than Burstyn could ever be, and I think her less official posture can have a freeing effect on actors. She can be startlingly frank, which gives her sessions a free-for-all quality; you can talk back to her in a way that you dare not with Burstyn. "Now shut up," Parsons said to one actor, "or else I'll forget what I'm saying. And maybe it doesn't matter anyway," she added. "Come on now, leave it alone," she reprimanded an actor who was pushing a point she didn't think worth pushing. In her reprimands and retorts, she sometimes sounds like the wacky schoolteacher she played so splendidly in *Miss Margarida's Way*, but her essential good nature comes through her occasionally barbed quality. She's terrifically likable.

I've seen her wit and outspokenness lift actors out of creative blocks. And her own toughened ego ("I always knew I was good—my God, any actor has to know that, or why continue?") helps to cut through actors' self-doubts. Where Burstyn, superb as she is, seems to be hewing to Strasberg doctrine, Parsons is a feisty independent who understands the value of the work but who will bypass orthodoxy if it doesn't serve the present instance. Drawing on her keen actor's intelligence to assist other actors, she is practical and intuitive rather than theoretical, as Strasberg often was. "Estelle comes at you as a working actor; what she says comes from her own experience, and that is very helpful to us," a new member says.

Compared to Burstyn and Parsons, Eli Wallach is easy. Wallach truly does nothing to call attention to himself, or to ruffle tradition. He's a Studio standard bearer, the Studio's equivalent of a company man, and valuable precisely because he speaks Studio doctrine in so pure a way: the catchwords and phrases that are the common currency pass through him unfiltered. He doesn't seize the room, the way Burstyn and Parsons do; while their sessions are powered by the interesting complications of their personalities, Wallach seems like a host, chatting amiably with everyone. A charter member of the Studio, he and his wife Anne Jackson have been around longer than practically anyone else. Anne Jackson always accompanies her husband and makes pointed comments that balance, corroborate, and expand on his.

Wallach's remarks are well-meaning, scattered, and above all traditional. He never gets stuck, but he never gives himself much space either —he's brief, often trenchant, but incomplete, as if he's issuing a series of topic sentences without the accompanying paragraphs. He takes notes, then speaks from them, moving quickly from point to point and embellishing with personal experiences, either from the theatre or from his private life.

"I remember when I was appearing in *Waltz of the Toreadors*," Wallach said, "and I could see a man in the front row who didn't seem to be reacting to anything I did. I wanted to get him to react, and I pitched my performance to him, which of course the actor should never do. I learned

Moderator Estelle Parsons, concentrating on the working actors.

DAN GLICK

after the show that the man was blind.

"When I was in *Antony and Cleopatra* . . ."; "when I was in a market yesterday . . ."; "I overheard a woman on the subway . . ."; "when my wife and I went to Adam Strasberg's Bar Mitzvah . . ."; "as I was saying to my wife . . .": his critiques are laced with these homey, domestic, personal recollections, which draw connections between what happens to the actor in life and what happens to him on the stage. Wallach's useful theme is that the actor's materials are all around him, in everything that he says and does and feels and observes consciously and unconsciously, waking and sleeping.

Wallach, Burstyn, and Parsons are all excellent working actors commenting on the work of other actors. They are not there to direct scenes or to interpret scripts or characters, but to aid the actor in learning to identify and then overcome whatever is inhibiting his theatrical expressiveness. When a director moderates, there are some subtle shifts in emphasis. The director-moderators tend to respond to the scene as a scene, a unit in a play, and tend to pay more attention to characterization than to actors' problems. Among the Studio's director-moderators, the one most eagerly sought is, of course, Elia Kazan. When Kazan is announced as taking a session, it's news. On a Kazan morning, you can feel a charge in the air downstairs.

The director who made "Method acting" a household phrase enters the room with what seems like a leap. Kazan has a smile for everyone, but beneath the convivial exterior is a strong resolve, manifested in two house rules that he insists on: no outsiders, sessions are for members only (although, given the way the Studio is run, this is difficult to enforce); and, at eleven sharp, just before the lights go down, the door is shut. Other moderators allow the door to remain open, so latecomers often enter while a scene is in progress. "During a Kazan session, the door is closed," people tell you, and behind their words is the implication that in these closed-door sessions the business of the Studio is conducted as it was originally meant to be.

Working for Kazan, the actors are steamed up; there is a sharpness and intensity in the work, a clearer outline than is often the case during other sessions. Actors say they wouldn't dare bring beginning work to Kazan, and so the work in these sessions feels more like finished acting and less like the kind of preparation and homework that is the usual menu.

Kazan violates Studio protocol to the extent that he views the work

Eli Wallach, a genial Studio moderator.

from a directorial point of view. "He likes the visual idea of what the scene should be," an actor told me. "He hates when actors do work on themselves rather than on the scene. 'Why don't you do it at home?' he tells actors who bring in private moments."

Michael Wager recalls that in the fifties actors wondered if Kazan would "pluck us from obscurity to stardom." When Kazan takes a session even now that expectation lingers, however submerged. "Maybe he'll make me a star, you think, even though you're not supposed to, and that that's not the reason you're at the Studio anyway," a new member says.

When Kazan moderates, he's crisp, concise, and frank; whether he knows the actors or not, he at once establishes a personal connection with them. His comments, like Strasberg's, contain an awareness of the actors' personalities—the problems they carry with them offstage that may block their impulses.

As he did on all his movies, Kazan goes to work on the actors' nerves and their imaginations with lightning-like speed. Although critical of him in other respects, Geraldine Page says Kazan is simply a born director who only "had to tell you a few words to make you want to go up and try it out."

To the disappointment of Studio members, Kazan moderates infre-

Kazan and Strasberg at the
Studio in 1979.

quently. After Strasberg's death, there was a rumor that Kazan would once again assume leadership of the Studio; but no, he was not to be lured back in any full-time way, just as he was not available as a moderator except on an occasional basis. And on that basis, Kazan is light on his feet, never insisting on who he is. He enters, he sparks everyone in the room with his darting intensity, he departs. And everybody wants more.

"Kazan and I are not doctrinaire to the Studio; we have our individual practices," says Arthur Penn, the most active of the director-moderators. Penn says he enjoys moderating to see if he is able "to do what Kazan can do. He's the finest director I've ever seen. Moderating lets me test my critical acuity, allows me to see whether or not I can be helpful and inspiring."

There is not a trace in Penn of neurosis, idiosyncrasy, or verbal indecisiveness—all the infamous Method insignia. Soft-spoken and even-tempered, he seems like an academic on holiday. Penn is surpassingly tactful, and gives the actors all the room they need to experiment with their talent or to fall flat on their faces if that is what they may need to do at the moment. Like Kazan, whose famous line is, "Of course I don't know anything about acting," Penn says he is not qualified to teach acting, and that as a director his job is to help actors realize the writer's intentions. But in fact he understands the Method as fully as anyone at the Studio and is better than anyone else in translating what he knows into language.

Penn is the Studio's resident intellectual. He's the most articulate if perhaps also the least dramatic of the moderators. He doesn't have an actor's temperament—he doesn't have Burstyn's aura or Parson's snap—and his calm manner and mental approach are antidotes to the intuitive, on-the-spot reactions of the actor-moderators. Placing the Method in a theoretical and historical framework, he often reminds the members of who and where they are. "We have a collection of the most talented actors in America," he told one session. After a scene with a large cast, he observed that only at the Studio could the piece have been performed so effectively and on such short notice. "Sometimes we forget how fortunate we are here, how much richness of talent is readily available." After a comic scene, he said, "People forget that Studio actors are wonderful at comedy, because our reputation is for drama." Penn told me he always tries to cast his films and plays with Actors Studio people "because they are the best actors around."

Arthur Penn directing Warren Beatty and Faye Dunaway in *Bonnie and Clyde* (1967).

10

A STUDIO SAMPLER

With Ellen Burstyn, Estelle Parsons, Eli Wallach, Arthur Penn, and others in the moderating chair, I would like now to return to another round of Studio sessions, though this time, instead of focusing on the moderator, I'll concentrate on how the actors work. At the Actors Studio the play is decidedly not the thing, but because it prepares the way for points I want to make later, I'm going to counter Studio emphasis (frankly, to cheat a little) by arranging examples according to the *kind* of play being worked on: how does a Method performer approach a character by Odets, by Shaw, by Shakespeare?

I. Kitchen sink realism, or "let there be shit on the diapers"

(a) A scene from *Clash by Night* by Clifford Odets

A woman sits at a kitchen table, slumped in her chair, staring vacantly into the middle distance as she appears to be going into a trance. Suddenly, she sits up, releasing a spray of sounds, sighs, and groans. "It's only a rehearsal," she whispers, "it's only a rehearsal." Then she slumps back into her chair, and says, "I can't talk." In an elaborate effort to relax muscles and parts of the body, she throws her head back and shakes her arms. She pours a cup of what looks like very muddy coffee. A man enters, dressed in a ratty bathrobe, his hair disheveled. His face looks creased. He, too, slumps at the table. They sit there in silence, looking past each other, preoccupied with their own thoughts. Two slobs sitting around a table: the acme of Actors Studio naturalism.

Slowly, with pauses that seem filled with resentment and that measure the distance between the characters, words are dredged up. Gradually, you get the sense of actors losing their self-consciousness and beginning to relate to each other. We're seeing actors find their own rhythm as they edge their way into the scene.

The woman goes to the counter and begins to cut carrots. One falls, she picks it up and washes it, going on with her lines.

Words aren't important in this scene. The words are only the outward sign of the feelings boiling within these two sad sacks. A few vocal eruptions scissor the thick silence that hangs over the room as the actors raise their voices to a level of near incoherence before quickly retreating to wordless glares. Emotion is being expressed primarily through action and gesture rather than language—the author's text is there to be kicked about, rearranged, improvised with, played off against. The characters drinking coffee, chopping carrots, collapsing in chairs: this is what you notice about the scene.

"I wanted to take the muscle out of the work," the actress says, though her work seemed nothing but muscle: torturous preparation. "I've felt the

KEN WEINBERG

need to perform, and I wanted to take that off and go back to zero, in order to go moment by moment to see what happens between Michael and me."

The actor says, austerely, "I wanted to work on the heat between these two people."

Arthur Penn, who's moderating, turns first to the actress. "We're taken by your gifts, when they get out. But you go through a misbegotten preparation agony. Preparation is not something you carry around like a camel carries a hump. I would like to see you stop working on yourself so much."

"You need an exercise to externalize rather than internalize you," an observer interjects.

"A lot of it has to do with working here," the actress says.

"Yes," Penn agrees. "A lot of people act in a certain way at the Actors Studio, and that's nonsense. Divest yourself of the exercises and go to work. You don't have to go back to fundamentals every time you work. The very essence of the work here is to get the fundamentals below the conscious level, and get on with the work. Don't start from ground zero each time."

In the scene as written, a baby cries offstage at one point, causing the woman to interrupt what she is doing. But today the actress omitted the baby's cry because she didn't feel it. "You denied the fundamental circumstances of the scene," Penn says. "You can't put so much weight on preparation and ignore one of the givens of the play.

"You must make a vigorous choice in relation to your partner, not in relation to yourself. Choose one thing: that man must get out of the house. Everything that happens in the scene will then be informed by that choice."

An observer praises the actress for her adjustment when the carrot fell and she picked it up and washed it. It's something everyone noticed, and seems to approve. In real life, after all, you pick up a carrot when it falls and you also probably wash it: it's this kind of logical, real behavior, the ability to react to things as they happen—even if and perhaps especially if they're not in the script—that is of prime value here. At the Actors Studio, the readiness is all.

When the actress spontaneously picked up the carrot, I was reminded of a moment in *A Streetcar Named Desire* when Marlon Brando takes a piece of lint off Kim Hunter's blouse. Surely, the lint-picking was not a directed action, but rather something that Brando improvised on the spot. That isolated gesture (what it reveals about the actor's relaxation and concentration) contains, I think, the essence of the magnetic aliveness that Method actors are always working for.

(b) *Clash by Night,* a second time.

Two weeks later, the same two actors bring in the same scene. This time it is a directed scene, and the director is present to explain what he wanted from the actors. Ellen Burstyn is moderating.

The actress, in tears—the character's, not her own—is at the table again, though now she seems to be *in* the scene from the beginning rather than preparing for it. Every action, like last time, begins in slow motion. The actor stumbles in, scratches his arm, takes swigs from a whiskey bottle, plants a hungry kiss on the woman. He slouches. She slouches. You have to strain to catch some of the words. Again, there are pauses within and between the speeches. Sometimes, the pauses are filled, expressing the building tension between the characters; sometimes the pauses seem empty, even preplanned, as if that's how you're supposed to deliver lines at the Actors Studio. This time, chopping carrots has been replaced by the actress washing clothes on a washboard, an action she performs throughout most of the scene even during heated moments. Covering a wide emotional range, the actor leaps from casualness to explosions. He seems at times to be writhing with pain, as his voice imitates the contortions of his body. His work is compelling; in comparison, the actress is stingy. She's still so much inside, concentrating on her inner monologue, that she remains inexpressive. And she keeps on scrubbing up and down that damn washboard.

"I told Corinne not to give an inch, not to let him know anything is going on inside of her," the director explains after the scene. (She followed

KEN WEINBERG

directions, all right.) "I told Michael to get her to respond. I was trying to set up obstacles, to lead them away from doing a big love scene. I told Michael I didn't want him to act at all, no punching or kicking. Just one thing, an inner thing. No histrionics. I wanted to bring them away from the theatrics of the scene, to do work on heat, coffee, diapers. I felt that in this rehearsal they trusted that."

Ellen Burstyn asks how the scene differed from the work done for Arthur Penn. "This time it was less internal, there was more going outward." The actress tries to form a sentence, but begins backtracking, or leaves her thought suspended in midair. "Finish the sentence!" Burstyn orders.

The actor, a new member, says, "After fifteen years of working, I've been relying on instincts, so half the time I don't know what I'm doing. It's scary. Here for the past two months I've been learning a new way of working, which is begging me to let go of acting and of preconceptions. I feel vulnerable."

"Good," Burstyn says. "You're learning the value of the way we work here. Your choices are rich and believable," she tells him. "Let the energy come out without worrying about being theatrical. Your fire comes out in a haphazard, unfocused way. Be specific. Don't play a general tone. Go over each line."

Turning to the actress, she says, "I felt your preparation. I saw the heat, the mother of a baby in a hot kitchen. Often in seeing your work, I don't know what you're doing. You have sudden explosions, and I don't know where they come from. Today you were just being on stage. The beginning of the scene is a private moment; I felt your inner monologue continuing whether he was there or not."

Burstyn, who wasn't familiar with the play, is surprised to learn that the scene is a courtship leading to bed for the first time. "What this looked like was a long-standing marriage that's ending. You need to work on the sexual heat. Work on it in a craft way. Sit knee to knee and explore each other's bodies with your eyes. Do the mirror exercise. Attune yourself to each other. Have your body know when he's near. You do that by breaking down the barrier that exists between actors: you do it with your creativity, not with your sexuality.

"The washing of the diapers was general. I would have chosen washing your husband's socks—clothes that would have stimulated you in a particular way. Never deal with a prop without it being infused with meaning. It doesn't mean you demonstrate; it means you respond to the reality of the object. If you decide to use diapers rather than socks, let there be shit on the diapers."

(c) *Chilly Scenes of Winter,* a scene adapted by the actors from a novel by Ann Beattie

A young man in a cluttered room. If you've been at the Studio for a while, you begin to look at stage props with a keen eye: what personal association does each object in that room have for the character? How much of the character's history is inscribed in the books scattered about, in the alarm clock, in the clothes strewn over the moldy couch?

Typically, the scene begins with behavior and no dialogue. The actor paces the room, picks up the phone, then quickly puts it down. He drinks from a can of beer. He smiles a sly, private smile: is it the actor himself who is smiling, or the actor in character for the scene?

He burps. He seems at home. You feel he lives here. This is a place he's created for himself, where he can be private, talk to himself, go crazy.

A young woman knocks on his door. As soon as she breezes in, we see she's a chatterbox: a vegetarian "into" gestalt, an all-around nut from California who has descended on someone we've already been introduced to as a New York neurotic.

They eat, through the detailed motions of which we catch the odd word and phrase. Both actors are appealingly casual and use a speaking tone, supplementing words with an array of personal tics. I feel like an eavesdropper, which I imagine is exactly what the actors intended.

The woman punctuates her sentences with "and, uh." They both have small, sudden gestures. He presses his knuckles, runs his hands through his hair, scratches his ear, speaks with his back to us. She presses her ankles, glances furtively off to the side, talks to herself. They're both charming, and so very easy.

Deliberately, they're not working at a performance level; indeed, they don't seem to be "acting" at all. Their energy is low, like that of real people in a real room rather than of actors on a stage with their motors turned on. But there's the promise of explosion.

"I wanted to get myself into a time when nothing's worked out," the actor says. "That's where this character is: the girl he's in love with is married, and nothing is going right for him. I tried to make the guy's stepfather real. And then I just let it alone, to see what would happen."

"I had certain people in mind for my lover," the actress says. "And I worked on sensory stuff, the cold. But I forgot to bring it in, and in a small way that discouraged me."

"You're both very natural on stage," says Eli Wallach, moderating, "but it's general. The behavior is easy, real, but what was going on in the scene? You both jump to the lines too quickly. Both of you are talking about things way out there, but the things they talk about are not really what they're talking about. So there's nothing happening but natural conversation. General behavior doesn't focus me into what your situation is. I don't see an engagement on the part of the two of you that involves me. Otherwise, without the subtext and the conflict, without some clear goals you set for yourselves, it's just easy, unforced behavior.

KEN WEINBERG

"Is it your choice that this woman just talks on endlessly? As an actress you have to know *why* the character talks all the time."

"I based the character on a woman in my building who knocked on my door at 4 A.M. to tell me there is a drip in her ceiling. She is totally unaware; she just went on jabbering. My character is unaware in just this way."

"When you select something before a scene starts, it has to vibrate off what your partner does. Each thing you do must be related to something. I still don't know why the character talks all the time. What is she hiding?

"Look, you both need an *action*. How about: how can they help each other?"

(d) Cop and victim: scene from a play by Marcia Haufrecht

A man pushes a woman into a room. From the opening moment, the air crackles with the possibility of violence. The man is a cop who has arrested the woman for shoplifting.

"Are you a hooker?" he snarls, in deep Brooklynese. As he taunts her, she alternates between bravado and paranoia. The scene's mounting power is fueled by the fact that the material is unfamiliar; we are seeing a scene from a play by the actress who's in it, and we don't know how it will end. As the scene moves through successive layers of physical and psychological violence, the playing space seems to close in. The cop is a sadist, and part of the tension is that you don't know how far he could go, you don't know his limits. And as the encounter evolves, you begin to realize you don't know hers either.

As I'm drawn deeper into the war between these two, I think, this is it: this is the kind of intensely realistic acting that the Studio is famous for. And it's marvelous! You couldn't see a scene like this played more skillfully anyplace else in the world. And for once, the work today doesn't seem like work or preparation, but a fully scored scene in which the actors aren't working on themselves so much as they are simply delivering the goods. Contrary to Studio practice, what we are seeing today is a performance; the two actors are obviously ready to go—and they take off.

The scene over, the audience bursts into spontaneous applause. "Don't do that," Arthur Penn says. To applaud scenes at the Studio is to violate the special covenant between actors and observers that says the actors are working not performing, and the observers are studying craft not surrendering themselves to the narcotized state of an audience. I appreciate that, but I don't think it's always possible to maintain. Strip away the laboratory setup, and you still have actors on stage engaged in some level of performance and observers who at some level comprise an audience, with some of the expectations an audience carries with it. An audience wants to be entertained; actors want to be applauded—even at the Actors Studio.

"I wrote this two years ago," the actress says. "At the time I was struggling with the writing not the acting; now I am approaching it as an actress. I tried to create today a sense of the character's forthcoming hysterectomy. In my preparation, I personalized this for myself. Also I worked with the place. And I was trying to work with my partner."

"I didn't know why I was doing this," the actor begins, with a diffidence nowhere in evidence in his insinuating performance. (In their statements, it seems to be traditional for actors to disparage what they have done. Just once I'd like to hear an actor say, "This is what I was working for, I reached it, and I'm pleased with the results.") "I want to make a science out of it," the actor continues. "That's why I'm here. Last night I did a preparation. I relaxed, to recreate that first feeling I had of danger when I read the script. I thought of an event in my life. When I came here this morning, I was really nervous, and I was in and out of concentration. I felt clamped."

The observers don't let him get away with this cockeyed self-assessment. "Your work had a sense of honesty and just being: the reality to be there. It was crackling. You may have been nervous, but you used it."

"You trust your intelligence. So many unexpected things happened."

"God, I was so moved by what you both did. There was a physical space between you that was terrifying—I didn't know what would happen when either of you crossed it. I'm sitting here in a sweat."

Sensitive as always to the general drift, Arthur Penn summarizes what was so impressive about the work. "It was filled with moving out toward the edge where it's really dangerous. There was a palpable sense of human danger inherent in the scene, an air of jeopardy: not knowing what a human being will do in a given situation. The one misstep was revealing the hysterectomy."

"I'm always hung up on words," the actor says, introducing a new concern.

"A constant problem for the actor is how soon are you married to the words of a play. I remember when Kim Stanley did a play with Garson Kanin. He asked her to come to the first rehearsal with her lines memorized. It was a new way of working for her, and she liked it!"

In some ways, the character Marcia Haufrecht wrote for herself expresses something of her dark side: her feelings about men and about herself as a woman. To release some of these anxieties through writing about and then enacting them is both therapeutic and, in a creative sense, galvanizing: her acting today was muscular and authentic—the separation between character and actress seemed to melt before our eyes, and we had the illusion of eavesdropping on a scene of terrifying reality.

In a role she wrote and that cuts close to elements of her own being, she is an exemplar of Method naturalism. Method technique has helped her to bring her own reality to that of her character; but can the Method help her to play a character not so close to home? Can the Method help her to be as real speaking words she did not write, enacting a character who is not a conduit for some of her own deepest anxieties? Can the emphasis on self, which the Method promotes, assist her (or any Studio actor) in playing Shaw or Shakespeare?

II. "SAY GIBBERISH!"

(a) Work on *Under Milkwood*

"I'm terribly nervous," the actress announces, looking at the moderator, Eli Wallach, but addressing the entire audience. "I haven't done a scene at the Actors Studio for twenty-five years."

When Eli Wallach announces that this is a scene from *Under Milk-*

wood, I think, ah, some poetry, the music of Dylan Thomas on stage at the Actors Studio. A temporary reprieve from washing diapers and drinking

KEN WEINBERG

burned coffee in ugly white mugs. But when the actress begins the scene by getting up from a bed and scratching her arm, I realize that Dylan's language is not going to be the first order of business. She pulls out a shopping bag, from which she takes a wig. She puts it on, as she mimes looking at herself in a mirror. Not liking what she sees, she hurls the wig onto the bed, and then starts to put on eyelashes, eyeliner, and lipstick, making clucking sounds all the while. She puts on a necklace, then picks up a red skirt that's lying on a chair. Examining herself in the mirror, she bumps and grinds. She hums.

Is this a private moment? The actress seems to be in a world of her own. I begin to believe in what she is doing; she seems like a real person in a real room, going through the private process of getting dressed before facing the world.

At the end of this apparently improvised ritual, the actress speaks some lines from the poem.

"Since I haven't worked here in so long, I thought maybe I could have some fun," she says. "I took a very short speech in the play, and I constructed a little plot around it. I wanted to work with props."

"When you went into dialogue, it was organic," a member compliments her. "Vocally, you didn't project more than what was happening internally at the time. And by the way, it was good that you admitted you were nervous; you gave yourself the luxury of that reality."

"This was a marvelous beginning for you to come back and work," Eli Wallach says. "You made decisions about each piece of clothing. Now give yourself a new element, perhaps something physical, perhaps something about time. The scene, which is only about fourteen seconds in production, took you almost ten minutes. That's wonderful. That's part of the luxury of being here, being able to go through all the steps. All this will feed you and enrich the final work."

The work today clarifies some basic Studio attitudes about language. I have been getting the sense for a few weeks now that words—the playwright's text—are often treated like the enemy, an obstacle to the actor's expressiveness. The inner work that is emphasized at the Studio is a way of helping to make the author's words real to the actor; the inner monologues that the actor creates, his personal excavation of the material, in effect turn him into a co-author. But I wonder if this stress on inner work always "feeds" the words, and is equally useful for all kinds and styles of language. At the Studio, inner work is seen as a means of laying a foundation out of which *any* playwright's words can flow organically, from deep within the actor's own creative wellsprings.

Today, I didn't see a connection between what the actress chose to work on and Dylan Thomas's poetry. What the actress set out to do, creating relationships with objects, she did well, and given the Studio rules, that is all that it is necessary or relevant to comment on. But since I don't belong to the Studio, I couldn't help feeling a gap between how the actress worked and the material she had chosen to work on.

Will concentrating on props and creating a detailed physical and psychological reality that precedes and underlies the language help her to *express* the language? I don't say that the inner work cannot carry her to Dylan's lyricism, but I can say that, on this occasion, at the point where she was in her work, it did not, for when she finally spoke some words she used a plain speaking tone and treated the words as an aside, a mere grace note to the sequence of realistic physical activity. To judge whether the preparation I saw today helped the actress to play the play, obviously I would have to see her in performance; but if it did not, if, that is, she continued to bring Thomas's poetry down to a small contemporary reality, then what was the value of working in this way on this particular material?

(b) Work on *The Millionairess*

Something unusual is happening today: the playwright's words are spoken as soon as the scene starts. But they're delivered with low energy and many pauses, and the distance between performer and language is deepened by the hat one of the actresses is wearing. It's a large hat that covers half her face: is it the actress who is hiding from the language and from us, or is it the character? She is hesitant and indistinct, under-rehearsed. (Not for the first time, I question the value of presenting work at so very rudimentary a level.)

"Are we improvising now?" her partner, who has been reading from a script, asks. "Yes," says the woman in the hat, who has been pacing back and forth, trying to do what? Released from Shaw's words, the two actresses charge into the scene with a newfound energy. The improvisation has relaxed them, and they're enjoying the response from the audience. Now they return to the lines, playing the scene as Shaw wrote it. They begin buoyantly, and the always sensitive, knowing Studio audience supports them with warm laughter. But again, the scene fizzles as the actresses begin to choke on Shaw's words.

"I'm going to stop you here, because you've lost a connection with each other," Ellen Burstyn interrupts.

"I was so tense," the hatted actress says. "I couldn't find a transition into the character's anger."

"What do you do when the text asks you to do something you find it difficult to do?" Burstyn asks, stating the actor's essential problem with lovely simplicity. "When you get to a point in a scene where you don't believe it, then you have to write a whole new scene for yourself to make it real to you. Why are you blocked? What's keeping you from that rage?

"Take that hat off! Take that thing off your shoulders! Take the rings off. Your shoes too. Now, release some of that anger. Don't worry about Shaw's words: say gibberish! Let it out! Think of somebody you hate. Just move and shout. Clearly visualize the face of somebody you hate; describe it when you can, the skin texture."

"I'm thinking of Cynthia, telling her off." Without hat or shoes, the actress moves restlessly about the stage, making guttural sounds, unleashing the energy that wasn't available to her when she was doing the scene.

"It's silly language. 'An unmitigated hog!' That's a silly thing to say. Anything real doesn't seem real in the language. I think it's the language that's getting in my way."

"Is it Shaw, an idea you have about Shaw?" Burstyn asks. "A preconception about the way you think he should be performed? Do you feel uncomfortable with Shaw because you are Italian? Bring the scene in in

Italian, see if it works for you then." She offers another suggestion. "Try an adjustment: that this is a dream reality. Keep on *playing* with this. When are you most playful? After drinking? After love-making? Do that as a preparation. Know that you're getting stuck on something that you can get over."

An observer makes a literary point about Shaw—I knew he was in trouble. "It is not a finished scene, to be evaluated in performance terms," Burstyn says.

Indeed, it is not Shaw's scene that we have been watching, but homework—using the inner technique to get the emotion the scene calls for when the play's given circumstances haven't triggered it. At that important craft level, it has been a valuable session. Before she could do the scene, the actress had to overcome whatever inhibitions were getting in her way; but once everyone agreed that she was ready to go to work on the character Shaw wrote, would matters of delivery, language, and (dread word at the Studio) style be given their proper place? From what I have seen in Studio sessions over the past few months, I doubt it. For good reason, the Actors Studio is not known for its Shavian prowess.

In Shaw, words matter. His characters express *everything,* including sexuality, through language, and like the playwright himself are immensely proud of their forensic abilities. Shaw's dialogue has to be delivered by loud, clear, trained voices, by immaculately well-spoken actors who savor the flow of wit and invective. Shaw demands the kind of vocal actor who can act with the superficial brilliance that the Studio's Method is opposed to.

The actress who thinks Shaw's language is silly is charming, and she'd be fine in a different kind of play. But she is not for Shaw, and Shaw is not for her, and probably most people at the Studio would think it irrelevant to tell her so.

(c) A scene from *Private Lives*

The actress moans. The actor paces. The lighting is dim. Words begin to creep into this minatory atmosphere like alien entities. A whisper here, a grunted syllable there. Pauses galore, as both actors seem to be diving into the shelter of their private thoughts between each sentence. There's a moody interchange between the performers, but it isn't the kind that the playwright imagined. Slow, weighted with subtext, with not even a vestigial glimmer of drawing room smartness and style, this is a decidedly Actors Studio version of Noel Coward.

"I worked on my animal," the actress says, startlingly, after the scene. "I went to the zoo to watch some leopards and lions and giraffes. I chose the giraffes as my model. They're so graceful. I worked on the spine and the rhythm of the giraffe. It made me feel enormously slow. Most of my concentration was going there, it muted other things, but it was important for me to work on that."

"Work on the animal helped your face to relax," an observer says. "The slowness was good for you. It made you lovely."

"Through work on the animal, I've been stiller on stage than I've ever been before."

"I used someone personal in my life who has given me a hard time," the actor says, explaining how he substituted his feelings for a real person to help him gain access to his character's feelings. "That bitch gave me a headache. For sensory work, I used the Coney Island Pier with lights. I lived with that pier for twenty-five years. But I couldn't get the ocean water today, perhaps because that drill outside was interfering with my concentration. Before the scene we did sensory work, touching each other's faces. And we did the mirror exercise. I wanted to work today minute to minute with my partner, to establish intimacy with her."

"The work was excellent," Arthur Penn, moderating, says. "I began to realize that there were people here who had independent existences, despite the sympathetic exercises you worked on. It's beginning to have contours." Sensing that the actors' choices were difficult and private, he used them to talk in a general way about the Method. "These two actors are demonstrative of aspects of the technique. We talk here a lot about sensory work, but unless you've been trained by Lee or have been around the Studio for a while, it's hard to know what is meant by it.

"What is sensory work, and how do we use it? Last week, confronted with playing Coward's character, Katherine asked herself, 'How do I play a woman of enormous wealth?' She said she felt *her* wealth was the Actors Studio and that she felt like an heiress. She used this as an analogy. But how do you get that down in the role? You're given the character in a play and yourself. How do you affect a rapprochement between these two alien beings? Where Lee was perceptive, he said you and the character both have sensory responses to physical elements. You're both cold, hot, hungry, etc. It's your first entry into a scene and is a constant reference point when the scene gets away from you.

"It's valuable to use your own reference point to take you *into* the scene. You bring as much sensibility to the material as the author. The substance is not the words but the circumstances as you have made them personal to yourself. Sensory work is right out of your experience. That's why we use it. But make the sensory choices rather more precious. Don't tell us about them."

"Lee did not ask the nature of the personal objects used," an old-timer interjects. "When someone would want to give details, he'd say, 'No, no, darling, don't tell me.' " There is warm laughter.

"Yes," Penn continues, "telling us about them can dissipate the private material. You can talk it away, like that image of the Coney Island Pier. Take an image like the giraffe and assimilate it. Don't make it literal. If the sensory images are literally there they don't feed you. Let the image stay there in a poetic state. It's not the giraffe we're interested in, after all, but Katherine playing Coward's character Amanda."

Which is exactly what, today, in very early work on the scene, we didn't and weren't supposed to get. We watched instead a talented, interesting actress "working on" a giraffe and a talented, interesting actor "working on" the Coney Island Pier. These animal and sensory exercises were chosen by the actors to help them enter faraway material through personal imagery. At this beginning stage, because they were more involved with their inner work than with the play or the external lives of their characters, the scene had a strangely dislocated quality—it was truly private in a sense Coward never intended.

In terms of the goals they set, the actors had at least partial success. Thinking "giraffe," the actress was indeed slow and graceful; is it relevant to ask, however, if these are the appropriate qualities for Coward's elegant, quick-witted, caustic character? The actor seemed lost in a personal reverie, which he told us was his reconstruction of the Coney Island Pier; is it beside the point to ask if Coney Island isn't as far as Timbuktu from the world that Coward's cosmopolite moves in? What, finally, do giraffes and Coney Island have to do with playing Amanda and Elyot in *Private Lives?* In terms of the actors' work on developing sensory sensitivity, giraffes and piers are undoubtedly useful; but as a preliminary entry into the brittle, glittering world of Coward's play, I'm not convinced. Their choices, it seems to me, only underscored their distance from the material. With their earthy proletarian quality, the two performers would be effective in any number of gritty American plays: but why shoot for the moon, when it is so clearly out of reach?

As before, I am struck by the disparity between the Studio's inner technique and the play it is being applied to, and between the actors' obvious talents and their unsuitability for and even disregard of the material they've chosen to work on. Like Shaw and Dylan Thomas, Coward is being used almost as an aside. Clearly what's important at the Studio is the first part of the Stanislavski System, the actor's work on himself, with the subsequent matters of building a character and creating a role seeming to take up comparatively little time. Since the actors' problems take precedence over the intentions of the playwright, every play is treated as being more or less the same as every other play. Shaw and Coward, Odets, Dylan Thomas, and a contemporary play about rape and hysterectomy are responded to as if they're by the same writer writing in the same way about the same kind of people. It isn't the world the writer has created that counts, it's the manipulation of the actor's own inner world that's most important and that, presumably, will lead him into the writer's imaginary circumstances.

It's this last, magical transference, from the actor to the character, from the actor's inner work to its external embodiment, that I didn't see enough of at the Studio. I want to go on record as saying that I believe in the work: the work works. But not for all kinds of plays, certainly not for plays where the rhythm and melody of words demand as much attention as creating a character's psychological reality.

III. Gidget Goes to Verona, or Shakespeare at the Actors Studio

(a) A private moment, and a monologue from *Julius Caesar*

An actor in gym tights prepares as the audience files in from a break. "Jesus Christ!" he keeps muttering. Waving his arms, he releases cries and gasps, ohs and ahs climaxed by a single, piercing yell. Still on break, members turn for a quick look, then go on with their conversations. It's a charming moment, the observers going back to their own reality as the actor continues to prepare himself for the scene. He seems oblivious to the buzz of the crowd as he proceeds from private sounds to sensory work on imaginary objects. He strokes the air, describing circles and rectangles with his hands.

The lights are lowered. Lee Grant, who's moderating today, announces the scene. The actor continues what he has been working on for ten minutes: in the private area where he is focused, there is no difference between lights on or lights off. I feel I'm looking at a private scene that is none of my business, and I suspect that that is exactly how I am supposed to feel. The actor puts on a tape of music (is it Beethoven?) which moves him to wrenching sobs. Gripped by emotion, he stalks about the stage.

The audience is bathed in a stillness that signals total absorption, and perhaps some discomfort as well. There's no telling how truly private the actor will dare to be. Gradually, scattered words and sentences, dimly recognizable as Marc Antony's funeral oration, filter into the chaos the actor has created.

"I wanted to use the exercises I learned from Lee," the actor says, breathing heavily after his workout. "I wanted not to feel silly about attending to imaginary objects. I wanted to keep away from words—I've always had a problem attending to Shakespeare's words—and to focus instead on sensory things. I had a commitment to what I was doing at all times; I allowed myself to trust what would come up to me at the time, and to allow myself to be fed by different emotional memories.

"I wanted to get traces of the scene, but I'm trying not to fulfill the scene, not to fulfill the needs of an audience. I was speaking to the Actors Studio and also I was Marc Antony talking to the assassins. I wanted not to be afraid to speak gibberish. I want to be able to speak the beautiful language, to speak the meter, but not to go to that first, to know I have this support behind me."

"You were in an emotional state to support anything," a member comments approvingly. "You're in a stage of work when you should be fragmented. Even so, I wanted you to say the lines."

"I saw you push yourself beyond where you needed to go," Lee Grant says, "and to connect to the situation in the play through your own emotions. You allowed yourself every place to go, and didn't give a shit what we thought. You stirred up enormous emotion; you became primal. The sounds say a world, say things you can't speak about. But then words break your concentration, and seem to belong to another element. To go from sounds to words is almost a cave experience; civilization enters you through words. You exposed yourself and then transmitted the emotion into language, but you push language that isn't contemporary to a place that's dry. You have to learn that language, like the memory of emotion, has buttons to push you too. Language is *not* an external. You have to learn to use the words as another kind of release."

Lee Grant's trenchant comments summarize a central problem at the Studio, translating emotion into words, learning how to be as turned on by a playwright's words (especially if the playwright isn't a contemporary) as by recalling a powerful image from your own life. The scene today was a perfect illustration of the chasm between feelings and words that seems to be a continuing hurdle at the Studio. When he was recreating a private moment, the actor had size and power—he was riveting. When he channeled that emotion into the scene, even though, as he stated, he wasn't trying to fulfill the scene, even though it was only fragments ripped out of the scene, there was a noticeable drop in temperature. Once he began to transfer the emotional reality he had conjured up from his private moment into the reality of Shakespeare's character and situation, the actor seemed diminished—all his terrific emotional preparation was dissipated right before our eyes.

(b) *The Winter's Tale*, a queen on trial

The scene is announced as being from *The Winter's Tale*, but there's nothing on stage that corresponds to my memory of that late, dark, fantastical Shakespearean romance. The actor playing a Shakespearean king looks and sounds like a refugee from *The Godfather;* the actress playing Hermione, a queen on trial for her life, moves uneasily between a sloppy conversational style and a higher tone of the fruity sort that is particularly suspect at the Studio. When, in a passionate outburst, she screams, words sail past in a blur.

"I haven't done any Shakespeare for six or seven years, not since a teacher of mine called me Gidget goes to Verona," the actress says good-naturedly. "I worked this time to get rid of the Gidget image. I've been doing contemporary comedy with lots of props, and I wanted something different: a queen put to death, a queen whose honor means more to her than her life. I investigated how honor could mean more than life to me, and I thought of one person I would die for," she says, starting to cry.

"Don't tell us," Ellen Burstyn says.

"Five of the judges I was speaking to as Hermione I personalized as five people in show business who have humiliated me. My life has never been threatened, but I was held up once at gunpoint; I used sense memory in relation to being held up."

"I'm not sure that's a right choice for you," Ellen Burstyn says. "Hermione's prepared, after all, she's been in prison for twenty-three days, which is a different kind of threat than a gun in her face. Here, it's a marshalling of all of her intelligence and eloquence to defend her honor. The image I had was: 'You can take my life, but my honor is not available to you.' Use your sureness of your feeling about that person you chose, then speak from the assurance of a queen."

Searching for a new substitution, the actress offers, "I will think of being an actress who prepares to be in front of people." (Her choices are too puny: instead of stretching herself, using her imagination to encompass the play's reality, she disfigures the play so as not to dislodge her own.)

"You don't have to lay in on the words," Burstyn suggests. "Don't direct the words. All the stuff you have now should be relaxed, and go to what works for you: that person you chose. Take that person's face that's potent for you and keep it alive for yourself. Direct your will." Almost as an afterthought, she says, "Do research on what a queen's life is."

To the actor who played the king, Burstyn says, "I heard some real nice tones coming from the chest, but I didn't always know what you were saying.

"How did you feel about condemning your wife to death?" she asks him. "Did you ever condemn somebody? Don't believe it so easily. Don't believe you can go so easily from him to you: transform yourself."

The actor sits on stage in a sullen stupor, rousing himself only enough to say, "I didn't have an opportunity to read the play." (What?)

"I think we should all be working on Shakespeare," Burstyn concludes. "It's time for an American Shakespeare company. Lee felt our internal way of working could bring a whole new value to Shakespeare. We get worried about our accents, but in Shakespeare's day they spoke more like us. Surrender the idea that we don't speak good English."

Burstyn told me that annually she puts on a production of *A Midsummer Night's Dream* in her garden. "Shakespeare should be liberated from the confines of our reverence," she says. "To treat Shakespeare in a literal way is to cheat Shakespeare. He is livelier, deeper, richer, more fun than we think." I like Burstyn's ideas about playing Shakespeare in a lively, vernacular American style, one which makes no attempt to compete with "British" Shakespeare, and the Actors Studio is the logical place where this unbuttoned approach can be explored. But I think many American actors, told for so long that they don't speak well enough to do justice to the language, have come to believe it; certainly the work on Shakespeare that I saw at the Studio avoided speaking the speech, substituting private moments and improvisations as ways of easing into the difficulties. Instead of all these strategies to make the actor feel comfortable, however, why not confront the hurdles of Shakespearean poetry by simply doing the poetry? I saw extravagant preparations for sliding into and sneaking up on the language, but I never once heard an all-out attempt to speak it. I realize that to go directly to the words contradicts Method procedure, but why not try it anyway? Everything the actor and the audience need to know about a character is contained in the words he speaks. As well as expressing the most intense private emotions, language sets the scene, describes the weather and the time of day. Surely if the Studio actor pays the same attention to Shakespeare's words as, in a modern piece, he does to what is *behind* the words, the feelings that he needs in order to fill in and to color the words might be provoked. For impelling the actor's imagination, Shakespeare's language is as good as any affective memory.

An actor I talked to (who wants to remain anonymous) recalled a session where Strasberg tried to help a black actress with strongly ethnic speech in a scene from *Twelfth Night*. "Lee took her far away from Shakespeare; he told her to roll around on the floor, because he said she was too wrapped up in the words, but she wasn't wrapped up enough. He pretended that this was the only way to do it, willfully ignoring the fact that if you can make contact with the music of the lines, if you can just speak the cadence, the appropriate emotion comes to you. I knew he was going about it this way because of his fear of Shakespeare. He was insecure, and so he avoided the language. It was pathetic and totally unhelpful and he knew it. He never simply said that he couldn't deal with Shakespeare, which was really the truth, and this was irresponsible because he was so powerful."

Burstyn's shyness with Shakespeare is thus part of Studio tradition. Her comments, as always, are incisive and her sentences shapely but there were crucial areas about performing Shakespeare that she didn't even begin to address. About the historical and theatrical background of the Elizabethan drama, not a word; nor did she have anything to say about poetry, imagery, meter. I realize that these are literary considerations, and that too much focus on them might make the actor's work too analytical and so take him away from the emotional areas where of course his focus has to be. But surely some attention to these matters is not only appropriate but necessary.

(c) Prince Hal and Falstaff

Today, at last, someone—brash, fearless, forthright, sensible Estelle Parsons—cuts through received Studio notions and prejudices and says what I feel it's necessary to say to Studio actors who stroll casually up to the monumental challenge of acting Shakespeare.

Henry IV, Part One: Prince Hal and Falstaff are having a drink at a tavern. They sing lustily and hoist their beers with gusto, though I'm distracted by a tavern maid who cracks gum. Although the scene has a jarring, modern quality, to have Hal and Falstaff roistering gives energy and fullness. The actors are allowing themselves to have fun with the scene, and the audience acknowledges this with laughter. Once words are introduced, the scene takes a precipitous nosedive from which it never recovers. Prince Hal is played by a handsome and, under more becoming circumstances, quite talented actor with a laidback Southwestern twang. He might have stepped into this English tavern from the best little whorehouse in Texas. The actor who plays Falstaff dips and swerves like a Bowery bum.

When the scene is finished, Estelle jumps in quickly. "I thought you were just saying lines. Whether you like it or not, this guy is a prince," she says to Falstaff, "he's not your friend who goes to Rudy's with you. This guy is going to be king. I didn't see the relationship between Falstaff and Hal—and it's a great relationship—I saw you and your friend, which is silly. You have to pretend he's someone else. Method-act, substitute someone else for him, sensorily create him. Look at your partner and see this other person. You two are very facile together, but this kid is royalty.

"This is not a fourth-wall scene. You can't forget we're out here. You can't do it naturalistically. Research for the scene doesn't lie in hanging around Ninth Avenue, or the Actors Studio. You have to pay attention to style.

"Words come out of emotion in Shakespeare. They come together. *It's in the word in Shakespeare, it's not in the subtext.* Action lies in the word. The character says what he means. You can't behave something and let the words get lost. You both need a lot of work on words. Your emphases and pauses were wrong. Copy out the words without punctuation. State wants. Ask at every rehearsal, what do you want? That's basic. Make specific choices. Take a specific thing each time, even if it's a wrong choice.

"You can work the rest of your life on this scene. That is what great work is all about."

11

THE LANGUAGE OF THE METHOD

As is certainly clear by now, they speak a language of their own at the Studio. It's a private language, tailored for professional insiders; it's a system of verbal talismans, riddled with formulas, passwords, and pet phrases that are repeated again and again, fervently, as if the very saying of them is an open sesame to good acting. ("There's nothing sacred about the words," longtime Studio member Lois Smith says. "It's a mistake when they get made sacred, because then they lose simple communicativeness, which happens at the Studio.")

What follows is a list of the code words I heard most often, arranged under six separate headings that describe a general sequence of how a Studio actor works and what he ultimately wants and does not want from the Method.

1. Words relating to an actor's instrument: talent; problems; colors.
2. Words for getting to work: preparation; relaxation; concentration.
3. Words to describe technical work (mostly internal): private moment; animal exercise; song exercise; affective memory; sensory work; adjustment; personalization; substitution; improvisation; as if; moment to moment; prior life; objects; inner monologue.
4. Words associated with work on the character and the play: tasks; wants; behavior; logic; subtext; given circumstances; choices; action; intention; through-line; spine.
5. Words of praise: truth; freedom; ease; aliveness; naturalness; being specific; spontaneous; conviction; casualness; organic.
6. Words of disapproval: general; mental; indicating; playing for results; memorized; cliché; conventional.

Indicating value or condemnation, describing problems, goals, and procedures, this thumbnail Studio lexicon is the Method actor's arsenal, the tools of his trade. Knowing what lies behind the words is the aim of the Method, and the Studio's reason for being.

Studio actors regularly say that there is no such thing as *a* method or *the* Method, and that putting "the" in front of the word was an invention of journalists. "There is no *the* method, the method is your own; there is no one Method, one comes to one's own through exposure to a lot of people," I was told more than once, the implication being that there are many methods, as many in fact as there are Method actors. "I did the Method before I knew what it was," Ellen Burstyn says, adding, "As Lee always said, Stanislavski didn't invent the Method, he set down what all good actors do." "The acting came first, then 'the Method' followed," says Estelle Parsons.

The resistance to labeling what it does as *the* Method is part of the Studio's protest that its work has been consistently misunderstood and misrepresented, but it also indicates the actors' healthy rejection of the idea that acting can be reduced to a set of rules. *The* Method sounds jarring to most Studio actors, because the use of the definite article makes it sound as if becoming an actor is like acquiring a scientific skill. To call the work *the* Method also sounds arrogant, as if you know some secret recipes for how acting works. Indeed, it's the popular presumption that Studio actors think they know it all that has given them a bad name with some of their non-Method theatrical colleagues.

Of course there can't be any hard-and-fast rules for so intangible and delicate an art as acting. ("The *art* of acting is always a mystery, the art is unteachable," says Ellen Burstyn.) Still, acting as it is practiced at the Studio does conform to some general principles and assumptions—sessions are not free-for-alls in which actors are allowed to try anything in any way they want to. Under Strasberg's vigilant leadership, Studio acting evolved out of a conscious technique, a body of guidelines, advice, maxims, and insights designed to direct the actor to a particular way of thinking about and practicing his craft. "Strasberg's work is a real process, with a logical, well-thought-out structure," says Sabra Jones. "He did what no one else did —it's the reason for his greatness as a teacher; he approached acting with a Germanic Prussian attitude, and sat down to work out a series of closely linked exercises."

"Your presence interferes with the purity of the work," I was informed by the Studio's production stage manager a few weeks after I had been granted the status of professional observer. Although her comment was a threat that held the promise of some dark reprisal, it also made sense to me. I knew that I was on borrowed time at the Studio, and I knew why. First, many Studio members believe that nonparticipants cannot really understand what is going on. "This technique is experiential," Madeleine Thornton-Sherwood told me. "It is impossible to know what it is like to be private in public, unless you do it." "The only way to understand it is to go through it," Ellen Burstyn says. "It took me seven years to be able to apply the work."

Studio members are certainly entitled to work in private, but I don't like the idea that studying acting is for actors only, or that acting is so deeply subtle a process that anyone who isn't an actor could not understand it or even deserve to watch it. I can't see how approaching your craft as though its materials are too sensitive to be apprehended by a sympathetic observer can be very helpful to the working actor.

Yet after I had been attending sessions for a few weeks, I too felt the seduction of the Method. Foolishly, having seen work that outsiders aren't usually allowed to see, and having listened to new, beguiling words and phrases like private moment and affective memory, I began to feel that I was becoming the custodian of some special knowledge. Belief in the work is catching, indeed transforming. Changed in some way during those two hours from eleven to one, I would find myself leaving the Studio in a daze; uplifted by having seen creators creating, I would consciously have to make an "adjustment" as I walked into the light of 44th Street. Heading for the wonderfully ratty Market Diner on Eleventh Avenue, where I would write down my impressions and judgments (and so, in a sense, be violating Studio house rules), I had to tell myself that now it was time to come back to the real world. The elitism that wafts through the Studio—and it exists, even if Studio propaganda sometimes denies it—is a heady elixir which on the one hand gives the actors a sense that they belong to a special community and on the other can fill them with some uppity notions. The atmosphere of the place is so intoxicating that even as an outsider, a visitor on temporary passport, I had glimmerings of both states of mind.

To begin to come to an understanding of what the Method approach to acting is, I think we have to start here with that intimidating phrase, "the purity of the work." "Work" is not for outsiders, the uninitiated, who automatically bring with them the expectations of an audience: "work" is not performance, and it isn't exactly rehearsal or work in progress either. It is instead a laboratory setup where the actor is released from the pressures of performance or the need to fulfill the demands of a text in order to investigate his own being, to locate his problems, and to set his own goals, which may not be those of the playwright, the director, the audience, or even the other performers on stage with him. Work is experimenting, trying out, sifting, measuring, and usually failing.

The respondents, moderators and members alike, have been trained by Lee Strasberg to be expert witnesses, looking below the surface at how an actor is using his tools. Comments are addressed only to what the actor tells you he intended to do: if an actor says he was trying to relax, or to work on heat or cold, or to create the place, or play moment by moment, then his work is scrutinized in those terms only. Strasberg set the tone as well as the substance of responses. Although, as we have seen, he could be feisty and sometimes lethal, and though it was one of his enduring beliefs that work could always be upgraded ("if Duse came to the Studio, we would point out ways in which she could improve"), Strasberg kept the general tone of comments skillfully suspended between support for the actor's attempts and upbeat suggestions for how he or she could do better.

The house, composed primarily of professional actors watching professional actors, is always sympathetic as colleagues share observations rather than make judgments, speaking a language everyone more or less understands. Because the actors know how much courage it takes to expose yourself, the working actor is treated with respect. While comments are often personal in the sense that members know each other, and have seen each other's work over a period of time and so can measure improvement or decline, I never saw any sign of personal likes or dislikes getting in the way.

Because it is homework, and so not intended or supposed to be finished, work often looks blurred, you can't always hear, and (this is an "audience" judgment) the pacing can be slow beyond belief. Evaluated as performance, which is what house rules will not allow members to do, a lot of the work can appear to be incompetent and self-indulgent: a bunch of slow-moving mumblers slouching and scratching. Work isn't supposed to be good or ready to go. Occasionally, when a scene that was finished or nearly so would be sneaked in, the actors were cautioned about the hazards of setting their performances too early. "This is the place to show all the steps," Eli Wallach once told actors whose work smelled of performance. "I don't care if it takes you thirty-five minutes to do a scene that would take only fourteen seconds in production."

I once saw what I thought was a remarkably well-played scene from *Death of a Salesman* where Willy Loman has come to beg his boss, a young squirt, for a new kind of job. Though I had been training myself to look at work as work and not as performance, I couldn't help getting engrossed in the scene on the level of drama rather than technique. The acting was terrific, I couldn't help thinking: intense, quick, rippling with emotions that seemed to be spontaneously generated as I was watching, and layered with small improvised gestures as when the boss grabbed his radio because he was afraid Willy might take it. At the end, I felt like applauding—then I remembered where I was. The comments surprised me: the actor who played the boss was criticized for speaking too loudly and for not showing enough seams, for not exposing homework and preparation. In effect, he was told that to bring in first work on a scene at so polished a level was to deny himself the unique opportunities of being at the Studio.

Work, then, is not for applause or for demonstrating what the actor can do easily and well. It's a deconstruction process, in which the actor examines and lubricates the squeaky parts of his instrument. Work often precedes where an actor would be at a first rehearsal in a professional production.

"If in production, the director tells you to move the glass, and you don't feel it, *move the glass*, don't start sticking up for the Method," Strasberg said. Work is work, he would remind his actors; a performance is something else—the moment the work goes public.

Working in the Studio way, the actor is suspended in an improvising state of mind. Unconcerned with how it looks to the audience, he's in an arena where he's willing to take risks and to act from the inspiration of the moment. The impulses that come up may not be right for the character or the scene, but that doesn't matter as much as the actor being free and loose and discovering what it feels like not to censor himself. Approached sensibly, work can ease an actor into a role by clearing his circuits. I saw one powerful example of how work can open up creativity.

In three separate sessions, I watched a performer dig beneath a scene, going deeper each time until after the third excavation it was clear she was now ready to begin to do the play. The first time she did the scene, a monologue from Gibran's *Jesus, Son of Man,* she was absolutely stationary, leaning her head against what she later told us she had imagined as a marble wall. Dressed in black, she was bathed in an ominous half-light as she spoke in hushed tones with significant though not especially weighty pauses. Members suggested that she needed to find some physical action to help her out of the reverential mold and that she ought to be speaking to a particular character.

Her second draft of the scene was radically different. This time, she was a contemporary woman talking to a friend over a picnic lunch about her feelings for Jesus. She spoke with animation, and she moved ceaselessly about the stage. Members approved of the changes but felt something was still missing because she hadn't created a strong relationship to her partner, and her breathless optimism seemed unfounded. Most people felt she was too tied to the lines.

The third draft proved a relevation. This is what "work" is all about, I thought, seeing how the actress had transformed herself and the material. Sounds, screams, laughter, and groans rose from the stage as the actress rolled around on a blanket. The actress, who is very contained on stage as well as off, had obviously broken through whatever resistance she had previously had. She was letting go, and her energy flooded the stage and washed over onto the observers. Undressing, she offered herself to a man who rejected her. "Fuck you, you son of a bitch!" she shrieked as she began to act out, at a primal level, the pain of sexual rejection, rolling around the stage, screaming, hitting her chest and thighs with tightened fists. She seemed demented. Viewed against her usual reserve, this marked an extraordinary release which indicated a trust not only in herself but in the working process at the Studio: if she stumbled, her colleagues would catch her.

"This is preparation; now you're ready to do the scene," Estelle Parsons, moderating, said. "Maybe you need physical release as a preparation all the time. It is marvelous work. This was a real breakthrough. You're not at the point where you can contain it; you need to let out all this energy first. Now you're more ready than you've ever been to do the scene."

The first time through, the actress had been tied to a mood, the next time to the lines; now, in sound and action, with only marginal attention

to the actual words of the text, she had captured the essence of the character. The actress had begun to find Mary Magdalene deep within her own
feelings. She had used the Studio in precisely the way it was meant to be
used: her three versions of the scene weren't the scene; it was only after
the third try, when she had all but dismantled Gibran's text, that she was
in the proper mood to receive the text, and so to begin to act it. These three
approaches to the scene were a triumphant example of what "work" can
do—now, as Estelle Parsons said, she was ready to start.

"The work can become a monster," said Frank Corsaro, a Studio
revisionist, during a session he was moderating. He reminded members that
the System was devised in a practical context—Stanislavski and his actors
were in class by day and on stage at night, where they applied their studio
discoveries directly to performance. Because the Actors Studio, except for
a brief part of its history, has not been involved in production, the sessions
exist in something of a vacuum, where the work is done for its own sake.
Since it is cut off from practical application—in a sense, from professional
accountability—it can become unprofessional. Work can become silly or
crippling, as if not to do it well is more pure than reaching for a performance
level, as if to hover experimentally on the edges of a scene is better than
to do the scene.

"The mystique that operates here that this isn't a performance is vastly
overdone," Corsaro said. Surely there's some truth to this, for no matter
how rarefied the atmosphere, no matter to what degree the observers can
divest themselves of an audience psychology, and no matter how skillful
the actors are in eluding their obligation to the letter of the text, still they
are actors on a stage, and there are people out front.

The Studio is the place where you can fail, several actors told me. "It's
a place to be bad," says Salem Ludwig. "Somebody said to me once, how
could I be so good on the outside and so bad at the Studio, and I said, 'If
you're bad here, you're not so bad outside.' " "We're supposed to do things
here that we could never do in public; this is the place to risk things you
can't or might not be able to do in a commercial setting," Ellen Burstyn
says, adding, "You can't grow without risk. Falling flat on your face has
no intrinsic value, but here if you do fall you're protected, you're in a safe
place." There were times, though, when I couldn't help feeling that at the
Studio doing a part for which you'd never be cast was a mark of integrity.

"I don't believe the idea around here that you should use the place to do what you can't do," Estelle Parsons says. "I think you should do what you *can* do." Following her own advice, Parsons says, "I did my best work at the Studio. I reached my heights there, and I gauge everything in terms of what I did there."

One way of looking at work is to see it as what the actor does *before* he begins to memorize his lines. It's how he gets underneath the text's words in order to make the play's world real to him. It's what he does to make someone else's words come alive inside him so that they seem to spring organically from his own behavior.

"We don't feel the words are going to do it for you, and so we work from the psychological gesture," says Madeleine Thornton-Sherwood. "Eventually you must get to those words—finally, the author's words are sacrosanct, holy." "To start with the words is to be too literal," says Ellen Burstyn. "The words are the last thing we come to." "The author's lines aren't yours until you make them yours," Eva Marie Saint says.

In Studio work, then, the author's words are less important than what the actor needs to do internally to help himself get to the words. (In the process, the words—the literal text—can take a terrific beating.) The work starts with "what do *you* feel? what do *you* want? before what does the character want? In the early stages, this can be conflicting," Marcia Haufrecht explains. Faced with the job of creating a character, the Studio actor begins with examining himself.

Through a private moment or a sense memory, the actor plucks images from his own life as a way of "feeding" his imagination. Once he's awakened a private emotion, the actor must transfer it to his character, channeling life into art. It's this part of the Studio's inner technique, rerouting a real feeling into a made-up world, that seems to me the trickiest part of the acting process. Imagine how the actor must protect the passage of emotion from one universe to another, ensuring that it undergoes just the right kind of sea change. The affective memory technique can work only if the entire sequence of recall and transference is second nature. "When you train it down, you can do an emotional memory in three or four seconds," Salem Ludwig told me. "In rehearsal, I reinvoke the memory at the beginning of the scene. I leave the play to do this: I'm tuning up the instrument. I start the memory six lines before the cue; with each rehearsal, I need less time; by dress rehearsal, I'm on the cue." (For all the actor-as-instrument metaphor that is standard at the Studio, the actor isn't touching notes on an object, he is doing something more delicate and perishable, he is "playing" feelings.)

Like all inner techniques where actors learn to make use of their own life experiences, the affective memory endows the performer with keen self-awareness. In effect, the technique tells actors that they have rich internal resources, a vast library of memories and impressions that contain the raw materials of theatrical art. "Every human being has a rich inner life, and the inner technique teaches you to train the emotional life, making it accessible," Estelle Parsons says. "We all build an emotional filing cabinet that we learn how to draw on quickly," says Madeleine Thornton-Sherwood. "It becomes like second sight. The work forces you to become aware of *all* your senses—we Americans mostly use our visual sense, and leave out the others."

Inner technique leaves it all up to the actor, who knows better than anyone else what turns on his motor. Trained to bring into rehearsal and performance a whole battery of purely private knowledge, he is monitor, judge, censor, and orchestrator of his own emotional keyboard; suspended over the precipice of his own quivering sensibilities, the Method actor has a heightened self-awareness that is both his potential glory and his potential downfall: a way into, and a possible decline of, his art.

From a controlled use of affective memory can come an eruptive emotionalism that has always been the hallmark of the best Studio acting. Actors who connect to something real and alive in their own past and then know how to direct those feelings into the play can bring to their work a charged intimacy: a sense of playing for real. "It helps you to stay fresh," says Estelle Parsons. "Pumping up something personal prevents you from going stale in a long run." "Actors who don't use this technique are faking it," says Salem Ludwig. "Teachers who reject it are afraid of it; their own personal experiences are too violent."

Hazards are a tortured self-consciousness and a neurotic sense of the actor's need for privacy. Strasberg cautioned actors to use an affective memory only when they were in trouble and only for peak moments in a play. (Echoing Stanislavski, Strasberg often referred to the Method as "notes for the moment of difficulty.") "If you're not reaching a certain point and need a different choice to get there, then you need the Method," says Kim Hunter. "The best is when it's there naturally: Shirley Booth doesn't have to resort to the Method." "You only use the work when you need it; knowing when you don't need it is also part of the craft," says Katherine Cortez.

But when you're exposed week after week to the kind of digging process that goes on during scene and exercise work at the Studio, you can begin to think that all acting must be hard-won. "It isn't always necessary to dig up your guts," Michael Wager says, "though at the Studio there's often a misunderstanding about that." "The exercises, the technique, are a pill to take when the actor is sick, but too often they can become an end in themselves," Sabra Jones feels. "The technique is fascinating, but can destroy the play by promoting the narcissism of the actor at the expense of the playwright. The work really contains a trap, which gets the actor stuck into believing he must do an exercise to explore the life in the scene. He's thinking about how his mother betrayed him at four instead of playing the scene. All the energy gets sucked up into the brain."

At the Studio, the playwright's words are approached sideways or from underneath; it is part of the process of work for the actors to chew them up, replacing them through improvisations where they find their own words, and finding personal analogies for them through emotion and sense memories. The worst thing you can say to a Studio actor is that he is *merely* saying the lines.

Stimulating his own Proustian rushes is one major way a Method actor has of diving beneath the playwright's words. Another important technique with the same goal is working on behavior (Stanislavski called it the method of physical actions, a term never used at the Studio as far as I know, perhaps because it sounds like a translation from a foreign language). Behavior is action: opening and closing doors and windows, washing diapers, chopping carrots, drinking coffee, putting on and taking off a hat, ironing, opening a letter, talking on the phone. Behavior is reacting to heat or cold, to the way clothes feel. It is the physical life of the character: how he holds his body, how he walks, listens, sits down, and gets up. It is what he looks like on the outside—his inner monologue made flesh. Contrary to popular impression, a lot of attention is paid at the Studio to realistic, logical, carefully thought out behavior. (When Strasberg coached Viveca Lindfors and Anne Bancroft in *The Stronger*, remember, he focused more than anything else on how Viveca drank her hot chocolate.)

Body language, gestures, physical reactions to sensory experience, and creating objects like doors and then being careful to walk through them as if they were actually there focus the actor's concentration and take his mind away from how he is going to trap the emotion that he needs for the scene. Paying attention to mundane reality—chopping carrots as if you meant it —grounds the actors. The physical actions that really count at the Studio are the kind that show what's going on inside a character: the slouch or grimace with soulful undertones. From a different angle than affective memory, behavior is a way of being private in public, another route to the *inside* of language and character.

Like affective memory, behavior occurs before the actor gets to dialogue. It is a way of impelling the actor into the script by allowing him to experiment with a parallel script of his own. And like the transfer of emotion involved in affective memory work, the movement from doing to saying can be treacherous. I have seen wonderful behavior at the Studio, where actors seemed to be deep inside the bodies of their characters. I have seen (imaginary) coffee drunk with great conviction, (imaginary) windows opened and closed and looked through with terrific earnestness and consistency. Time after time, scenes would begin with an actor alone on stage doing something real—pacing, smoking, jiggling his feet, twining rope, drinking, slumping—as the physical life of his character was gathering shape. Usually, the actor would be improvising, taking his cue from the play's circumstances as he worked out a detailed physical scenario to help anchor him in the scene. Often, physical business would go on for several minutes before the scene as the playwright wrote it would get under way.

After what was usually a prolonged and convincing sequence of doing things, the first spoken word would often smash the reality the actor had been carefully constructing: the actor's behaving had internal validation while the playwright's words were still an enemy agent, not yet absorbed into the actor's or the character's being.

I think it's significant that the most memorable work I saw at the Studio grew out of private moments, affective memories, and physical actions, where emotions were expressed at a level beyond the need for words.

Before I get to some general conclusions about what Method acting is and is not, I'd like to go outside the Studio for an instructive detour.

"I don't want to see a Method actor ever: give it all to Lee! I want to see actors."

"Stanislavski didn't need that Strasberg insanity. You don't have to be at home in Shakespeare: there's absolutely nothing you can do about Elsinore, sweetheart."

"Strasberg teaches, bring your life onto the stage. All teachers teach the Strasberg way now—Uta [Hagen] too. But on the stage you have to lose your life. You have to find a way out from this sickness that is killing every actor. YOUR LIFE IS ONE-MILLIONTH OF WHAT YOU KNOW. YOUR TALENT IS IN YOUR IMAGINATION: THE REST IS LICE."

These juicy quotes are from Stella Adler, Strasberg's professional archenemy, and a look at Adler's Method will help to place Strasberg's in clearer focus. The rift that developed between these two renowned teachers when Adler began to offer her own classes to Group Theatre members was never settled. Even after his death, Adler has continued to wage battle against the Strasberg Method.

Physically and vocally, Adler is very grand. She's larger than life, a beautiful statuesque blonde with sovereign carriage and impeccable mid-Atlantic diction. (She speaks better than anyone at the Studio.) Strasberg, who did not speak well, was small and squat. While everything about Adler seems to point upward, Strasberg seemed always to be looking down and in. As she moves through the crush of students waiting outside her classroom, Adler grabs the space around her; Strasberg often looked as if he wanted to get lost in the crowd.

Stella is theatrical royalty who instills in her students a sense of the nobility of acting. "As actors we must have dignity," she says. She dares her students to *act*, to lift their bodies and their voices, to be larger than themselves. Strasberg seemed like the prole to her aristocrat, the downtrodden immigrant to her imperious queen. If Adler exhorts her students to stand straight and to talk up, to love language and ideas, Strasberg spent a lifetime trying to cut acting down to the dimensions of real life, encouraging actors toward a hushed, tensed innerness. Where Strasberg wanted acting that didn't look as though it was, Adler says, "The actor's impulse is to want to act, not to be yourself."

"Oh, sweetheart, we don't need your emotion; we need the text," she tells a student, with a wicked smile. "Don't bring it down to the level of the street"; "don't bring it down to your own small selves," she repeats, over and over, deploring the kind of casualness and intimacy that is often in evidence in Studio work. "The intimate tone is the tone you use in life; it's boring, disgusting, like seeing a couple of dogs playing; you think if you're being intimate, you're democratic, which is useless for art, and boring without end. That low tone is for the mice." "Get a stage tone, darling, an energy: *never* go on stage without your motor running." "Get rid of the notion that you're just like everyone else."

Speak up ("your voice is geared toward a cup, and this and that"); sit up straight; stand tall: in her instructions, Adler sometimes seems like a fussy schoolmarm telling students how ladies and gentlemen are supposed to behave; but her corrections are intended to hoist students out of their limiting contemporariness. Mumbling, slovenly posture, and mere averageness of voice and carriage are to Adler indications of a collapsed spirit.

With a passion surely fired by her animosity to Strasberg's ideas, she urges students to explore the given circumstances of the play rather than those of their own private lives. Unlike work at the Studio, where literary values, themes, and styles are virtually never referred to, Adler classes are filled with comments about plays and playwrights. "You must know why you're on the stage, from the author's point of view," she says. "You have to work in the style of the piece." "The ideas are in the words, and you have to fall in love with the words." "A text is there to reveal an author's sense of truth." "You're too involved with your own feelings, and so the words get lost."

She makes no pretense of being a literary critic but instead talks about plays as scripts for actors, and on this level, mining a text for performance clues, she is always provocative and original. One of the trends I found disconcerting at the Studio was the unspoken assumption that every kind of part in every kind of play could be approached in the same way, whereas Adler insists that "there is a difference between classical truth and modern truth" and that (heresy at the Studio!) "the most important thing you can teach actors is to understand plays." For playing Shakespeare and Shaw, her two favorite authors next to her beloved Chekhov, she has one set of instructions; for a modern realist piece, where "the characters are good and mixed up," she has another, urging actors to cue their own style to the play's.

In Shaw, she says, "fall in love with the speeches, and don't try to fill them in too much. I don't want psychological pauses. Shaw understood

Stella Adler at the time of the
Group Theatre.

music and speech for him is aria: he doesn't need a convulsed American
actress. Thinking, which is what Shaw's characters do, does not require
muscle. We use muscle because we are inarticulate. You can't put pause and
inarticulateness into Shaw—it ruins the style. Speak out, that's what Shaw
wants: you are white, British, and articulate."

While Adler is partial to theatre where words alone can carry the actor,
she appreciates a few of the modern realist writers as well. Refreshingly,
she calls realism a style: "It's the biggest style, the hardest form of all. You
have to be an expert, and yet you all go to it first, and it's the thing you
do worst of all. It's not all this piddling business," she says angrily, berating
students whose idea of being realistic is to fuss with props, to slouch, to
talk quietly, to turn their backs to the audience.

"In the modern theatre words are not everything," she admits, with
a trace of reluctance. "The whole aim of the modern theatre is not to act,
but to find the truth of the play within yourself, and to communicate that.
If you play simply for the lines, you're dead; if you do that, try Shakespeare,
where he will carry you. In the modern theatre, place is everything. If the
place doesn't feed you, you can't act in a realistic play." "You have only
the words, you have no place," she says to a student attempting Nora in
A Doll's House. "The snow outside isn't yours, you don't know the life of
the piano in Nora's room."

Echoing Studio doctrine, Stella urges students not to rush to the words even though they may seem so easy and accessible. "You must get beneath the words before you can say them. The text must be in you. You can't borrow the words. It is your job to fill not to empty the words; you have to create and agitate the words. They can only be used if they come out of what you need to say."

On how an actor confronts language in a contemporary realist drama, Adler thus hews to the Studio line. But where Strasberg encouraged actors to enrich the author's words by writing a subtext triggered by emotional and sensory memories, Adler tells students to remain within the place and situation of the play. "Create the place; work with props—a prop will make you act; reach out to your partner; prepare a past for your character—if you don't build a past, you insult the stage and me." "Stanislavski said not to start with the language, start with movement. Acting is action, action is doing: find ways to *do* it, not to say it." Adler's idea is that the actor claims personal possession of the playwright's words not through self-analysis, as at the Studio, but by stepping out of himself, allowing his imagination to take flight from clues the author has planted.

For all the real differences between the two titans of American acting teachers, there are many striking similarities as well. They each started to think seriously about acting at about the same time and in the same place, as students of Richard Boleslavski at the American Laboratory Theatre. (Stella says, "Strasberg and Clurman attended Boleslavski's lectures, but I was the only one who actually was a student of his.") As original members of the Group Theatre, they shared some of the same ideals about good acting and good theatre. Temperamentally, too, they had more in common than either of them would ever admit. What they have to say may differ, but both have an evangelical style and a talent for saying things in memorable ways. Their students delight in quoting their pungent phrases and catchwords, their gnomic tag lines and ex cathedra pronouncements. Speaking a language of their own, compounded of earthy Yiddish folk wisdom and theatrical toughness spiced with Stanislavski, they're both wickedly witty, aiming for the verbal kill. Strasberg never coached a successor because he felt no one could replace him; and when she was asked recently who would continue in her footsteps after she was gone, Stella answered, "No one."

Although both started as actors, they spent more time offstage than on. When he appeared in *The Godfather*, Strasberg hadn't acted since 1931;

Adler hasn't appeared in New York since 1945, and her last performance was in 1960, in a London production of *Oh Dad, Poor Dad, Mama's Hung You in the Closet and I'm Feeling So Sad.* For both, teaching acting was a form of acting, a way to release their own acting impulses. In front of a class, both had showmanship. "Lee loved to perform," says Marcia Haufrecht. "His style was underplayed, but he could be extroverted too. He was a great comedian. And he had a flamboyance like Clurman's." Week after week at her scene study class Adler continues to give what are surely some of the most energetic performances in New York. Her students treat her like a diva, applauding her at the beginning and end of each class. For two hours, sharing personal anecdotes, theatrical reminiscences, and bits of philosophy (she teaches her students about life as well as acting: "You have to have a daily way of enriching yourself," she says), getting up from her thronelike chair to show how an action should be played, raising her voice to a bellow to bring home a point, running her hands through her hair, and demanding a response from the class (she is greeted with a more or less continuous chorus of "yesses"), she never stops radiating: the acting teacher as bravura actress.

If Strasberg was the remote Jewish father, withholding approval behind a stolid mask, Adler is the domineering Jewish mother, forever tisking and scolding. Stella certainly seems the warmer and more approachable parent, though her comments can be harsher. Strasberg always allowed actors to finish before he responded, and he almost always found something encouraging to say about the work; Stella, who does not suffer fools gladly, often stops students after only a minute or two. "You're a dear, sweet boy, but you can't play this part; it isn't in you"; "No, no, sweetheart, you can't do it this way."

"Jesus Christ, you've got no talent: nothing affects you!" she yelled at one actress struggling her way through a Shakespearean monologue. To another woman with a sloppy contemporary style, she said, "You have no diction, no depth, no deportment: so what are they going to do with you?" "Everything is Hoboken to you!" she leveled at a young actor affecting the casual style she loathes. (Outside her studio is a sign: "Stella wants everyone to know that criticism in the theatre is not personal. Nothing in the theatre is personal.")

The Actors Studio is for professional actors; Adler's conservatory is for students, some of them markedly unprepared, and the bitterness she occasionally unleashes indicates impatience with how far her students are from her own high standards. Her anger comes also, I think, from her feeling that she is fighting an uphill and solitary and probably losing battle against the invasion of "the street" onto "the platform." "You won't see any more great acting, at least not in your lifetimes," she says. For her, the great theatre is the theatre of the past, the kind of theatre that her father ran, and that her husband, Harold Clurman, attempted to build with the Group experiment: a theatre that teaches the audience "how to survive by making it understand something about Man." Her kind of theatre is one dedicated to revealing the intentions and the truths of the great writers. "There's nothing more important than Shakespeare: he's God, darling!"

Stella is waging a gallant fight, one for which she is uniquely equipped. But she knows at heart, and her students know, that there is more work for actors who can mouth soap opera banalities than for ones who can do justice to Shakespearean poetry or Shavian wit. "Nobody wants us any more because we don't speak well," she tells students threateningly; but do they believe her, when they see actors on television earning fortunes by sounding like truck-stop waitresses and stevedores?

When the Method was first adapted as a conscious technique in the Group it challenged the artificial, standardized acting—the acting that looked like acting—that afflicted the commercial theatre. Then as now the Method's enemy is acting by rote, the kind of acting that at the Studio is often referred to as the "British school." To gauge the American flavor of the Method, I think it will help to take a quick look at attitudes toward its opposite number.

"In the American style, you have to create a great deal within you to say the words; in the English style, you just say the words. The English don't bother with the emotion; it sounds nice, but it's not too good," says Stella Adler.

"The English theatre is certainly skillful, as in a cemetery," Lee Strasberg said. "Everything is so beautifully engraved, but you're willing to let it rest. The English style is outdated. It is *acting*, it is not humanity or reality. I love the theatre environment in London, but I don't like the theatre."

"They always speak Shakespeare beautifully, with wonderful articulation—and you couldn't care less," Carroll O'Connor said at a Studio session I observed.

"I'm never taken by surprise in the British theatre, not even by Olivier," Arthur Penn says.

"I saw Laurence Olivier do *On the Harmfulness of Tobacco*," director Martin Fried reported, "and I'm sure that if I saw it again, he would do it in exactly the same way."

Estelle Parsons goes farther. "Olivier could use a little Method—he's terribly technical."

John Strasberg disapproves of the Studio's British bias. "It's all so silly and self-defeating," he says. "The British are the best storytellers in the world. What they do they do better than anyone else."

The Studio's notion of traditional British acting, then, is that it is well-spoken, external, cultivated, and manicured, like a well-tended English garden; that it is set and rigid, with no room for the adjustments and improvisations that the Studio actor prizes; and that, as a result of its meticulous attention to form, it leaves you cold. At the Studio, British acting seems just that: acting—behavior that has been trimmed and arranged for public display.

Against British poise the Studio espouses countervalues, in which British formality is answered by American spontaneity, British reserve is smashed by American intensity. Militantly anti-classical, the Studio style is rough-and-ready, instinctive, improvisatory, proletarian, physically active, and defiantly emotional. Although it is not true that all Studio actors mumble or speak poorly, it is true that they are not encouraged to speak well: to speak like declaiming British actors. Strasberg gave lip service to the necessity for work on voice and projection, but his covert message was that too much attention to external matters would not be good for the actor's soul.

Set up to smash theatrical tradition, the Studio now sits on a long and distinguished (and occasionally notorious) tradition of its own. For over thirty-five years, as it has dedicated itself to exploring ways to help actors be "real," the Studio has come to stand for a certain kind of acting style, a hyper-intense American realism. "Studio work has genuinely spread out to the theatrical community—to the world,[3]" says Arthur Penn. "It's the accepted technique of American acting." The style the Studio studies is a roomy one and of perennial value, but like any style it is susceptible to a creeping conventionalism: "doing it the Studio way" can interfere with an actor's development.

At the end of one session I observed, an actor said that when he was at the Studio he felt he was expected to act in a particular way. I think there's an insidious truth in that. Members are keenly aware of Studio tradition; they carry with them, the way outsiders do, an idea that the Studio "produced" Marlon Brando and James Dean. ("Do you think Marlon Brando used this urinal?" I heard someone say in the men's room during a session break.) Estelle Parsons says "No particular kind of actor comes from the Studio, except all the actors have to use themselves totally; if they can't, they need therapy." Still, if you're a young actor at the Studio, you act rather like Marlon Brando circa *On the Waterfront.* Studio work is saturated with actors who scratch, look nervously off to the side, value casualness and working-class sexiness, and react to heat and cold with magnified sensitivities so that they won't be like scrubbed British actors whose training shows but who (apparently) feel nothing.

Not to act (in a particular way) continues to charm Studio actors, a notion that can lead to a mannerist style, an entire battery of verbal and physical hesitancy that's Studio shorthand for neurotic agitation. The cult of being real, which floods the place, can encourage vehement displays of *hiding* craft. ("Craft, a word to treasure, was a dirty word at the Studio," says June Havoc.)

Many Studio members argue against the popular notion that the Method simply invites the actor to show off his own pumped-up tics and eccentricities at the expense of playing his character. "The Method is not playing yourself—that's one of the misunderstandings people have about the Studio," Eva Marie Saint says. "The Method helps you to observe, to see life, to look outside yourself. For instance, as I get older, my mother, now eighty-seven, is in much of my work: that's using the Method." "The Method is a way to get away from myself: to bring all of myself to the character," Estelle Parsons says. "The Method is all internal work *on the character,*" explains Ellen Burstyn.

But I was sometimes bothered that the distance between the actor and the character—the inevitable gap between simply being and giving a performance—was not clarified, as if to be yourself in a believable way was enough. Knowing how to relax in front of an audience is an important part of the acting process; but at the Studio, it seemed to me that the actor would often stop at a point where he was loose enough to be able to uncover his own wounds and blemishes. When it's arrested there, the process can become one where the *actor's* insides are revealed rather than the character's. "In the seventies, the Studio became a dying organization devoted to neurotic exercises in self-revelation that led away from the craft of acting that Lee had originally created," Sabra Jones says. "Lee knew it was happening, and he was enraged."

Sabra and her husband, John Strasberg, who felt confined by Strasberg's regard for honoring the actor's own emotional history, broke from the Studio and the Institute to start teaching on their own. In August 1979 they opened their own school, the Real Stage, and in December 1983 they founded an ambitious repertory company called the Mirror Theatre. "Our work is oriented to the expression of life within the form of the play," John Strasberg says. "My father's work dealt almost exclusively with the expression of feeling. That's not the same as creating life on the stage. He was incapable of expressing his own feelings, so he always reverted to that in his work. He simply couldn't express himself on deep levels except in his work. Some actors will tell you he could, that he was a warm man: I know he wasn't. He would tell actors, 'Express yourself, forget about the story.' He thought it was important to develop going with impulses and self-knowledge, and he fell short in interpretation. He got lost in the need for people to express themselves, because it was *his* need; he never resolved his own problem. He knew better, but he didn't say it enough publicly: the play is your best friend. American actors tend to have an anti-literary bias, and it's Lee's fault.

"He said art is for the individual to express his view of life—but art has to have form. The individual's need for self-expression: that's what everyone loves about America. And that's why the Studio fails.

"Life at its best is always spontaneous: good acting is to be spontaneous within the form of the play, to learn to rely on your knowledge of the play. A play has a structure, like music, and that structure has to be followed. It's only in the theatre that people think that knowing a lot can inhibit you. That's an attitude that comes from the Studio, and from my father."

"We felt Lee had got stuck on one thing, the expression of feeling," Sabra Jones says. "So we branched out at our school, where we want to combine the best of English and American training. (I guess we are reactionary, in a sense.) We have courses in fencing, speech, music, voice. Lee thought voice was an accessory, an adjunct class. John's great gift is for synthesizing; we feel the best theatre has always combined feeling with form, form freshly interpreted each time out. Lee had separated them, emphasizing feeling at the expense of form.

"When we founded the Real Stage, Lee took it very badly, as a total insult and unbelievable betrayal. Encouraged by Anna, he wouldn't talk to John or me, wouldn't let us in his house. Yet it was not a rebellious act on John's part; we were trying to provide an absolute truth. Because Lee was so powerful and famous, nobody studied voice and speech for twenty-five years; everybody was busy analyzing himself, and dredging up emotions. We're trying to correct that."

Used rather than abused and applied with conscious control, as Strasberg insisted it had to be, the Method is an inescapable technique for illuminating modern realistic plays. With the Method's process of self-investigation, the actor can create characters with ripe, complex inner lives that bathe words and actions; far from being anti-verbal, the Method, used well, adds dimension to dialogue. "The Method works for everything," Geraldine Page says. "This work fills the text—any text," says Ellen Burstyn. "Every play has a subtext, just as every character is more than what he or she says. And whether you're doing verse or realistic dialogue, you work on the humanity of the character."

Though I have yet to see a Studio actor (or, for that matter, an American actor) shine in Shakespeare or Coward or Shaw, Sophocles or Congreve or Molière, I have seen many Studio actors unleash lightning flashes in plays by Williams, Miller, Inge, Chekhov, and in realistic movies. The Method is the ideal technique for giving life to stories about our mixed-up American contemporaries. "Shakespeare, Molière, Congreve—the European classics—are not part of our tradition," Ellen Burstyn points out. "We don't come from a tradition of rhetoric the way the British do. Though I believe our work prepares the actor for all kinds of plays, it's true that at the Studio we excel in American theatre: we are the leaders of the *American* style."

As a quick summary of what's good and not so good about the Method, I like Arthur Penn's comments: "The Method gives acting a truth, an honesty, a sense of a character's inner life, all radiating from the actor's genuinely personal core; its pitfalls are self-absorption at the expense of the play and a lack of preparation of other areas of the instrument."

12

AUDITIONS, ACTIVITIES, FINANCING

A ny actor over eighteen can audition for membership in the Actors Studio. Although the Studio secretary is allowed to discourage obvious crackpots, "most people know that the Studio is for professional actors not for beginners, and so beginners usually will not audition here until they have had training," says Mary Mercier at Actors Studio West. Auditions are held once a month during the season. (Presently, actors must sign up approximately six months in advance.) There are a few rules for auditioners: no monologues, no Shakespeare, no scene longer than five minutes. On the first day of the month the actors signed up for that month (thirty actors is the usual limit) call the secretary to find out what day the auditions are scheduled for; and on that day, the applicants call to find out what time that evening, between six and eleven, they are to perform their scene. In order to be properly relaxed, auditioners are encouraged to arrive at the Studio an hour before their time. Then, pair by pair—the actor who is auditioning and the partner the actor brought along—they are called upstairs to the theatre where three judges are waiting.

"Their way of doing it is so anonymous," Redvers Jean-Marie, an actor who auditioned in November 1982, told me. "It was indistinguishable from any other audition I've ever been to. I got an impersonal form letter telling me that 'we are unable to pass you. You are of course eligible to audition one year from this month.' I would have preferred a personal letter; I would have appreciated *anything* of a personal nature: what I need to work on. They are irresponsible to their auditioners. And because of what they represent, it is more destructive when they do it."

"It's a terrifying experience," says Ted Zurkowski, a successful auditioner. "I failed eleven times," Estelle Parsons admits. "Each time I froze —I've never been so scared as at my auditions for the Studio." One of the Studio legends is that Geraldine Page auditioned seventeen times—the number grows each time the story is told. But Page, who laughed when I reported this rumor to her, says she never actually auditioned. "I was too scared to, I didn't want to be rejected by a group that I so much wanted to be a part of. I partnered people who were auditioning, and after the fifth time—it was a scene from *Awake and Sing!,* with Shelley Berman, who's a wonderful actor—they asked me to become a member."

It's rare when more than a few people from each preliminary audition are invited to the finals; in many months, no one makes it to the finals. "After decades of looking at actors, I can spot talent in a minute," Cheryl Crawford says. "I look for a unique, special energy," Arthur Penn says. "And people who have a certain commercial viability." Strasberg said he was looking for the kind of talent that could profit from working at the Studio, which meant that he wouldn't always choose the most technically accomplished or professional candidates. The judges say they're looking for actors with originality whose work is free of clichés, but it's my hunch that they're most impressed by actors who fit into the mold the Studio has itself fashioned: actors who already have the Studio stamp.

The finals were traditionally judged by Lee Strasberg, Elia Kazan, and Arthur Penn (Cheryl Crawford, in the early days) with John Stix holding the clock. For this annual ritual, the membership at large is invited, and now there may be as many as seventy-five people in the house. Usually, the actor who has made it to the finals is asked to bring back the same material; sometimes he is asked to change his partner; less frequently, he is asked to bring in some other piece.

Those who pass are called that night ("as an act of kindness," says Janet Doeden, a former Studio secretary); the others receive a letter encouraging them to try again. The voting takes place at eleven and the lucky actors are called by the secretary after midnight, sometimes as late as one or two in the morning. Ted Zurkowski remembers that the night of his final was bitterly cold. After his scene he went home exhausted and certain that he hadn't passed. So he went to sleep. Several hours later, he was awakened by a call from Janet Doeden, who said, ritualistically, in a code that he understood, "Come in Friday, Lee wants to meet you." After hanging up,

Ted released a cry of joy that ripped through his still, cold apartment: he was now and forever a member of the Actors Studio.[1]

Since its founding, the Acting Unit sessions have been the core of the Studio, but over the years other kinds of activities have been offered. In the fifties, there were classes in speech, movement, and fencing, and periodically there have been Units for directors and playwrights. Since the late sixties, there has been a series of open house staged readings and full productions, and in the late seventies a Playwrights Lab was in residence. Under Strasberg's leadership, the Studio devised a way of working for actors that has had an enduring and widespread influence; reasonably enough, the Studio has not had a similar success with its playwriting and directing workshops. (In the sixties, the two units merged into a single body, the P/D Unit.) "The actors are the heart of the Studio; the others come and go," says June Havoc.

Because of its reputation, the Studio has always been able to attract prominent writers and critics to its playwriting labs, and at various times in its sporadic existence William Inge, Edward Albee, Elia and Molly Kazan, Harold Clurman, Arthur Penn, Arthur Kopit, Jack Gelber, Jack Richardson, Frederick Knott, Clifford Odets, and Robert Anderson have moderated the playwriting sessions. Among the plays developed in the Unit were Albee's *Zoo Story*, Michael Gazzo's *Hatful of Rain*, and Tennessee Williams's *Night of the Iguana;* but it must be said that the Studio has not produced a body of significant American drama. Perhaps the only play that might never have been written except for the Studio was *A Hatful of Rain*, which was developed, piecemeal and through improvisation, on the premises—it's the only play that the Method directly gave birth to.

The Studio's weak literary record is no reflection on its achievement: the Studio was never intended to serve the playwright. And, furthermore, can writing be addressed within the kind of group forum that works so well for actors? The actor dares not create in isolation, while the writing of plays can never be a collaborative process. Although writers have to know about structure, character development, and dialogue, writing surely can never have a method the way acting can, and therefore the kind of group investigation that goes on in acting sessions is not automatically transferrable to a group of writers.

In addition, writers were never made to feel a part of the Studio. They were not members, and their presence was always somewhat resented. Meade Roberts, who was a member of the first Playwrights Unit, run by Robert Anderson in 1955, recalls that it was "divorced from the main body of the Studio. The idea was that ultimately we would create projects that would be brought to the Acting Unit. But that kind of exchange never really happened. 1955 was a good year for the Studio: that was the year *Hatful of Rain* opened. But the Studio didn't go on to provoke a whole body of plays. Why not? Well, there wasn't a cry for Actors Studio productions partly because when *End as a Man,* which also was developed at the Studio, moved uptown, it died: it was too 'off-Broadway' for uptown, and perhaps commercial producers thought that anything that emerged from the Studio was ipso factor 'off-Broadway.' But more crucially—and closer to home—there was Strasberg. His feelings about the Playwrights Unit, at best, were ambiguous. He wanted to control all the units, and the literary area was simply not an area where he was strong at all. He really resented us being there. I remember a symbolic moment in one of the acting sessions. An actress was working on heat and cold in *Macbeth;* she mumbled. Strasberg said, 'Fine, fine, darling, words come later, after costumes and lights and so forth.' One of the writers from our unit spoke up then, and asked, incredulously, 'With Shakespeare?' and Lee threw us out of the acting unit."

Roberts remembers that Strasberg's phrase "the actor is his own instrument" made him nervous, because it implied that "the actor is a *creator* more than an *interpreter.* The actor's instrument, after all, is to transmit notes on paper. A method is not an end, it is a means to a dramatic truth. I think too often at the Studio exercises are confused with playing the scene. You have to find the core of the play as the author had conceived it, not in the actor's intention."

What can the writer learn from watching an actor's creative process? How might it help the actor to know something of how a writer creates characters? Can a knowledge of the Method inspire a writer to think in dramatic terms, and to create richly actable characters? The Studio, surely, is just the place to explore these questions, but it hasn't because it has never quite shaken the idea that actor and writer occupy separate tables. The suspicion of the text that haunts the Studio added to the high value placed on the actor's right to work in private made writers seem like intruders.[2]

In the late seventies, Harold Clurman turned the Playwrights Unit into a lively open forum. Once a week, he would talk about playwriting to an audience of more than one hundred rapt listeners. Strasberg was not pleased.

But the idea that there is a place for the writer at the Studio is still alive. In 1982–83, a new P/D Unit was run by Elia Kazan, Arthur Penn, and Joseph L. Mankiewicz. Unlike actors, writers and directors have never auditioned for space at the Studio, they are invited: the three directors asked about forty people whose work interested them to join their group. The sessions, held on Mondays from four to seven, were open to Studio members, though only members of the Unit were allowed to comment on the work. As it turned out, the sessions were concerned more with writing than directing (one director told me that the directors felt underused). The general format was to have a play read, usually by Studio actors; sometimes it was a directed reading, sometimes an act of a new play was performed, sometimes a writer brought in one act and said he didn't know where to

"You don't write from your soul! You write from yesterday's hit!" Harold Clurman tells a Playwrights Unit in 1979.

© SYEUS MOTTEL

go with the material. After the work was presented, one of the three moderators would open the discussion, asking the writer about what he had tried to do, and what did he want from the house? Following discussion ("toward the end of the season, it got too polite," I was told), the moderator summarized. Each week, the session drew full houses. New plays by John Hopkins (with Shirley Knight) and by an as yet unknown writer named Bonnie Walsh ("What a playwright! Remember her name!") were particularly well-received.

The new unit has expert guidance. "As a teacher of playwrights, Kazan is exciting, forceful, dynamic, brilliant," Meade Roberts says. "He generates such excitement that you go running home to the typewriter." Arthur Penn's quiet intellect is a fine balance to Kazan's straight-from-the-hip style; and with his reputation for making movies with literate characters, Mankiewicz is also well placed in a writer's symposium. Furthermore, Strasberg can no longer run interference through jealousy or suspicion of writers, so it may be at long last that the writer will have a real base at the Studio.

For those who follow the Method, directors are on the other side, to be linked with writers as a potential threat to creative autonomy. Historically, therefore, within the Studio the director has fared little better than the playwright. Like writers, directors had to be invited in, and once there were rarely more than honorary guests on temporary visa. Over the years directors were called in because Strasberg (or Kazan or Penn) was familiar with their work and interested in it; unlike actors, who are admitted for life, directors had to be asked back, and so had to keep proving themselves. Because the Studio never made a full commitment to the directors, most of the directors didn't make a full commitment to the Studio. Attendance was casual, anywhere from five to seventy-five or one hundred directors in any one session.

"It was always a mystery as to how people were selected," recalls Syeus Mottel, who lasted longer in the Directors Unit than anyone else, from its inception in 1959 to the mid-seventies (with periodic intermissions when the Unit was disbanded). "I was there because I had taken a course in directing with Lee at the American Theatre Wing in 1954. At the end of the course he suggested I apply to the Studio. But I found out you had to audition as an actor. When they formed a unit for directors, in early 1959, Lee asked me to join."

Directors Units lasted longer than those for writers because Strasberg, who was a director but not a playwright, was around to run them. "Lee never delegated authority," Syeus Mottel says. "Sometimes he just wasn't there." A typical session was conducted much like the Acting Unit, this time with focus on the director's problems. A scene might last from five to thirty minutes, after which the director would explain his intentions; then there would be open discussion. (Sessions were open to the general membership and occasionally to observers, who were asked not to comment.) Mottel recalls that Strasberg usually did not participate in the open discussion, though he would sometimes get into "passionate battle about something blatant, an audacious comment or misstatement." Occasionally he would redirect the actors to make a point, but his remarks were for the most part "philosophic rather than didactic. He would usually sail off on his own insights rather than address points already made. His statements would be filled with theatrical lore and anecdote; sometimes what he talked about had nothing to do with the scene.

"A lot of people used the Unit as a tryout for new material. Quite often Lee would not want to talk about the play: 'That's for the Playwrights Unit,' he would say. Some directors kept bringing the same work back again and again, particularly if they were working on a new play, hoping that Lee would give them the magical cue for Broadway success; he never did."

While there is a surprising range of material brought in to the Acting Unit, "most people tried to play safe in the Directors Unit," Mottel says. "There was a lot of Williams and Inge, the classic fifties and sixties slice-of-life school. There was practically no Shakespeare, very few classics, and few comedies: it was mostly heavy drama, because that's probably what most of the directors thought they should be working on at the Studio."

"Strasberg was a marvelous theorist and teacher, but a shaky director," says Frank Corsaro. "I watched Harold Clurman directing, and he described characters beautifully. But he didn't know where to start when it came to work, giving the play a shape and form. In his own way, Lee was very much like that. He and Clurman had what I call immigrant fear. As a director, Strasberg held back on himself—he was like a badger. But Strasberg and Clurman created Kazan: he could do it; he was not afraid. He was like a primal creature." If Strasberg was possessive about running the Directors Unit, Kazan was the director everyone at the Studio looked up to. "Kazan is the greatest director I know of, the greatest director I've ever seen work," says Arthur Penn.

Kazan knew how to coax greatness out of actors, and Kazan's style became the inspiration for Studio directors, the way Marlon Brando's work became a model for Studio actors. Subtly and pervasively, Kazan's methods influenced the directors—Penn, Corsaro, Delbert Mann, Martin Ritt, Sydney Pollack, Mark Rydell, Jack Garfein—who came within the Studio's sphere. But the Studio didn't shape the sensibility of a generation of directors the way it did that of actors: if it has never been a school for actors, the Studio has certainly never been a director's conservatory. It has simply offered a weekly workshop on a sporadic and unsystematic basis where directors have been exposed to Method language and technique.

In the fifties the Studio occasionally supplemented its free-form sessions with classes in external technique. The one that was most popular and lasted longest was Alice Hermes's speech class, the goal of which was to teach actors how to speak pure general American. The first year Hermes taught on Tuesdays and Fridays, following the acting sessions; for the next three years, she came once a week only, on Fridays.

"It felt good to be at the Studio," Alice Hermes says now, though at the time there were frustrations: arguments over money, Strasberg's rudeness, and irregular attendance, with students working at different levels of accomplishment. "I never knew who was going to show up. Like everything else at the Studio, it was all rather casual. Gerry Page came for three months, and then she just disappeared. There was a great range in the class, from people who spoke well like Gerry to people who could hardly speak at all. More and more of the foreign observers came, and I think the American actors began to feel they'd be left behind. Lots of people were too shy to turn up, and when they got famous, it was as if they couldn't show up. Gerry never felt that way, certainly, and neither did Shelley Winters or Estelle Parsons, who studied with me privately."

Alice Hermes, who speaks beautifully—in a way that is referred to as English or "upper-class American"—feels that her class balanced Strasberg's sessions, where "there was no emphasis on speech at all. I do drill work, which is useful not only for actors but for anyone who has to speak. My course takes a long time. I begin with the sound 'a' in 'cat.' In ninety-minute sessions, I give examples, then ask students to imitate. It amounts to a kind of ear training. After a long while, students would get to sentences. We wouldn't get to an actual text for years, and when we did do reading —we read some Shakespeare sonnets, for example—it would be for speech values, not for interpretation."

During her four years at the Studio, Hermes went regularly to the acting sessions "to see what was going on. Of course, when they get to a scene, actors have to forget they are working on speech." She recalls that there were many complaints from observers who could not hear the actors, "but three-fourths of the members of the Studio had the best speech on the American stage. People who talk about the mumbling don't know anything about the Studio. The reputation is based on Stanley Kowalski and the fact that lots of the actors were just slobs. Some had no money, some came out of the army, though many of the slobs may have spoken well. Brando, by the way, mumbled only when appropriate. He was in my first class, at the Piscator Workshop in the forties. He read something, and I said you are a Midwesterner. He said he was from India: how far back he was delighted with the exotic! He also did a little private work with me in the fifties. He respected the work, and oh, he was tremendously observant."

Hermes sees no correlation between speaking well and being a good actor. "Eli Wallach speaks badly, and he's a marvelous actor. Shelley Winters speaks badly—she has lower-class Midwest speech—and she came to me to learn to speak well for a play, *Girls of Summer,* in which she played a woman of education and taste. She spoke beautifully then.

"American theatre hasn't demanded good speech, so actors put that in the back of their minds. I'm afraid nobody really cares about it very much," she sighs, "and many actors in fact worry about what's going to happen to their personalities if their speech gets improved. Of course, with a bad New York accent, you can play a character with a bad New York accent."

That the Studio hired a speech teacher—the best one in the field, a teacher for whom properly formed English sounds are as important as emotionally truthful acting was to Strasberg—underlines the fact that Strasberg never denied the importance of external technique; he merely felt it was less significant than inner work, and that there were other places where actors could go to receive this kind of training. Understandably, making room at the Studio for "the other side" never took hold, and for the Studio to have offered a full roster of classes in addition to speech would have turned it into something it was never intended to be.

After the departure of Alice Hermes, the Studio did not continue to offer classes in speech. Apart from the regular acting sessions, and the less regular meetings of the P/D Unit, the facilities are now used for rehearsals of scenes or for the staged readings and projects that have become customary since the late sixties. The projects are presented on a strictly workshop basis. "We're definitely not interested in critics or in having any press coverage; we don't have our eye on Broadway," says Jann Tarrant, until December 1982 the Studio's production stage manner. "We are offering the productions as work in progress. We're not offering any final work—the script may change during production."

Theoretically, projects are open to the public but the public is hardly encouraged to come. There is no publicity about what's playing at the Studio. There is a mailing list, but I have never received a mailing, although I listed my name on six separate occasions. Like everything else at the Studio, then, the projects are not really for outsiders. They are extensions of the acting sessions to the degree that the work is meant to be exploratory and unfinished.

Like many things at the Studio, how projects are developed is something of a mystery. "Nobody knows how they got there," a new member says. But Jann Tarrant says there *is* a method to the apparent madness. "Someone—it can be any member, or a member of the P/D Unit who might not technically be a member of the Studio—will submit a script to the reading committee. Scripts are usually original, though we do some revivals. If they pass on it, there will be a staged reading. If that goes well, or at least looks promising, the Board decides on whether or not to give it a production. If they pass, it then comes to me, and I supervise the production according to the showcase code."

There is a rule of casting 50 percent of all projects with Studio members. "Ideally, all projects should be cast from within the Studio," Jann Tarrant says, "but realistically it just can't be done that way. We're not a repertory company, and we sometimes have requirements that members can't fill. Last year, for instance, we needed a midget, and now [February 1982] we have two fifteen-year-olds [the parts were cast with Lee Strasberg's two young sons]. But we definitely encourage our members to work here."

Some of the members, particularly the newer ones, resent the 50 percent casting rule. "Why aren't Studio people cast in projects at the Studio?" they ask. "If a play is written, directed, and cast with at least half outsiders, how can it fairly represent the work of the Studio?" Members complain also that the limited Studio space is taken up by outsiders working on a project that has no clear-cut connection to the Studio.

Inside the Studio it was well known that Strasberg wasn't pleased with the projects, because their small scale was a reminder of the failure of the large-scale Actors Studio Theatre. "Why do we have the projects? I'll tell you," the late Carl Schaeffer, the Studio's treasurer, said. "I pushed them to keep the place active, to keep the ball rolling, at a time when Strasberg had begun to move away from the Studio. I had to stimulate interest among the members now that Strasberg's attention was elsewhere. And I had to have something to show my Board of Trustees. If they were going to give money to the place, they had to see some sign of activity."

The projects, clearly, are a compromise. Nobody is really pleased with them; nobody believes they represent the kind of work Studio actors are capable of. And yet they continue as both a stopgap measure, a sign that the Studio is still alive and kicking, and, as one new member told me, "an implied carrot, that maybe the Studio through these penny-ante projects is gearing up toward big-time production again."[3]

In the 1982–83 season, the Studio's first year without Strasberg, there were no projects at all. "There were no public projects this year because the thrust has been to get back to the basics of the work," Mathew Anden says. "We realized that most actors don't know the work. We've had to go slow this year. Also, Ellen [Burstyn] wants to have a repertory company, and that will take one or two more years in the planning stages."

Two projects were nearly launched, though, one that fell through because members were enraged when Harvey Keitel hired an outside casting director; and another, with Arthur Penn directing Estelle Parsons in a one-woman show, *Adulto Orgasmo Escapes from the Zoo*, that collapsed over "artistic differences." One project did get on, for members only and for select producers: a new play based on the Clytemnestra legend, written and directed by Elia Kazan and cast entirely with Studio actors. (In November 1983, this production opened at the Hartman theatre in Stamford, Connecticut, to strongly negative critical and audience reaction.) In March 1984 the Studio presented an ambitious project (a cast of forty!)—*Cabal of Hypocrites* by the Soviet dissident Mikhail Bulgakov.

Its small size, its modest facilities, its limited number of activities, its avoidance of classes, its semisecret projects—all these are emblematic of the Studio's nonprofit status. Aside from its short-lived Theatre and "going public" in a minor way with its open house projects, the Studio has spread its wings only once, when it established a West Coast branch.

"After the debacle of *Three Sisters* in London in 1965, they were going to put the padlock on the Studio. I thought it was a good time to do something on the West Coast," recalls Jack Garfein, who was instrumental in organizing the Studio's Los Angeles home. "I was determined to start a Studio in the spirit of the late forties and fifties. I remember talking to Paul Newman, who said that something had been lost at the Studio in New York, that it was no longer a haven and that being there was like being on Broadway. It was to rediscover the *original* spirit of the Studio that we dedicated ourselves.

"I called a meeting of Studio people who were on the West Coast at the time: my wife, Carroll Baker; Dennis Weaver; Lee Grant; Karl Malden; and Alfred Ryder. I told Strasberg, and he was all for it. I said I would do all the basic organizational work but that I wanted it to be financially independent and to run its own affairs. Carl Schaeffer sent us one thousand dollars, with the understanding that Strasberg would be the overall artistic director."

Garfein wanted the new Studio to be separate from the New York outfit but with "regard for it." "Among our West Coast members, Karl Malden was especially adamant that the Studio be kept away from Lee's interference, that people admitted by the New York Board not be allowed to turn up simply as a matter of course. He felt we should find some other name for it besides Actors Studio West. We thought he was wrong, but he turned out to be right. People from the East came in and said, 'This is ours,' and yet we had built it up. Karl left as soon as he saw that what he feared would happen was in fact happening, but the rest of us still wanted the alliance and still believed, naively, that we could control the place."

The West Coast group wanted the new Studio to do full-scale productions, in effect becoming the phoenix that had risen from the ashes of the Actors Studio Theatre. "I wanted the Studio finally to fulfill the role of producer that it should always have had," Garfein says. "I wanted it to be a place where new plays could be developed and then given first-class productions. I invited Bill Inge to start a Playwrights Unit and I went to UCLA to talk about a possible association with them. They were interested, and we presented our first program there, a double bill of one-acts by Inge *(Do Not Go Gentle)* and Calder Willingham *(How Tall Is Toscanini?)*. We were a fast sellout, the reviews were wonderful.

"Word got out to New York, and there was an exodus because an Actors Studio Theatre seemed to be forming in Los Angeles. A New York group came in and started to agitate that I was doing too much direction. I said anyone could direct but the first work had to be done in the Studio. Meanwhile we ran into problems our second season at UCLA. When I came to the Actors Studio Board in New York, they chose to interpret that the break with UCLA indicated that our work was not on a certain level. They didn't want me to go on, because they felt our work wasn't up to it. But I found another theatre for the season, though when elections at the Studio came up, I was defeated. It was just as well because if there was to be no production arm I was no longer interested. After I left, the Actors Studio West opened in what was called the Merle Oberon Theatre and had two disasters. Dan Sullivan, who was the new [Los Angeles] Times critic, bemoaned the fact that the Studio wasn't doing Chekhov and Odets. That was the end of Actors Studio West as a producing organization."

In its struggles for power, in Strasberg's dominance, and in its failure in production, the West Coast branch mimics the history of the parent organization. But like its parent, Actors Studio West endures—and in much the same fashion. It values its isolation and protects its members' rights to work in privacy. Its heartbeat is the Acting Unit session which meets once a week for twelve months a year. The audition procedure is the same as in New York—Strasberg always had the final word on candidates. And instead of big-time productions, there are modest Studio projects, sometimes as many as five a season, sometimes only one or two, or even none, as projects "go into abeyance when actors get paying jobs," notes Mary Mercier. Unlike the projects in New York, these get reviewed, although there is no money for advertising. The P/D Unit, as in New York, has had an irregular life. "Lee disbanded it because we could not get enough moderators that he okayed," Mary Mercier says. "Lee wanted top people, but it's hard to get the quality people that Lee would okay because of the time commitment. People simply go off when they get jobs and you can't blame them."

Against the wishes of the original West Coast group, New York members are free to come in when they're in town. "At least half the total membership is out here," Mercier says. "The tougher things got in New York, the more actors came out here. But people go back and forth."

© ROGER GOULD

Actors Studio West in Los Angeles, located in the house of silent screen actor William S. Hart. Offices and rehearsal rooms are located in the main house; sessions are held in Hart's former garage.

As in New York, when Strasberg moderated there was "a packed house." When others moderate, "we do pretty well as far as attendance goes."

The Studio is located in a house that once belonged to silent screen actor William S. Hart, who left it in his will to the city of Los Angeles. Barely visible behind a clump of trees and surrounded by a yard which is a public park, the house is on a shady side street in a ravine one block south of an elegant art deco apartment tower on Sunset Boulevard. Like the location of Actors Studio in New York, far west of Broadway in Hell's Kitchen, Actors Studio West, nestled beneath glittering Sunset Boulevard, stands in symbolic confrontation with the world of commercial show business.

"It's a simple little place," Mary Mercier says. "Everything is more relaxed out here." The phone doesn't ring as much, and the small, bare rooms of the movie actor's former house have an eerie unoccupied feeling. The whole setup has the touch of the anomaly that it is, with East Coast intruders making a home out of the remains of Old Hollywood money and depending on the generosity of the city of Los Angeles.

As in New York, the decor is clearly early donation. In the office, there are three significant photos: of the Group Theatre, Elia Kazan, and Marilyn Monroe attending a session. Upstairs, there is a rehearsal room and a prop room, and private quarters for the caretakers ("the city insists that we have people on the premises"). Outside the main house is Hart's old garage, which has been converted into the theatre where sessions are held. There are picnic tables in the park, and trees, with new ones planted whenever a member dies.

"In Los Angeles, the Actors Studio is a good place for members to go as an alternative to enjoying the weather on the one hand and [entering] the wasteland of television work on the other. It's easy for actors to hang out in California, and to let time slip by," Mary Mercier observes. "In New York there are so many off-off theatres that actors can always work even if they don't always get paid. Here, actors can be seen at certain restaurants."

In addition to Strasberg, the Studio has rarely had more than two or three paid employees. In 1982, it had only two, a secretary and a production stage manager who between them ran the place. The secretary has charge of "the book," in which actors sign up to do scenes at sessions and for rehearsal space (always limited and in demand). She also schedules the monthly auditions; answers phones; supervises the working observers; and, since there is often no one else around, does everything else that needs to be done. "There's no end to the job," Janet Doeden, who left it in the fall of 1981, told me. "It could take over your whole life if you let it." The stage manager, the second employee, is in charge of all the actors' technical needs for their scenes, and supervises the production of staged readings and projects.

It's possible to keep the Studio running with such a skeletal staff because of the working observers (beginning acting students, or actors who have passed preliminary auditions) who are allowed to sit in on acting sessions in exchange for eight hours of work a week answering phones, typing, and assisting backstage. The number of working observers varies, anywhere from ten to twenty-five or thirty when the production schedule is full. They are admitted for a season, September to December or January to May, and can reapply.

(There is a second category of observers: directors, playwrights, established actors who are not Studio members, and critics, who must submit a résumé to the Board. If passed, they are admitted for three months, after which they too can reapply. Traditionally, most professional observers are from abroad; they've heard about the Studio and want to see its work first hand. Because of Strasberg's hospitality to foreign observers, Studio sessions often have an international flavor: in the back rows there is a babble of different languages.)

Although working observers make it possible to keep the Studio going on a low budget, many members think of them as a necessary evil. Professional observers, except for the occasional visiting luminaries, a Laurence Olivier or John Gielgud, the Moscow Art Theatre or the Peking Opera, are regarded as out-and-out intruders. In session, observers are second-class citizens, who must sit only in the last two rows and cannot participate in discussion. "I can see the day when there will be one hundred observers and no one working," Kazan said as long ago as 1955. Indeed, to admit any non-member is a violation of the closed, tight-knit community of peers that the Studio has always made a point of offering its actors.

Even with a group of eager young actors performing routine chores for the privilege of attending sessions, the Studio is always in financial peril, and so over the years, like Blanche DuBois, it has had to depend on the kindness of strangers. Many have worked to keep the doors open, but two people can be called the Studio's patron saints: a charming woman named Liska March, the Eleanor Roosevelt of West 44th Street, and a shrewd, feisty attorney with a lifelong interest in theatre, the late Carl Schaeffer.

"I've been at the Studio for over thirty years," Liska March says with quiet pride. For many of those years, she planned the annual benefits that more than anything else helped to keep the Studio afloat. (Often, these were the premieres of films directed by Kazan or starring a Studio actor—*The Rose Tattoo, East of Eden,* and *Baby Doll* were all major Studio benefits.) But Liska March has done more than organize benefits. She's been den mother, unofficial public relations officer, and financial helper. She answers the phone, supervises the office staff, takes a personal interest in the actors. Many actors speak warmly about her, recalling an act of generosity, a show of interest when interest was needed. During sessions, she gives her undivided attention to the actors. And I could tell, from her posture and her absolute concentration, that what drew her to the Studio over thirty years ago, and what keeps her there still, is a real love of actors and acting.

If Liska March is reticent about her contributions, the Studio's other lifesaver was decidedly not. "I don't show ego, I'm never in the forefront, yet I've been behind 99 percent of the work at the Studio during the last fifteen years," Carl Schaeffer told me in the summer of 1981. "God has been good to me; I've been successful in everything I've done. I don't believe in accumulating money, so I want to do good with it."

Like Liska March, Schaeffer loved actors—he was star-struck. "They're all my children," he said of Studio members. "They're my gang. It's my family. I'm proud to be the only non-actor member of the Studio."

Schaeffer's involvement with the Studio dated from the time in 1964 when Cheryl Crawford came to ask his help with the Actors Studio Theatre production of *Three Sisters.* "It's difficult for the Studio to raise monies— it will always be difficult," Schaeffer told me. "Who the hell is interested in giving money to develop an actor? When we went to public corporations they said that their function is to raise monies for clients not to give to charities, and the bulk of their charity money is to colleges not to performing arts. Private foundations will not contribute to develop an actor. Public foundations say, 'Produce plays, we'll give you part of the money.'

"People ask why the big artists aren't supporting it. Remember, we instill in them, from their first day, that the Actors Studio wants no money from them. We have had so many pressures to charge fees, and the answer is absolutely no. I was told that if Steve McQueen had had to pay ten dollars a week, he would never have come, and he would never have developed. Eighty percent of our actors are unemployed. We have many members who are as talented as our big stars, and they're starving. They will not do soap operas because it will affect their talent. I have never met a collective group who have been so insecure: even the stars are insecure, and this does not enable them to contribute. If I called on the Newmans, they'd give ten thousand dollars, but I am reluctant to do this because I have to depend on them for other things—to do an affair for nothing.

"Our people don't save their monies, or their salaries have been greatly exaggerated. We have tremendous stars who have no money. The fact is, the money is not forthcoming."

Because he could not go to corporations and could not depend on the generosity of successful members, Schaeffer decided to "impose on personal friends to become part of a Board of Trustees. But I can't just say to this Board, 'We're developing actors.' We have to keep the Trustees excited, so I put on workshop productions. Then I have something to show them, and then I extract x amount of money from them.

"The average outfit our size would need hundreds of thousands a year;

I can do it on one hundred thousand, because we can have aspiring actors come and work gratis, to be near greatness."

In the past few years, the Studio has had a windfall in the form of a quarter of a million dollars in royalties from *The Best Little Whorehouse in Texas*, which was written and developed at the Studio. "I wanted to present it under Actors Studio auspices on Broadway," Schaeffer said. "We recognized its potential. We had it where you could identify with each whore. It was a *play* with music. As is, it is vulgar. But how can you argue with success?"

In failing health since 1980, Carl Schaeffer had begun to move away from the Studio, feeling it was time for new blood to take over. Musingly, he wondered what had kept him at the Studio for so long, trying to raise money for an organization whose only equity is the intangible one of artistic talent. He never said so directly, but I think part of it was what drew everybody else to the place: the lure and the challenge of Lee Strasberg.

"All my life I looked for somebody who could make an original contribution," Schaeffer said. "I went for an Albert Schweitzer, a Norman Cousins . . . a Lee Strasberg. Financially, I helped them all. If you judge Strasberg on artistic merit, you have to admire that man—he made acting respectable. I don't want to get into him as a person, that would be negative. I had the backbone to stand up to Lee, I was one of the few because I never needed him for anything. He doesn't need me now," Schaeffer said, six months before Strasberg's death. "He's very powerful." But for many years, Strasberg and the Studio very much needed Carl Schaeffer.

"I have done innumerable things for him, to ease up his life. Everything he owns I was behind. I set up the Strasberg Institutes. I gave him a gift of that building on 15th Street which houses the New York Institute. I helped him buy his house on the Coast. I kept the Studio open. In Lee's last years, the artistic leadership was vague. Kazan stays away because he doesn't want to step on Lee's toes. Arthur Penn is busy; he's practical. Lee came around for two hours a week: you call that leadership? I had to flim-flam, otherwise we lay dormant. I produced a documentary about Lee and the Studio. It was a monument for Lee: flowers before his funeral."

Beneath this litany can be heard the traditional lament of the ingratitude of the receiver and, as if to say, look what my largesse has turned him into, Schaeffer asked, "Have you ever seen the way he entertains? I was to dinner, they brought out twelve lobsters. The fruit there! And how he dresses now!''

Having helped Strasberg to attain his power, Schaeffer seemed also to want to undercut it. "Remember no one person can be responsible entirely for someone else's talent. Very few of our members owe *all* their talent to Lee Strasberg or the Actors Studio, though Ellen Burstyn, Jane Fonda, and Al Pacino give Lee full credit. Brando, you know, talks negatively about Lee.

"Down through the years, I pushed Lee to increase the number of corporate members who are allowed to vote and who elect the officers— they're the equivalent of the stockholders. I don't believe in a thin corporation. I couldn't get him to increase the number beyond five for years. I leave it to your imagination why he resisted it. You know, in business we train younger people. Lee said that doesn't work artistically. 'When I die,' he would say, 'somebody will arise.' You have a right to question that. Are there other motivations at work? Insecurities?''

Making it possible for Strasberg to gain control, Schaeffer wanted to gain control of Strasberg. "He wanted to leave the Studio at one point; I convinced him to stay." Schaeffer felt spurned when Strasberg got too big for the role Schaeffer had helped to create; it was easier dealing with Strasberg when he wasn't a "lion," when "Kazan, the big director, and the big actors considered themselves superior to Lee Strasberg, a poor little teacher without clout." In the late seventies, Schaeffer brought Clurman into the Studio to take over the P/D Unit. "It was not to Lee's liking," he said. Surely he must have known it wouldn't be.

Like Strasberg, Schaeffer was a cunning man whose desire to have power over others resulted in notable good works. Having both started out as poor kids from the Lower East Side, both men craved status and recognition, yet both were also in a way selfless, and keenly devoted to the actors they thought of as their children. Genuinely philanthropic, impressed by worldly success, slippery and complex, their motives partially masked, Lee Strasberg and Carl Schaeffer were brilliantly matched for the struggle that was waged between them, covertly, for fifteen years.

Some members wondered if the Studio would be able to survive Strasberg's death. Happily, it has. In the fall of 1982 Ellen Burstyn and Al Pacino were appointed artistic co-directors, with Paul Newman as president of the Board of Directors. "Ellen is a strong leader," says longtime Studio member Mathew Anden. "She's very ambitious for the Studio. She's a tough administrator. She fired the old staff, the secretary and production stage manager, and now we have an entirely new staff: a house manager, a lighting designer, an executive secretary to handle grant applications, and a secretary who is in charge of day-to-day business. There are no more hangers-on as there used to be. And if there's any fucking up, the roof trembles."

The building that houses the Studio remains disarmingly modest—it's a dump—but these days it has a cleaner, sharper look; upstairs, they have replaced plush theatre seats with ascetic folding chairs and the stage platform has been removed to give the theatre a trim workshop ambience. Downstairs the bulletin board looks more lively than I've ever seen it. The place has been painted, and the wobbly-looking balcony has been bolstered. Outside, a new flag flaps broadly.

"I hadn't been back in many years, and I was delighted to see the Studio was so alive and vital—it will continue," Eva Marie Saint said in the spring of 1983. "The place has a good spirit, and some old members are coming back," Madeleine Thornton-Sherwood reports. "It's been revitalized since Ellen took over. She wanted the job, and I'm glad she got it. She's becoming more and more articulate. I haven't seen Al Pacino since Lee's funeral, but I understand he goes to corporate board meetings and gives money, and his name obviously means something." (In the spring of 1984, Ellen Burstyn became the Studio's sole artistic director.)

To its members, the Actors Studio is family, shelter, gym, lab, church, nesting place, a home away from home, craft guild, social club, a school that charges no tuition, offers only one course, and accepts you for life. In an insecure profession, pitted with tough competition, intermittent employment, frequent rejection, and temporary alliances, the Studio endures, providing its members with a sense of community and continuity. Through the failure of the Actors Studio Theatre, the jokes about Method actors, and the death of its leader, the Studio has held onto its legend. Like any institution, it has its rituals and traditions, but unlike most institutions it has retained its original scale. It started as a small, select, secretive, familial meeting place for professional actors and such it has stubbornly remained. What Elia Kazan said about it in 1955—"the Studio is a clean place in a dirty business"—is still true.

Lee Strasberg (as Hyman Roth) and Al Pacino (as Michael Corleone) in *The God-father Part II*. As Hyman plans a lethal double-cross, he tells his protégé, "You're a wise and considerate young man."

Part 3

THE ACTORS STUDIO
ON STAGE AND FILM

13

THE HESITATION WALTZ

On the first day of rehearsal for the Actors Studio Theatre production of *Three Sisters*, Lee Strasberg said to Geraldine Page, "Sit behind the desk, look up at the balcony, and talk loud!"

"I couldn't believe it," Page recalls. "I was in shock. How could he be doing this?"

At a later *Three Sisters* rehearsal, Arthur Penn remembers Strasberg shouting at Luther Adler: "Move this way!"

At a rehearsal for the London production of the play, Strasberg exploded as Sandy Dennis stammered her way through Irina's speech at the end of Act I. "My God, what are you doing up there? Are you trying to ruin my play?" After a thunderous silence, sitting very still center stage, Sandy Dennis said, "You can't speak to me this way. I'm a human being," as, flushed and overwrought and only a few months away from a nervous breakdown, Kim Stanley interjected, "Why are you screaming at her? I'm the one you really want to yell at."

After all the talk, the theory, the idealism, after all the preparation, the practice, the exercises, the work on self and on inner technique, it finally came to this: a director screaming at his actors as he gets a show ready in an atmosphere of haste, deadlines, rising tempers, and clashes of will and personality that seemed no different from a standard commercial production. Where was the ensemble spirit, the sense of community that had been promised and that seemed, after all, to be the logical extension of the high-mindedness that had always been the mark of the Studio? Where was the chance for the actors to try out the Method in production? At the Studio, actors had always been encouraged to take whatever time they needed to ease themselves into the spirit of a scene, reveling in sensory and emotional recall, having the luxury to discuss aims and to look closely at results; yet in production, their creative rights seemed to be withdrawn as they listened to their teacher turned director telling them where to move and how to say their lines.

Now that an Actors Studio Theatre had become a reality, where—and what—were its goals, its ideals, its vision?

The idea of a theatre had been in the air, at least as a possibility, since the founding of the Studio in the fall of 1947. Indeed, why shouldn't it have been? Although Cheryl Crawford says emphatically that the Studio was not intended to be a producing outfit, events—and common sense—suggest otherwise. "It was founded as a theatre," John Strasberg insists. "I grew up in that world, and I know that it was the Studio's intention from the beginning to become a theatre. Theatre people aren't interested in training for training's sake—naturally, they want to see how training works out in production. People who say the Studio wasn't meant to become a theatre are really trying to justify its failure to become one."

Strange Interlude, the first production of the Actors Studio Theatre, opened on March 11, 1963. Probably no theatre in the world has had so long a period of gestation, has been—before the fact—so heatedly talked about. For sixteen years, through a series of false starts, reiterative debates, and broken promises, the idea of having a theatre of its own was woven into the fabric of the Studio's history. No matter what anyone says now, from the start an Actors Studio Theatre was a possibility. Though at various times it seemed both the best and the worst of ideas, it was finally the thing that had to be done.

Four times in the years between its founding and the opening of *Strange Interlude* the Studio (more or less) produced a play. Four times, at any rate, pieces that began in a workshop context were transferred to professional production. Each time the Studio went to market, seismic shocks swept through the ranks, prompting yet a new round of debate about long-range goals. Each time there were bruised egos and a barrage of accusations and reprisals. When the Studio minded its own business, remaining a private place where Strasberg moderated sessions, problems of leadership did not surface; but when it went public the Studio exploded with administrative crises. Looking back, it's possible I think to read the failure of the Actors Studio Theatre in the story of the Studio's four ragged, half-hearted, plague-ridden ventures into management.

It's a rarely recalled fact that the Studio put on a play on Broadway in the very first year of its life. In September 1948, almost a year to the day of its founding, a production labeled clearly as "produced by the Actors Studio" opened the new theatre season. The name of the play was *Sundown Beach;* the author was Bessie Breuer, a short-story writer married to the painter Henry Varnum Poor. The play was cast entirely with students from Kazan's class at the Studio.

"Kazan had been looking for a play for us, with a large cast," recalls Joan Copeland. "We were about the same age, and we were all kind of raw; we were the younger actors, Robert Lewis's class the more experienced ones, and anything we did certainly wouldn't have drawing-room polish. We didn't want that anyway: we wanted a natural luster. With *Sundown Beach,* Kazan felt he had found just the play to show us off in." Copeland says the production of *Sundown Beach* was not meant to set a precedent but that it was "natural that Kazan would think in terms of production."

Before the play was first presented to the public during the summer of 1948 at the Westport Country Playhouse, Kazan said in an interview, "The company of actors that is performing *Sundown Beach* has been together one season. I didn't know a single one of these young actors when I interviewed them last fall. We worked on the play for the fun of it. . . . When we liked what came to be, we decided to show it. Nothing else."

In a letter to Cheryl Crawford, shortly before the play's premiere, Bessie Breuer offers a fascinating insight into the kind of bond that connected the novice actors to their dynamic director. "The chief point and reason for my being a little bit dubious about the present cast," she writes, "is that when Gadge is away the performance falls to pieces and is like children reciting. . . . Yet the moment Gadge appears, it's as if they were puppets and he held the strings, and he was their voice. In other words it is not an internal organism but an outer one that propels them. Well, how would that affect their continuing without him, when they have not yet— due only to their tender years—the IRON, the aesthetic discipline within *themselves,* the knowledge of life, to go on when he is no longer their parent, on the critical professional stage?? I have never in my life seen or imagined the extraordinary combination of faculties that is Gadge. For me it has been a great and exhilarating experience. And I daresay that is true of these young actors."

Sundown Beach was, in a sense, a thesis production—the first public demonstration of Actors Studio technique. It may have looked like an acting school exercise, but what a school! These were Kazan's kids, the chosen ones, the best young actors in New York (among them were Julie Harris, Martin Balsam, Cloris Leachman, Phyllis Thaxter, Steven Hill, Edward Binns, Lou Gilbert, and Warren Stevens) personally trained by the best young director in the American theatre. "Although most of the critics faulted the play, they were aware of a company feeling, an ensemble feeling," says Joan Copeland. "We all spoke the same artistic language."

Cheryl Crawford recalls *Sundown Beach* as "a good play, a good ensemble piece" which did well out of town. "We brought it into the Belasco the first week of September. The theatre was very hot. Kazan came in and jazzed it up. It became frenetic." The play closed after a meager seven performances, "putting a damper on further productions at that time," Crawford says.

Sprinkling sex and psychiatry over thirty high-strung characters as it dramatizes the problems of a group of war veterans and their wives and sweethearts, the play was a fine showcase of Method intensity. Here's how reviewers reacted to this first exhibition of the Studio style: "An Actors Studio practice piece, it would have been wiser to keep it to themselves"; "an emotional vaudeville"; "the mental and emotional disturbances are the real stars of the play"; "Miss Breuer lays on her psychoses thick and fast: a mother complex, a father complex laced liberally with a sissy, or non-virility complex, a religious complex, and a few light cases of paranoia and schizophrenia—the women are approximately as sick as the men."

One reviewer wrote that "the Actors Studio is a high-minded group of players motivated solely by love of the theatre. It seemed as if the ghost of the old Group Theatre was haunting the Belasco." My own sense in reading the play that it was rich Studio material was confirmed when Arthur Penn told me how seeing *Sundown Beach* had affected him.

"It was one of the illuminating experiences of my life. I was shaken to my very core. After seeing it, I walked the streets. It discarded everything that had come before. It completed the Group Theatre's attempt to shake the Theatre Guild gentility, which is as corrupt as it could be. *Sundown Beach* was Actors Studio grubbiness, which is what life is all about."[1]

Julie Harris and Steven Hill in *Sundown Beach*. Produced on Broadway in the fall of 1948, this was the first public demonstration of the Studio's Method.

End as a Man, the next Studio project, was the effort of an ambitious young Studio director, Jack Garfein. "At a party I met Calder Willingham, who said he had made a play of a novel: a three-hundred-page play about a Southern military school," Garfein recalls. "At the time, 1952, Calder didn't think much of the Actors Studio. To him, Broadway was the only thing that mattered. But I convinced him to let me have a go at the script at the Studio.

"I went and cast all the new people. Ben Gazzara begged me to let him read the part of Jocko de Paris. James Dean created the part of Starkson. I was obsessed with getting ensemble work for actors; to get actors to create human souls. I did the play only for the work.

"We rehearsed late, on the top floor of ANTA where the Studio was located then. One night about 2 A.M. we heard footsteps coming down the corridor. It was Kazan, who wondered what we were up to. He watched rehearsal for a while and said he thought we really had something. But Strasberg was leery.

"When we put it on as a project, it was the first time outsiders had been allowed to see work at the Studio (I remember the audience list had to be approved by the Old Guard)."

End as a Man was so well-received that Garfein was able to transfer it to the off-Broadway Theatre de Lys (for five thousand dollars). Garfein recalls that Clifford Odets came down to see the show and loved it. "He said there should be continuity, that the actors should be put into something else." Except for Kazan, the Studio leadership did nothing to encourage Garfein or to promote the idea of an ongoing theatre. Only reluctantly did they agree to have the Studio's name mentioned in the program.

"The Studio brass came down only after we had opened to great reviews," Garfein says. "Strasberg was nervous; he felt it was too precarious to let the reputation of the Studio ride on one production."

The response downtown was so strong that the producers decided to move uptown to a regular Broadway theatre. But *End as a Man* didn't do well as a Broadway offering, and this gave Strasberg further ammunition for his belief that the Studio should not become a producer.

Because it was an isolated phenomenon, an inside project that made it to the outside world, *End as a Man* has acquired a high place in the Studio's history. Overrun with nutty characters, the play helped to give the Studio its reputation for doing murky, claustrophobic dramas.

The play's anti-hero, the phonily named Jocko de Paris, is the school bully, a cunning sadist. (It's a fat part that made Ben Gazzara a star.) Jocko, dominating students who are less knowing than he and who therefore aren't shrewd enough to be on to him, is reptilian—truly sick. But his pathological behavior is never examined. Willingham simply presents Jocko's evil actions as a spectacle; he's the star of a Freudian freak show. It's up to the actors to supply the inner lives that the playwright has neglected.

Garfein put the Method to work, discovering conflict and ambivalence in the characters and hurling his actors through a series of improvisations that helped them to get to know each other as well as to build prior lives for their characters. Even critics who didn't care for the play noticed the wired ensemble acting, the atmosphere of a group of isolated men aboil with suppressed violence. "This group of young performers who have been working together at the Actors Studio are shrewd, studied, thoroughly sensitive," Walter Kerr wrote.

The third time the Studio went public, it was with a play that had been developed through improvisations. Michael Gazzo, a member of the Studio's inner circle, brought in an idea about a veteran who is a drug addict and who tries to conceal that fact from his wife, and he wanted actors to improvise scenes. Garfein recalls that Gazzo "wanted improvisations to *create* the play. I wasn't interested in this approach. I felt improvisations were for the actor, not for the writer, to get to the reality of the characters. But I remember watching many steamy improvisations between Eva Marie Saint, who was playing the wife, and the Italian Mafia, Ben Gazzara and Anthony Franciosa, who played the addict and his brother. Eva quit, and Carroll Baker, my wife, went in. We nearly had a divorce over her sexy improvs!"

Frank Corsaro, who directed the play, called *A Hatful of Rain*, says that Gazzo was "willing to give us three different versions of a scene." The piece that finally emerged from the give and take between the writer and the actors was thus a true collaboration, a made-to-order Method text.

As with *End as a Man*, it was clear from the excitement that the scenes were generating during sessions that this was material that ought to be shown to the public. Again, Kazan was bolder than Strasberg; he liked what he saw and wanted the project to be seen "on the outside." And again, Strasberg resisted.

In the summer of 1954, *A Hatful of Rain* was presented at the Studio for five performances. When it opened on Broadway on November 9, 1955, with the same cast of Studio actors (Shelley Winters replaced Carroll Baker), it was produced by outsiders. Strasberg refused to attend opening night, going only after the play had received excellent notices from magazine critics. Once it became a solid hit and was sold to the movies, the Studio claimed the play as its own.

Since in fact it was created on the premises, *A Hatful of Rain* has come over the years to seem the quintessential Studio piece, a problem drama with a tenement setting and anxious working-class characters who speak with raw vernacular vigor. Unlike either *Sundown Beach* or *End as a Man*, it felt less like a Studio exercise or a collection of ripe scenes for intense Method actors than a full-fledged play, a prime example of American naturalism, fifties style.

Its main character is a drug addict, but *A Hatful of Rain* is really a family drama of the sort that has always appealed to Studio actors. A father who doesn't know his sons, a wife who sleeps beside a man she doesn't know is a junkie, two brothers who compete for the love of their remote father and of a woman who is torn between them—these characters are the grist of the Method. In the play's scheme, drug addiction is like homosexuality in Tennessee Williams's mid-fifties drama, *Cat on a Hot Tin Roof:* unmentionable. As in Williams's play, confession is therapeutic; it takes Johnny Pope almost three acts to be able to tell his father and his wife that he's an addict, but once he's able to speak the truth recovery becomes possible.

A year after *A Hatful of Rain* opened, another play by Michael Gazzo was developed in the Studio, again using actors' improvisations. This time, Strasberg refused to let the Studio's name be associated with the play when it was produced on Broadway. "We almost did *Night Circus,"* Strasberg told an acting session after the play had been produced by an outside team. "But we didn't do it because, if we had, there would have been great discussion

Jack Garfein directing Ben Gazzara and Pat Hingle for the film version of *End as a Man,* released in 1958 as *The Strange One.* In England, the film was advertised as "the first motion picture from New York's famed Actors Studio."

and argument. We felt the play started off in one direction and then went somewhere else. We lost the logic of the play. The background which I reacted to when the play was done here was missing on Broadway. The characters, who live in a bar, were pulled out of their environment; it appeared too abstract and general. Remember, it started from an effort to find a theatrical form for jazz—the main character is a jazz addict. Certainly Mike's dialogue was vivid, but at the end of the play nothing happens from the talk: so why should anything happen to us? On stage, the author must show the logical end of action. If there's no conclusion, that is not a play, it is a novel."

Night Circus closed quickly, and you could hear the relief in Strasberg's voice when he said, "If we'd come in on Mike's production, we'd be in trouble. You know I'm not afraid of argument, but in production there has to be authority. Your confidence in our judgment must be carried into production work."

The last time the Studio edged sideways into production, before it established its own Theatre, the results were apocalyptic. And in the backstage struggle for control of the play was a preview of what went wrong with the Actors Studio Theatre.

"It was a shattering experience which destroyed so many things for me," says Jack Garfein, who directed. At Piscator's Dramatic Workshop in the forties, Garfein had developed an interest in Sean O'Casey's plays, and, ten years later, he chose O'Casey's *Shadow of a Gunman* as a piece to be studied profitably in a Studio environment. Like *End as a Man, Gunman* is an ensemble play, a drama about an isolated group, the residents of a shabby Dublin boardinghouse whose lives are scarred by the struggles between the I.R.A. and the British. It's a challenging play, in language and temper beyond the range of anything Garfein had yet worked on. O'Casey's dialogue has a lyric intensity quite different from the psychological intensity of plays about American neurotics, which had become Garfein's specialty. But in its focus on a *group* of characters—loquacious, high-strung Irishmen —the play seemed to lend itself to a Method approach.

Shadow of a Gunman developed into a Studio project with production possibilities. "We rehearsed it the way we had *End as a Man*," Garfein recalls. "First we worked on character relationships and circumstances. These had to become real to the actors. We did a lot of improvisations and created scenes that took place before the action of the play. The actors grew

Shelley Winters and Ben
Gazzara in *A Hatful of Rain*,
created through improvisations
at the Studio.

to know their characters and each other before we did any work with the
dialect or with O'Casey's words."

When the play was first performed, Lee Strasberg wasn't there. "I
pleaded with him to come down," Garfein says. "It was the old problem.
He didn't want this one production to represent the work of the Studio. He
was always so nervous about the Studio: that was all he had. Kazan liked
it and felt the production should not be taken over by a commercial management. Reluctantly, Lee agreed.

"And then the trouble started. The moment the Actors Studio got
involved, Lee Strasberg wanted stars, Rod Steiger and Gerry Page. I felt
any stars coming in could not move with the ensemble—an enormous
amount of work had been done already and though there were faults
(some of the character people couldn't get to some of the Irish lyricism),
I wanted to keep the ensemble, which was necessary to the spirit of the
play.

"Lee said I could go ahead, but he told everyone that I was dictatorial.
I refused to go with stars—that was not the the Actors Studio. I wanted
actors who would work well together. Strasberg was not part of the casting.
I did cast some non-Studio actors (including Bruce Dern, not then a Studio

member) because no Studio people were right for some of the parts. But I worked with them as though they were Studio actors.

"Paula Strasberg suggested Susan Strasberg for the lead female. I thought she was right for it, and cast her. This only intensified Lee's nervousness. Lee asked to come to a rehearsal. I said all right, but I didn't want him to talk to the actors directly. He came to the first preview (I had scheduled two weeks of previews). Afterwards, I was asked to meet Strasberg, Paula, and Cheryl Crawford at Downey's. Lee said, 'What do you think?' I said, 'It should be all right.' He turned to Cheryl and said—and I will never forget his tone—'If he thinks that, close the show tomorrow night. I don't think it has any kind of reality.'

"Stunned, I called Carroll [Baker] and said, 'Let's buy out the Actors Studio and produce it ourselves.' She agreed. We made the offer to Cheryl Crawford, who said, 'I'm not going to be bought out. Permit Lee Strasberg to work on this, or we'll close.' I called Kazan, who felt Lee would not really make changes, that he would be too intimidated. 'Introduce him as an adviser,' Kazan said. I listened to Kazan's advice, called Lee, and told him he could come in. He arrived the next day and started immediately to restage Susan's scene in the first act.

"I left the theatre and called my lawyer. 'Have my name removed from the program,' I said. Strasberg started to rework the raid scene. The Studio actors were terribly intimidated by him. He said to the non-Studio actors, 'Go ahead and do whatever comes to you,' whereas I had held them down. Bruce Dern wouldn't take direction from Lee. It was all so careless, the opposite of what Lee had been teaching about the proper creative atmosphere for actors.

"Mrs. O'Casey came to the opening and said that it was the best production of Sean's play ever done. I went over to tell Paula, who huffed, 'A lot she knows, all of O'Casey's plays were flops.' And I thought to myself, 'Where was the idealism Strasberg had always talked about?' It had all become so crass and commercial.

"Opening night, around ten-thirty, everyone started to clear out. It was funereal. I started to have doubts. Brooks Atkinson gave us a rave; he wrote that it was the best ensemble work he'd seen since the Moscow Art Theatre! We also got a rave from the *Daily News*. Walter Kerr was negative, except for Bruce Dern.

"I was encouraged by the reviews, on balance, and I asked to call a rehearsal. I felt if we continued to work, we'd really have something. Cheryl Crawford said she didn't want any calls at all.

"The final blow was two-pronged, from Paula. She called the *Times* and said that Lee Strasberg had actually directed the production. But Brooks Atkinson said, testily, that he knew whose work he had seen and it wasn't Strasberg's. And around this time Paula began to say that it wasn't true that I had been a concentration camp survivor. She even envied me that!"

After the play opened, Strasberg began to direct a series of rehearsals and ads billed Susan Strasberg as the star (there are no star parts in the play, and Susan's role, though vivid, amounted to only two scenes). Cheryl Crawford's company manager informed Garfein that he would need a ticket to enter the theatre; when he stormed in, the company manager screamed, "Get him out of the theatre!" and called a policeman, who had the final word: "This looks like a family quarrel."

A newspaper strike and dwindling business caused the play to close in a few weeks' time. Garfein, deeply wounded, felt Strasberg had betrayed the ensemble ideal that, in theory, he had always upheld; once the play went into production, Garfein saw his mentor give in to commercial thinking, promoting his daughter's career at the expense of the company and the play. "For me, after that, he became a failed Messiah," Garfein says. "Lee Strasberg did not follow through on his promises, and all of us, who were then in our twenties, were let down and began to move away from the Studio."

For Strasberg, the *Shadow of a Gunman* ordeal only reinforced his anxieties about professional production. "The essential problem was between the director and the Actors Studio," he told an Acting Unit session in a postmortem discussion. "The production was in charge of Cheryl Crawford and Joel Shenker. We did not interfere in any of the work the first two and a half weeks. We came in the third week, and we felt the production was in an appalling state. We couldn't understand what the talented director was trying to do. It fell into a conventional idea of what people would expect to see. It was tepid, there was little movement, it was slow, there was no reality and conviction in the way I try to describe to you. Under ordinary conditions, you fire the director. But we have a responsibility toward the talent of our people, and we felt it was not irretrievable. Gadge did not want the Actors Studio to be blamed for what was on the stage. So we decided I should come in and sit with Jack and do whatever had to be done. I came down on Friday night, Jack said it was a great shock to him. (I don't know why it should be a shock.)

"A director in the Group Theatre had complete charge. On *Shadow*, that wasn't equally true, but we had full conferences with the director at the beginning. We should have been accepted with open arms; instead, it became personal. Jack's assumption was that in the Actors Studio he should be free to do anything he wants. When we came in, he felt that was a usurpation. We felt where the Actors Studio takes responsibility, we must take authority. If the Studio's name is used, the Studio has responsibility. The Studio has no intention of lending its name in situations where its authority would not be implicitly accepted. I will not permit the Actors Studio to be used as a stepping-stone. It has been a bitter pill, because of personal recriminations. We are not willing to be placed in such a position by the younger people."

I can see his point. If the Studio has its name on a production, audiences naturally assume that the Studio's leaders stand behind the work. Since Strasberg had always been reluctant to have the Studio used as a showcase, and since, as a result, the Studio's name appeared in public so rarely, its association with O'Casey's play had far more significance, to the Studio as well as to outsiders, than it ought to have had. It suggested that the Studio—that is, Strasberg and Kazan and Crawford—really thought they had something to show, unlike the other productions which were for members only. Strasberg's handling of the matter obviously lacked diplomacy and raised questions about his leadership abilities, but I think he was entitled to say something like "No, this does not represent the quality of work we aspire to at the Studio; this production does not meet our standards."

It's ironic that one of the fiercest internal battles in the Studio's history was over a play that the Studio had no business putting on in the first place. Why, when the Studio had historically been so reluctant to produce anything, did it happen to produce a lyric Irish tragedy that was outside the range and background of most of its actors? And why was the production almost ready to open without Strasberg having seen it? That he found it in "an appalling state" says as much about his artistic and administrative leadership as about Garfein's direction.

Instead of acting the tyrant he was often accused of being, Strasberg hadn't been tyrant enough. Because of his ambivalence about producing, he had not exercised his executive privileges from the start. He hadn't established the ground rules, and when he did barge in, after having allowed Garfein control of the production, Garfein was understandably dismayed. Suddenly he had a disapproving boss to contend with when all along he had become accustomed to the apparent indifference of the front office. Strasberg claimed too much authority too late.[2]

An organization that could botch so small an enterprise is not likely to overcome the obstacles of establishing its own theatre. Nonetheless, putting on *Shadow of a Gunman* revived the idea of the Studio becoming a full-fledged producer and forced Strasberg to confront his doubts.

"I tremble whenever we come to making a decision," he announced to an acting session. "About the second or third year of the Group, I gave a summary that was not well received; conflicts were developing and what I tried to make clear was that, as in a marriage, when the Group was a dream, everything was ideal; when the dream became reality, there are natural disagreements, and this must be recognized. The people here are not aware enough of the problems—they were the problems of the Group Theatre." But despite the problems, despite the scars over *Shadow*, and the awareness that what had happened was but a taste of what might occur again and again, Strasberg was tempted by the possibility of heading his own theatre: perhaps he could now have his Actors Studio Theatre the way Clurman had had his Group.

"We would never have gone ahead on the Bijou project [*Shadow of a Gunman* was presented at the Bijou Theatre] unless it had been part of a larger vista," Strasberg told Studio members. "It arose out of the feeling that we might as well take the bull by the horns."

Strasberg began to talk himself into going public. "The Moscow Art Theatre had only six top people. The Group didn't have that many. We have twenty or twenty-five. We would be able to engage on a greater variety of levels than any theatre there ever has been. . . . We could do work that Stanislavski might never have dreamed of. We have laid the basis here in the Studio to put into the world arena the best in ensemble theatre. The combination we have, of actors and directors and professional experience, is unparalleled. We have in the Studio a strange and unusual blend of age and youth, of talent and artistic conviction and commercial awareness. It's the first time in the history of the theatre.

"It took ten years' time to do. It was done easily and freely. We have a unit which could make the best theatre and the best movies. We have a wealth and richness of talent without the holding on that took place in the Group.

"We are today at a peculiar moment. Think about it, be aware of it. We can't go into it haphazardly."[3]

14

THE ACTORS STUDIO THEATRE

As early as 1957, Strasberg was mentioning the possibility that the Studio might be asked to form a theatre as part of what was then called the Lincoln Square project. In 1962, the Lincoln Center Board asked Elia Kazan to become co-director (with Robert Whitehead) of the Center's Repertory Theatre. Pointedly, the invitation did not include Strasberg or the Actors Studio. "My father was stunned," John Strasberg reports. "He and Kazan didn't speak for many years. My father had few real friends, and he had felt, mistakenly, that Kazan was one of them."

"Gadge had always told Lee that he was going to be head of the training program at Lincoln Center," Geraldine Page recalls. "Then, at the last minute, he said, 'No, it will be Bob Whitehead.'"

Whenever he had talked about an Actors Studio Theatre, Strasberg had always linked Kazan's name with his own ("Gadge and I are highly regarded in the professional theatre"); the two of them were to be the leaders of a world-class company. Hooking up with Kazan, America's top director, allowed Strasberg to share the reputation of the younger man who had been his protégé in the Group. Now, with Kazan defecting to Lincoln Center, Strasberg could no longer lean on the glitter of Kazan's name.

"It was a dependency relationship," says Michael Wager, who was instrumental in organizing the Studio's Theatre. "Strasberg and Kazan were bound to each other with umbilical cords of piano steel wire. In some ways, Strasberg realized he could not function in the theatre without Gadge, who was the one who had the theatrical success."

"Lee envied and admired Kazan so much," Geraldine Page says. "When he directed, he wanted to prove that he could be tough and commercial like Kazan. He wanted to be Gadge when he directed; Gadge thought Lee was a teacher, not a director. When we confronted the Studio directors with the fact that we wanted our own theatre, Gadge said to Rip [Torn, Page's husband], 'Don't do this to that old man, he should be left in his teaching chair.' Gadge is a born director but he wanted to be like Harold Clurman and sit and talk about the play. Harold talked about the play and the character beautifully, but he didn't give you anything to get up and try. Gadge would be so vivid—a few words from him, and you couldn't wait to get up and go to work. It was all weird and schizophrenic, Lee wanting to be Gadge, who wanted to be Harold."

Losing Kazan naturally reinforced Strasberg's wariness about forming a theatre. "I had always felt that we were laying the groundwork for a complete theatre," a shaken Strasberg said at the time of the Lincoln Center rejection. "Now I have begun to question our reason for existence."

"We were as dependent on Strasberg as he was on Kazan," Michael Wager says, "and we sensed that when Kazan left, we *had* to push Lee into

Geraldine Page and Betty Field in *Strange Interlude,* the opening production of the Actors Studio Theatre. "A historic date for the American theatre," Lee Strasberg announced.

forming a theatre; we felt that if it didn't happen now, it wasn't going to happen. If somebody didn't do it for him, he wouldn't do it."

"The idea of finally forming our own Actors Studio Theatre really came from Rip," says Geraldine Page, who is eager to set the record straight. "Every year Cheryl came in and told us how the Studio was out of money. That year—1961—Mendy [Michael] Wager leapt up and said, 'Let's form a committee to raise money.' Rip brought up the fact that we all go out and earn money for producers, why not do our own productions? Rip was elected chairman of the committee, which in order not to get Lee alarmed we called The Committee to Ensure the Long-Range Financial Stability of the Actors Studio.

"Rip worked out a plan whereby Studio actors who wanted to be part of the Theatre would give five months a year to it—this Rip figured was the amount they could afford to give without interrupting their careers. When we presented our plan to the members, everyone screamed 'Yes, we should do it.' Rip had structured it so that Lee would be the final authority. We called the three directors and told them the entire membership of the Studio was *demanding* to start a theatre.

"We took Rip's proposal to the Ford Foundation. Over the years, Gadge and Cheryl had tried unsuccessfully to get Ford to give a grant to the Studio. Nan Martin knew Mac Lowry at Ford; he said, 'On the basis of this plan, I will give you a quarter-million provided you raise a matching amount and that somebody responsible would be in charge of the funds.' He said he would approve of Cheryl for that job. He felt secure about her. So she got railroaded into a job she didn't want. She wanted the Actors Studio to be a workshop to develop people to put into her productions that would make money for herself. *We*—the committee—raised the money. Cheryl Crawford was a figurehead.

"Rip and I went to see Billy Rose, who said he'd give us his theatre for a dollar a year, and the matching grant. We immediately called Lee to confirm. Paula answered; she said she'd tell Lee. We waited, but he never called back. Billy got hurt and withdrew his offer.

"Then Rip attacked Roger Stevens, who agreed to match the Ford grant. We called up Lee again; this time he answered the phone. Rip told him to come over to Roger's apartment to sign the papers. He said, 'It's snowing out, I can't come.' Rip got in a taxi to fetch Lee to Roger's. Lee really was terrified.

"It was only Rip's fanaticism that caused the Theatre to happen."

On August 1, 1962, the Actors Studio presented a prospectus to the Ford Foundation for a theatre. "Previous attempts to create a permanent American theatre have foundered on the problem of how to get a sufficient number and variety of top people to play in a wide repertory over a long period of time. . . . Our flexible program makes unique provisions for this." The prospectus presented a budget based on the first five years of continuous operation, with three to five new productions (to be kept permanently in the theatre's repertory) projected for each year. Shrewdly, the plan mentioned that it is "not realistic to assume that this theatre can establish itself economically in one or two years."

Maintaining that the Theatre's "primary responsibility" is toward "the American playwright—especially the new play," the proposal envisions building a repertory of American classic plays (*The Contrast, Winterset, Battle of Angels, Awake and Sing!, The Show-Off,* among others, are mentioned), contemporary European dramas (Pirandello's *Henry IV,* Camus's *Caligula*), and foreign classics *(Phaedra, Uncle Vanya, The Country Wife).* In announcing so wide-ranging a repertory, the plan clearly tries to dissociate the Studio from the contemporary American realist play its reputation was based on.

Liking what it read, the Ford Foundation awarded a grant of a quarter of a million dollars. "Foolishly, Ford thought it was going to make a lot of money," Cheryl Crawford says.

The Actors Studio Theatre gave its premiere performance at the Hudson Theatre on March 11, 1963—a day, said Strasberg at the time, that "might well be recognized in the future as an historic date for the American stage." Speaking for the Production Board, he said that their dream was a theatre that will "live long past the lives of those who founded it."

The opening attraction was Eugene O'Neill's nine-act *Strange Interlude,* a play so long it required a 6:30 curtain and a forty-five-minute dinner interval. The second production, *Marathon 33,* written and directed by June Havoc, opened on December 22, 1963, at the ANTA Theatre. *Dynamite Tonite* opened (and closed) at the off-Broadway York Theatre on March 5, 1964. Paul Newman and Joanne Woodward starred in a new comedy, *Baby Want a Kiss,* by James Costigan, which opened at the Little Theatre on April 19, 1964. James Baldwin's *Blues for Mister Charlie* premiered at the Plymouth on April 23, 1964, and the Actors Studio Theatre's final (and best) production, *Three Sisters*, opened at the Morosco on June 22, 1964. As of July 24, 1964, the Theatre's deficits were $38,346.11. The only play that showed a profit (of nearly $10,000) was *Baby Want a Kiss*. The history of the Actors Studio Theatre closes, disastrously, with the company taking two of its productions, *Blues for Mister Charlie* and *Three Sisters*, to the Aldwych Theatre in London in June 1965 to be part of the World Theatre Season.

After two short seasons and six productions, Strasberg's off-again, on-again dream of transforming his Studio into an American national theatre collapsed. Financially, and according to many people artistically, the Theatre was a major disappointment, a case of good intentions soured by expediency, miscalculation, in-fighting, foul play, and spinelessness. Veterans of the Theatre have hardly a good word to say about the experience—harsh feelings linger to this day; and these two seasons are generally seen by Studio members themselves as a blot on the Studio's history: Strasberg's folly.

I don't agree. Far from doing discredit to the Studio, the history of its Theatre seems to me to indicate extraordinary promise—its record is certainly more substantial than Kazan's misbegotten seasons at Lincoln Center.[4] Before its premature death, the Studio's Theatre showed signs of becoming a genuine diamond competing bravely with the costume jewelry that is the usual Broadway fare. Of course there were mistakes in judgment and administration; but the quality of the work that was completed was sufficiently challenging to have earned the Theatre more time. Its two seasons offered good actors in plays that were worth their efforts. In *Strange Interlude, Blues for Mister Charlie, Three Sisters*, and *Marathon 33*, there were many thrilling moments, flashes of brilliance and daring in acting, writing, and staging.[5]

"It would have taken five or six years for the Theatre to find its face," says Frank Corsaro. It was the five or six years that, miraculously, the Group managed to claim for itself, and it was the five or six years that the Moscow Art Theatre had needed to discover the rhythm of its own particular genius. It is the five or six years that the Actors Studio Theatre desperately needed and had both earned and deserved. It's the five or six years that, as a theatregoer, I feel cheated of. And who, at this late date, can I blame? The Ford Foundation, for not supporting the Theatre for a longer period of time? Strasberg, for being star-struck, for having made promises over the years that in the heat of battle he was unable to keep, and for being too possessive and therefore unwilling to appoint someone who knew how to run a theatre? The Studio members themselves, who let the Theatre that had been their dream as well as Strasberg's slip away from them in an orgy of arguments that betrayed both its real achievement and its intoxicating promise? Michael Wager says, "The failure of the Theatre can be traced to Lee Strasberg and our weakness vis à vis him; we were all accomplices and accessories."

The Actors Studio Theatre failed because it didn't show a profit, and in the American system there has almost never been room for an organization that can't pay its own way. And it failed because, after the Ford Foundation withdrew, Studio members weren't willing to do what had to be done to save their Theatre. Too easily, it seems to me, they gave up. It failed, too, because it didn't build a subscription base that would have assured some continuity, and instead presented its shows on the open market, one at a time, in different theatres, looking like any commercial producer. And it failed because the Studio had waited too long and started too big.

"The Theatre should have been started earlier," says Frank Corsaro. "The actors would have been willing to start a real ensemble in the fifties and the star aspect would have happened by itself then. And the Theatre should have started more modestly." Like Corsaro, Arthur Penn feels that putting on major productions on Broadway right from the beginning was overreaching. "But Lee was not willing to evolve. He wanted to begin big. It was a mistake to begin with several large-scale productions, all at almost the same time. Lee thought too big and he wanted to be funded for these major productions: those funds will never be forthcoming."

Some of the reasons for failure were the Studio's fault, some of them were not, but what I kept hearing again and again was that the greatest obstacle of all was the personality of the artistic director. "Lee Strasberg was single-handedly responsible for the failure of the Actors Studio Theatre," Edward Albee says in a tone of absolute finality. "The Theatre needed an entrepreneurial genius like Joe Papp," Arthur Penn points out, "and yet that kind of person could not have worked with Lee." "Lee could not function in a professional situation: that was the great tragedy," Michael Wager feels. "Lee believed he had a commercial instinct, but he didn't," Gordon Rogoff says. "Under pressure, his faults magnified," says Frank

Corsaro, "and yet he insisted on maintaining artistic decisions." "Lee was a weak center who wanted to control, and did so by vacillation," says Jack Gelber, who was on the Production Board. "He had total power, it was his baby. And he used that power negatively. He just didn't know how to run the Theatre."

"My father could never work with anybody else on an equal basis," says John Strasberg. "Theatre is a collaborative art—you can't do it alone. You have to work out your dream with everyone else. Yet to have an ensemble spirit you need a strong leader. The Actors Studio Theatre failed from lack of leadership; my father never took open responsibility for the failure. However, to me, it was his fault. He wasn't willing to say no or to say this is what we are going to do. He'd blame the failure of a production on the designer or the actors. His whole history in the theatre was leaving it whenever it got tough, as in the Group. He would get mad at people when they wouldn't do what he wanted; and he only gave to people when they fed him what he wanted. He was an infantile man, who was always surrounded by people who took care of him. But they were all like a bunch of kids fighting for power: they weren't adult enough to put together a theatre. Doing it bigger and better and being famous were more important than the Theatre and the organization. They were all self-serving, with no one big enough to rise above their own needs. It's the problem of America. The Actors Studio Theatre is an idea that ought to have worked: but it didn't because it lacked the right kind of leadership."

Under fire, the teacher that Studio members revered turned out to be merely mortal, and poorly cast in the role of theatre administrator. He couldn't do everything that needed to be done in the daily running of a theatre and at the same time be sensitive to the needs and problems of individual actors in the way he was in Studio sessions. It wasn't fair of the actors to expect Strasberg as producer to be the same man who patiently examined their acting problems in sessions—but when there was so decisive a gap between Strasberg in class and Strasberg wearing a producer's hat many actors felt let down. "Strasberg had continually dangled the dream of the creation of a theatre," says Michael Wager, "and then, when we finally had it, he betrayed this glorious dream." When it came time to put theory into practice, and to move from the informality of a workshop to the responsibility of running a theatre, Strasberg stumbled.

"It was typical of the rudeness at the Studio that Lee never told me whether I'd gotten the part of Irina [in *Three Sisters*]," recalls Lois Smith. "It was just like a commercial management: I had to find out from Shirley Knight, who got the role." Michael Wager left the Studio, permanently, when Strasberg failed to tell him that he wasn't going to London with *Three Sisters*. "He had every right to cast whoever he wanted," Wager says, "but that he wouldn't have told me his decision was something I couldn't accept. I was astounded by his perfidious conduct. I felt betrayed. And I had to leave the Studio then—I would have had no self-respect if I hadn't."

Anne Bancroft felt Strasberg had promised her Masha in *Three Sisters*. When he said, off-handedly, "Play Natasha instead," she left in a fury. "No, no, darling," she snapped, "I play Masha or nothing."

Geraldine Page and Rip Torn left the Studio, never to return ("except when someone died"), when Strasberg and Cheryl Crawford fired Rip from the London-bound *Blues for Mister Charlie*. "The fracas started during rehearsals," Page recalls. "They had only one week to get it ready because they kept putting off the decision whether or not to go to London. As Rip had predicted, it had to be recast. When Rip, who was an original cast member, started making production suggestions, as he always had, Lee got very testy. 'We've been in the business forty years, we know what we're doing,' he said. Burgess Meredith, the director, turned on Rip and yelled, 'Who are you? You're just an actor.' (Rip had gotten Burgess the job!) When Rip said not to cut speeches in order to appease British censorship, Jimmy Baldwin said, 'Who are you? You're just an actor!' Rip was only trying to protect the play the way Jimmy had written it. Jimmy and Burgess told Lee to fire this 'upstart' actor. Lee hoped it would all go away. Rip was executive producer for everything the Theatre had done—there wouldn't have been a Theatre without Rip. Yet now they decided he was just a loudmouth actor. Cheryl came in then and said [Geraldine Page does a wicked imitation of Crawford's deadpan delivery], 'Didn't you get the letter?' [in which Rip Torn was fired]. I left the Studio that day. I just couldn't go back again, even on a social basis. Rip said, in the late sixties, 'Lee has a new wife. Let's go to a party for her.' Rip had had a violent eruption with Lee. Rip gets so mad he wants to kill, but it works itself out of him. Me, I'm too civilized. I'm always polite. And I never forgive anybody."

Crushed egos, bitter feuds, unkept promises, temper tantrums in the heat of the moment, high-handed firings—these are standard backstage behavior. But the thrusts, cuts, and wounds behind the scenes of the Actors Studio Theatre were acts of fratricide and parricide from a bloody family drama whose aftermath was as strewn with bodies as the fifth act of a Jacobean revenge tragedy.

Many veterans of the Theatre believe it might still be alive but for a first catastrophic mistake, its failure to open with the best American play since *Death of a Salesman* and *A Streetcar Named Desire*, Edward Albee's *Who's Afraid of Virginia Woolf?* A new Theatre that turns down such a play is a Theatre determined not to succeed. (Albee was an in-house writer, a member of the Playwrights Unit as well as of the Theatre's Production Board, which makes the rejection of his play even more puzzling.)

When the Board decided against his play, Albee left in a huff from which he has never recovered. "The great Theatres had their playwrights," Michael Wager persuasively argues. "But whose theatre were we? And who knows what would have happened to Albee's career if he had written for an Actors Studio Theatre?"

We can't know, but opening with this play would have shown that the Actors Studio not only knew how to play Broadway's hit/flop game but could play it better than anyone else. And the resulting credibility and luster might well have given the Theatre the five or six years it required to ensure its long-range survival.

The opening night of *Who's Afraid of Virginia Woolf?*, October 13, 1962, at the Billy Rose Theatre, was the kind that theatre lovers dream about: the audience responded to Albee's puncturing wit with a fusillade of laughs and gasps as its rising excitement embraced the actors, lifting them and the play into orbit. Rarely has there been an opening night like it since, or a new American play so powerful or original. That night should have belonged to the Studio but it didn't. Why not?

"About *Virginia Woolf*, I refuse to mourn," Geraldine Page wrote to Cheryl Crawford (in December 1962). "I think it would have been wonderful for us to do if it could have been surrounded and padded by at least three and preferably five more positive plays—I think it would have been disastrous as our first production. It is very theatrical—well-written, etc., etc., but it is an intensely ugly play in a way the Tennessees are always accused of being but never are—it would have put a stamp on us of bitterness, hostility & infantilism that would take us years to struggle out from under. We had a very narrow and very *providential* escape. It was a temptation because it's so good but can you imagine the effect of this play compounded with our widespread reputation for being sweaty smelly scratching beatniks who do God knows what behind closed doors—'So—they've opened the doors & it's just as we thought!' I know Lee wouldn't mind, he loves to alienate people and not in the Brechtian sense."

This lively, sassy letter indicates that Page writes as well as she acts: but her judgment! Michael Wager reports that it was Page's strenuous objections that put the finishing touch on the Studio's decision not to produce the play. "She kept saying, 'I don't want to play this part, I want to play a part where I can wear beautiful clothes.' " ("Is he kidding?" Page says.) Page herself told me, "Lee said I should play it. He said if I had any loyalty to the company I *would* play it. Edward wanted me to play it. I said, finally, that under duress I would do it. My last role had been in *Sweet Bird of Youth* where I had played a hard lady, a drunken loudmouth, and I didn't want to do that kind of thing again so soon. But also I don't respect that play: I hated that play. It would have had trouble passing the Board anyway because Roger Stevens and his wife didn't approve of the naughty language. And, you know, if the Studio had done it, critics wouldn't have reviewed the play the way they did."

I don't agree. And I also think Geraldine Page, who has just the wit and ripeness and theatrical size for Albee's character, would have been a sensation, or at least as good as her former teacher Uta Hagen, who starred in it. But if Page didn't like the play, surely there were other Studio people who did, and who could have played Martha as effectively; for a start, I can think of Anne Bancroft, Patricia Neal, Joanne Woodward, Shelley Winters, and Kim Stanley. A rotating cast of Studio actors (stars and non-stars alike) in *Virginia Woolf* might have been the making of the Actors Studio Theatre.

"Not doing *Virginia Woolf* was the beginning of the end," Michael Wager says.

"Every time anyone suggested a play to open with, Lee said it wasn't quite right," Geraldine Page remembers. "We found out that he would approve something by O'Neill. Rip kept saying *Strange Interlude* over and over, until we were ready to kick him. I was embarrassed, because here was my boyfriend pushing a play with a nine-act starring part for me. We got Cheryl to approach Carlotta O'Neill (whom she knew) for the rights. We kept nagging and nagging Cheryl, who reported that Carlotta said all the O'Neill plays had been promised to Lincoln Center. We were outraged. It was like hearing that only the National Theatre could do Shakespeare. Jason Robards told us that that wasn't true, because Ted Mann and José Quintero were going to do *Desire Under the Elms* at the Circle in the Square. Rip got himself cast in it, and started to go to work on José. José is usually a reluctant dragon, like Lee, but Rip persuaded José, getting him excited about working on *Strange Interlude* for the Actors Studio. And José got the rights from Carlotta in a flash. Then we tricked Lee, getting him to say he would agree if we got the rights; we knew he thought the rights were all tied up at Lincoln Center. When Lee found out, he went to bed for three weeks."

As an opener, *Strange Interlude* was a solid choice: a major play by the playwright who, practically on his own, had made the world take notice of the American theatre for the first time; a play so long that it can be played only with a dinner interval. Producing *Strange Interlude* countered the popular notion that the Studio wasn't interested in revivals and linked the Studio with an early and great period in American theatre history. (First produced by the Theatre Guild in 1928, and starring Lynn Fontanne, *Strange Interlude* was the culmination of a series of daring experiments in form and language that O'Neill had undertaken throughout the twenties.)

O'Neill's vision of what he wanted to accomplish often exceeded his grasp of language and dramatic structure: the plays that he wrote were usually not as majestic as the plays that were in his mind. Sometimes his subject was too vast for him, as in the epic *Mourning Becomes Electra*, where he tries to interpret the story of Orestes in American terms; with *Strange Interlude*, the play's grand form seems too weighty for its subject. A wild mix of Sophocles, Ibsen, Strindberg, Freud, and Elinor Glyn, *Strange Interlude* is about fathers and daughters, mothers and sons, husbands and wives, wives and lovers, promiscuity, frigidity, the burdens of passion, the sins of the father haunting his children—but at heart, the play is about an extramarital affair.

At the center of the sprawling psychiatric canvas is Nina Leeds, one of the great neurotics of modern drama, a woman obsessed by the memory of her lover, Gordon Shaw, killed in the war before their affair was consummated. Nina blames her father for her virginity. After the shock of Gordon's death brings on her first nervous breakdown, she becomes compulsively promiscuous, and then marries a man, Sam Evans, she doesn't love, only to learn from Sam's mother that there is insanity in Sam's family. Pointing darkly to a crazy aunt sequestered upstairs, Mrs. Evans urges a pregnant Nina to have an abortion and to give Sam a child by someone else—which Nina does. Sam's child, named for Nina's dead lover Gordon, is by a doctor (Ned Darrell) who has the dark sexuality that good-egg Sam lacks. Hanging around through the years is Nina's surrogate father Charles Marsden, the man she ends up with in the end, a prissy mama's boy who writes genteel novels.

Divided between her loyalty to her unsuspecting husband and her smoldering passion for the man who fathered her child, Nina seems like a manic-depressive, oddly becalmed in one act, mordant and hysterical in the next. Is she O'Neill's idea of the Eternal Feminine, a wicked Circe, alternately tempting and rejecting her three suitors?

Guilt-ridden, tied to the past and to smothering parents both alive and remembered, sexually stalled, torn by ambivalence, O'Neill's monumental neurotics are fertile ground for Method actors. O'Neill has even written the subtext the actors would normally have had to supply for themselves, in the form of a continual stream of asides which represent the characters' private thoughts, what at the Studio would be called their inner monologues. Forever telling us what his characters are thinking, O'Neill has in fact removed much of their mystery and ambiguity. O'Neill's "method" here is thus the exact opposite of Chekhov's—where Chekhov suggests and implies, O'Neill holds up each character's insides like laboratory specimens that require careful labeling.

"Strange Interlude didn't stand a chance of representing Studio work at its best," says Arthur Penn. "The production was good but one wished one were watching a better play. The play suffered from the passage of time —the naiveté of this early Freudian drama constantly eroded the acting effort." Countering O'Neill's blood-and-thunder diction, the actors shrewdly underplayed. The work on inner technique that has always been the Studio's focus was evident in the company's quiet approach to O'Neill's declamatory style and in the fact that the actors discovered some of the depth and privacy that O'Neill himself had systematically removed when he had his characters talk their thoughts. As Nina, Geraldine Page looked every bit a great actress rising to the demands of a great role. "When I read the play for the first time at school, I felt I knew it—I felt Nina was in me, and I was in her," Page says. "How I loved doing it. I thought it was a wonderful production." Page caught the character's lightning shifts of mood: at times, her Nina was cryptic and sour, and capable of stabbing cruelty—a woman who remained apart from the men she taunted. At other times, she was ablaze with sexual fever.

Ben Gazzara as Nina's lover was too oily and clenched, and not convincing as a proper New England doctor, but Jane Fonda as the hard-bitten fiancée of Nina's son, Pat Hingle as Sam, William Prince as Marsden, Franchot Tone as Nina's possessive father, and Betty Field as Sam's controlling mother were strong. And though Page necessarily dominated the evening, it was the play that was really the star.

Expectedly, the response was mixed. "The Actors Studio has taken a step forward," wrote the *New York Times*. "It may turn out to be a giant step forward for the good of the American theatre." The *Village Voice* (with its bias against uptown theatre) said unfairly, "If the Actors Studio is attempting to advance the art of the theatre, this is a poor beginning. If they intend to compete with David Merrick and Alexander Cohen they have more or less succeeded. This rediscovery of L.B. Mayer and the star system suggests a new failure of nerve at the Studio."

"Any theatre would have been wrong for *Marathon 33*," says its writer and director June Havoc. "It doesn't live in a theatre. An armory would have been a good setting for it, or a prize fight arena, or a faded, abandoned old ballroom. Theatre doesn't have to be in the theatre."

Marathon 33 is Havoc's documentary-like account of a Depression phenomenon, the dance marathons that became a livelihood for many starving young people. (Most audiences are probably familiar with marathons from the 1969 film *They Shoot Horses, Don't They?*, adapted from a hard-boiled novel of the thirties by Horace McCoy.) Onto a crowded dance arena Havoc brings phantoms from her own life: the cynical, exploiting producers; the hollow-voiced carnival barkers; the driven, dazed dancers; and the audiences who come to the spectacle with blood in their eyes and ice water in their veins. The author's self-portrait, young June, enters the marathon when the vaudeville circuit on which she had been raised dries up. With visions of going legit—having a career on Broadway—June becomes a marathon contestant without realizing how much it can damage her spirit. Toughened by her vaudevillian life, June is not quite tough

enough for the marathon world. But with her native shrewdness and optimism—her belief that somehow things manage to turn out in the end—she
survives.

"I loved that period of the marathons, despite its horrors," Miss Havoc
says in retrospect. "And I knew the period. My sister [Gypsy Rose Lee]
didn't care for authenticity, she wanted money and fame, and our family
story as told in *Gypsy* is not the truth. That wasn't the way it was. In
Marathon 33, I told the truth."

But between Havoc's original truth and the final production there was
much interference. "June wrote a fantastic piece," Geraldine Page recalls.
"But people started saying, 'It's not a play, it's not a play.' Well, so what
if it wasn't a play in any conventional, well-made sense? It was June's raw
remembrance. It was real. It was her unique, fabulous experience. What the
play was and what they did to it—oh my. I could kick myself because I
didn't keep a copy of the original."

Marathon 33 does not communicate in script form. If ever there was
a play that depends on production values—a tawdry American underworld
has to be meticulously recreated on stage—this is it. Havoc herself says that
the published text is merely a series of notes to guide a director and his
cast, who must create a full score out of scraps of colloquial dialogue and
dashes of vivid local color.

A longtime Studio member active in both the Acting and Playwrights
Units, Havoc realized that the Studio was just the place to go to work on
a play like this. "It was not written at the Studio, but I knew that there
I could work on the core of the piece, and that I would be allowed to share
with the actors the astonishing truths of that shady world. The play was
optioned originally by David Merrick and Gower Champion, but I gave it
to the Studio out of a sense of cockeyed loyalty. 'I'm losing a big smash
of a musical, another *Gypsy*,' I said to myself at the time."

If she sold the rights to David Merrick, she knew she would also give
up any continued creative access to her own material. Merrick and Champion would have transformed her authentic account of a bygone social
phenomenon into a rip-roaring musical extravaganza and sentimentalized
it beyond recognition, while under the Studio's auspices she would be able
to protect her work.

Months before the play went into production, Havoc began investigat-
ing what she calls "essence": "We worked on the semi-fanaticism that

characterized the marathons as I knew them, and on squirreliness, which is a special brand of madness that broke out like an epidemic during the marathons." June's trenchant autobiography, *Early Havoc*, became required reading at the Studio, and Havoc recalled first-hand experiences from her marathon days to give the actors a sense of the period in all "its squalor and its strange beauty." In December 1962, a full year before the play was mounted, she offered a special evening at the Studio during which she discussed the marathons as ten teams and a floor judge (composed of Studio members) demonstrated rules, habits of behavior, sounds, and movements "peculiar to the time."

But once they went into production, the atmosphere got meaner. A first problem, one which still brings up bitter feelings, was who was to direct. "I was originally to have directed June's play," Frank Corsaro claims. Corsaro feels that Strasberg allowed June to "mangle her own play. It was whittled down to conventional form—Lee permitted her to do it; he didn't exercise his prerogative."

June Havoc feels that Strasberg exercised entirely too much preroga-

Julie Harris as June Havoc in *Marathon 33*.

tive. "They went through three or four directors with concepts Cheryl and Lee did not want. Cheryl all along wanted me to direct, as from the beginning I had been led to believe I would. Lee finally agreed. But he interfered with my work. He was enamored of the comedic in it, but he was also destructive of it, because he didn't understand it. Broad comedy after all was not exactly the Studio's forte. I had been raised in vaudeville; I knew first-hand how these characters should move and sound. And I knew what they were like inside, too. I worked like mad to protect the comic elements —I didn't want to make the piece too heavy, but Lee's work made it seem like Dostoevski."

"Lee wrought chaos upon Havoc," Michael Wager puns. "He didn't like what June was doing. He wanted to impose a consecutive story line. The material, so diffuse and so large scale, ideally needed a Guthrie or a Reinhardt to whip it into shape." "Lee kept working with Julie Harris [who played June] to make it more sentimental," Geraldine Page recalls.

Despite the fact that Havoc still feels the Studio "shortchanged" her play, despite Strasberg's well-intentioned but misguided notions about marathons, and despite the fact that it wasn't given the environmental staging it needs (it was originally to have been put on in a ballroom), June Havoc is proud of the work she did on it. "We managed to make truth on that stage," she says. "I was nominated for a Tony Award as best director, and the production got four Tony nominations. No other Studio production got that." Cheryl Crawford says she "loved *Marathon 33*, I don't care what anybody else says about it—it was one of my favorite productions."

I don't understand the coolness of Studio members who worked on it; though it may not have been all it was originally intended to be, *Marathon 33* was riveting. From the first moment, I felt steeped in a teeming, riotous environment. This was a sound and light show of extraordinary complexity, with two or three simultaneous actions interwoven with fragments of conversations and overlapping music to create the illusion of a thickly textured reality, a strange new world. This play about dancers was densely choreographed, with intricate contrapuntal movements beginning and ending abruptly—all the movements seemed to emerge organically from the grueling lives of Depression down-and-outs. With so much happening all at once, with characters swarming in from the wings and sliding up from the floor, with continual microphone announcements, and with multiple mini-dramas of heartbreak and blasted romance squeezed into the corners of the action, watching the play was a challenge—we were hurled into a setting whose ground rules we discovered only gradually. Recreating the glaring reality of the marathons as she knew them, Havoc wasn't interested in making it easy for us.

Julie Harris had originally encouraged Havoc to turn her first book of autobiography into a play because she wanted eagerly to play June herself, a prospect which made the project attractive to the Production Board: an authentic Studio-created star returning to her alma mater in a showpiece role. But Harris felt in the end that she had let down the Studio. In a letter to Cheryl Crawford (January 23, 1964), she wrote, "I wish with what's left of my heart that *Marathon 33* had been a stunning success for you and June and Lee, and will always feel guilty that I didn't make you get a sparkling young lady." Harris's performance was grave and refined when something more earthy and with a comic touch was called for, but she gave the role the full force of her lyric intensity, playing June with a love for the character that captures the real June's great warmth and enthusiasm. Most important, Julie Harris played unselfishly—she remained part of a closely drilled ensemble. *Marathon 33* was a group effort, a true company production, and, like Cheryl Crawford, I loved it, I don't care what anybody says.

Dynamite Tonite expired after a single performance, and has been all but written out of the Studio's official production history. "Nobody believed in it," Michael Wager says. Like *Marathon 33,* but in a more extreme way, the play suffered a sea change when it was moved from the Studio's workshop environment.

"It was wonderful at the Studio, but then when they gave it a full production, they made it pretentious," says Geraldine Page. In the Playwrights Unit, where *Dynamite Tonite* was developed out of improvisations between the play's author, Arnold Weinstein, and Studio actors, the material seemed promising; but as it congealed into a fixed, final form, it began to lose some of its original snap, and by the time it opened to the public it had become a Studio stepchild. How did the production get as far as it did if the Studio had so little faith in its potential? And wasn't there enough money in the reserve fund to keep it running for a few weeks at least, to test its possible audience appeal and to avoid the disgrace of a one-performance flop? In the face of such sloppy, cowardly management, we might well ask: who was minding the store? "In this case, Mendy Wager was minding the store," Geraldine Page says.

Dynamite Tonite was part of the Studio's "experimental phase," for which it received a Rockefeller Foundation grant of $56,400. Called, variously, an actors' opera, a comic opera for actors, a travesty on the idiocy of war, it is a pungent cabaret satire with a dissonant score in the style of Brecht and Weill that takes potshots at opera, actors, musicals, war, and religion. The style is brash and irreverent, an anti-musical for the sixties. This wasn't a wise choice for the Studio, at least not so early in its Theatre's history. *Dynamite Tonite* flew in the face of what audiences and critics expected (and had every right to expect) from the Actors Studio. After the Theatre had become firmly established as an interpreter of American realism, Weinstein's abrasive comic opera might well have had some point—a playful piece to demonstrate the range and virtuosity of Studio talent. (In fact, because it was such atypical Studio material, the cast was augmented by performers from the Second City, a group of comic actors from Chicago skilled in improvisation.)

The week of April 20, 1964, the Actors Studio Theatre opened two productions, a comedy with Paul Newman and Joanne Woodward, and a blistering, out-of-control play on race relations.

Working for scale, the Newmans did James Costigan's *Baby Want a Kiss* as a favor to Strasberg and to the Studio. Since their names alone ensured a healthy box office, it didn't really matter what play they acted in: why did they choose this one? "Paul and Joanne wanted to shine in a little vehicle, and this was the play they really wanted to do," says Frank Corsaro, their director. "We had fun with it. I think it had a certain appeal as an absurdist piece, but it really was not a good choice: it exemplified a fallacious side of the Studio."

To a failed writer's remote country house (decorated in high-camp Gothic) come two friends, world-renowned movie stars Emil and Mavis, for their first meeting with Edward (played by Costigan) after a rupture of fifteen years. Uneasily, the guests banter with their host, recount incriminating dreams, revel in their beauty and fame, take turns seducing Edward, and finally offer to take Edward back into their lives. When Edward refuses, there is more numbing small talk as Emil and Mavis reassemble their made-up personalities before departing, leaving Edward, as at the beginning, in sole possession of his mausoleum.

"What is it?" asked Howard Taubman in the *New York Times*. What it is, is two acts in search of a play. For ninety minutes, James Costigan's three decadent characters talk at each other as they weave in and out of a tangle of themes, abruptly switching tone from chit-chat to accusation. Trying to cover a conversational vacuum, they're like guests at a party who have been deserted by their host and who say anything—the first thing that pops into their scattered minds—to avoid an embarrassing silence. Sometimes, in a volley of enigmatic monosyllables, the characters speak a studied, sub-Pinteresque lingo; other times, trying for an arch gaiety, they sound like demented refugees from a Noel Coward drawing room. And when, at climactic moments, they tear off their masks of affability in order to tell the truth about themselves and each other, the shade of Edward Albee at his bitchiest hovers in the air. Papered over this schizophrenic small talk is a stale reality/illusion contrast that is strictly bargain-basement Pirandello. I suppose the playwright is saying something about what fame does to the worshipped as well as the worshippers—beneath their cultivated image of ageless beauty, these beloved movie stars turn out to be faking it, physically as well as emotionally.

Although I wouldn't like to see them try, Elizabeth Taylor and Richard Burton might be able to give Costigan's manufactured characters a semblance of wit. But Paul Newman and Joanne Woodward were far too sensible for these preening, corrupt characters. Far from playing themselves, far from playing even a travesty of themselves, they were both hopelessly out of their element: Joanne Woodward too likable and down-to-earth for the sort of cartoon character that, in her decline, Tallulah Bankhead always played, even when she wasn't supposed to; Paul Newman too solemn and constrained for his character's insinuating self-mockery.

The play made money, but *Baby Want a Kiss* probably did more damage to the Actors Studio Theatre than any other production. To have sold a cheap bill of goods on the basis of attractive star names was a betrayal of the kind of theatre that Strasberg had always talked about, and when the Ford Foundation saw this production they began to reevaluate their commitment to him. "It was a desperation measure," says Arthur Penn; a ploy to keep the Theatre afloat in the hope that a box-office hit—and the kind of artistic compromise that that seemed to require—would enable the Theatre at a later point to do the kind of work it said it wanted to do, to become the Theatre it said it wanted to become.

"Lee was so happy that Paul, the big star, wanted to do something," Geraldine Page recalls. "Lee said, 'Paul has a play he wants to do; if we do it, he'll bring in some money.' I thought it was a good idea to balance out our offerings with a light comedy, but this wasn't it. I suggested *Any Wednesday*, but nobody was interested. Lee and Mendy Wager kept saying about *Marathon 33* and *Blues for Mister Charlie*, 'It isn't a play, it isn't a play.' Did they think *Baby Want a Kiss* was a play? I hated it! All I remember about it now is that there was a bird on stage and people kept saying to it, 'Cheep, cheep, cheep.' "

James Baldwin's *Blues for Mister Charlie*, a sprawling play of epic magnitude about race relations in the American South, was exactly the kind of material that a theatre company eyeing greatness should have undertaken. Baldwin is not a born dramatist, his play is too long and awkwardly structured as it moves between present and past action, and there are occasional purple patches where his dispossessed characters sing out their grief, but this enormous work is lit throughout by its author's anger and power.

The play opens with a bolt of theatrical lightning. "And may every nigger like this nigger end like this nigger—face down in the weeds!" shouts Lyle, Baldwin's representative white Southerner after he has killed an upstart black man named Richard. In the three long acts that follow, Baldwin examines the causes that led to this murderous encounter. Interweaving fragments from the past into the present turmoil that follows Richard's death, Baldwin attempts to reveal the conscience of a color-divided community. At the center is the victim, a young black who went north to New York to work as a musician and found there the same traps that he left the South hoping to avoid. Drifting into a subworld of whoring with ravenous white women, he descends into a pit of self-loathing from which he tries to escape with drugs. Burned out, spewing bitterness, eaten up with hatred for Mr. Charlie, his white oppressor, he comes home determined to turn a redneck Southerner like Lyle into his executioner. "I'm going to make myself well," he intones to his pacifist grandmother, in one of the play's many incantatory speeches.

I'm going to make myself *well* with hatred—what do you think of that? ... I'm going to learn how to drink it—a little every day in the morning, and then a booster shot late at night. I'm going to remember everything ... all those boys and girls in Harlem and all them pimps and whores and gangsters and all them cops. And I'm going to remember all the dope that's flowed through my veins. I'm going to remember everything—the jails I been in and the cops that beat me and how long a time I spent screaming and stinking in my own dirt, trying to break my habit. I'm going to remember all that, and I'll get well. I'll get well.

Taunting the stupid white man Lyle, insulting Lyle's masculinity and playing on his primitive fears of blacks, Richard courts his own death, sacrificing himself in order to ignite his people.

Wildly uneven, *Blues for Mister Charlie* is a play about which it is possible to have serious reservations. The hatred of white people that wells up from Baldwin's impassioned dialogue has the stench of race prejudice. This is an incendiary play; this is theatre with blood in its eye, and in 1964, at the height of the Civil Rights movement, it was especially timely. The Studio almost passed up the chance to produce this landmark drama.

"Jimmy had been around the Studio for quite a few years," Arthur Penn recalls, "and we felt we owed him something. Lee had made some promises to him; and besides, we all felt we should get a black playwright up there, since there was no black theatre at that point." Still, when the Production Board had Baldwin's final manuscript in front of them, the vote was split down the middle. Several members were put off by the play's fierceness as well as its sprawling shape; they felt it wasn't yet ready for production, and that it wasn't, at this early point in their history, the kind of play they wanted the Studio to be associated with. "The Baldwin play should not have been done," Frank Corsaro says. "The Studio was afraid of it," says Geraldine Page. "It was a long hot summer, and people were worried about the impact the play might have. Four of us on the Board loved the play and wanted to do it. Five didn't want to do it. Only Arthur Penn hadn't voted—and we had trouble getting him into town from his place in the country. Rip told Arthur, 'You know the Actors Studio ought to do it, if it has any ambitions to be relevant.' Arthur said, 'It's not a play but it says something that ought to be said. I don't want to direct it, but I'll vote for it.' So the vote was even—five for, five against. Rip turned to Lee and said, 'It's up to you.' Lee got up and said, 'I have to catch a plane for California.' He left us sitting there. An hour later, Paula called from the airport to say, 'Lee says to do the play.' "

After it passed the Board, they couldn't find a director. "Burgess

Meredith wanted to direct it passionately," Page recalls. "Rip persuaded them to let Burgess direct. He said, 'Nobody else wants to do it and he's dying to do it.' " Before production, Page says there was "another big battle when Cheryl Crawford, who was appalled at the play's horrible language, got out her blue pencil. Rip told her she couldn't touch the play. 'I promised Jimmy Baldwin we'd do it the way he wrote it,' he said, which is interesting in light of what happened with the British censor."

Frank Corsaro thinks the play *ought* to have been interfered with. "Lee permitted Baldwin to exercise his controls in a way that was detrimental," Corsaro says, "and the results were desperately disappointing."

Three years later, responding to a scene from the play that two members had worked on, Strasberg recounted calmly and with clarity the troubled production history of *Blues for Mister Charlie*. "There were conflicts between Jimmy and myself. He was encouraged to make it propaganda; I felt it should have stressed more of the human elements. Jimmy's passion as a writer has humanity for both white and black, objectively. Jimmy was trying to raise our understanding, showing the human currents which affect political motivation. It is in the play, sometimes roughly and primitively done, but finally the play backed off from things it propounded. The third act, where people came out at you, to speak their inner thoughts, never quite solved its problem, as writing or theatre.

"Originally, Corsaro was to direct. He wanted the stage to be not abstract but to take on a sense of community. Behind every scene was to be an improvisation of communal life. Then we got into trouble because Jimmy disagreed with some of the things Frank asked for in the writing. Burgess Meredith found it difficult to carry through the idea of the continual presence of the community. I had hoped the production would be visually more exciting, to bring out the life of the people. The Swedish production filled in all the scenes realistically—which was the right idea. Our production was visually sparse. It started off well, with starkness and simplicity, but it needed more color—it got much too one-toned, too gray. While exciting in many aspects—Rip Torn, Diana Sands, and Pat Hingle were excellent—it did not add color and aliveness. I was disappointed in it. We weren't able to control it organizationally."

Strasberg, Corsaro, Penn, Wager, and other Production Board members may have been disappointed, but I agree with Geraldine Page who says, "It was fabulous—wonderful," and who remembers "the terrific excitement of both white and black audiences." "It is this kind of play (one with national significance) which can once more restore to the theatre the excitement, the passion and the dignity it had in other times when it was not merely an entertainment for buyers and their expense account guests," the *Journal American* announced. "When the Group Theatre was functioning many years ago, it had something to say. It said it ardently, and people flocked to it. It is their [the Actors Studio Theatre's] belief that that audience still exists. It simply has had no place to go." "In its impact," Howard Taubman wrote in the *New York Times,* "it resembles *Waiting for Lefty* of three decades ago. It's a play with fires of fury in its belly, tears of anguish in its eyes and a roar of protest in its throat."

The production was filled with acting that met the power of Baldwin's writing head on—like Baldwin, the actors reveled in their emotional force, releasing feelings of operatic intensity and dimension. I will never forget Diana Sands's monologue in the third act when, before she takes the stand to bear witness for her slain lover, she recalls a night of passion. Midway in her character's outpouring of grief and longing, she bent into a panther-like crouch as her voice reached a shivering pitch. Her words seemed to come from some place deep within, from a privacy I had never before seen on a stage. Her pulsing cry had a primordial power. This is how Greek tragedy must have been played, I thought, with this kind of ecstasy and wonder, with this kind of shattering eloquence. After her aria, shaken and exhilarated, the audience cheered wildly, its own restraints freed by the spectacle of Sands's force.

Three Sisters, directed by Lee Strasberg: this was an event, and everyone knew it. For Strasberg, the pressure was intense. A born talker, he now had to trade the comfort of a workshop session for the demands of putting on a play. He hadn't had a full-fledged directing success since 1934, with *Men in White,* and now he had the challenge of a classic Method text, a play that had helped to shape Stanislavski's ideas about inner technique. Chekhov's delicate play; a high-strung director unsure of his ability; a handpicked cast of longtime Strasberg students, waiting for the miracle, wondering if their teacher could transfer to production the remarkable qualities of his work in Studio sessions—the stage seemed to be set for a disaster.

"The experience was a major disappointment in Kim Stanley's life," reports Arthur Penn. "She had expected for years that work at the Studio would be carried over into production, but in rehearsal the goal was to get the play on; and it was unthinkable as a logical extension of Studio work." "Strasberg directing *Three Sisters* was a strange mixture of not quite practicing what he preached," says Frank Corsaro.

Yet how could it have been? To direct a play the way he worked with actors at the Studio would have taken years of rehearsals. He proceeded more quickly, as indeed he had to, but Strasberg did not abandon or betray his Method. For all the disappointment his actors felt at the (inevitable) difference between Lee Strasberg in class and in the director's chair, his production had exactly those qualities he always praised in class. It was a demonstration of Strasberg's enduring belief in the beauty, the charm, and the moral value of art made up to look like life.

The long, detailed party scene at the end of Act I put Strasberg's technique on brilliant display. As a large group sat down to dinner in celebration of Irina's birthday, there was a buzz of overlapping conversations broken by stabs of laughter as glasses clinked and knives and forks clattered against plates. "Strasberg gave us a good thing to work on," Geraldine Page recalls. "He said, 'Go on with what you're doing when other characters are speaking; move around like normal people. Everybody go on about your business—don't stand there and be polite.' That's what we all did, and the party scene had a terrific lifelike quality as a result."

Overall, the production was weakest in creating a sense of the period in which Chekhov lived and wrote—Imperial Russia at the turn of the century. In voice and movement and gesture, in emotional tenor, the company was rooted in New York, transforming Chekhov's high-strung aristocrats into more or less modern neurotics. This was a decidedly New York *Three Sisters*, and as such it was a happy contrast to the arch, brittle British approach. At the National Theatre or the Royal Shakespeare Company, Chekhov is made to seem a cousin of Congreve or Wycherly, with the actors treating Chekhov's lean, muted poetry as if it were a string of epigrams. The Americans were less polite, thank goodness, interpreting Chekhov with an emotional fullness that he rarely receives.

The three sisters were played by three of America's foremost naturalistic actresses. Geraldine Page, with her voice fluttering at high pitch, her hands adjusting her hair, her eyes and face pinched from the fatigue of work and set in the mold of her spinsterdom, suggested Olga's deep disappointment as well as her great patience, her abiding spirit that makes her the family leader. With her porcelain beauty undercut by a sour expression, Shirley Knight steered clear of making Irina a sentimental ninny by giving her a tart, viperish quality. Physically restricted, her Irina seemed to be struggling for release from a prison of her own making. As Masha, Kim Stanley gave a performance that has become one of the legends of the American theatre. From the opening moments, as we saw her reclining on a chaise longue dressed in black and smoking a cigar as she flipped distractedly through the pages of a magazine, her Masha was startling, a woman on the edge of madness suffering from a terrifying sense of isolation. When she spoke, in a hushed voice lined with irony, it felt as if she was stabbing the air. With her mocking smile and hints of sadism, she was a Krafft-Ebbing Masha, pitiless, haughty, and tragic.

Stanley played Masha with such darkness that her lunge for the handsome soldier Vershinin seemed doomed from the outset, the last hopeless struggle of a woman who knows she is fated to remain with her idiotic husband, the provincial schoolmaster Kulygin. When, in Act IV, Masha says goodbye to her lover, Stanley was wrenching; her character seemed almost visibly weighed down by the lifetime of unused emotions that awaits her.

"The Actors Studio talks a good deal about the truth," Jerry Tallmer wrote in the *New York Post.* "Last night at the Morosco it nailed for our lifetime the right to do so and Lee Strasberg proved to a world waiting twenty years that he could direct a play . . . with all the creative truth and strength a human being can command." The Studio's superior *Three Sisters* ought to have proved the validity of the *idea* of its Theatre. "In a sane culture, the logical place for the Studio to end up would be as a national theatre," says Arthur Penn. "We've worked together for thirty years." But *Three Sisters* was the Theatre's last stand in New York.[6]

Unfortunately, there is a postscript. In 1965, the Studio was invited to participate in the World Theatre Season at the Aldwych in London. The Studio accepted the offer, and decided to bring over two productions, *Blues for Mister Charlie* and *Three Sisters.* To raise the fifty-five thousand that was needed, the Studio undertook a long fund-raising campaign. Since it was to be the sole American representative to the World Theatre Season, it applied to the State Department, which turned it down on the basis of its repertory. The State Department objected to Baldwin's play as being "controversial, badly written, and noisy—more cartoon and sermon than play at all," and to *Three Sisters* as bearing "little kinship to America" though possessing "great merit."

The Studio finally raised most of the money from its own membership. The London appearance now seemed especially significant because the Theatre had not had the funds for a third season; and many members felt that a well-received London engagement could renew the interest of the Ford Foundation.

Peter Daubeny, artistic director of the World Theatre Festival, interviewed in the *New York Times* five months before the Studio's London debut, reported that the Studio's announced visit was generating "great anticipation and excitement. The Actors Studio is not only a national institution without national support, but an international one that has benefited actors all over the world and influenced a whole generation. Through their realism we have discovered a whole way of life—we have discovered America. The Studio was selected to represent American theatre because we're tremendously interested in Lee Strasberg's work and teaching which means a great deal to us. We consider them the psyche of American drama." "Their visit is surely the most eagerly awaited event in London since the first visit of the Studio's elder sister, the Moscow Art Theatre," reported a British critic in a London newspaper a month before the Studio Theatre's scheduled performances. Weeks before the May 3 opening, both Studio productions were entirely sold out.

As it turned out, the Actors Studio Theatre season in London was a disaster from which the Studio's ego has never, in fact, entirely recovered. Strasberg's most virulent enemy couldn't have devised a more ghastly finale for his Theatre.

Its production of *Three Sisters* represents "the suicide of the Actors Studio," Penelope Gilliatt wrote in *The Observer.* Turning the house of Chekhov's cultivated sisters into "an expensive private asylum," the production trivializes Chekhov's heroines into "a slob, a tiresome little professional virgin, and a wardress for junkies." Watching this "coarse-grained" performance, Gilliatt continues, was like "playing the harpsichord in boxing gloves, like filling the Spanish Riding School with hippopotami." In *The Spectator,* Anthony Burgess decried the Studio's "rendering, or rending, of *Three Sisters.* Chekhov, Stanislavski, Strasberg: the middle term ought to unite the two outer ones, but it didn't." Seeing them play Chekhov,

Burgess wrote, is like spending "four whole hours to demonstrate the inefficacy of the Method when unleashed on a 'classical' acting text. There was no sense of a real *fin-de-siècle* Russia, but a doomed South waiting for a terrible slow sword, with *Gone with the Wind* officers to match." "The atmosphere is like a tenth-rate American psycho melodrama that would eventually be filmed with a trio of Hollywood's hammier elder stars," R.B. Marriott wrote in *The Stage*. "This is the worst production, purporting to be serious, I have ever seen. On the opening night it was booed."

Blues for Mister Charlie fared only marginally better. "It's old-fashioned without having the richness of a tradition"; "it is a straggling, overloaded propaganda tract with little fire in it."

In a quick defensive action, a badly shaken Lee Strasberg explained to the British press: "We are not a repertory company, and have had a company for only a year. We have no regular actors under contract. We thought it might be interesting for you to see us from the beginning, and then follow our work and progress. *Blues for Mister Charlie* and *Three Sisters* are not necessarily representative of the work of the Actors Studio. They are only part of the effort of the first year." To the dismay of many Studio members, Strasberg even apologized for James Baldwin, saying that the writer had not quite succeeded in getting his message across. "There is confusion in the play between Mr. Baldwin's dynamic anger at the racial situation and the human involvement beneath it. It is partly his fault, partly ours, if the human emotions are not sufficiently conveyed in the production."

Behind the opening night catastrophe of *Three Sisters* were the kind of logistical, administrative, and temperamental problems that had plagued the Theatre from the beginning. Because some of the original company decided they either couldn't or didn't want to go to London, certain roles had to be recast, thereby undermining the ensemble balance that had been achieved in the summer of 1964. In London, there was very little rehearsal time, and virtually no time at all on the stage of the Aldwych itself. "The management at the Aldwych was terrible," says Salem Ludwig who, as Equity deputy for the company, was closely involved with administrative details. "The backup was poor. Awful. We had no rehearsal space. They gave us tennis courts and armories, never a theatre. Then when we finally got access to the Aldwych, we found that it was a raked stage, with an eighteen-foot apron—we didn't have time to adjust to this. The costume fittings were all wrong. Lighting was not strong enough and it wasn't the same lighting plot as in New York. We didn't get a lighting man until the day before we opened. There was nothing but flat lighting for the third act. And because we had had almost no time to rehearse on the Aldwych stage, we kept falling into the apron, where we were covered by almost total darkness. We rehearsed up until six o'clock on the day we opened. Everyone's nerves were strained to the breaking point. We knew we just weren't ready to open. As deputy, I called a dinner break at six, the curtain was at seven. What with all our unfamiliarity with the playing area, and the British crew's inept scene shifts, opening night had twenty-eight minutes of extra playing time."

Cheryl Crawford, who hadn't seen any of the rehearsals, sat in the Aldwych opening night in a state bordering on shock. "They were all fucked up in London," she says. "So many things went wrong. The lighting was so dark you could hardly see some of the actors. There were miscast substitutes. The raked stage seemed to throw people off. The tempos were all wrong. I was very upset, and I criticized Strasberg for saying actors could be substituted—not those substitutes, at any rate."

Playwright Meade Roberts, who had seen and loved the New York production, says that in London "there wasn't a trace of Kim Stanley's performance of a year before. It was a travesty of what it had been in New York. Sandy Dennis [who replaced Shirley Knight as Irina] stammered continuously, had a silly Marilyn Monroe hairdo, and holes in her shawl. Kim looked like a mammy in white face. Nan Martin [who had replaced Geraldine Page as Olga] looked inappropriately elegant, like Gertrude Lawrence. And George C. Scott [who had replaced Kevin McCarthy as Vershinin] had been busy beating up Ava Gardner at the Savoy and barely knew his lines. It looked like a lot of actors doing a lot of scenes."

It was an opening night that, as Strasberg later said, was in reality a dress rehearsal. Later performances naturally improved, but the production never touched what it had been in New York.

Returning from the wars beaten and derided, Strasberg reported his version of what had happened to a June acting session. "The performance of *Three Sisters* fell apart," he said, his voice weighted with fatigue. "It was no one's fault. I didn't want to go to begin with, I would like to go four years from now, when our repertory is established. The critics there are used to companies coming and showing the result of fifteen years' work. We had to reassemble and re-rehearse the plays, something none of the other companies had to do. If our original company had gone, it would have been different. We weren't experienced enough and the people there steered us a little bit wrong. The other theatres are theatres, whereas we were totally unprepared for technical and administrative problems.

"I had to agree with the critics because of what went wrong opening night. They went too far in efforts to draw final conclusions—they were ready to draw those conclusions no matter what. The woman next to me opening night was in tears. I was in tears, too, but for different reasons. It was one of the few occasions in my lifetime when I was forced into the ignominious position of agreeing with the critics: there is nothing worse.

"Well [a long sigh] it was just one of those things. Now we will have to face basic matters of the functioning of the organization."

15

THE METHOD AND THE
MOVIES: THE ANTI-HERO

A n airport. Reporters and photographers swarm around an old man, buzzing him with questions and a flash of light bulbs.

"I am a retired investor living on a pension," the man says in a calm voice that yet has a razor's edge. Except for his wary, darting eyes, his face is masked.

A shot rings out. The man falls to the ground. Panic.

The old man, who clearly was not who he said he was, is Lee Strasberg in *The Godfather Part II*, acting with a naturalness that vindicated a lifetime of teaching. His performance was not only a personal triumph but a symbolic one as well, for the Method and for the Studio. When the film's director, Francis Ford Coppola, at the urging of Al Pacino, the film's star, offered Strasberg the role of a Jewish gangster, Strasberg was reluctant to accept it. The last time he had acted was in a 1931 Theatre Guild production of *Green Grow the Lilacs,* and he knew that his work would be looked at closely.

Playing Hyman Roth, a mobster whose every word is a lie, Strasberg does exactly what he had always counseled his students to do: he avoids all the clichés. His grandfatherly gangster is an elder Jewish statesman, an uneducated immigrant who made good. Plain-spoken, his character sounds and looks like any other nice, simple Jewish man of his age and background, someone you'd see in an art deco Miami Beach cafeteria where they have $3.95 dinner specials before five. Strasberg gives the character a touch of piety—like many men who've overcome great obstacles to make a good life for themselves, he's got a holier-than-thou attitude. A preternatural calmness encases him, as if he has nothing more to prove. Yet his absolute quiet is unsettling and alerts you to the ruthless killer just below the casual facade.

Again following the advice he always gave to students, Strasberg plays not for the surface value of the words but for what's going on beneath them: his performance has a bristling subtext, so that even the most off-handed conversational exchanges contain promise of the violence and cruelty by which this man has carved out his career. Paternalistic yet intimidating (like Strasberg at the Studio!), his honeyed words covering his murderous intentions, Hyman Roth has learned how to hide out in public. Obviously, Strasberg drew on his own experiences as a leader to create this underworld kingpin, a man with godlike power over others. The strength and determination that kept him at the head of the Studio oozes from his character. His gangster has the assurance of a born tyrant.

Perhaps because I had never seen Strasberg act before, I thought of him as a non-actor brought in to play a role for which he was a natural. Certainly I never once caught him acting. Playing Roth in an intimate, low-key style, Strasberg is wonderfully real, at once simple, fresh, spontaneous, alive, and at ease. Strasberg's beautiful performance lends final proof to what was obvious since the founding of the Studio, that the Method is primarily and ideally a film technique.

After *The Godfather*, Strasberg was employed in films for the rest of his life. He never again had so rich a role in so strong a film, but he was consistently natural. In *The Godfather*, he was startlingly effective, in a way that may be possible only when you see an actor for the first time. In his subsequent film work, there were no surprising variations in mood or range, though his technique remained invisible, without fuss or theatricality.

In *The Cassandra Crossing*, he plays a concentration camp survivor. The sketchy script offers no firm details about the character's background but Strasberg by his presence alone and by the flicker of pained memories that crosses his face in close-ups suggests a tortured past for his character. Through weighty silences and a face that registers fleeting thoughts and feelings, Strasberg speaks to the camera—he doesn't need any dialogue. In *Going in Style*, Strasberg is really outclassed by two master comedians, Art Carney and George Burns, though he has two strong scenes, the first when he recalls the time, long ago, when he hit his son; the second, when he's in an ambulance after having suffered what will prove to be a fatal stroke, and wordlessly looks up at his friend. It's one of the simplest and most eloquent death scenes I can recall. Even in the seldom-seen *Boardwalk*, where Strasberg as a modern-day Job, a middle-class Jewish man beset with woes, has to wade through a contrived script and to play against a grotesquely miscast Janet Leigh (an archetypal shiksa trying hopelessly to be Strasberg's Jewish daughter), he performs with simplicity and conviction.

Although some Studio members were skeptical about their leader's movie successes, there is a positive way to think of them, as a significant part of Strasberg's legacy to future generations of acting students. Strasberg's rapport with the camera underlined the fact that it is through the film work of its most famous members that the Studio has made its most enduring contribution to the history of American acting.

There is indeed a demonstrable "Studio line" in American film acting that stretches from John Garfield and Montgomery Clift to Marlon Brando and James Dean, from Paul Newman and Steve McQueen to Dustin Hoffman, Al Pacino, Robert De Niro, Robert Duvall, and Jack Nicholson, and that, on the female side, moves from Julie Harris, Geraldine Page, Shelly Winters, Anne Bancroft, Lee Grant, and Kim Stanley to Ellen Burstyn, Estelle Parsons, Sandy Dennis, and Shirley Knight. This roster obviously includes some of the most distinctive and accomplished actors we've ever had, and at some point in their development their talent was nurtured, sharpened, rechanneled, or clarified by exposure to the Studio's Method. These performers share what I think are some common ingredients, and it's those qualities I want to examine in the following pages: the qualities of the Method actor in the movies.

It is a historical irony that the true fulfillment of the Studio style would be attained on film rather than in the theatre, since the Studio inherited the Group's disdain for movies. The Group actors who pledged themselves to Harold Clurman's experiment regarded movies as mass-produced products that had nothing to do with the art of acting; fortunately, however, neither Kazan nor Strasberg shared Clurman's unrelenting anti-film attitude. When he co-founded the Studio, Kazan was already an established film director commuting between New York and Hollywood. Although Strasberg would occasionally repeat the Group's traditional objections, he in fact was more concerned about what could happen to an actor's talent if he hit it big in Hollywood than about movie acting as cheapening work-for-hire. Strasberg realized that there was simply more work, and better-paying work, in films than on the stage.

At the Studio there still exists, however, a value distinction between the New York actor, devoted primarily to the stage, and the Los Angeles actor who is thought to have sacrificed craft concerns for well-paying hack work. Acting on stage still counts for more than "Coast" acting. Acting on stage is like continuing to attend Studio sessions, even after you've become successful: it's a sign of authenticity.

Ostensibly, work at the Studio prepares actors for the stage—most actors use the Studio to learn how to create and sustain a part in a play. Movie acting is rarely talked about; and no actor dares to bring in a scene from a film script. Most Studio actors I talked with frankly prefer theatre to films, claiming like Geraldine Page that films are for directors (or cinematographers) while theatre is for the true actor, the actor who loves to act. "On stage, you make all the decisions," Page says. "In movies, you say to yourself, 'It's not my fault! It's not my fault!' In movies, the director's got it. It's his playpen. You have no responsibility. In theatre, you can do what you want, and the director has to wait until the curtain comes down to yell at you. In films, they can cut it out."

Nonetheless, movies put the Actors Studio on the map. The stunning success of Studio actors like Brando and Dean brought a kind of fame that could never have happened if Studio members had acted only in the theatre. Two crucial questions: What was so excitingly new about Brando and Dean? And to what extent was their style indebted to the Studio's Method?

Historically, top movie stars like Clark Gable, Gary Cooper, James Stewart, Spencer Tracy, Humphrey Bogart, and Edward G. Robinson had always been prized for their naturalness. Their work seemed instinctive, without apparent technique and devoid of the rhetorical flourishes or vocal self-consciousness that was traditionally associated with stage performance. They were at their best working a narrow, repetitive range, playing parts that seemed close to their own real-life personalities. Ease on camera and the gift of creating the illusion of being real, for which Brando and Dean were praised, were in themselves nothing new; but Brando and Dean added qualities that gave their work a kinetic charge—a revolutionary intensity. They appeared to be more fully and interestingly alive on screen than any generation of actors before them. Their realism was deeper, more layered and more complex, than that of a Tracy or a Cooper; Brando and Dean were fascinating neurotics, exuding a primeval sexuality. Emotionally, they were knottier and more vulnerable than actors had seemed before, daringly androgynous, even feral. Reaching into their own psyches, they were intuitive and spontaneous. When Brando and Dean first appeared in films like *On the Waterfront* and *East of Eden,* they seemed startlingly rough-edged: untutored. You felt they were actors who acted because they had to, to release the demons within.

Using their voices as naturally as they did their bodies, they sounded like real people. Brando's fabled mumble, in *A Streetcar Named Desire* and *On the Waterfront,* turned out to be an act, but James Dean, with his thick Midwestern twang and his slurred delivery, really didn't speak well. The inarticulate style they made famous, whether feigned or real, was a signal that words were inadequate to convey the tangle of inner feelings. Their war with words—the failed struggle toward verbal expression that became an emblem of a generation—told us, in effect, that they had emotions that went deeper than language. To instinctive characters like Terry Malloy (in *On the Waterfront*) and Jim Stark (in *Rebel without a Cause*), words were hard to come by and not to be trusted because they usually didn't honor the full complexity of feelings.

Brando and Dean were members of the Actors Studio in its earliest days, and so were exposed to the Method primarily through Kazan rather than Strasberg. Brando's stage performance as Stanley Kowalski was in fact created before there was an Actors Studio, and Brando over the years has downplayed his indebtedness both to the Studio and to Lee Strasberg. After Strasberg's death, he stated that he resented Strasberg's attempts to claim credit for his development, maintaining that the teacher who had done the most to help him in his early days was Stella Adler.

Brando had never been deeply involved in the Studio, having attended only sporadically in the late forties and early fifties. Dean also kept a wary distance. Once, when Strasberg criticized him after he had performed in a scene, Dean was so stung that he didn't return for months. And when he was at the Studio, he would typically sit sullenly in a corner, or cower, head down, body collapsed, in the front row.

"Brando would have been Brando even if there never had been an Actors Studio," Carl Schaeffer said, adding, "Lee certainly helped talented actors to develop, but he can't claim responsibility for their talent, or for making talented actors into stars." John Strasberg says that it is simply "a myth that the Actors Studio created Brando and Dean. Their discovery really belongs to Kazan, not to my father or the Studio per se, which passively took the credit."

Nonetheless, the reputations of the two actors are inseparable (I think justifiably) from that of the Studio. Their work is exemplary of the Studio's style of luminous American realism. To act like Brando and Dean remains a strong (if unspoken, perhaps sometimes unconscious) pull for many Studio members. Indeed, it has been said that the Studio is an acting factory that produces cut-rate Marlon Brandos. Brando may be the epitome of the charged psychological realism that Studio actors are working toward, but it seems to me unfair to dismiss Studio acting as imitation Brando. The point of being at the Studio is for actors to unlock their own individuality, to be odd and interesting in their own way, not in Brando's. But as Stanislavski discovered early in his career, imitation holds sway over an actor's subconscious; and so Brando-isms linger in the Studio atmospehre, and sometimes actors forsake their own way of being real for that of the actor many of them consider the world's best.

A man "roughly dressed in blue denim work clothes" carrying his bowling jacket and "a red-stained package from a butcher's" enters with a bellow whose echo can still be heard on stage and screen. "Hey, there! Stella, Baby!" "Don't holler at me like that," Stella answers, not really meaning it. "Catch!" Stanley throws the package to her, calling out "Meat!" as he and his friend Mitch prepare to leave. "Stanley! Where are you going?" "Bowling!" In another second, he's offstage.

In 1947, Marlon Brando as Tennessee Williams's passionate, inarticulate Stanley Kowalski in *A Streetcar Named Desire* acted with a joyful realism that seemed like a reprimand to all previous styles. Slurred, nasal, guttural, rising to a growl in bursts of temper, descending to an insinuating purr in moments of sexual intimacy, the voice that Brando created for Stanley had a jolting blue-collar coarseness. Like the Moscow Art players, he turned his back to the audience. He chewed gum, he talked with his mouth full, he picked his teeth, he scratched his chest, and most memorable of all, he stalked the stage in a ripped t-shirt. After a fight with Stella, he went down on his knees and howled like a stricken animal. In the heat of battle, he wouldn't bother to finish a sentence, or even a word. And then, in a quiet moment with Stella, in a gesture of appeasement, Brando took a piece of lint off her dress. He didn't do it in the same place every night, recalls Kim Hunter, and he didn't necessarily do it every night. But that he did it at all, a little undirected bit of business like this, was evidence of an actor's creative state that Strasberg spent thirty-five years talking about.

Playing moment to moment, trying out ways to keep the play fresh for himself, Brando never froze his performance; long after opening night, he continued to explore, adding and changing and removing, adjusting his performance according to how he felt on the spot. To act on stage with him was like running an obstacle course. It was an experience exciting to Kim Hunter and Karl Malden, who were to become part of Kazan's inner circle at the Studio, but a trial for Jessica Tandy, who has always avoided the Studio. "The one or two times I went," she says, "the work seemed amateurish and unprofessional."

From night to night, Tandy (Blanche DuBois) was never sure how Brando would behave, what new colors or values he would add, or at what point he would add them. And Kim Hunter says that over the course of the play's long run, Stella's relationship with Stanley underwent some surprising shifts. "By the end of the New York run, we were doing more yelling than loving. The characters' relationship had become strained and tense, and so when we made the film Gadge was careful to bring us back to the original values—to play that Stanley and Stella were madly, passionately in love, and Stella's love for her husband overrode her love for her sister."

Brando in a ripped t-shirt, like Brando in his leather jacket and blue jeans in *The Wild One,* became a generation's symbol of rebelliousness. Yet Stanley is a strange character to be accorded rebel status, since he stands for nothing more and nothing other than sensual gratification—he's Williams's most potent version of what was to become his recurrent fantasy figure, the stallion who levels every woman (and most men) he meets. There's nothing heroic about him except his sexual prowess, and he doesn't have the personality to qualify as an anti-hero. Yet with Brando playing Stanley the character took over the play in a way that Williams hadn't fully intended.

In Williams's great play, Stanley is the body to Blanche's soul, the natural man to Blanche's cultivated aristocrat. In the titanic battle that ensues between Stanley and the sister-in-law who invades his house and calls him common and who must be expelled, nature fights art, and wins. As a Southern aesthete, Williams was himself deeply attracted to Blanche's air of refinement, her sensitivity and intelligence, and he is on one level

Vivien Leigh and Marlon Brando in *A Streetcar Named Desire* (1951).

horrified by Stanley's Neanderthal strut. (On another level, he's titillated by it.) Williams regards Blanche's defeat—she is taken off, strait-jacketed, to a mental institution—with pity and terror. To him, Stanley's victory means the triumph of darkness over the forces of enlightenment, and represents his fear that the meek shall not inherit the earth after all.

Even so, Williams has a sneaking respect for Stanley and a vestigial distrust of Blanche, whose guilt-ridden sexuality stands in eloquent contrast to Stanley's sexual openness. And it's the playwright's own powerful, ambivalent feelings for the characters, his uncertainty about and attraction to each that lifts the play far above the level of thesis drama and gives it moral fervor and beauty.

On stage, with Brando's lusty Stanley and Jessica Tandy's arch Blanche, *Streetcar* became Stanley's play. Brando was so vivid that he unbalanced the playwright's original scheme, and the play's villain became its hero, the straight-talking sensualist who cuts down an uppity dame. Stanley was the character the audience liked—he was honest and funny whereas Blanche with her love of illusion and dim lighting was devious. Ironically, then, Williams's pitiless victor was transformed through the radiant naturalism of Brando's presence into a sort of rebel hero. Brando's Kowalski became a cultural emblem: the sexy slob as America's new natural man.

For the 1951 film version, Kazan restored the play's original balance. With Vivien Leigh as a more haunted and majestic Blanche than Jessica Tandy, *Streetcar* became Blanche's tragedy rather than Stanley's comedy. Brando is arresting, of course, steamy and life-affirming, but he is never allowed to dominate the film.

If Kazan didn't allow *Streetcar* to become Brando's film, he made up for it by giving the actor *On the Waterfront*; and as Terry Malloy, the bum who could have been a contender, Brando gives the finest performance in American films. What's important about Stanley Kowalski is his body and the way he talks; what's important about Terry Malloy is how he thinks. The real drama of *On the Waterfront* is an internal one, what goes on in Terry's mind.

A hanger-on of a corrupt waterfront union, Terry has learned to survive by doing what his bosses tell him to do. He is a good henchman, dumb and pliable, who gets by by not asking questions. But when he discovers that he has been used to set up the murder of a dock worker who spoke out against the union, he begins to think, for the first time in his life. The movie is really about the birth of his moral conscience, and his heroic act is to testify against the union at a Congressional hearing. (Many critics have read the film's support of Terry's testimony as a vindication of Kazan's notorious cooperation with the McCarthy hearings, where he named names and so made lifelong enemies.) In speaking out, Terry grows up. He returns to the docks, faces the union boss in a fierce fight, and then bloodied and covered with glory leads the men into the warehouse to begin the day's work.

From the beginning, Terry is thrown into a moral crisis he is unprepared for, and as he moves through the film, a double drama is going on: what Terry says, and the jumble of feelings colliding beneath the words and overt actions. Brando shows us how his character thinks—you can see the flicker of inner thought passing over his face and eyes, can hear how his insides jam up his voice. Look at him as he's trying to express himself to Edie Doyle (Eva Marie Saint), the sister of the man for whose death he was unwittingly responsible, and you can feel the war that's raging inside him, the conflict between his guilt and his growing love.

When Terry finally discovers the words that match his feelings, as he does in the famous taxi scene, he's purified. "I coulda been a contender, I coulda been somebody, instead of a bum, which is what I am," he tells his brother simply, in a renowned speech of self-recognition.

Brando's third landmark role of the early fifties was in *The Wild One*, where, dressed in leather jacket, shades, and blue jeans, he plays the leader of a motorcycle gang that invades a narrow-minded small town, one of those sleepy communities that recur frequently in American films of the period. In script, direction, and supporting performances, it's strictly a B movie. Audiences now laugh at the film's first image of Brando astride a motorcycle, but all dressed up as a fifties hood he is a powerful icon, the stuff that legends are made of. Brando's presence and the tingling subtext that he brings to every word and gesture are really all the film has to go on—his performance is a stirring demonstration of the Studio's inner technique.

"It begins here for me on this open road," his character announces in a voice-over as the film opens. "Mostly I remember the girl . . . she got to me, something changed in me. I don't know how to describe it." In *Waterfront*, Terry's inarticulateness was an organic part of his character— Terry's struggle for words was the film's subject—but here the "I don't know how to describe it" is more an expression of the film's inability to be articulate rather than the character's. ("Everything these days is a lot of pictures and noise," says a hostile old bartender of the punks who have taken over his town. "Nobody knows how to talk. They just grunt at each other.")

"I don't get your act at all," the sheriff tells Brando at the end, after there have been a number of clashes between the gang and the town. "I don't think you know what you want to do, or how to go about it." Brando sits there, filling the silence with provocative resonances: what he doesn't say is almost more powerful, certainly more tantalizing, than whatever it is he might say.

In two scenes Brando creates a richer script than the one he's been given. "Man, you are too square," he says with a mixture of moral disapproval and sly humor to the waitress he's attracted to. "I have to straighten you out. [He's explaining where you go, when you "whale."] You don't go any one special place. That's cornball style. You just *go!* . . . the idea is to whale, to make some jive. Do you know what I'm talking about? If you're gonna stay cool, you got to whale." The way of life he manages to suggest is far more exotic than the filmmakers could possibly have imagined. As Brando talks about it, investing it with poetry and sexual promise, "whal-

The classic Method performance: Marlon Brando as Terry Malloy in *On the Waterfront* (1954). The real drama is internal.

ing" becomes like the theme song of a generation. Brando, then, almost manages to write his own movie, an American loner's romance with the lure of the open road.

At the end, just before his gang is ready to move on, he returns to the cafe to say goodbye to Mary. He leaves a trophy with her—although he never won it, he's leaving Mary with a part of himself. He pushes the trophy down the counter, and then, unforgettably, he smiles. He's redeemable, that smile tells us. It floods the screen, an expression of the character's spirit, and a privileged moment.

Torn t-shirts, blue jeans, sweaty sexuality, the mumble, the stutter, the scratch, the stare, the anti-social attitude—these insignia of Brando's performances became the general public's idea of Method acting. And just as most moviegoers associate the Method with Brando's early toughs and hoods, so Brando is usually linked to the lower-class anti-hero he originated despite a career dedicated to asserting his versatility.

Brando didn't regain his reputation or rejuvenate Method realism in a major way until his two great early seventies performances in *The Godfather* and *Last Tango in Paris.* Between them these two films define the two poles of Brando's genius: the first is his greatest disguise performance, the second his most unsparing act of self-revelation.

Brando's Don Corleone is the kind of vaudevillian performance that Olivier might have given. It has a flashy surface—Brando with a new look —but it also has Method innerness. Playing an old man, Brando remakes himself: he takes on a stooped, slowed-down movement and acquires a gravelly wheeze of a voice. It's a good show, a great actor's great stunt, and it's more than that: there's a full character beneath the masquerade, a man who carries with him the weight of his past. Like Strasberg playing the vicious Hyman Roth as a quiet, kindly Jew, Brando endows the Don with a surprising stillness. On the surface he is grandfatherly and seemingly benign, but this man has an inner ferocity. His evil core, his true, appalling coarseness, can be felt in tremors behind the statesmanlike facade. As with Strasberg, there are depth charges firing away within.

Brando's presence in the role is so strong—the hushed voice rasping out commands in darkened rooms, the hand raised in a benediction that looks like a death sentence—that he dominates the long film even though in actual screen time he has a supporting role. Wounded early in the action and offscreen for long stretches, Don Corleone remains a potent memory

Brando as *The Wild One* (1954).

in the minds of the other characters as well as of the audience.

In *Last Tango in Paris*, as in *A Streetcar Named Desire* and *On the Waterfront*, Brando introduces a new level of realistic film acting. *Last Tango* is about an affair in which the lovers, strangers who meet in an unfurnished apartment, agree to tell each other nothing about themselves as they act out a kinky porno fantasy. This "last tango" is dirty sex as a death wish: Brando's character Paul ends up just as he wanted to, killed by his anonymous lover.

As Paul, Brando plays a character who resembles what we know about Brando—Paul is a former actor who treats exotic women brutally. Drawing on details from his own life, Brando seems to have constructed his character along the lines of an extended Actors Studio exercise, employing a full battery of affective memories and private moments in a style that is blatantly improvisatory. For the first time in nearly twenty years, Brando delivers dialogue with the Method paraphernalia he himself patented, breaking up his lines with a chorus of pauses, mumbles, backtrackings, and syntactical rearrangements. He seems to be making up a lot of his lines on the spot, recklessly throwing himself on the resources of his fabled instinct.

Paul recalls the archetypal wild one, grown up and become terminally sour. He is the apotheosis of the outsiders, the twisted fringe characters, that Brando has always been drawn to. Brando plays the part by taking

Method neuroticism to the brink as he unleashes erotic fantasies and emotional explosions that seem to come directly from him rather than his character. It's as if we're seeing the purest kind of Method acting, a fireworks showcase of how an actor draws on his own reservoir of memories, anger, and anxieties to create a character. Brando doesn't seem to transform his own emotional reality into that of a fictional character, a writer's creation: here, astonishingly, he seems simply to be displaying a dark side of himself, so that the film finally—on one level at least—is about what it's like to be Marlon Brando.

In the notorious sex scenes, Brando opens up new dimensions of being real on screen. It isn't only that he's revealing his body, he seems also to be acting out his own fantasies of anonymous, violent sex. As the line separating actor from role seems to be altogether erased, I remember feeling a momentary panic: I have no business watching this, I thought. Brando assaults the boundaries of the actor/audience contract, carrying to the limit the fact that all performance involves the actor exhibiting himself and that being the observer of a created scene is indeed a kind of voyeurism. Transcending matters of taste, Brando's work in *Last Tango in Paris* reveals the greatest actor in the history of American film staking out new territory. This may be it, Brando's last pioneering hurrah, the final, stabbing comments on Method realism from its most famous practitioner. His work since amounts to no more than footnotes, and Brando has said that he is no longer an actor.

James Dean's death at twenty-five on September 30, 1955, froze him in time at the exact midpoint of the decade. His tragic fate has cast him forever in the role of the brooding fifties rebel crying out against the bland conformity-ridden world he has unwillingly inherited from his elders. Unlike the rest of us who grew up and out of the fifties, Dean is trapped there forever, hovering on the verge of juvenile delinquency and bathed in the pain and confusion that spoke for his generation. As his films recede in time, Dean himself continues to connect to new generations of teenagers. Aspects of his movies may date, but *he* continues to seem real.

Where Brando *imagined* himself into different kinds of roles, Dean seemed to interject who he actually was into the three roles, in *East of Eden, Rebel without a Cause,* and *Giant,* that are his epitaph. Dean never had the chance to prove he had range, and it doesn't matter; what he created in his first two films (he's less effective in *Giant*, where he has to play someone else) is an indelible image of what Pauline Kael has called "the world's first teen-ager," a mixed-up kid—wounded, aching, unable to express in words all the turmoil and longing that he feels. In his two "signature" roles, he is deeply personal, as he seems to be putting his own life on view, revealing his wounds for all to see. Watching him, we feel he is acting just for us, allowing us through him to indulge in and to expiate our own sense of feeling without a place. It's the intimacy of his style that sustains his appeal from decade to decade.

Like Marilyn Monroe, James Dean had the kind of outsized, troubled personality to which people have powerful reactions. Many Studio actors I talked to had vivid opinions about him nearly thirty years after his death. I was told he was "Dostoevskian," "driven by demons," "a sybarite," "a male whore," "a nasty little boy who refused to grow up and hid behind a show of helplessness," and "a kid who couldn't handle his huge success." I was told that Kazan was "revolted" by him, and that Strasberg thought "he belonged in a nut house." And I was told that he was really a sweet fellow, shy, introverted, loyal to friends, and grateful to those who helped him in his career. "I feel privileged to have known him," says Geraldine Page. "If I hadn't met him, I'd be left with all this nonsense that's been written about him. He was wonderful! An incredibly magical human being! And he was a marvelous director. When we were having trouble with the third act of *The Immoralist*, he privately gave me some directorial suggestions. They had rewritten it so many times I didn't know what I was doing, and yet a few words from Jimmy and it all made sense. I was told he directed much of *Rebel*, and I can believe it. He could upset people, we saw that. He was direct, he dealt with you, and it made some people nervous. People were jealous of him. But I responded to him, and I have wonderful memories of him."

East of Eden opens with a low-angle shot of Cal (Dean) crouched on a curb. Huddled at the bottom left corner of the frame, peering up at a woman in black who's walking by him, Cal is established at once as a moody adolescent outsider.

The woman growls at him, asking what he wants. "Any law against following around the . . . t-t-t-town . . . madam?" he stammers in a twangy rural voice thick with tension. As he rides back to Salinas on the top of a train after his brief encounter with this woman whom he believes to be his mother, Cal curls up in a fetal position, his face framed against the brooding American landscape.

We glimpse him next behind a grove of trees, isolating himself from his brother Aaron and Aaron's fiancée Abra as they walk hand in hand. Fiddling with switching sticks, he mumbles responses to Aaron's questions. He lurks in the background again as his father talks to a business associate about a plan for keeping ice refrigerated. Impulsively Cal runs up the chute to the barn where his father has stored the ice. In the ice house, he peers at Aaron and Abra from between blocks of ice, softly hitting his head against one of them.

"He's scary," Abra says, not aware of Cal's presence. "He looks at

James Dean in *East of Eden* (1955), pleading for love from his remote father (Raymond Massey).

you, sort of like an animal." Impulsively again, Cal grabs a pick and starts to chip away at the ice, then in a sudden fit begins hurling chunks down the chute.

"Why did you push that ice down?" his father asks at dinner that night. Cal, his back to the camera and hunched over, mumbles, "I don't know." In Kazan's cunning mise-en-scène, Cal and his father are seen in long shot and at a tilted angle at opposite sides of the long dining room table. Their estrangement is measured by the space between them, and by the silence that seeps between words and sentences.

"Talk to me, father," Cal pleads, asking Adam (Raymond Massey) to tell him about the mother Cal never knew. Talking in a low voice, Adam says, "I never knew what she was like. She wasn't like other people. [A long, sad pause.] She was so full of hate." When Cal asks his father why he never talked about her before, Adam says, "I wanted to save you pain." "Pain?" Cal shoots back, his voice trembling; and with that one word, Dean summons up a lifetime of his character's anguish.

"Talk to me, please," Cal repeats the words, this time to his mother (Jo Van Fleet), as he clings to the wall outside her office. But his naked need is too much for this toughened woman, and she has him thrown out. When, on his second visit, he penetrates her private office, he asks her for five thousand dollars so he can start a business planting beans to sell to boys in the army. "Is it true that you shot Adam?" Cal asks. "I shot him because he wanted to hold me down, to keep me on a stinking little ranch. Well [a powerful, resonating pause] . . . nobody holds me."

There are heavy silences, pauses, and hesitations like those between strangers or between people who haven't yet adjusted to each other. Yet there is a strong bond between these two, a communion beneath their halting words. As she's been talking about her life, she's been sizing up this son of hers, concluding that he's a good boy with a spirit similar to hers, and she decides to give him the money he's come for. As she hands him a check, he attempts awkwardly to take her hand. As if touched by electricity, she backs off from this gesture of strangled love. "Go on, get out of here," she snarls, in her low, gravelly voice, and beneath the dismissal we feel how deeply he got to her.

Before the party at which he is going to present his father with money he's earned from the sale of his beans—money that's meant to replace what Adam lost when his refrigeration scheme failed—Cal runs into the house.

Nervously checking to see that the decorations are in place, he puts his finger in a glass of wine and then licks his finger absent-mindedly. When his father rejects his gift, telling him he can't accept money that has been made from soldiers, Cal hugs Adam closely, holding on to him the way he has held on to walls and doors and objects throughout the action, as if in defense against going mad. Inarticulate with grief (Kazan's tilted angle makes it seem that Cal's world has been turned upside down), he runs out of the house, expelled from Eden, to hide beneath the branches of a large tree. "You're mean and vicious and wild," Aaron taunts the outcast, "don't touch Abra again." Emerging from the darkness, Cal asks in an insinuating voice as he hatches a plot to show Aaron who his mother is, "Can you look at the truth just once?"

"I did an awful thing," Cal confesses to his father, who has had a stroke brought on by Aaron's sudden drunken departure for the war after Cal has shown him their mother in her whorehouse. When his father wants to speak to him, Cal leans in to hear the old man's enfeebled voice. At last, his father has spoken to him, asking Cal to stay to take care of him. As Abra opens the door to leave, Cal, his face alight, gives her a look of confirmation that is transcendent.

As Steinbeck's tortured anti-hero, Dean in his film debut gives a Studio performance remarkable in its physical and vocal intensity. Filled with suddenness, with gestures and glances that spring from the moment, Dean's is acting in the present tense. Leaping in and out of scenes, touching and leaning into and against objects and people, he's catlike, lithe and spontaneous. Dean's pauses, his loaded silences, the way he sneaks into and around his sentences, say more than the words themselves. And what Dean does physically, the way his body registers pain and alienation, also fills in the words, anchoring them in the character's quivering emotions.

Spotting Dean at the Actors Studio, Kazan sensed the potential behind the actor's often sullen manner, his quicksilver rages and withdrawals. In the film, he gives those qualities visual underlining, placing Dean behind bars or objects, or at the rear or side of the image. Seldom photographing him from a neutral angle, or in the center of the action, he calls attention to Dean's strangeness. The tilts, the odd disfiguring angles, the shadowed lighting, and the distances that separate Cal from other characters reinforce his outsider status. Shrewdly, based on his own intuitions of Dean's quixotic personality, Kazan presents his actor as peering out of the shadows, cowering at the corners of his own story.

Although *East of Eden* is a period piece, set at the time of the First World War, it had a distinctly fifties glaze to it—in his moodiness and isolation and his battles with language, Cal seemed contemporary. The anti-hero imagery that rests lightly over Dean's first film became the heart of his second one. *Rebel without a Cause*, like *The Wild One*, is a shallow movie that nonetheless captured the anxieties of an era and that was redeemed and even to some extent transformed by a star performance.

The title of this famous teen drama places it in the middle of the Eisenhower decade: as the title of a film about teenagers in the sixties it would not only have made no sense, it would have been a mockery. But in this film that more than any other from the fifties has come to seem a pop artifact that portrayed a generation's collective despair, kids couldn't define the terms of their rebellion. They cut up because they were vaguely unhappy, because they had it too easy, because their parents didn't love them, because the culture placed so much emphasis on conforming to rigid values. Unlike their counterparts in *The Wild One* or *Blackboard Jungle*, the restless teenagers in *Rebel without a Cause* are distinctly middle class. They feel confined by the characterless cleanliness of their parents' homes, escaping whenever they can—but to do what? Like Brando's wild one, these youngsters have no goal. They squander their time on cars—on speed and machines. "Why do we do this?" Jim Stark (Dean) asks the leader of a car gang. "Well, we gotta do something," he answers. Far from having any thoughts about changing the world, like the sixties rebels, the mixed-up fifties kids just want to have car races as a way of proving their manhood, and as a kind of unconscious rejection of the weakness they see in their fathers. The code they set up is as restrictive as their parents', however; the film is about the efforts of the new boy in town to crack this closed society of affluent demi-hoods only to realize that what the punks have to offer is no better than the small gutless world his parents have made.

Jim Stark finds what he needs in a temporary idyll with two lost friends, Judy (Natalie Wood) and Plato (Sal Mineo), in an isolated mansion where they form the nourishing family unit that the outside world withholds from them. (The scenes of the three confused teenagers forming a healing alliance against a world that doesn't understand them are especially moving now because the three actors all suffered ghastly, premature deaths. Our knowledge of the real-life vulnerability of the three doomed stars casts an additional mythic layer over the film.)

Like Brando in *The Wild One*, Dean laces the essentially bland material with an underlying threat of danger and the unexpected. The first few minutes of *Rebel* show how Dean's Method galvanizes the pulp-like story. (This time Dean had another canny director, Nicholas Ray, who like Kazan provides visual italics for the actor's quirkiness.) *Rebel* opens with a strangely angled close-up of Jim Stark, dead drunk on a street, curled up with a toy teddy bear—an image that's more provocative and neurotic than anything else in the film. In the police station, where the opening scenes are set, we hear Jim making the sound of a siren before we see him spread out on a chair, head thrown back against the wall; his physical looseness hints at violence. When his parents come to the station, he jolts upright, as if he's ready to attack. They move back, frightened by the tension in his body. Dean hasn't said a word, and yet his character is already established.

When he does speak, it sounds like thunder. "You're tearing me apart!" he cries as his parents pick away at each other in a galling public display of their small-mindedness. Jim's explosion is primitive, animalistic —and it hangs in the air over the rest of the film.

"Please lock me up," he pleads with the juvenile officer. "I'm going to hit someone and I don't . . ." Unable to complete the sentence, he starts furiously pounding a desk. "I don't know what to do anymore, except maybe to die. . . . If I had one day I didn't feel all confused, and felt I belonged somewhere," he says at the end of the scene. Dean turns these sketchy statements into a threnody; passing through him, the words acquire romantic vibrations.

Here are some further examples of how Dean communicates through actions rather than words. Before he leaves his house for the chicken run, Jim cuts himself a thick slice of chocolate cake. The choice to cut the cake seems improvised, the actor's on-the-spot inspiration. Halfway out the door, he turns abruptly, goes to the table, and slices. It's only a grace note, and I don't want to make too much of it, but the whole passage, Jim moving through the room, turning, slicing, eating, has a wonderful freshness and intimacy that tell us, through movement, how Jim thinks. In another passing action, Dean hugs a milk bottle to his cheek. You can feel the coolness of the bottle against his skin as Dean luxuriates in the tactile pleasure it gives. It's a private moment that registers the character's sensitivity. (Dean understood intuitively the wisdom of Stanislavski's method of physical actions.)

When he discovers his father wearing an apron and picking up food off the floor, Jim says, "Dad . . . don't . . ." He can't finish the thought, and he doesn't have to. The feelings are expressed in his choked voice and in the way he touches his father with a mingling of love and disappointment.

"What's a chickie run?" Plato asks Jim. As Jim answers, he lightly shadow-boxes with Plato, a playful action that expresses Jim's protective instincts toward his new friend. As he talks to Plato at the end, trying to reason with his terrified friend, he touches the jacket he's just given Plato, punctuating his words with gestures that seem spontaneous.

Dean makes furtive, abrupt movements throughout the film. He seems now like a jackrabbit, now like a squirrel, as he leaps, ferrets, pole-vaults in and out of the action. His character always seems half-cocked, and ready to shoot. The jack-in-the-box movements together with the symphony of extra-human sounds—moos, sirens, bellows—are signals of what's happening inside.

Edging beneath the script's bare words, embellishing them with movement and a litany of pauses and stumbles, Dean validates the Studio's inner technique. Working at what seems a deep intuitive level, he transforms a routinely written character into an enduring symbol of the fifties, a beautiful sufferer, quick, real, and true.

"I coulda been a contender," says Robert De Niro playing prizefighter Jake La Motta studying himself in a mirror in the last scene of Martin Scorsese's *Raging Bull* (1980). Although the film is nominally about the rise and fall of Jake La Motta, *Raging Bull* is at the same time, and more interestingly, a tribute to *On the Waterfront* from De Niro and his director, the Brando-Kazan of the seventies and eighties. Attempting to beat the masters at their own game, De Niro and Scorsese aim to be more real, more intense, more Method than *Waterfront* as they blast us with two hours of virtuoso acting and directing.

With its studious imitation of the kind of gritty New York realism that Studio people helped to popularize in the fifties, *Raging Bull* is a movie about its own brilliance. It's about De Niro, the finest naturalistic film actor of his generation, setting himself the challenge of being better than Brando at his best. In the film's opening and closing shots, Jake sits in a dressing room staring at himself in a mirror. He talks to himself, reciting fragments of a poem he has written. He stops mid-sentence, mumbling to himself.

We're made to feel as if we're eavesdropping, and the combination of intimacy and improvisation in these framing scenes is the keynote of De Niro's realism. To play the aging La Motta in later scenes, De Niro gained fifty pounds, and at the first view of him, his stomach hanging over his pants, his face bloated almost beyond recognition, audiences gasp, as much for the actor's evident dedication to realism as for the unsightliness of his appearance.

De Niro's performance is a résumé of proletarian realism in film acting, a tradition that goes back at least as far as the poor city guys played by John Garfield in the forties. It's a tradition that can be traced through many actors, including Brando, Steve McQueen, Paul Newman, Al Pacino, and Dustin Hoffman. What do the Method-trained actors, from John Garfield to Robert De Niro, have in common? They're private, moody, intuitive, deeply sexual; their toughness is qualified by flashes of sensitivity and humor. They are finely tuned American drifters, outlaws, and anti-heroes. Riddled with contemporary malaise, the archetypal Method star is a man of the city.

The link between the Method and the city can be traced to John Garfield, harbinger of the new kind of actor to emerge from the Studio. A refugee from the Group Theatre, Garfield was the first Method-trained actor to achieve wide audience acceptance. He wasn't as unusual or as quixotic as Clift or Brando; he was less entangled, and yet he seemed more troubled and more real than the standard movie hero. Exploiting the vulnerability underlying Garfield's tough street kid veneer, Hollywood typed him a ghetto loser, the poor boy who makes bad.

Garfield also differed from the Hollywood norm in his New York accent. He didn't sound as if he'd been trained by a vocal coach and the lingering regionalism plus his ethnic appearance and his intense sexuality made him seem raw, unpolished. With one glance at Lana Turner in *The Postman Always Rings Twice*, Garfield conveyed an anthology of X-rated fantasies. In the forties, he became Hollywood's token Jew, or at least token ethnic: the outsider as anti-hero. Although he never quite broke through to the full neuroticism of his most forceful Method successors, the image Garfield created in films like *Body and Soul, Humoresque,* and *Force of Evil* of a downtrodden city boy alienated by appearance and temperament from mainstream America is one that had special relevance to the iconography of later Studio actors.

Robert De Niro (with Joe Pesci at right) as prizefighter Jake La Motta in *Raging Bull* (1980). For the role, De Niro wore a false nose and gained fifty pounds.

The typical Method actor, then, is the opposite of a straightforward, conventional he-man like John Wayne. In the interestingly cast *Red River* (1948), in fact, there's a vivid contrast between the Duke, a monument even then of stalwart, unimaginative Old Hollywood, and Montgomery Clift, one of the apostles of the new-breed Method performer. In this cross-country cattle trek, Wayne as the tough reactionary leader plays his usual obdurate hero as Clift, in the role of his rebellious adopted son, introduces a Freudian note into the code of the West. With his blazing eyes, trembling voice, his physical and emotional fragility, Clift makes an unusual cowboy. He is mercurial, anguished, covertly homosexual. The script pits the two men against each other; beginning the journey as father and son, they soon quarrel over leadership and a woman. By the end, Clift has earned his manhood by overcoming his mentor and thereby bringing a more enlightened perspective to the taming of the American wilderness. Although he's cast as a liberal in contrast to Wayne's pragmatic conservative, Clift turns out to be more than the script asked for, because he's not so much liberal as peculiar, and there are moments when Wayne looks at him quizzically, as if asking himself, what manner of man have we here. In retrospect, this odd casting and Clift's last-reel victory over Wayne are symbolic of a new trend in movie acting, the ascendancy in the fifties of the quirky Method hero.

Like Clift in *Red River,* all the famous Method actors enrich and sometimes alter the script's literal significance. With their subversive, tunneling style—the "filling in" that the Method has trained them to do—true Method actors can burrow into even the most pedestrian script. They're all potential termites.

The close-up is the ideal foil for the subterranean Method style. Through furtive movements of the eyes, a twitching lip, a facial tic that might not register in the long shot within which all stage action takes place, a Studio-trained actor can cue us in to the dark side of the psyche. Al Pacino's performance in *The Godfather,* for instance, is centered in his eyes, which, in close-up, record his character's gradual evolution from a pleasant young man holding himself aloof from his father's crime syndicate to a ruthless Mafia kingpin. The nervous, sidelong glances of the insecure young Michael and the steely gaze of the later chieftain tell us all we need to know about the character—like all good Method actors, Pacino doesn't need dialogue to tell a story.

If John Wayne's bluster is un-Method, so is Charlton Heston's larger-than-life heroism. (Imagine a Method actor as Moses or El Cid!) Ambiguous sexuality and the possibility of cruelty and self-destructiveness hover over the Method performers, who bear their psychic wounds like so many medals. No matter what role he's playing, for example, Jack Nicholson seems like an inmate; his characters carry their anger and scorn, trailing a lifetime of self-contempt. Pacino also radiates twistedness. When he tried to depart from this image in an upbeat family comedy called *Author! Author!,* he looked pained. Despite his best intentions, he tore into the film's Neil Simonized script as if he were once again acting with Strasberg in *The Godfather.*

Most Method actors, like Pacino and Nicholson, have a saturine quality. Seldom released at full blast, it is always there, palpitating just beneath the surface of whatever role they are playing. Even if he's strikingly handsome, like Clift or Brando or Newman, the usual Studio actor has other qualities that curdle his looks—an air of menace or intimidation, as often with Newman and Brando, an extreme frailty, as with Clift, a blistering,

John Garfield, the first
Method-trained actor to
become a film star.

Montgomery Clift with
Joanne Dru in *Red River*
(1948).

possibly deforming intensity. Method actors instinctively distrust the smooth good looks of the movie star as male model; a regulation handsomeness is read as the sign of a bland spirit.

In his best roles, Paul Newman plays against his classic looks, mocking them, or undercutting them with harsh characterizations, as in *Cat on a Hot Tin Roof* and *The Hustler*. As Hud, Newman is so chilling that his male beauty seems more threat than benediction.

Since a sculpted face is a possible threat to art, interfering with the Method's emphasis on being real, Method aesthetic welcomes actors who look like regular fellas. The colloquial reality that Method actors work for sits more easily on someone who looks like Dustin Hoffman than it would on Errol Flynn or Tyrone Power. (We don't expect people who look like that to do any acting at all.)

The appeal of a Dustin Hoffman, an actor who looks like everyone else, can be traced back to the cult of the little guy that signaled seriousness in the fifties. In movies like *Marty* and *Bachelor Party* (both written by Paddy Chayefsky, the fifties' answer to Clifford Odets) and in some plays from television's so-called Golden Age of Drama, being average, lacking color and flash, became a mark of integrity. The grayer the character and the performance, the truer the acting was supposed to be.

If one strand of the Method legacy is a knotted up, high-strung individuality, another is the elaborate display of being "cool" like Newman and McQueen. McQueen was the epitome of the casual Method actor, the Actors Studio Clint Eastwood. For certain kinds of vernacular American characters—those who are low-keyed and laid back—McQueen's is an ideal camera manner. McQueen wasn't in the same league as his other famous Studio colleagues, but his work did represent a legitimate aim of Studio technique: relaxation. He didn't seem to have a tense muscle (he also didn't have any depth). But his cool style was enough for a *Cincinnati Kid*.

How the Method's lessons are applied depends on the temperament of who's using them. One of the myths about Studio acting is that in training actors to examine their own experiences, it simply promotes self-dramatization, encouraging actors to play hyped-up versions of their analyzed selves. If one kind of Method actor works this way, playing variations on his own neurotic "instrument" (James Dean is the preeminent example), another, like Brando, craves versatility. Of the actors in my pantheon, Dean, Nicholson, McQueen, Clift, and Garfield tend to be the self-repeaters, acting within a confined range. We go to see them because they are believable or arresting. They seem real, and their reality on screen seems to come directly from who they are rather than from a cosmetic, prefabricated image. Jack Nicholson is always Jack Nicholson, people say: the same droning, ironic voice, the same misogyny. As "Nicholson," he is always convincing, playing "himself" in the relaxed, truthful way that is the byword of the Studio.

Actors like Brando, De Niro, Hoffman, and Robert Duvall, on the other hand, seem always to challenge the criticism that the Method actor merely cultivates a neurotic persona which he transports from role to role. These actors, as much as Olivier, exult in the chance to wear different kinds of clothes, to hide behind makeup, to alter the way they move and sound. Think of Hoffman dolled up as Tootsie or as limping, dishevelled Ratso Rizzo in *Midnight Cowboy;* De Niro hidden behind fifty extra pounds in *Raging Bull;* Brando as a Japanese wheeler-dealer in *Teahouse of the August Moon,* or a beautifully spoken Marc Antony in *Julius Caesar;* Duvall, virtually unrecognizable from role to role, moving from the faceless family retainer in *The Godfather* to the demented warmonger in *Apocalypse Now* —for these actors, impersonation and self-transformation are positive values. Their experiments are varyingly successful—De Niro as the literate, withheld Irving Thalberg in *The Last Tycoon* ranks as a good try rather than a finished interpretation, just as his quiet priest in *True Confessions* is notable more for the contrast to the fireworks of his preceding role as Jake La Motta; Pacino trying light comedy in *Author! Author!* or, on stage, making a stab at *Richard III* earns praise more for the attempt to stretch his range than the quality of the work itself. Among some of the best-known Method actors, then, the desire to try something different is a continuing aim, although the Method continues to be most useful close to home. The most famous Method actors have reached greatness playing characters like Terry Malloy, Jake La Motta, and Ratso Rizzo, outsized American lowbrows and downbeats struggling for survival on the margins, in big city alleyways and back room tenements.

16

THE METHOD AND THE MOVIES:
THE ANTI-HEROINE

American films have a tradition of rebels and anti-heroes, most of whom have been created by Studio actors. But who are the anti-*heroines,* the women who trespass the norm? A hero who's a loner, aberrant and nonconforming, is a character type the culture can absorb in limited quantities if the actor playing him is personable enough. But a female loner, a woman who bypasses the customary roles of wife and mother and who lives by rules of her own is a rare character indeed.

Because parts for women who are intense and idiosyncratic—the kind of woman likely to be attracted to the Method—are scarce, no Studio actress has had the same artistic or cultural impact as the most successful Method actors. Kim Stanley, Geraldine Page, Anne Bancroft, Joanne Woodward, Maureen Stapleton, Estelle Parsons, Julie Harris, Carroll Baker, Patricia Neal, Shelley Winters, Eva Marie Saint, Ellen Burstyn, Anne Jackson, Shirley Knight, Lee Grant, Sandy Dennis, Lois Smith, Viveca Lindfors, and (as a special case) Marilyn Monroe are among the most well known of the actresses whose work was significantly molded by working at the Studio. Among them, to be sure, are Academy Award winners who have been widely praised; but there isn't one who hasn't been misused or underused and whose film career hasn't had curious gaps and changes of fortune. Not one has had the chance to compile a dossier like that of Brando or Newman or Pacino or Hoffman. Unwilling (or perhaps unable) to play the sexy image that American movies often force on women, these actresses have either returned to stage work whenever they could or else been cast in supporting roles as an assortment of oddballs and weirdos. Dressed in fright wigs and camouflaged with garish makeup, they have sometimes been cast unflatteringly, their individuality mocked rather than protected by the romantic aura that cradled Montgomery Clift and James Dean. In American movies, to be sensitive, high-strung, unusual, defiant, maybe even a little crazy, and female doesn't get you as far as to be all those things and male.

The film career of Julie Harris is typical of the fate of the Studio actress in movies. Harris's first major theatrical success was in the Actors Studio production of *Sundown Beach*. The promise she showed in that short-lived play was fulfilled two years later, when, in a performance almost as shattering as Brando's in *A Streetcar Named Desire*, she played Carson McCullers's twelve-year-old Frankie (Harris was twenty-seven) in *Member of the Wedding*. On stage, the performance was electric; on film, a year later, it was exhaustingly intense. With her short-cropped hair, her overwrought manner, and her almost startling homeliness Harris is strange, and she radiates more than the close-up movie camera can comfortably absorb. Is there a movie heroine before this who was quite so singular? Here was no contract player groomed to conform, but a fierce young actress, independent and offbeat.

Watching Julie Harris in *Member of the Wedding* you can see why she never became a movie star. As she tries to remove a splinter from her foot, Frankie grabs a large kitchen knife, a gesture that epitomizes the character's zest for overstatement. Frankie's theatricality belongs in the theatre; on film she's too much. "Do I give you the creeps? Do you think I'll turn into a freak?" she questions Berenice (Ethel Waters), her surrogate black mother, wondering how people in the outside world, in the world beyond the kitchen where she spends most of her time, view her. She's like a weather vane blown this way and that by the force of her feelings. In one scene, moving back and forth, she works herself into a frenzy as she imagines a future in which she'll have thousands of friends and be a member of the whole world. Quivering with excitement, she seems about to explode. "I'm beginning to feel I just can't breathe anymore! I want to tear down the whole world!" she cries out. Burying herself deep within Carson McCullers's freakish, wondering tomboy, Julie Harris plays with extraordinary feeling a character continually thrown by the strength of her feelings. It's a bravura, one-of-a-kind performance that typed Julie Harris as a Method oddball.

Four years later, working for Kazan in *East of Eden*, Harris is more muted though still unconventional. She's lovely as Abra, luminous and yielding as she plays quietly against James Dean's raw intensity. But after this, she has not been used importantly or interestingly in films while she has continued to work steadily on stage.

Estelle Parsons, Shirley Knight, Sandy Dennis, Maureen Stapleton, Geraldine Page, and Kim Stanley are other Studio members whose film work is only a footnote to their careers in theatre. On film, they have sometimes seemed shadowed by neurosis and trauma, while in the theatre they've found roles they could tear into without fear of being labeled eccentric.

Consider the case of Estelle Parsons. Like many Studio people, she respects theatre far more than films, and after a flurry of movies in the late sixties and early seventies she has all but abandoned the medium for stage work, traveling anywhere she's offered an attractive role. She went to Hawaii, for example, because she wanted to play Lady Macbeth. Parsons says her commitment to acting is a commitment to the theatre; to her, movies are journeyman's work, a director's rather than an actor's medium, and a way to support her interest in doing challenging parts in noncommercial theatre. A superb character actress who doesn't know how to be conventional (her Oscar performance in *Bonnie and Clyde* is very brave, high-pitched in voice and feeling), she's earthy and individual—and, in Hollywood terms, she's destined to play colorful supporting roles rather than leads. But on stage, where you don't have to look like a movie star to be a star, she has continued to find great roles (like the mad tyrant in *Miss Margarida's Way*) where she can cut loose.

Unlike most Studio actresses, Shirley Knight had the looks of a Hollywood starlet. Blond, with dainty features and a translucent complexion, she might have become the conventional ingenue, playing a string of decorative roles. But anger churned beneath that pretty facade, and a sour expression—a stingy smile tinged with irony—promised thunder. Knight was simply too batty and too interesting to have a pallid career on the Hollywood treadmill. Even in *Sweet Bird of Youth*, where she played the hero's romantic interest, Heavenly Finley, a part Tennessee Williams hardly paid attention to when he wrote it, she is subversive. As she goes to work on Heavenly, adding physical tics and a turbulent inner life, the character becomes a Southern Gothic curiosity who seems to suffer from far more than a hysterectomy.

Sandy Dennis is another who's too quirky to sustain the leading lady

Hollywood image. Because of what she does to an English sentence, she's been called a walking compendium of Actors Studio clichés: the Method actress as full-fledged neurotic. Approaching language as an obstacle to expressiveness, she feints with words, jabbing at them and pulling them apart. Her fractured delivery, decorated with snivels, wheezes, and guffaws, amounts to a prolonged stammer. Add to the verbal curlicues hands sawing the air in inarticulate accompaniment to the sputtered sentences, a raised finger preceding an "uh" or "and um," an arm raised to wipe a perpetually runny nose. In *Who's Afraid of Virginia Woolf?*, as hysterical, dim-witted Honey, Sandy Dennis has an improvisatory freshness. After winning an Oscar for the performance, she became a film star, but only fleetingly. Though obviously skillful, she was simply too specialized to sustain general audience acceptance.

Sandy Dennis practices what the Studio preaches—to a fault. I don't mean to belittle Dennis, who has come in for more than her share of brickbats; she's always interesting and inventive, an American original whose persistent mannerist excesses in the service of psychological realism have turned her into a sideshow rather than mainstream attraction.

Like Dennis, Geraldine Page lets you see her at work. She's always in danger of upstaging herself. She made a splash in films in the early sixties, with her Tennessee Williams double-header in *Summer and Smoke* and *Sweet Bird of Youth*, though it was evident even then that she was too theatrical—too much in love with acting up a storm, too meticulous a technician—to have an extended film career.

Page made her name, on stage (in 1952) and in film (in 1960) with a definitive portrayal in *Summer and Smoke* of Alma Winemiller, Tennessee Williams's spinster turned whore. Like Brando's Kowalski, it was a performance that had enormous influence on the work of other actors—Page herself has spent a career trying to escape from its shadow.

"When I did *Summer and Smoke*," Page recalls, "I took something Uta [Hagen] said in class: 'People in life do not know what they're going to say.' I took this to heart, and I outraged the rest of the company in the pauses and the broken phrases I used to make Alma sound real. Maybe I got carried away with it downtown; pauses were new then, everyone was still trying to speak the pure line. It's become a Method cliché. Now to get attention you say a sentence all in one breath, and you hear pauses in toothpaste commercials." In the over thirty years since her famous New

York debut, Page has continued to brandish an idiosyncratic delivery, puncturing the rhythm of sentences with unusual stress patterns, going for abrupt changes in volume from booms to whispers and back again. At times, with her piping breathy voice and her bold emphasis of key words, she almost seems to be singing. She's a Method mannerist with a sneaky humor.

Repeatedly placing her hand to her chest, fussing with objects like fans and gloves, holding herself at stiff angles, her hands flying up to arrange her hair as her high-pitched manic laughter cuts into her words, Page outfits Alma with a jittery physical reality that's the surface of her inner boil. When Page is at her best, as in this role, her emphatic "acting" is a direct route to the character's core.

Of the Studio actresses who have proven too intense to sustain Hollywood careers, Kim Stanley is the most admired. Like Brando, the ultimate actor's actor, she commands enormous respect among theatre professionals. Virtually every Studio member I talked to cited Stanley as the finest actress he or she knew of. The impact of her style on Studio actresses has been as keen as Brando's on Studio actors. Yet hers is a name little known by the general moviegoing public, who are likely to get her mixed up with Kim Hunter, "the actress who was in *Streetcar.* "

During the height of her stage career, Stanley made only two films (in addition to the film version of *Three Sisters*): *The Goddess* (in 1958) and *Séance on a Wet Afternoon* (in 1964). Happily, Stanley is working again, as an occasional guest star on television dramas and in films (*Frances, The Right Stuff*). In the late seventies, she taught at the Strasberg Theatre Institute and did some producing; and she would now like to form her own theatre company.

I spoke with a young actor, Kristofer Batho, who studied with Stanley, and his observations are a good place to begin: "Stepping into her class, one instinctively got very quiet. It was very still there. It was almost as though moving into her personal space was an intrusion, for she was, all at once, personal and far away. When she coached you before an acting exercise, she would put her hand on your back and whisper in your ear very quietly. One felt like a child next to his mother; outside of us, all was noise and ruckus, but here for this moment it is very still. She whispered to something deep, perhaps buried, within us—a far cry from some of the screaming, lunatic teachers in the building. Here in the highest room in the Institute, the higher parts of ourselves were touched by this almost invisible goddess. (She covered her body completely from head to toe in a long caftan, her face looking out through a kerchief.) Sometimes she did not show up for class, but more often she allowed the class to run on into the night, following her own intuitive time clock. Living in a world that seemed to have a very delicate equilibrium, she had immense privacy, and a sensitivity which made almost everything seem too much. Sometimes, when the world outside of acting got too close she seemed almost paranoid. 'What are you looking at?' she barked at me once, when, smitten by the sunlight framing her silhouette at the top of the stairs, I dared to look too long. Unapproachable—yet she wrapped us all in her magic gauze."

The qualities Kristofer Batho perceives in Stanley as a teacher are those that come through in her acting: a sensitivity so extraordinary that it seems mystical; a luminous quietism; a privacy shadowed by measureless sorrow. As teacher and performer, Stanley is a woman who sees; no wonder she's often been cast as mediums, psychics, zealots, world-renowned actresses—as people who have special knowledge or power.

Playing a tortured movie star in *The Goddess,* and an obsessed medium in *Séance on a Wet Afternoon,* Stanley brings to both these extreme and "gifted" characters an intimation of madness. *The Goddess,* written by Paddy Chayefsky, is a thinly disguised biography of Marilyn Monroe told in three parts: Portrait of a Young Girl, 1930; Portrait of a Young Woman, 1947; Portrait of a Goddess, 1952. Stanley takes the character from a sad-eyed, wistful, small-town girl dreaming about going to Hollywood to an embittered, drug-ravaged movie queen, someone whose dreams unfortunately came true. The film has a conventional view of the price of fame, showing what happens to a neurotic young woman deprived of love once she conquers Hollywood. Chayefsky's dialogue is characteristically overwrought, and audiences at revivals often break into laughter. "You don't know what loneliness is. You don't know the great ultimate ache of desolation," says the man who is to become Emmie's first husband. Later he tells her, "I'm too damaged for you. You have a passion for respectability, I have a horror of loneliness: that's love." By the time this characters says, "I need help, I'm suicidal," contemporary audiences are in stitches. But while the writing is often hysterical and "literary" in a stultifying way, Kim Stanley manages to counter Chayefsky's artifice with her actor's truth. Here are some examples of her alchemy.

Emmie, a self-conscious teenager known as the town tramp, talks

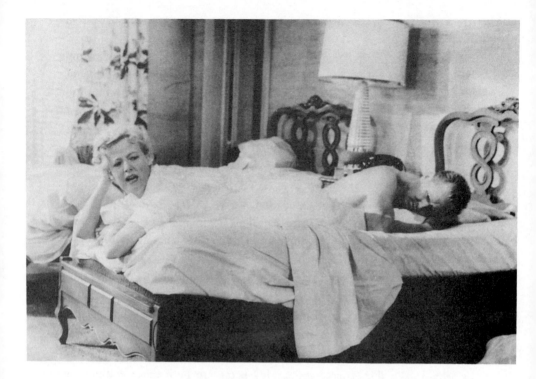

Four views of Kim Stanley in *The Goddess:* as neurotic wife (with Lloyd Bridges); uneasy movie queen; religious convert; and drug-ravaged has-been (with Elizabeth Wilson and Steven Hill).

compulsively to a boy who's asked her out on a date. She knows why he's asked her out, and yet she pretends to herself and to him that she is just an ordinary girl on a date. As the character chatters, Stanley plays against the words, revealing through her glances and busy hands and an occasional catch in her voice Emmie's fear that she will never be loved.

Now a young woman with a crying kid, Emmie turns on the radio to cover the child's noise, snapping her fingers nervously and looking distractedly around her dingy apartment. In a flash, she creates the character's desperation. Working herself into a fit, she starts screaming at the child. In the climax to this short, searing scene of incipient madness, she yells at her mother, "I don't want my child!"

"I got transferred to a combat outfit," her husband (Steven Hill) reports, adding, "I hope I get killed." A menacing pause. "I hope you do, too," she says, in a devastating tone.

"Do you love me, Dutch? Do you love me?" Emmie asks, crouching at the feet of her second husband (Lloyd Bridges), a former athlete. Clinging to him and pleading in a hushed, little girl's voice, Stanley conveys a naked vulnerability.

In Part Three, after she's become a Hollywood star and has had a nervous breakdown, Emmie talks to her mother as she wrings her hands, pats her dress in a compulsive, meaningless gesture, and fingers a glass. "Mama, I can't stand to be alone. I feel like I'm going insane." The words are pronounced with a deathly stillness. Later Emmie tells her mother that she has found God. "I feel Him near me, mama," she says as they both get down on their knees. As she speaks of her religious conversion, she seems transformed: washed clean. For the first time in the film, Stanley doesn't look tired, and her gestures have none of their usual frenetic quality. Later, sitting quietly in a chair, she recounts how she was saved, speaking in a grave voice that suggests serenity achieved through despair.

"I want to die!" Emmie cries out, at her mother's funeral, prostrate with grief and needing two people to hold her up. Her harrowing cry comes from some deep place in Stanley herself.

"Ooh, that would be a nice feeling, just to lie and float and have the water come up over you" (she lifts her hands up). She's talking to her first husband, whom she hasn't seen in years, calling up an image of peaceful retreat as she rises from drug-induced sleep. Her character's speech thickened by drugs, Stanley plays the scene, as she does the entire last section of the film, as though hypnotized. If in the scene where she announces she has found God she seems to ascend, here she seems to be underwater.

In *Séance on a Wet Afternoon,* she plays a medium who kidnaps a little girl and then pretends to locate her through her powers. She wants her husband (Richard Attenborough) to kill the child (he can't bring himself to do it) so that the little girl can be company in the next world for their own child Arthur, born dead. The character doesn't think of herself as a fraud; she believes in her gift, and explains, "I have to do this little lie, so they can know the whole truth."

Playing a woman lost in her own world, Stanley seems at first unprepossessing, a plain, overweight woman, shabbily dressed in a baggy sweater. "It was nice, being different," she recalls, remembering how she was asked to show off her powers as a little girl. Standing at the foot of the stairs she looks into space, and Stanley's force is such that we can visualize the strange little girl she once was, performing for guests in the very place where a ravaged, middle-aged woman is now standing.

The heart of Stanley's performance is the two séances, where, as the medium wills herself into a daze, Stanley's voice takes on a breathiness that's eerie. Like her character, she's moving in and away, toward a mystical privacy. (Watching Stanley go into a trance is like seeing an actor enter Stanislavski's creative state, becoming available to unconscious promptings and signals.) The film's final séance is like a master demonstration of a private moment, an epitome of Method privacy and intimacy. As she enters her trance, the people around the table move back, as if to protect themselves from the fluttering of wings, the palpitations of the spirit. Cradling an imaginary child as she recollects her primal trauma—the death of her child—Stanley's voice is hushed. She gasps, as if in response to images in a dream, her face twitches involuntarily, and tears course down her cheeks.

"It's so bright, after a séance," she says, returning from her inner darkness into the light. "The brightness seems to fall from the air." "Did I do it all right, Billy?" she asks her husband as he looks at her helplessly, realizing he's lost her.

The Goddess and *Séance on a Wet Afternoon* are flawed, even hokey films which Stanley redeems through her art. Arthur Penn calls her the American Duse. Her kind of realism, instinct with spirit and a life beyond language and reason—beyond the conventionally knowable—is exactly the kind Stanislavski dedicated his life to.

It's ironic that Kim Stanley, America's greatest actress of the fifties, played a character based on Marilyn Monroe, who wanted to be America's greatest actress of the fifties. Stanley was the First Lady of the Studio; when Monroe first became interested in the Studio and began sitting in on sessions, she was the First Lady of Twentieth Century-Fox, a studio she didn't respect. Exposing herself to the Method surely did Monroe no harm, but it's my feeling that she went to the Actors Studio to learn what in fact she already knew. In 1952, before *Gentlemen Prefer Blondes* made her a big star, she played a psychotic babysitter in *Don't Bother to Knock*, giving a splendid Method performance before she'd even heard of the Method.

"Use yourself," Studio actors are continually admonished. "Use your past, use your pain." Monroe understood instinctively how to do this. Her vulnerability, her fear of inadequacy, her sense of not belonging—all these qualities of the real woman beneath the actress are channeled artfully into her role as the babysitter. After *Gentlemen Prefer Blondes* made her a Hollywood commodity, she felt trapped in the traditional dumb blonde caricature, playing characters not allowed to have any insides, and she escaped to the Actors Studio and to private classes with Strasberg whenever she could. From the point in the mid-fifties when she became part of Strasberg's family until her last film, Arthur Miller's excruciating *The Misfits* (1961), she gave a string of well-crafted performances; but *Don't Bother to Knock* indicates that if she had had more trust in herself she might have been able to reach those performances without help from anyone.

John Strasberg, who in a sense grew up with Marilyn ("we became like a family for her"), has some illuminating observations. "Hers was an American tragedy. The way people treated her contributed to her despair, and made life not worth living. She didn't have enough of an ego to fight back. She was like a child. People looked at her like a thing; they thought about what she was worth to them. She wasn't murdered or involved in some political cover-up, the way they're trying to make a case for: she killed herself. She had not much intent to harm. She was certainly very kind to me. She understood my suffering. She had the fortune and the misfortune of being taken care of by my parents. They protected her. I remember when she first came to our house, after Milton Greene called my father to ask him to help her, she tiptoed in and out."

Two of Monroe's Strasberg-influenced performances (Paula Strasberg was her on-set coach), in *Bus Stop* and *The Prince and the Showgirl*, are models of Studio style. "I been trying to be somebody"; "It was real nice the way you made everybody shut up in there like you had respect for me":

her lines in *Bus Stop* as William Inge's lost floozie aching for respectability and a legitimate career as a singer (a role originated on Broadway by Kim Stanley) have continual references to the actress herself. "I just want to be sure that the guy that I marry has some real regard for me, apart from . . . (here she pauses, closes her eyes, and retreats into memories of private pain) that loving stuff," she tells her cowboy Romeo (Don Murray). At the end, he hands her his jacket, which she puts on as if it's a coat fit for a queen—she runs her hands along the rough fabric treating it like cashmere. These two moments illustrate her mastery of the inner technique: the pause before "that loving stuff" ripples with affective memories and her "relationship" to Bo's jacket is sensory work of the sort that is holy writ at the Studio.

The Prince and the Showgirl presents a clean contrast between Monroe's inner American Method and Laurence Olivier's external British technique. Olivier, as the foppish prince of a Transylvanian duchy, is all dressed up for his part, the actor himself hidden beneath layers of makeup, an elaborate costume, a monocle, and a thick accent. Clearly he is giving a performance; his work is fussy, brittle, artificial, and as such exactly what the part calls for. Monroe hides behind nothing, exposing herself both physically and emotionally. She wears a revealing white dress and talks the way she always does. Olivier seems to be playing a role, while Monroe seems to be playing herself; Olivier is knocking himself out doing a turn while Monroe sails through the movie without any visible acting effort.

The contrast in acting style serves the material, a light comedy derived from a play by Terence Rattigan about a courtship between a pompous monarch and a dizzy American showgirl. Over the years, Olivier has made no secret of the fact that he couldn't stand Monroe: he found her vulgar, inconsiderate, and thoroughly unprofessional, and he had nothing but scorn for her devotion to Paula Strasberg and for the Method. He couldn't understand her compulsive need to analyze character and motive, to justify action. Nonetheless, Monroe's Method steals the picture. In one famous scene, Olivier is on the phone as Monroe picks away at a buffet. Olivier has all the lines, shouting into the phone, as Monroe comments on his remarks in the way she selects and eats her food. Like a practiced Method actor, she doesn't need dialogue to create character and mood—she "speaks" beautifully through movement, relating to place, props, and partner at a level beyond words.

In the few films where she had a chance to go outside a Hollywood stencil, Monroe's work reveals all the qualities that are sought after at the Studio. I don't mean to argue that Monroe was a great actress, in the same league as Kim Stanley or Geraldine Page. She wasn't, and she was hampered by a voice badly in need of training: she *did* sound stupid, and she spoke in odd rhythms with a little girl breathiness and with affected pronunciation that helped to keep her locked into the image she hated.

Monroe has passed into history as a phenomenon rather than as an actress. If her beauty hindered her development personally and professionally, conditioning the way studio bosses and the public were willing to see her (and contaminating the way she saw herself), it also protected her from seeming truly crazy and therefore subversive. It helped to contain the public's view of her, so that she didn't seem seriously unhinged, the way a plainer-looking woman who had many of the same symptoms might have. As a result, though she was a deeply disturbed woman, she had the lustrous movie career denied to Studio actresses who were more talented and eccentric in more obvious ways.

Marilyn Monroe is the most famous of a group of actresses who found refuge from Hollywood at the Actors Studio. Shelley Winters, Anne Bancroft, Viveca Lindfors, Ellen Burstyn, Sally Field, Rita Gam, and Jane Fonda all traveled the same route, from West to East, to sharpen their craft after having felt misused and undervalued in their movie work. "When Lee told me movies hadn't used me, I knew I had come to the right place," Viveca Lindfors says. Since study with Strasberg was often accompanied by therapy, the actresses felt like born-again Christians remaking themselves in the light of a new vision. In every case, after their conversion to the Method, the work of the Hollywood exiles shows remarkable growth.

The development of Shelley Winters, Anne Bancroft, and Ellen Burstyn, for instance, reveals how strong an influence Strasberg's Method can have on a willing student. All three began their careers as contract players imprisoned in roles that their own strong natures chafed against; all three were too feisty to fit into the slots the Hollywood studios had waiting for them. With his talent-spotting ability, Strasberg saw in each of them a naturalistic actress bristling with nerves and energy, and he helped to release the temperament Hollywood had had no use for. Transformed by the Method, all three had the satisfaction of returning to movies in triumph, playing meaty roles that won Oscars for them.

17

PRIVATE MATTERS:
THE FILMS OF ELIA KAZAN

"The films of Elia Kazan are the true legacy of the Actors Studio," Arthur Penn says. Indeed, Kazan's cycle of major films in the fifties provides a showcase of great "Studio" acting. *A Streetcar Named Desire, On the Waterfront, East of Eden,* and *Baby Doll* place the Method on display. Strasberg and Kazan made a great team: what Strasberg spent hours talking about, Kazan was able to elicit on the spot, in production.

What does Kazan say or do that frees his actors, enabling them to be intensely expressive? Here are some clues from actors who retain vivid impressions of what it was like to be directed by him. Lois Smith, unforgettable as the frightened bar maid in *East of Eden,* remembers above all Kazan "taking people secretly aside. He always seemed to have his arm around Jimmy [Dean], and they were off to the side, conferring. Kazan was so good to him. It was always chatty, intimate things he had to say to you, things that seemed to occur to him on the spot and that he felt it was right to share with you, and only with you. Kazan was always whispering to someone. Privacy and secrecy are important to an actor, especially on a movie set. How hard it is to retain that privacy—yet Kazan's 'secrecy' helped us all to achieve that."

Kim Hunter, recalling how Kazan directed her in both the stage and film versions of *A Streetcar Named Desire,* says he was "always personal, though never severe. He would get to know the actor, and take us into private matters. It was always private, between you and him, focusing on what the problem was and how to overcome it, with our own inner resources. He would never burden you with result terms, but with how to arrive. He pushed people as far as they could go—and he could always push the right key."

"Filming my first scene in *On the Waterfront,* where I give Terry my brother's coat, I was terrified," Eva Marie Saint recalls. "First, I was in awe of Marlon Brando. Then there were so many people behind the camera, how was I to concentrate? And then I felt I had to prove why they'd given this great part to me, when so many people had tested for it. But Gadge pushed all the right buttons. He took me aside and said to me, privately, 'You are a Catholic girl and you're frightened. You're not out with a young man very often.'

"Later, when I had to do a scene in a slip, I got quite nervous again. I was a modest young woman. Kazan kept talking about my husband Jeffrey and that relaxed me, so I felt very free and comfortable. How quiet and personal Gadge always was. He said things that were specific to me; Marlon wouldn't hear them. It was so completely different when I worked with Hitchcock on *North by Northwest.* Hitchcock never talked to me about my character—he just gave me external things, like 'lower your voice.' With Kazan you always had these private conversations; with Hitchcock, never.

"A Kazan set is very special. There's constant rehearsal. You're never on the phone to your agent. You have to stay in character. One day Kazan reprimanded me for talking too much on the set, warning me not to dissipate energy, of which each of us has only a limited supply. It was strictly a closed set where, when you weren't on camera, you were working, rehearsing, and improvising. The famous glove scene was something Marlon and I discovered in rehearsal. I dropped the glove accidentally, Marlon picked it up and put it on his hand. We both realized that that was the catalyst, that was what we needed to keep me there talking to him. We repeated the action that had happened as an accident for Kazan, and he liked it.

"Marlon and I were constantly rehearsing. He was so dear to me. I don't know him personally, and I've only seen him once since *Waterfront,* fleetingly, at a party in Hollywood in 1955. He gave me so much as a fellow actor—he was so kind, and had such a good sense of humor. When I auditioned for the film at the Studio, Kazan gave me a set of circumstances and Marlon another set, then we improvised: Marlon disturbed me, I reacted—Kazan liked that, and on the set he encouraged us to keep that improvising spirit. I've kept what I learned from both of them working on *Waterfront,* and I've applied what I learned there to all my later work."

My own experience with Kazan revealed aspects of the way he negoti-

Kim Hunter and Marlon Brando
in *A Streetcar Named Desire.*

ates with his actors. Responding to my request for an interview, he called
me into the Studio one day after a Board meeting, then told me he couldn't
talk to me about "opinions or inner things" because he was writing his own
memoirs. I thought I'd try anyway, but when I asked my first question,
"What drew you to the Group?" and he responded with, "Jesus, fella, that's
a book!" I knew that the interview I had dreamed about was not to be.
Seeing my disappointment, he put his arm around me. "Gee, buddy, I'm
sorry to do this to you. Ask me facts. Facts I'll answer."

When I went to the theatre for the interview, the Board meeting had
just ended. Paul Newman, Joanne Woodward, Arthur Penn, Ellen Burstyn,
and Kazan were grouped around a punchbowl set up on the stage. Seeing
me come in, Kazan waved as if I were an old friend and motioned me over
to two chairs in the corner. It was just the way he treated his actors, I
thought, taking them off to the side to hold a private conference. Aspects
of the non-interview we proceeded to have were nonetheless revealing. Even
when Kazan was off in a corner with me he seemed to be at the center, the
person the others naturally gravitated to. At seventy-two, Kazan moves like
a young man. After the interview, he bounded out of his chair and back
into the middle of the group of colleagues who seemed to be waiting for
him.

"Before we started filming *America, America,*" Salem Ludwig recalls,
"Kazan took me aside and gave me a single note about my character. 'He
sleeps with his hands between his legs,' he said. I was puzzled at first. I
didn't know what he meant. But then I remembered a period in my own
life when I used to sleep with my hands between my legs. It was just after

the war, when I lived in a cellar on West 45th Street, and I was totally withdrawn. The image Kazan 'fed' to me threw me back to that period, and I was so full before we got to shooting, so weighted with powerful emotional memories, that I could hardly contain myself. He touched everybody in that way—he got to everyone."

"I know a lot about the personal lives of actors," Kazan told Michel Ciment for an interview book called *Kazan on Kazan.* "At the Actors Studio I knew the actors not only as technicians but as people. The material of my profession is the lives the actors have led up to now." The way Kazan examines his actors is the core of his method. "The basic channel of the role must flow through the actor," Kazan said. "He has to have the role in him somewhere. He must have experienced it to some extent."

"One thing in the Stanislavski System that I always stress . . . is what happened before the scene. I not only talk about it, I sometimes improvise it. By the time the scene starts, they're fully in it, not just saying lines they've been given. . . . All these things are cinematic in that they take the reliance off the dialogue, off the spoken word and put it on activity, inner activity, desire, objects, partners. . . . There's a basic element in the System that has always helped me a lot in directing actors. The key word . . . is 'to want.' 'What do you want?'—I always asked that of actors; what they're in the scene to obtain, to achieve. The asset of that is that all my actors come on strong, they're all alive, they're all dynamic—no matter how quiet." Kazan's actors enter a scene sideways, coming not from the wings or from off-camera but from a prior life. "Initially and immediately I try to break down any declamatory, old-fashioned theatrical remnants in the style of the performer. And very often, when I've worked with a performer and then I don't see him for a while, and he appears in someone else's picture, I realize he's gone back to over-theatricalism. . . . I've tried to stress . . . a basic simplicity; that is, listening to the person who's talking to you, and talking to him, not declaiming.

"One of the basic things in the technique of the Method is to use objects a lot. All objects are symbols of one thing or another . . . it's like making an act out of a feeling, through the object. Of course, it helps actors who are self-conscious, because if they concentrate on the object they won't be concentrating on themselves." Thus, things, possessions, and objects of all kinds assume a life of their own in Kazan's movies. The swing, the rocking horse, and the cradle in *Baby Doll* are all symbols of the characters' pubescent sexuality. Blanche DuBois's furs conjure up a vision of the antebellum South in which the character's fantasy life is rooted, and the shades that Blanche insists on putting on the naked overhanging light bulbs she finds in her sister's apartment say much about her need for illusion and enchantment. James Dean caresses a handful of earth from a beanfield, Brando courts Eva Marie Saint by holding onto her glove. Through these gestures, common things are charged with personal meaning, infused with sensory and emotional memories. The heightened value that objects acquire is a mark of Kazan's heightened realism, a sign of how his work celebrates the poetry of the ordinary.

Although Kazan has a social conscience that may be a lingering heritage from the Group, his truest films are about characters knotted with neurosis and fatally divided against themselves. It was their ambivalence and unexpectedness that drew Kazan to the characters of Tenessee Williams. "Williams once made a remark to me that stuck in my mind: 'There should always be an area in a dramatic character that you don't understand. There should always be an area of mystery in human characters.' " What Kazan appreciated in Williams is the duality that plagues his characters, the intimation of an inner often potentially destructive life that beats just

Carroll Baker as Baby Doll.

In a Kazan movie, psychological conflicts are expressed physically. Eli Wallach, Karl Malden, and Carroll Baker in *Baby Doll.*

beneath the surface. Blanche DuBois is a genteel Southern lady on the outside, a sexual tiger within. Kazan was fascinated by her psychological as well as sexual doubleness. "Blanche DuBois, the woman, *is* Williams. Blanche DuBois comes into a house where someone is going to murder her. The interesting part of it is that Blanche DuBois–Williams is *attracted* to the person who's going to murder her. That's what makes the play deep."

Working on a character like Blanche contributed as much as did Method technique toward Kazan's mature style in his films of the fifties and early sixties. As Kazan has said, sifting the charged ambivalences of *Streetcar* helped him to clarify his own attitudes about "the ambiguity in character. I saw this attraction/repulsion, fear/love thing all around me. I see it all the time . . . in love-connections where there's resentment at the same time as there's love. It isn't only that I'm attracted to it as an artist—it is the *truth* for me, and I think that when you don't have that in a work, the work suffers, not in regard to subtlety only, but in regard to truth-telling. As I began more and more to assert my own view of life, I expressed these contradictory impulses in my films."

Ambivalence, contradictoriness, abrupt changes of feeling, the pressure of unresolved emotions—these ignite Kazan's movies. *Streetcar* is a thicket of internal wars. *On the Waterfront* is about moral ambivalence. In *East of Eden*, the "bad" brother played by James Dean has more "good" in him than the virtuous brother. Part of the continuing appeal of Dean's performance is the way he makes Cal a steaming brew of love and hate; in the climactic moment where his father rejects his gift, love and hate look like the same emotion, as his embrace of his father seems also to want to crush him. The three characters in *Baby Doll* are each locked in a comic conflict of attraction and resentment. Baby Doll's husband, denied his conjugal rights by his childlike bride, is literally driven wild by lust and fury. He's so horny he could kill her. Baby Doll, though, is excited about Vaccaro, a swarthy intruder who is her husband's business (and, as it develops) romantic rival. Vaccaro seduces Baby Doll as a way of getting even with her husband, who set fire to his cotton mills—at the same time that he is mocking her, taking advantage of her gullibility, he also really desires her.

In a Kazan movie, space, as well as people and objects, is kinetic, charged with symbolic implications. Wisely, Kazan decided against opening up *Streetcar* with location photography and filling in the drama with atmospheric details of life in the French Quarter. Although most of the action is confined to the Kowalskis' dingy apartment, where the walls seem to be perspiring, *Streetcar* does not look like a filmed play. Kazan uses close-ups, angles, shadowed lighting, and enclosed spaces to underscore the psychological claustrophobia of the characters. The probing camera isolates characters in their own frame, creating literal as well as symbolic separations among them, and allows us to read their inner thoughts.

Kazan's dynamic visual style—his tilted angles, scrutinizing close-ups, pointed contrasts between areas of light and dark, his use of space to indicate division and alienation, his claustrophobic framing—reflects states of mind. Frequently overheated and startling, like his actors, Kazan's mise-en-scène transmutes reality through skillful calculation. Like the Method which he relies on as his directing base, and like the work of his favorite playwright, Kazan's visual technique is impassioned realism, realism transcending itself as it probes beneath everyday people, objects, places, and situations to uncover a palpitant poetry of the commonplace. This is the kind of realism that Stanislavski's original System had as its aesthetic aim (emotional reality transformed by creative vision) and it's the kind of realism that has always been pursued at the Studio. It's a realism that includes mumbling and scratching where those qualities are appropriate, but it rises loftily about them, to true psychological revelation. It's the kind of realism that, in America, has so far received its fullest and most enduring expression in the fifties films of Elia Kazan.

Undeniably the Studio's heyday was in the fifties, when Brando and Dean exploded onto movie screens and Kazan's string of film hits were in effect a showcase of great Studio acting. "The Studio was the only place to be in 1950," Jack Garfein recalls. "The best of the Broadway people were there, and being there meant a certain kind of acceptance and recognition. The actors had an ease and humanity, and twice each week they illuminated something in the play which hadn't been touched before. I felt these people had gotten close to the spirit of Stanislavski's book *An Actor Prepares*, which had been the original spark for me. In 1950, there was a fire there, like the fire of the Vestal Virgin. I never walked in without my heartbeat speeding up."

Madeleine Thornton-Sherwood recalls that when she became a member in 1959 people were "already talking about the Golden Age, and they told me I had missed out on the best of it." New member Julie Garfield feels that "they talk about the past too much—about what it was. You can feel the shadow of the Group hanging over it."

For some members, the pursuit of psychological realism has lost its allure. "The light at the Studio got too thin," June Havoc says. "I have gone back dozens of times, searching for inspiration plus, and I didn't find it. The work is too small—it leaves too much up to you and your analyst. As a workshop, the emphasis is only on some of the work. These are times that require a big power, not the Studio's introspection. There was a time for the Group, and a time for the Studio: I think it served its time."

"It's like a junkyard," is the complaint of Frank Corsaro, who nonetheless moderates occasionally and who directed a play at the Studio in the spring of 1982. "It's become all the things it's accused of—a rampant self-indulgence has taken over; it's like a sandbox where kids play. Stanislavski requires discipline. They've never gone beyond the ABC of Stanislavski. They're still doing naturalism, for God's sake!"

"The Studio is passé and everyone knows it," John Strasberg says. "There's no new force there. New artists don't seek it. Most people who want to be successful don't go to the Studio. In its heyday, up through the Actors Studio Theatre, it was a focal point for the *best* in American theatre. The type of acting that came out of the Studio was a cultural choice: American theatre is after all a tradition of realism. We are defined by realism. In Russia, Moscow Art Theatre realism is only part of the theatre; here, it's everything. The Studio has been important as a reflection of the kind of theatre that the culture wanted: that's a more important legacy than training the people, which is the Studio's myth.

"The Studio is now a remnant of what it once was. It will be hard to get people together again in the way the Studio did in the fifties. Any new force that would change the Studio would have to come in and criticize it. They don't want that. Ellen Burstyn runs it as a homage to my father: everything she does is in his honor. When you go from Jesus to Paul, you're in trouble, and the Studio is repeating that. I don't know if it's possible to cleanse the sickness at the Studio. You have to change; I don't know if they really want to."

Obviously the Studio can't keep up with the evolving interests of individual members, but as I see it, its exploration of psychological realism is of perennial value. I don't agree with its critics who claim that the Studio should widen its sphere to experiment with anti-realist forms, or that it should "graduate" from Bronx kitchens to the Forest of Arden. There is much talk about actors using the Studio to stretch themselves in the classics (and in fact there is probably more scene work from Shakespeare than any other playwright, although he is often treated as if he were Paddy Chayefsky), but its real purpose, one I have absolutely no quarrel with, is to sharpen the actors' abilities to perform the kind of realistic material that they are likely to be hired for. After attending for a semester, I was impressed by how challenging a style contemporary realism is; to be able to play it with truth and ease demands a lifetime's dedication.

The blend of reality and illusion that the Studio is interested in will always be valid. The last time I was at the Actors Studio I overheard a comment in the downstairs office. After one actor had finished recounting an amusing incident, his listener asked, "Was that from a scene, or did it really happen?"

KEN WEINBERG

In a world that at this writing, the perilous fall of 2001, is undergoing radical changes, how comforting to report that little has changed at the headquarters of the Actors Studio on West 44th Street in New York. The Studio's modest building looks the same as it always has; in this bare-bones, no-frills gymnasium for actors, sleekness, modernizing touches, indeed traces of any style at all, have been banished. As it always has been, the aggressively unassuming mise-en-scène is a skillful camouflage—you could never tell that the place is world-famous.

It isn't only the building that has resisted alteration. The heart of the Studio's activities continues to be the two-hour Method-based sessions on Tuesday and Friday from eleven to one when members bring in work at various levels of preparation to be commented on by fellow actors and a rotating roster of moderators. And, also hewing to tradition, these sessions remain closed to outsiders. Now well into its sixth decade, the Actors Studio honors its original purpose: It is a place where its members can work on their craft in an environment in which actors' problems are treated with reverence and addressed in the language of the Method as it evolved during the long tenure of Lee Strasberg, the Studio's still-controversial, incisive, problematic Artistic Director.

If the Studio's house and its primary agenda are undisturbed, since Strasberg's death in 1982 there have been some shifts on the local level. Strasberg's immediate successor, Ellen Burstyn, moderated sessions (very capably) in the spirit of her mentor, spreading the Word according to Lee. Over the years, however, the hieratic atmosphere has become less intense, and the conviction that Strasberg alone had ultimate knowledge about how to achieve truthful acting has been challenged. The two most influential iconoclasts have been longtime members Arthur Penn, the Studio's president from 1994 to 1999, and Estelle Parsons, the Studio's present artistic director. (At this writing the Studio is under the leadership of co-presidents Ellen Burstyn, Harvey Keitel, and Al Pacino.)

"I make no bones about my position," Arthur Penn told me. "I felt Lee had become a despot who was completely out of touch. What Lee failed to see about himself was his fundamental impracticality." Whether consciously or not, during his regime Penn (who is modest, accessible, and universally liked) began to remodel the Studio in his own image, stripping it of the exclusivity that had become ingrained during Strasberg's long watch and the lingering effects of Strasberg's "personal grandiosity." Penn resisted Strasberg's Holy Grail: the belief in a singular, anointed route on which to achieve illuminated realism. "I don't believe there is such an exquisite or encapsulated thing as 'the Method' that only we have the secret of. Isn't the so-called 'Method' in some variation what all good actors do?"

Penn felt the system had to be re-examined from the "perspective of several generations of actors who had been trained in this so-called Method to teach and to develop their own exercises." With "exclusivity no longer a real factor," the Studio seemed poised for a new chapter. "Unlike in the old days, the Studio [in the years after Strasberg's death] was no longer the only game in town," added Penn.

The impetus for a major outreach program came from James Lipton, a member who serves on the Studio's Board of Directors. "I was privy to the Studio's financial struggles, which [in the early 1990s] weren't getting any better," Lipton told me. (Indeed, as Penn attested, "Over the years the Studio lived modestly on the kindness of strangers and friends. But frankly, the Studio continued to be able to function mostly on [longtime member] Paul Newman's generosity.") After one particularly disheartening Board meeting, Lipton was "seized" by a plan of drawing upon the Studio's extraordinary roster—"greater than that of MGM in 1939"—in order to establish an acting program at the New School University in New York. "I called the President of the New School and asked him, 'What if at the stroke of a pen we could restore the glory of the [legendary] Erwin Piscator Dramatic Workshop [which operated at the New School in the 1940s]?' 'Where is the pen and when do I sign?' the President said. I returned to the Studio's leadership and asked, 'Are you interested in opening the Studio's doors, not to let the world in, but to let the Studio's process out?' There wasn't a moment's hesitation." An outreach program of this kind was "the only thing that made contemporary sense," Penn said.

Over a year and a half, working with Penn, Parsons, Burstyn, and Lee Grant, among others, Lipton developed a three-year MFA program called the Actors Studio Drama School. Sensitive to the traditional criticisms of the Actors Studio style, the committee laid down a broad-based curriculum. "There was a germ of truth in the old journalistic and popular perception of the 'Method' as narcissistic," Penn said. "There are aspects of the work in which the actor is training what Lee referred to as the 'instrument,' and the exercises are necessarily self-contained and introspective. But this is like a musician doing scales, and it was never a part of the philosophy or practical intention that it be carried into production or performance: a violinist doesn't perform practice exercises on the stage of Carnegie Hall. In our program, people start the day at Alvin Ailey, for body work; then they work on voice with teachers from the Metropolitan Opera. This is before they work with Studio teachers on emotionally freeing exercises." Reflecting the fact that, in Lipton's words, the Studio "today is eclectic—Arthur Penn is a product of Michael Chekhov, Strasberg, and Kazan, while at the Studio on the West Coast Sydney Pollack and Mark Rydell are Meisner-trained—the Drama School embraces all of the tributaries of the Stanislavski System. We exclude no one, and this is good."

At the Actors Studio Drama School, actors, writers, and directors take many of the same courses, but also work separately on their disciplines; in the third year, the students present their work to the public in a repertory season at the Circle in the Square Theatre on Bleecker Street. Lipton, who from the beginning has been the Drama School's Dean, speaks with pride about its unprecedented three-track acting, playwriting, and directing program: "Our system is not analogous to the set-up at the Studio [where the Playwriting and Directing Units have had erratic histories] or, for that matter, to any other school. So many directors come out of film school who have never talked to an actor or to a living writer."

"Both the New School and the Studio underestimated the magic that the Actors Studio name still carries," Arthur Penn said. "Our program [which was accredited by the state in August 1994 and welcomed its first class that September] has been successful beyond anyone's expectation. We have thousands of applications for each class size of about ninety." The best advertisement for the program has been *Inside the Actors Studio*, a television interview series hosted by Dean Lipton; according to the Drama School's catalogue, the series "appears weekly in more than 40,000,000 homes in the U.S., in all of Canada and Latin America, and in many European and Asian countries." As Lipton recalled, "I asked well-known people, who would be too busy to teach a course, if they could give me one day of their lives to come to talk to our students: 'Will you come inside the Actors Studio to teach our students?' I realized that the valuable sessions should be recorded, and we contacted the networks; Bravo was immediately interested. We're the only university with a series on the air. At first we had to do a lot of importuning, but now seventy-five percent of our guests come to us, to ask to be on the show."

Early guests were Studio members, but, as Lipton maintained, "We would have been off the air in a year if we had limited ourselves to the Studio. We want our students to have a thorough education, and after all people like Julia Roberts and Sylvester Stallone, who have appeared on the program, *do* have something to say." Opening the show to celebrity non-members has inevitably occasioned some criticism about the Studio tarnishing its heritage, and about the Studio, in effect, capitulating to the commercial limelight. But the open-door policy is in fact a natural outgrowth of Penn's ecumenical agenda—and, though nobody says so, it's also a reflection as well of Lee Strasberg's (notorious) attraction to movie stars. ("Would Strasberg have approved of the show?" I asked Dean Lipton. "I don't know, I didn't know him, but I'm sure he would have approved of the fact that as a result of the show's phenomenal success the Actors Studio is a secure institution forever." As Arthur Penn remarked dryly, the Studio now has what it never had before: "a little extra money, a little more than we need.")

In another way, inviting movie stars who may never have set foot in the Actors Studio or who may never have been exposed to any branch of the Method, makes perfect sense. Although film acting is not taught at the New School program, "our system is the way to learn film," Lipton claimed. The techniques—the inner work, the exercises in relaxation, focus, and imagination—that are practiced at the Studio and at the Drama School are those all good film actors draw on instinctively in order to create truthful behavior for the prying gaze of the camera. The connection that *Inside the Actors Studio* implicitly forges between the Actors Studio and the movies is historically justified. However variously interpreted, the kind of acting pursued at the Studio since its founding and now (in a more expanded and structured way) in the MFA program at the New School University, is the quintessential Hollywood style.

The Actors Studio may no longer be the exclusive high temple of the Method, which in various versions is taught in virtually all acting schools, and its "secrets" may no longer be confined behind the still-closed doors of that plain-as-paint building on West 44th Street, but the Actors Studio's influence has never been greater. And its simple rationale as a place for actors to "work out" has transcended the many internecine battles that have marked the Studio's history and has withstood the occasional ridicule and many misinterpretations that its vaunted "Method" has provoked. Happily, in an increasingly uncertain world, the Actors Studio looks like a sure thing.

Foster Hirsch
New York
October 2001

NOTES

Part One

1. Unlike Andreyev, Tolstoy was unmoved by Chekhov. Instead of waxing poetic about Chekhov's dance of objects and sounds, he made this comment after seeing *Uncle Vanya* on January 24, 1900: "Good Lord, a guitar and a cricket—all this is so nice that I don't see why I should look for anything else."

2. A French psychologist, Théodule Ribot, first described how affective memory works. Stanislavski devised his sensory and emotional memory exercises after having read Ribot's *La psychologie des sentiments* (1896) and *Problèmes de psychologie affective* (1910), in which the way past emotions and experiences are reexperienced is exhaustively analyzed.

3. Stanislavski's many books are written with untiring urgency. Following his own directorial methods, he is always specific, arriving at general statements only after he has offered a number of examples. In the seminal *An Actor Prepares,* he presents his material in the form of classroom exercises in which he casts himself as an autocratic teacher named Tortsov. The classroom drama—the lively opposition between the demanding teacher and his often defiant students—offers the System as practical solutions to immediate acting problems rather than a series of rules. Challenged by disbelieving students, Tortsov is forced to make his points through enlightening example.

4. "We have created a technique and methods for the artistic interpretation of Chekhov, but we do not possess a technique for the saying of the artistic truth in the plays of Shakespeare," Stanislavski wrote. That the Method works for some plays and not for others is a continuing problem at the Actors Studio.

5. Although he disagreed with Stanislavski's ideas, Meyerhold never spoke negatively about his former teacher, maintaining that Stanislavski was at heart more of a rebel and fantasist than his work indicated but that he was restrained by his deeply bourgeois partner Nemirovich-Danchenko and by the Moscow Art Theatre Council. Meyerhold and Stanislavski remained personally cordial, and it's worth noting that near the end of his career, when he was in official disfavor, Meyerhold was appointed to head the Stanislavski Opera Studio.

346

6. Michael Chekhov, nephew of the playwright, was another Moscow Art Theatre émigré who as teacher, director, and actor had a major impact on American actors, inspiring his own band of disciples. Like Boleslavski, Chekhov helped to translate Stanislavski's spiritualized realism to earthbound American actors. Chekhov's book on acting, *To the Actor* (1953), is as much a standard reference as *An Actor Prepares* and *Acting: The First Six Lessons*. Like other actors and directors trained at the Moscow Art Theatre, Chekhov differed with some of Stanislavski's theories and went on to develop his own adaptation of the System with Stanislavski's encouragement.

"Chekhov went a step further than Stanislavski," says Beatrice Straight, who co-founded the Michael Chekhov Theatre School in 1936, and who reorganized the school in 1980 nearly forty years after it had closed. "Chekhov went beyond emotional and sense memory, which he thought was too limiting. He felt it limits you to a small world, and is destructive in working for an ensemble. He believed that the actor should be encouraged to develop his imagination. He was criticized as being too spiritual, particularly by people in the Group Theatre who admired Chekhov as an actor but not as a teacher. They distrusted Chekhov's devout belief in the work of Rudolph Steiner and were suspicious of his theory of radiation, which is reaching out to your partner and to the audience, sharing, beaming an aura, sending out qualities, in an almost mystical sense. But I think we're coming into a time when that spirit is necessary."

Chekhov's most famous contribution to acting technique was what he called the psychological gesture. "Chekhov used this as a way to help actors get to the feeling they needed, without thinking," Beatrice Straight says. "He felt actors trained in the System became too intellectual and that they had to be trained to use their bodies as a spontaneous instrument. Everybody uses psychological gestures all the time, in real life—these gestures, which we use unconsciously, express feelings. If we actors learn to use them, we can awaken feelings without having to analyze so much."

In his classes, Chekhov above all wanted his students to free their bodies. "We did eurhythmic exercises," Straight recalls, "the body doing sounds, sensing through the whole body what sounds are, and then applying that to speech. You could spot any Chekhov student by how he spoke on stage," Straight laughs, "—not in the right way. Because he was so scared of the intellect, Chekhov emphasized gestures: our work became too much the *gesture* of the line rather than the idea of it. The lines had a singsong, incantatory quality. As an actor himself, Chekhov incorporated gesture as so much a part of his character that he seemed able to communicate fully without language. Everything he did seemed to be happening at the moment—it was so full and alive. When I saw him in *The Inspector General*, he didn't seem to touch the ground.

"Chekhov was a marvelous, patient, loving, demanding teacher. We felt, working with him, that we had to change the world. I feel that what he had to teach is valuable whether you become an actor or not. Poise, self-assurance, developing the imagination, freeing your body, sharing, communicating, *radiating* (to use his term)—these are the things his work promotes, and that's why I've reinstated the Chekhov School."

7. Cheryl Crawford cites the following incident as an example of the Group's inspired realism. "In rehearsal one day, the actors were carrying Morris Carnovsky who as Uncle Bob Connelly had just committed suicide. They were crying and grieving over Morris, when

the doorman rushed in asking what had happened and should he call for an ambulance? Their grief seemed so real."

8. Morris Carnovsky remembers that "one critic said that *1931* gave a false image of America by showing bread lines, when, he said, there were none. In fact, there was one right outside the theatre."

9. Interestingly, the film version of *Men in White* was directed (with routine competence) by Richard Boleslavski.

10. Odets was a ripe target for parodists. Here's a selection from S.J. Perelman's wicked take-off, called *Waiting for Santy, A Christmas Playlet (With a Bow to Mr. Clifford Odets):*

> RIVKIN: I got a belly full of stars, baby. You make me feel like I swallowed a Roman candle . . .
>
> RISKIN: I tell you, it's like gall in my mouth two young people shouldn't have a room where they could make great music . . .
>
> (Stella Claus enters . . .)
> STELLA: Love me, sugar?
>
> RIVKIN: I can't sleep, I can't eat, that's how I love you. You're a double malted with two scoops of whipped cream; you're the moon rising over Mosholu Parkway; you're a two weeks' vacation at Camp Nitgedoiget! I'd pull down the Chrysler Building to make a bobbie pin for your hair!
>
> STELLA: I've got a stomach full of anguish. Oh, Rivvy, what'll we do?
>
> PANKEN: Here, try a piece fruit.
>
> RIVKIN (fiercely): Wax fruit—that's been my whole life! Imitations! Substitutes! Stella, tonight I'm telling your old man. He can't play mumblety-peg with two human beings!

11. Group actors have at last had a chance to do Chekhov. Within the last year, I have seen three Group alumni play aged Chekhov servants. Doing the legend of the Group proud, Ruth Nelson in *Uncle Vanya* at Yale, Margaret Barker in *Three Sisters* at the Manhattan Theatre Club, and Morris Carnovsky in *The Cherry Orchard* at the Long Wharf in New Haven brought a wonderfully seasoned quality to their work.

12. In 1946, Harold Clurman went to Hollywood to direct a film, *Deadline at Dawn*, with a screenplay by Clifford Odets based on a novel by the crime writer Cornell Woolrich. It's an atmospheric, nicely acted *film noir*, filled with claustrophobic close-ups and a studio-created New York that is appropriately hot-looking and oppressive; over the years, Clurman said many unkind words about the film, no doubt because it represented an unhappy time for him. Working on material that he felt no real connection to, he also realized that film was not for him; he felt he didn't have the touch for it.

Part Two

1. Here are two case histories of the audition process.

"I was afraid of auditioning, being John Garfield's daughter," says Julie Garfield. "My father was very close with Lee. The place was loaded down with symbolism and tradition for me. I would go there to observe sessions, and then I would run away. It all meant something to me that was so heavy. I was so worried that I would be compared to my father, and that I'd pass the audition, or I wouldn't, because I was John Garfield's daughter. Instead of thinking about the work, I was involved with my own fears.

"About two years ago, something happened to me. I had a better understanding of what it meant to be an actress. I felt I was able to stand up and say I could take a chance. I started to work for myself. I became less involved with other people's opinions, and more involved with the pure thing: the work.

"I auditioned with a scene from *Two for the Seesaw*, which I had just done professionally. The part was close to me (they say you should do that). I passed the preliminary, and for the final I was told to do the same scene but to change my partner. I got a job at Milwaukee Rep. just at the time of the final in January, so I had a perfect excuse to miss it, thank God! I waited till next year. I did the preliminary in November 1979, I missed the final in 1980, and did the final in March 1981. Again, I got a job just at the time, so I had another excuse to avoid it. But I thought, 'This is silly, this is not last year, I've had a year of fruitful work, all stretches,' and so I arranged to fly from my job at Indiana U. in order to take the final. I did my scene from *Seesaw* at 8:30, found out I got in when I got a call from the secretary, and then flew back to Indiana at 6 A.M. It was the best circumstances under which I could face the final because I was preoccupied.

"Oh, I hated that final. The scene didn't go well, but I managed to relax enough to know what was going wrong. My partner freaked out, but I didn't push. They must have seen that. I played moment to moment: my partner turned from flesh to wood in front of my eyes, and I was so relaxed I was like a rag doll. I had made up my mind that no matter what I was going to be relaxed. Before going upstairs I did a relaxation exercise. I sat in a chair and relaxed my whole body, as I worked on a sense memory. I relaxed so things would flow through me.

"There are moments when I think they took me because I'm John Garfield's daughter. But I never got anything being his daughter; nobody ever gave me any presents, believe me. I know I wouldn't have survived the audition if I didn't have something. Even when I'm bad, I'm good, I'm told."

"I studied with two Studio people, Sandy Dennis and Salem Ludwig, who both talked about the Studio," says Ted Zurkowski. "They both encouraged me to audition. I did two preliminaries. The first one was *Lunch Time* by Leonard Melfi. They said come back in a year, which is the usual time they ask you to wait, take another partner, another scene. There were five judges then, now there are three, and it's just you and them in that upstairs theatre that drips with history: it's terrifying. I did a scene from *The Woods* by David Mamet. I passed the prelim. Boy, the pressure at the finals: Kazan, Penn, and Strasberg were there, and about sixty or seventy members. They had told us to bring back *The Woods*. We got into character, my partner and I, well before we were called up. We improvised a lovers' argument and other people who were waiting to go up thought it was for real. They thought all the tension had made us start to fight. When our turn came we sprinted up the stairs and charged right into the scene. We were real, I guess, since I got in."

Out of hundreds of actors who audition each year in New York and Los Angeles only a handful are admitted. In 1982–83, the first post-Strasberg season, four new members were accepted. Getting in, against such odds and under such tense circumstances, is a genuine accomplishment and an important indication of talent. And in an uncertain profession membership in the Actors Studio is a sure thing: the honor of belonging to it can never be taken away from you, and it's a reminder that people like Lee Strasberg and Elia Kazan and Arthur Penn believed in you.

2. Typical of the distance between playwright and actor at the Studio was the recent example of the Playwrights Lab run by Israel Horovitz almost as a parody of the secrecy of the acting sessions.

"Playwrights don't need to know about acting. My lab was not between playwright and actors, but between playwright and playwright," Horovitz says. "The lab had a specific format. We were a group of ten working professional playwrights: no students, no beginners, no one in the pluperfect: everyone actually *is*," he says, with evident contempt for anyone who isn't.

"We made one essential agreement: we all started working on a play at the same time. Everybody schedules their lives around starting work in October. Every Wednesday we met for two hours in closed-door sessions. We ate enormous amounts of fruit. We read five pages at each session, in sequence. We had a playwright's approach to writing and it was a kind of criticism an outsider wouldn't understand, a kind of criticism you'll never find in another kind of room. It was not mannerly. It was educated, specific, concise. Our comments were never general: it's of no use to a writer to be told a particular section is boring.

"Once a month, we let people—actors—come in and observe the sessions. In the spring, we did readings of plays for that year. In the early part of the year, we did full productions of work done the year before." Horovitz mentions some titles of plays that were created in the Lab: David Rimmer's *Album*, Peter Proud's *Sorrows of Stephen*, and Wendy Wasserstein's *Uncommon Women*, all of which were given off-Broadway productions. "We've developed twenty-five to fifty new American plays in a world that doesn't need them.

"I selected the writers. I chose on the basis of somebody's compatibility as a critic, as well as their talent. I kept a very low profile as to publicity, otherwise you'd have an unsightly stock of scripts. I'm not willing to read the work of unknown writers—they have to be making their living as a playwright."

Horovitz admits that the kind of play that got written in the Lab was the kind of play associated with the Studio acting style. "It was never planned that it would be a workshop for naturalistic plays, but that's how it turned out, I suppose inevitably. The kind of writer that is attracted to me is attracted to the Studio style. I always cast my plays with Studio people. The Studio actor is so good for naturalistic plays. They have a particular kind of

preparation in building a character. They build a role the way a writer builds a character."
(Then why wasn't he interested in opening a dialogue between actors and writers?) The
Studio and Horovitz did not part happily. "He just disappeared," said Carl Schaeffer, who
had made it possible for Horovitz to bring his Lab to the Studio. "I never heard from him
after 1980. He never called to thank me, he never told us if he planned to reactivate
the Lab for the following season. A fine how d'you do. Most of the writers despised
him."

"Don't mention his name to me!" one of the playwrights said, groaning. "He marked
up my script with red ink on every page."

Every Wednesday for four years, Lab writers sneaked into the Studio as protective of
their privacy in the back room downstairs as most of the actors are of theirs in the upstairs
theatre. Because space at the Studio is so limited, many actors resented the Lab: to them,
it meant that once a week ten outsiders were taking up time and room that could have been
used for members working on scenes or projects. Furthermore, they resented the shut-door
policy that in effect kept them out of their own home.

3. Typical of the kind of play the Studio has presented as projects are *On Bliss Street in
Sunnyside* (spring 1981) and *My Prince, My King* (winter 1982).

Written by Studio member Marcia Haufrecht, herself an excellent naturalistic actress,
Bliss Street is a high-strung family drama about a forty-year-old woman who has come to
live with her mother and stepfather after having cracked up. The woman's father and his
second wife, a psychiatrist, come for a visit, entering gamely into what has the feel of a
prolonged Studio exercise. All the characters are filled with accusations springing from the
unfinished business they carry about with them like so much excess baggage. Abandoned
in childhood by her mother, the troubled daughter is a potentially gifted artist who has rotten
relationships with men; she's a victim of the sexual wars. At the climax, she locks herself
in the bathroom, threatening like all devout hysterics to slash her wrists. Intense, humorless,
scrupulously real in language and action, the ironically titled play is loaded with opportunities for sensory work and affective memories. Although it was too much like too much else
I have seen at the Studio, it was extremely well acted and directed.

My Prince, My King, which opened the week of Strasberg's death, ends with the death
of a Jewish patriarch. In the cast were Lee Strasberg's two young sons, playing the sons of
a father who dies. When the father in the play died, people in the audience gasped: art
seemed so closely to be imitating life, as Strasberg always said it should.

Set on the edge of World War I, the play is a series of anecdotes about an immigrant
family on the Lower East Side, dispossessed Jewish socialists dreaming of utopia. The family
patriarch is a failure in the practical world but a beautiful dreamer who is good with words
(his wife, whom he courted and won with his verbal skill, calls him "my prince, my king").
Their daughter has a bourgeois boyfriend shocked by her radical family—in addition to their
socialist ideas, the Wolfsons never bothered to marry. There is a rich sister, Irish boarders,
a family friend who secretly loves Mr. Wolfson: ethnic types. Short on story but rich in
atmosphere, the play mines familiar ground. It's a minor genre piece, watered-down Odets,
without the social or political urgency that drove Odets's family plays.

Part Three

1. Another early Studio venture into production, one that nobody at the Studio seems to remember or talk about, as if it never happened, was a television series that lasted for two seasons from September 1948 to March 1950. There were fifty-six shows in all, mostly dramatized short stories. The opener was a Tennessee Williams one-act play, *Portrait of a Madonna*, starring Jessica Tandy and directed by Hume Cronyn (neither of whom are Studio members). Each play was rehearsed at the Studio for two weeks and then broadcast live. The series was well reviewed and even earned some money for the Studio. It won the Peabody Award for distinguished achievement. Historically it was the first sustained effort to present serious theatre on the new medium. And it provided a showcase for Studio actors, among them Eva Marie Saint, Kim Hunter, Mildred Dunnock, Julie Harris, Jo Van Fleet, Eli Wallach, and Lee Grant.

The Actors Studio on television was a terrific idea—and it worked. Why didn't it last longer than two seasons? Again, there seem to have been problems with leadership—Studio directors like Cheryl Crawford and Elia Kazan were busy with their own careers—and Lee Strasberg wasn't interested. Too, preparing shows on a regular basis strained the Studio's facilities; it was a big job, requiring a steady flow of acting and writing talent and it may be that two seasons taxed the Studio's ability to keep up a consistently high level of production.

Coming as it did so early in the Studio's history, the television series is further refutation of the idea that the Studio was intended to be a workshop only. Within its first two years, it had a show on Broadway and a continuing television series: clearly, the young Studio was eager to find ways for its actors to be seen. That these public forums were not continued is a surprise and a disappointment. The Actors Studio didn't really decide to be a strictly private institution until the early fifties when Strasberg in effect took over.

2. The story behind the scenes of *Shadow of a Gunman* became the basis of an absorbing though largely unsuccessful novel by Daniel Stern called *Who Shall Live, Who Shall Die?* It's about a fierce struggle for control of a Broadway play: *At the Gates*, like *Shadow of a Gunman*, is a play about war's impact on private lives—this time, reflecting Garfein's own experience, the background is the Holocaust. Jud Kramer (read Jack Garfein), himself a survivor and now a Broadway director, is about to prepare his most ambitious project when a dark stranger, a survivor named Carl Walkowitz who bears the visible scars of a limp and one half-shut eye, insinuates himself into Jud's life, seducing his beautiful movie star wife (read Carroll Baker) and attempting to take Jud's new play away from him. Jud discovers Carl's identity and his motives only at the end in a last-minute revelation that is melodramatic hokum: in the camps, Jud had worked in an office where, when he saw a list of names marked for extermination, he erased those of his own family and added the names of Carl's family as replacements. Now Carl has tracked Jud to claim an eye for an eye.

Jud is twice bedeviled since his artistic mentor Paul Rovic (read Lee Strasberg), the director of the Theatre Workshop (read the Actors Studio) where Jud studied and where *At the Gates* was developed, also betrays him. The nervous producer wants a play with stars and a little humor and asks Jud to make some script adjustments; when Jud refuses, Paul, who *is* willing to be commercial, agrees to replace Jud as director. Jud buys the play from the original producer and breaks with Paul.

If Stern had concentrated on the struggle between Jud and Paul, he would have had a good backstage story about the kind of people who would sell their souls in order to bring in a hit show. But in aligning a theatrical soap opera with the Holocaust and introducing a complex allegorical character like Carl Walkowitz, whose mania seems Dostoevskian compared to the show business neurotics who populate the novel, Stern is out of his depth.

3. The *Shadow* fracas forced Strasberg to size up the distance between running a workshop and putting on a show. On the one hand, closing the gap represented the Studio "living up to its responsibilities"; on the other, it was something "we've been pushed to do and are reluctant to do." Strasberg told an Acting Unit session that "a Studio is not concerned with production, and so it doesn't matter whether what you do here is good or bad." (He is speaking early in January 1958, while the fires over *Shadow of a Gunman* were still raging.) "In a Studio, differences of opinion are valuable: leadership helps, but a Studio is not the prerogative of one man. A Studio can be formlessly organized. A Theatre is a totally different kind of organization. In production, all that matters is that it should be well done. A wide area of disagreement and difference of opinion is possible in a Studio; in production you cannot have that. A production has one director. There can be only one person at the top: there is no theatre without firm artistic leadership." What is troublesome here isn't so much what Strasberg is saying—a Theatre needs a leader, and a vision such as Clurman had for the Group—as the truculent way in which he is announcing who is boss.

"I am responsible for this hospital," Strasberg reminded members at the time of his disputes with Garfein. "There must be sufficient regard for the people at the head of the Studio—Kazan and I and Miss Crawford in terms of other things, as at the Moscow Art Theatre for Stanislavski and Danchenko. In the final stages, Stanislavski and Danchenko would come in and check each production: Danchenko was more interested in dramaturgy, Stanislavski in acting. What they said went. In any professional activity, there is responsibility and authority. It is never questioned. Why it is questioned here, I do not know."

As Strasberg envisioned an Actors Studio Theatre, five years before the fact, he brought up ideas about casting that would later cause bitter argument. "There are certain kinds of plays which with hit notices will not do hit business. But if that same play has stars, it will do hit business. What do you do? This is a problem that has to be faced if the Studio becomes professional. If you can get the best names of the Studio, then you have something a production on the open market cannot do." On the one hand, Strasberg talked about "the variety and distinctiveness of talent here that has to be used in an ensemble way: then you'd have something like the Moscow Art Theatre and a little like the Group, with the background work full." And, on the other hand, he said that if a Theatre is created it will be done "with the best of our people available," adding some sentences that would come to haunt him: "The best known are after all not the worst actors here. It demands from our people with names a certain sympathy."

What Strasberg was proposing was, in effect, a Group Theatre with stars. To rely on stars makes box-office sense, but it also defeats the ensemble spirit that a true, not-for-profit repertory company must nurture. "He tried to combine David Merrick and Stanislavski," Frank Corsaro says. "It was like watching a schizoid personality: art and commerce didn't go together."

4. The two-year regime of Elia Kazan and Robert Whitehead at Lincoln Center was notably less successful than the concurrent two-season Actors Studio Theatre. First, the actors weren't as good as the Studio's, and second, there was the choice of plays. Excepting *Baby Want a Kiss* and possibly *Dynamite Tonite,* the Studio's selection was balanced; the Kazan-Whitehead repertory was less defensible: Arthur Miller's *After the Fall,* S. N. Behrman's *But for Whom Charlie,* and a revival of O'Neill's *Marco Millions* were the first season's offerings.

Since part of Miller's long play dramatized his marriage to Marilyn Monroe, *After the Fall* qualified as an "event." But the fact is that the play is a windy, rhetorical, self-aggrandizing embarrassment. It's a work of remarkable hubris that cannibalizes history as it assaults the memory of Monroe. Miller's protagonist Quentin confesses to a disembodied Listener (it's like a high-minded *Portnoy's Complaint* in its open-ended confessional structure), alternately beating his breast like a modern-day Job and patting himself on the back. Quentin pictures himself as the conscience of his race, seeing all and forgiving all, as he places his personal failures, his purely local and domestic problems—his trouble with women—against historical catastrophes, the collapse of his father's business during the Depression, the betrayals of friend against friend during the McCarthy hearings, and the inhumanity of man against man during the Holocaust. To link Quentin's private drama with the cataclysms of modern history is morally and theatrically unwarranted—in fact, outrageous. Quentin isn't a big enough character to stand up to so cosmic a setting: all this talk, all this history, and what's really on Quentin's mind is how he has failed the women in his life and how they have failed him. The character's inability to communicate is reflected in the lack of communication in the play which is in essence a marathon monologue, Quentin-Miller talking to himself and evidently admiring the sound of his voice as the other people in his life are reduced to ghosts who come and go, summoned by his memory. At the end Quentin's new woman friend Holga calls out to him from the topmost level, "Hello." "Hello," he says, holding out his hand as he climbs up to meet her. Theatrically, it's a poetic ending, but nothing in the play has prepared for it; nothing has happened to Quentin to lend conviction to this last-minute rescue.

As the opening attraction of a company that everyone hoped would evolve into an American national theatre, *After the Fall* earned a historical significance it doesn't merit. But Kazan's direction was exciting. The play's open form—the action takes place on different levels within Quentin's mind—was suited to the openness of the thrust stage of the ANTA–Washington Square where the Lincoln Center Theatre was located (before its permanent home at the Vivian Beaumont was ready), and Kazan's staging, with characters moving in and out of spotlights and appearing and disappearing on the varying levels of the abstract, unlocalized set, was crisp and fluid. Aided by Barbara Loden's immense performance, the Monroe section was electric—with just the kind of coiled, sourish domestic drama that Kazan has always been drawn to. The highly overrated Jason Robards was a one-note Quentin, blurry and boring.

But for Whom, Charlie was equally disappointing. There was no urgency about the play, no sense of occasion. Civilized and literate, like all of Behrman's work, it is also strangely amorphous. It concerns a foundation for writers; the man who runs it, Charlie, is a character type familiar from Behrman's earlier work, being an opportunist with a slippery and utilitarian morality, opposed in the play's scheme to a truly good guy, his boss and old friend Seymour, a genuine philanthropist. For Kazan, this cup-and-saucer kind of comedy-drama was dainty pickings; and if he was using his prerogatives as co-director of the Theatre to choose vehicles designed to show off his versatility, he chose wrong.

Like the first two offerings, *Marco Millions* was the work of a famed playwright in an off season. O'Neill's fantasy of American capitalism hadn't been revived since its original production in the twenties, for good reason. And again, the play was ill-suited to the company's talents; where a sense of playfulness and an imaginative projection into another time period are called for, the actors were stuck in a flatfooted contemporary naturalism.

The second and final season was worse. *Incident at Vichy*, another new play by Arthur Miller, was selected, leading skeptics to proclaim that Kazan wanted to turn the Lincoln Center Company into the Arthur Miller Repertory Theatre. Though well directed by Harold Clurman, it was a solemn thesis drama, negligible as a theatre piece. Set in German-occupied France during the war, the play is about a group of men waiting to be interviewed by German officers. The waiting victims are all easily recognizable types. Each is allowed his position-paper speech while the central debate is between a Gentile Austrian aristocrat arrested for having helped Jews and a Jewish doctor for whom the Austrian ultimately gives up his own life. *Incident at Vichy* is a mock-debate, as it is a mock-play, a drama on a powerful subject that courts the appearance without supplying the substance of tragedy.

The second play was *The Changeling*, a Jacobean revenge tragedy which was Kazan's one venture into noncontemporary drama. Kazan had little feeling for the imagery and rhythms of the language, and he permitted Barbara Loden to give a shallow, ill-spoken performance, verbally, emotionally, and physically mute. Kazan received the most scathing reviews of his career, a true critical bloodbath.

The third offering, Molière's *Tartuffe*, was a well-received import from the Actors Workshop of San Francisco, who were to be Kazan's successors at Lincoln Center. At the end of the second season, Kazan withdrew from the Theatre to write a series of novels.

5. In reading through the contemporary notices of the Actors Studio Theatre productions, I can't help thinking that some of the reactions betray an anti-Studio bias. Not for the first time, the Studio seems to have become a victim of its image as a secret society; now that the Studio was at last going public after years of insisting on its right to exclude the public, critics had a chip on their shoulders. They carried a show-me attitude into the Studio productions and emerged with a shrug, as if to say, "Is this all there is to it? Is this what your sacred Method is all about, finally?" Many journalists held up Studio productions to higher standards than they would have for regular commercial offerings with the result that the Studio's work, which was markedly superior to almost all other Broadway attractions, actually ended up being talked about as if it wasn't as good.

6. A film of *Three Sisters* was made in 1965, with Paul Bogart more or less repeating Lee Strasberg's direction for the stage. Although it looks like filmed theatre rather than a movie, it nonetheless preserves some notable performances—Kim Stanley's Masha, Geraldine

Page's Olga, and Shelley Winter's surprising Natasha, the most subtle and intelligent work I've ever seen from her. Not filming other of the Theatre's productions seems like another of the Studio's missed chances. Surely, if the films were carefully handled—sold to television or schools rather than depending on regular theatrical distribution—they could have brought in some money for the Theatre.

BIBLIOGRAPHY

Aaron, Daniel. *Writers on the Left: Episodes in American Literary Communism.* New York, Octagon, 1974.

Adams, Cindy. *Lee Strasberg: The Imperfect Genius of the Actors Studio.* New York, Doubleday, 1980.

Allen, Frederick Lewis. *Since Yesterday: The 1930s in America.* New York, Harper & Row, 1972.

Allsop, Kenneth. *The Angry Decade.* New York, British Book Centre, 1958.

Anderson, Maxwell. *Night over Taos.* New York, Samuel French, 1935.

Ardrey, Robert. *Thunder Rock.* New York, Dramatists Play Service, 1950.

Baldwin, James. *Blues for Mister Charlie.* New York, Dell, 1964.

Boleslavsky, Richard. *Acting: The First Six Lessons.* New York, Theatre Arts, 1949.

Braun, Edward. *The Theatre of Meyerhold: Revolution on the Modern Stage.* London, Drama Book, 1979.

Brenman-Gibson, Margaret. *Clifford Odets, American Playwright: The Years from 1906 to 1940.* New York, Atheneum, 1981.

Breuer, Bessie. *Sundown Beach.* New York, Grindstone Press, 1973.

Buckle, Richard. *In the Wake of Diaghilev.* New York, Holt, 1983.

Chekhov, Anton. Best Plays. Translated by Stark Young. New York, Modern Library, 1956.

———. *Letters.* Translated by Michael Henry Heim, with Simon Karlinsky. New York, Harper & Row, 1973.

Chekhov, Michael. *To the Director and Playwright.* Compiled by Charles Leonard. Westport, Connecticut, Greenwood, 1977.

———. *To the Actor. On the Technique of Acting.* New York, Harper & Row, 1953.

Ciment, Michel. *Kazan on Kazan.* New York, Viking, 1974.

Clurman, Harold. *The Fervent Years.* New York, Da Capo, 1983.

———. *Lies Like Truth.* New York, Macmillan, 1958.

———. *The Naked Image: Observations on the Modern Theatre.* New York, Macmillan, 1966.

———. *On Directing.* New York, Macmillan, 1972.

Cole, Toby. *Acting: A Handbook of the Stanislavski Method.* New York, Crown, 1955.

357

Cole, Toby, and Chinoy, Helen Krich, editors. *Actors on Acting.* New York, Crown, 1970.

Corsaro, Frank. *Maverick: A Director's Personal Experience in Opera and Theatre.* New York, Vanguard, 1978.

Costigan, James. *Baby Want a Kiss.* New York, Samuel French, 1966.

Cowley, Malcolm. *Exile's Return.* New York, Peter Smith, 1983.

Crawford, Cheryl. *One Naked Individual.* Indianapolis, Bobbs-Merrill, 1977.

Dostoyevsky, Fyodor. *The Brothers Karamazov: Six Scenes from the Novel.* Translated by Jenny Covan. New York, Brentano's, 1923.

Easty, Edward Dwight. *On Method Acting.* Orlando, Florida, House of Collectibles, 1966.

Edwards, Christine. *The Stanislavski Heritage.* New York, New York University Press, 1965.

Filler, Louis, editor. *America in the Nineteen Thirties: A Collection of Contemporary Writings.* New York, Horizon, 1963.

Fiore, Carlo. *Bud, the Brando I Knew.* New York, Delacorte, 1974.

Flanagan, Hallie. *Arena.* New York, Ayer Co., reproduction of 1940 edition.

Freed, Donald. *Freud and Stanislavski.* New York, Vantage, 1964.

Funke, Lewis, and Booth, John E., editors. *Actors Talk about Acting.* New York, Avon, 1961.

Garfield, David. *A Player's Place: The Story of the Actors Studio.* New York, Macmillan, 1980.

Gazzo, Michael V. *A Hatful of Rain.* In *Famous American Plays of the 1950s,* selected and introduced by Lee Strasberg, New York, Dell, 1962.

Goldstein, Malcolm. *The Political Stage: American Drama and Theater of the Great Depression.* New York, Oxford University Press, 1974.

Gorchakov, Nikolai M. *Stanislavski Directs.* Translated by Miriam Goldina. Westport, Connecticut, Greenwood, 1974.

Gorelik, Mordecai. *New Theatres for Old.* New York, Octagon, 1975.

Green, Paul. *The House of Connelly and Other Plays.* New York, Samuel French, 1931.

————. *Johnny Johnson (The Biography of a Common Man).* New York, Samuel French, 1937.

Havoc, June. *Marathon 33.* New York, Dramatists Play Service, 1969.

Hethmon, Robert H., editor. *Strasberg at the Actors Studio.* New York, Viking, 1965.

Houghton, Norris, editor. *Great Russian Plays:* Gogol, *Inspector General;* Turgenev, *A Month in the Country;* Tolstoy, *The Power of Darkness;* Chekhov, *The Cherry Orchard;* Andreyev, *He Who Gets Slapped;* Gorky, *The Lower Depths.* New York, Dell, 1960.

Jones, Ernest. *The Life and Work of Sigmund Freud.* Edited and abridged by Lionel Trilling and Steven Marcus. New York, Basic, 1961.

Kazin, Alfred. *Starting Out in the Thirties.* New York, Random House, 1980.

Kirchon, V., and Ouspensky, A. *Red Rust.* New York, Brentano's, 1930.

Koteliansky, S. S., editor and translator. *Anton Chekhov: Literary and Theatrical Reminiscences.* New York, Haskell, 1974.

Lawson, John Howard. *Success Story.* New York, Farrar & Rinehart, 1932.

————. *With a Reckless Preface: The Pure in Heart; Gentlewoman.* New York, Farrar & Rinehart, 1934.

Levy, Melvin. *Gold Eagle Guy.* New York, Samuel French, 1934.

Lewis, Robert. *Advice to the Players.* New York, Harper & Row, 1980.

———. *Method—or Madness?* New York, Samuel French, 1958.

Ley-Piscator, Maria. *The Piscator Experiment: The Political Theatre.* Carbondale, Illinois, University of Southern Illinois Press, 1967.

Magarshack, David. *Chekhov, a Life.* Westport, Connecticut, Greenwood, 1970.

———. *Stanislavski, a Life.* Westport, Connecticut, Greenwood, 1975.

Mailer, Norman. *Marilyn.* New York, Putnam, 1981.

Maltz, Albert, and Sklar, George. *Peace on Earth.* New York, Samuel French, 1934.

Matthews, Jane De Hart. *The Federal Theatre 1935–1939: Plays, Relief, and Politics.* Princeton, Princeton University Press, 1967.

Miller, Arthur. *After the Fall.* New York, Viking, 1964.

Mordden, Ethan. *The American Theatre.* New York, Oxford University Press, 1981.

Morella, Joe, and Epstein, Edward Z. *Rebels: The Rebel Hero in Films.* Secaucus, New Jersey, Citadel Press, 1973.

Munk, Erika, editor. *Stanislavski and America.* New York, Fawcett, 1967.

Nemirovich-Danchenko, Vladimir. *My Life in the Russian Theatre.* Translated by John Cournos. New York, Theatre Arts, 1968.

Nijinsky, Romola. *Nijinsky.* New York, AMS Press, reproduction of 1934 edition.

Obolensky, Chloe, and Hayward, Max. *The Russian Empire: A Portrait in Photographs.* New York, Random House, 1979.

O'Casey, Sean. *Three Plays: Juno and the Paycock, The Shadow of a Gunman, and The Plough and the Stars.* New York, St. Martins, 1966.

Odets, Clifford. *Six Plays: Waiting for Lefty, Awake and Sing!, Golden Boy, Rocket to the Moon, Till the Day I Die, and Paradise Lost.* New York, Grove, 1979.

O'Neill, Eugene. *Strange Interlude.* New York, Boni & Liveright, 1928.

Ostrovsky, Alexander. *Enough Stupidity in Every Wise Man.* Translated by Polya Kasherman. New York, Brentano's, 1923.

Piscator, Erwin, and Goldschmidt, Lena. *The Case of Clyde Griffiths.* Ms., 1936, New York Public Library, Lincoln Center.

Pitcher, Harvey. *Chekhov's Leading Lady: A Portrait of the Actress Olga Knipper.* New York, Franklin Watts, 1980.

Pritchett, V. S. *The Gentle Barbarian: The Life and Work of Turgenev.* New York, Random House, 1978.

Rabkin, Gerald. *Drama and Commitment: Politics in the American Theatre of the Thirties.* New York, Haskell, 1972.

Roberts, J. W. *Richard Boleslavsky.* Ann Arbor, UMI Res. Press, 1981.

Rosenfeld, Lulla. *Bright Star of Exile: Jacob Adler and the Yiddish Theatre.* New York, T.Y. Crowell, 1977.

Saroyan, William. *My Heart's in the Highlands.* New York, Samuel French, 1941.

Sayler, Oliver M. *Inside the Moscow Art Theatre.* New York, Johnson Reprint, reproduction of 1925 edition.

———. *The Russian Theatre.* New York, Brentano's, 1922.

Shaw, Irwin. *The Gentle People.* New York, Dramatists Play Service, 1939.

Sifton, Paul, and Sifton, Claire. *1931—*. New York, Samuel French, 1931.

Simmons, Ernest J. *Chekhov: A Biography*. Chicago, University of Chicago Press, 1970.

Simonov, Ruben. *Stanislavski's Protégé: Eugene Vakhtangov*. Translated by Miriam Goldina. New York, DBS Publications, 1969.

Slonim, Marc. *An Outline of Russian Literature*. Oxford, Oxford University Press, 1958.

———. *Russian Theatre: From the Empire to the Soviets*. Cleveland, Ohio, World, 1961.

Smiley, Sam. *The Drama of Attack: Didactic Plays of the American Depression*. Columbia, Missouri, University of Missouri Press, 1972.

Spencer, Charles. *The World of Serge Diaghilev*. New York, Viking, 1979.

Stanislavski, Constantin. *An Actor Prepares*. Translated by Elizabeth Reynolds Hapgood. New York, Theatre Arts, 1936.

———. *An Actor's Handbook*. Edited and translated by Elizabeth Reynolds Hapgood. New York, Theatre Arts, 1963.

———. *Building a Character*. Translated by Elizabeth Reynolds Hapgood. New York, Theatre Arts, 1949.

———. *Creating a Role*. Translated by Elizabeth Reynolds Hapgood. New York, Theatre Arts, 1961.

———. *My Life in Art*. New York, Theatre Arts, 1952.

———. *The Sea Gull Produced by Stanislavski*. Translated by David Magarshack. New York, Theatre Arts, 1952.

———. *Stanislavski's Legacy*. Edited and translated by Elizabeth Reynolds Hapgood. New York, Theatre Arts, 1968.

———. *Stanislavski on the Art of the Stage*. Translated by David Magarshack. New York, Hill & Wang, 1961.

Steiner, George. *Tolstoi or Dostoevsky: An Essay in the Old Criticism*. New York, Knopf, 1959.

Strasberg, Susan. *Bittersweet*. New York, New American Library, 1981.

Tolstoy, Count Alexei. *Tsar Fyodor Ivanovitch*. Translated by Jenny Covan. New York, Brentano's, 1922.

Torporkov, Vasily Osipovich. *Stanislavski in Rehearsal: The Final Years*. Translated by Christine Edwards. New York, Theatre Arts, 1979.

Wolf, Friedrich. *The Sailors of Cattaro*. New York, Samuel French, 1935.

ACKNOWLEDGMENTS

Stella Adler; Edward Albee; Mathew Anden; Margaret Barker; Kristofer Batho; Michael Bavar; Phoebe Brand; Ellen Burstyn; Lisl Cade; Morris Carnovsky; Martha Coignay; Joan Copeland; Frank Corsaro; Katharine Cortez; Cheryl Crawford; Janet Doeden; Lillian Friedman; Jack Garfein; David Garfield; Julie Garfield; Jack Gelber; Mordecai Gorelik; Gayle Greene; June Havoc; Marcia Haufrecht; Alice Hermes; Israel Horovitz; Kim Hunter; Sabra Jones; Elia Kazan; Dina Kley; the late Sharon Lilienfeld; Viveca Lindfors; Joanne Linville; Salem Ludwig; Liska March; Mary Mercier; Sonia Moore; Syeus Mottel; Ruth Nelson; Geraldine Page; Estelle Parsons; Arthur Penn; Maria Piscator; Sylvia Regan; Meade Roberts; Gordon Rogoff; Eva Marie Saint; the late Carl Schaeffer; Carol Houck Smith; Lois Smith; Maureen Stapleton; Beatrice Straight; John Strasberg; Jessica Tandy; Jann Tarrant; Madeleine Thornton-Sherwood; Michael Wager; Ted Zurkowski.

The Motion Picture Section of the Library of Congress; The New York Public Library, Lincoln Center; Wisconsin Center for Theatre Research, at the University of Wisconsin, Madison.

PHOTO CREDITS: MB Archive (pp. 64, 147, 216); The Center for Russian Studies (pp. 14, 23, 27, 29, 45, 46, 48, 55, 57); Cinemabilia (pp. 178, 244, 301, 306); Roger Gould (p. 237); Dan Glick (p. 176); Syeus Mottel (frontispiece, pp. 127, 128, 136, 137, 140, 152, 154, 158, 179, 228); The New York Public Library at Lincoln Center (pp. 61, 69, 76, 80, 83, 86, 92, 97, 100, 163, 251, 256, 263, 276); Bill O'Connell, Ltd. (pp. 11, 173, 180, 254, 298, 303, 313, 315, 324, 332, 335, 338); Ken Weinberg (pp. 110, 182, 184, 187, 190, 339).

Page numbers in **boldface** refer to illustrations.